Edited and designed
by David Dew

Contributors

Richard Birch
James Burn
Graham Dench
Dave Edwards
Richard Forristal
Dylan Hill

James Hill
Bruce Jackson
Paul Kealy
Jon Lees
Steve Mason
Kevin Morley

Ben Newton
Dave Orton
Mark Scully
Brian Sheerin
Nick Watts

Cover artwork by Jay Vincent
Inside artwork by Nigel Jones and Stefan Searle

Published in 2016 by Racing Post Books, Raceform, 27 Kingfisher Court, Hambridge Road, Newbury, RG14 5SJ

Copyright © Raceform Ltd 2016 All rights reserved. No part of this publication may be reproduced, stored in a retrieval system, or transmitted in any form or by any means, electronic, mechanical, photocopying, recording, or otherwise, without the prior written permission of the publishers. The Racing Post specifies that post-press changes may occur to any information given in this publication. A catalogue record for this book is available from the British Library.

ISBN: 978-1910498521

LOWDOWN FROM THE TRAINERS

RACING POST EXPERTS

THIS SEASON'S KEY HORSES

STATISTICS

Magical season on cards for hungry trainer with wealth of ammunition

FRIDAY, March 18, 2016, Cheltenham and Don Cossack is leading the Gold Cup field down to the final fence. Bryan Cooper counts the strides in his head, something he has done a million times before, but these are the strides he's been preparing for throughout his whole career. One, two, three and Don Cossack responds to negotiate the jump and scoot up the Cheltenham hill with over four lengths in hand from his nearest rival.

Don Cossack, a Gold Cup winner. Time now for his trainer Gordon Elliott to exhale. In truth, he had been holding his breath for long enough, as the young trainer waxed lyrically about the son of little known sire Sholokhov when he was only learning his trade in bumpers. But that is a different story for a different day. Now, the Gigginstown House Stud-owned gelding had delivered, and in turn, provided 38-year-old Elliott with the greatest moment of his career.

"I actually sat back and watched the race for the first time in a while the other day," Elliott says. "It would put you in good form looking at it. The Gold Cup is the biggest race in the world for me and of course it was the best day in my career."

Whether Don Cossack will be able to defend his Gold Cup crown next March remains to be seen, but Elliott is cautiously optimistic he can nurse the nine-year-old back to full fitness following the tendon injury that ruled him out of the Punchestown Festival in April.

"Every day could be their last day after a leg injury, but he's back doing road work and his latest scans were all good so he'll be back here with us at Cullentra House in early October all being well.

"If we get a clean run with him, we'll probably get one race into him before he goes back to defend the Gold Cup. The Kinloch Brae Chase at Thurles served him well last season and that could be the place to go with him again this season as it will be late enough before we'd have him ready and options are pretty slim at that stage."

No More Heroes had looked a hugely exciting prospect for Elliott, but sadly his career was cut short when he was fatally injured in the RSA Chase at Cheltenham.

"That was a massive blow. We thought he was going to be our next Gold Cup horse. He'd probably done more as a novice than Don Cossack had achieved at a similar stage and we were all very excited about him. But that's the game we're in and you have to give yourself a shake and keep going."

'Don Cossack is back doing road work and his latest scans were all good so he'll be back here with us in early October all being well'

DID YOU KNOW?

Gordon Elliott used to be a jockey. An amateur in Ireland, he won ten races in 1996-97 and in 2002 he won a race at Cheltenham for Martin Pipe. Elliott came from a completely non-equine related background – his father was a mechanic – but he always had an eye on training horses and was already doing so with point-to-pointers in his riding days. When he won the Grand National with Silver Birch in 2007 he hadn't trained a winner in Ireland, but last term he had 123 back home and 28 in Britain.

5

Some 30 minutes after that blow, Elliott was provided with the best possible tonic when **Diamond King** weaved his way through a wall of horses to win the Coral Cup, and he is set to go novice chasing this season.

"We were lucky he delivered at Cheltenham. Talk about the ups and downs of the game. He'll be out early in the season and is probably going to be aimed at the Drinmore Novices' Chase at Fairyhouse. I'd say he doesn't really want winter heavy ground so we'll probably have him ready for some of those novice chases run earlier in the season, give him a break during the hardest part of the winter, and then get him ready for Cheltenham. The JLT Novices' Chase could suit him."

Prince could be 'very good'

If there is going to be a horse to step forward and become the top-notch staying novice chaser Elliott so desperately craves, **Prince Of Scars** may be the one to deliver.

Having progressed from handicap hurdle company to winning a Grade 1 staying hurdle at Leopardstown last Christmas, Elliott has always viewed him as a chaser and counts last season's exploits as a pleasant surprise.

"He could be a very good horse over fences this year for us. He's come back in looking a lot stronger this season and he was always going to be a chaser."

"I know he's won a Grade 1 over hurdles but chasing is his game. He looks a million dollars and he's definitely one I'm looking forward to."

In the same Gigginstown House Stud colours, Elliott has the likes of Tombstone, Tycoon Prince and Ball D'Arc to look forward to, but admits splitting up his novice chasers will be a new and exciting challenge this season.

"I've never had as many good novices over fences so it's a great problem to have," he says.

"**Tombstone** ran very well to finish fourth in the Supreme at Cheltenham but has had a few problems since that. He's another who is going to go chasing, but I think his trip is going to be 2m4f as opposed to 2m. He's delicate but he has a big engine. He isn't the easiest to train

Prince Of Scars: expected to shine over fences this season

but if we can keep him right, I'd be looking forward to seeing what he could do around the good tracks.

"**Tycoon Prince** has had a wind operation. We aren't entirely sure if he'll go chasing or stay hurdling yet. He's extremely well handicapped over hurdles. He has a very big engine and could be a horse who is just growing into himself now. With the wind operation he could be all right this year. He's a massive horse but doesn't lack for pace – he's very fast.

"**Ball D'Arc** is another to look out for. He's not slow and we'll be going 2m novice chasing with him. He has a big engine, too."

The real deal

Asked about some of the horses who won't be carrying the maroon and white jersey of Gigginstown, Elliott is quick to mention the JP McManus-owned **Sutton Place**, a horse who steadily improved from winning a bumper at Fairyhouse last January before finishing his

GORDON ELLIOTT
LONGWOOD, COUNTY MEATH

	Races Run	1st	2nd	3rd	Unpl	Per cent	£1 Level Stake
Non-hcp chases	341	58	77	43	163	17	-161.40
Handicap hurdle	209	28	21	25	135	13.4	-75.69
Non-hcp chases	151	35	40	24	52	23.2	-32.75
Handicap chases	123	15	23	10	75	12.2	-43.75
NH Flat	95	13	21	11	50	13.7	-51.11
TOTAL	**919**	**149**	**182**	**113**	**475**	**16.2**	**-364.70**

BY MONTH

	W-R	Per cent	£1 Level Stake
January	9-74	12.2	-54.02
February	14-50	28	+3.00
March	13-94	13.8	-20.69
April	4-49	8.2	-33.67
May	15-83	18.1	-33.52
June	14-72	19.4	+5.39
July	16-91	17.6	-46.37
August	5-90	5.6	-53.19
September	10-45	22.2	-10.71
October	21-89	23.6	-46.08
November	14-88	15.9	-32.98
December	14-94	14.9	-41.51

FAVOURITES

	W-R	Per cent	£1 Level Stake
Non-hcp chases	37-79	46.8	-7.45
Handicap hurdles	16-58	27.6	-11.93
Non-hcp chases	22-37	59.5	+2.92
Handicap chases	6-27	22.2	-6.50
NH Flat	10-27	37	-4.43
TOTAL	**91-228**	**39.91**	**-27.39**

Statistics relate to runners in Ireland during the 2015-16 season

Sutton Place: Elliott has high hopes for the three-time winner

Ladbrokes

ONLINE & MOBILE

BEST ODDS GUARANTEED PLUS

PRICE TAKEN 3/1   WINS AT 7/2   PAID AT 4/1 *

WHEN THE **FUN** STOPS **STOP**™

gambleaware.co.uk

18+

...ilable on all UK and Irish races. Online & Mobile only. Maximum stake for BOG+ to apply is £200. Single bets only. Maximum payout as a result of BOG+ is £25,000. Not available on Tote or ante post bets. Ladbrokes reserves ... withdraw this offer at any time. See Ladbrokes.com/tc/bogplus PLEASE BET RESPONSIBLY. gambleaware.co.uk Need help? Call the National Helpline free on 0808 802 0133

season with a battling Grade 2 success over hurdles at that same track over Easter.

"He looks the real deal. He'll be ready to start off late October and he could be anything. We'll start him off small and see how he progresses but he seems to have the right attitude and we'll let him tell us whether he wants 2m or 2m4f. He's definitely a very nice horse."

It is unlikely Elliott would have expected to have **Free Expression** among his novice chasers for this season, but the son of Germany failed to get his head in front in three starts over fences last year and his trainer hopes he can find the key to him this time.

"He's a very good horse but at the same time he's been a little bit frustrating. He'll start off in a beginners' chase and we'll take it from there. He definitely has the ability and hopefully we can find the key to him."

'I can't wait for Missy Tata'

Before conversation switches to novice hurdlers, **Missy Tata's** name is mentioned as a possible dark horse as a chaser.

"I can't wait to see her over fences. We'll start her off against her own sex before taking full advantage of her age and sex allowance against the geldings. She'll win plenty of races, that's for sure."

Fagan is another who will be campaigned modestly to start off, with Elliott keen to take baby steps with last season's Albert Bartlett Novices' Hurdle runner-up before aiming at something like the four-miler at Cheltenham.

Best staying novice hurdler

Death Duty was a highly promising bumper horse for the stable last season winning two of his three starts, and his sole defeat at Fairyhouse came at the hands of subsequent Grade 1 Punchestown Champion Bumper scorer Blow By Blow.

Elliott says: "He could be very good and I'd say he's our best staying novice hurdler. We'll be campaigning him over 2m4f to 3m and he's one I've always liked a lot. He's a real nice horse and we'll start him around a good big galloping track."

The former jump jockey-turned-trainer has assembled the most powerful bunch of novice chasers yet, some cracking novice hurdlers and plenty of old familiars who will be taking high rank in some of the most prestigious handicap chases either side of the Irish Sea throughout the winter.

Irish National firepower

Mala Beach was unlucky not to get his head in front last season. The Chris Jones-owned eight-year-old was narrowly beaten in the Thyestes Chase at Gowran Park before falling at the second-last fence when travelling like the winner in front under Davy Russell in the Bobbyjo Chase at Fairyhouse.

"He was unlucky he didn't win a big one last year so, touch wood, we can make up for it this time. Something like the Irish National could be right up his street and I wouldn't rule out reverting to hurdles."

Jones could have another decent staying handicap chaser on his hands in the shape of **Noble Endeavor**, who would have gone very close to winning the four-miler at Cheltenham but for coming down two fences from the finish.

"His jumping let him down in the second half of the season. He was running a big race in the four-miler before he fell and I'd say he wasn't going to be too far away," Elliott says. "He'll be competing in staying handicap chases, and again, he could be bound for the Irish National."

While Elliott has yet to win the Fairyhouse showpiece, there was a notable first success in the Galway Plate this summer when **Lord Scoundrel** got a deserved day in the sun having bumped into some top novice chasers last season.

"He came out of Galway great. We're aiming him at Gowran Park for the PWC Champion Chase on October 1. After that we'll be looking to Down Royal for the second-season novices' chase and then we'll take it from there."

The Game Changer will be kept to the minimum trip for the majority of the season and will be seen at his best when encountering better ground.

Asked for three dark horses, Elliott is keen to put forward the relatively lightly raced four-time winner **Ned Stark**, whom he purchased out of Alan King's stable.

"He could be a horse for a nice handicap – maybe something like a Paddy Power Chase at Leopardstown over Christmas.

Last Minute Man can win plenty of races

"Of the younger brigade, **Last Minute Man** is a lovely horse by Yeats who we think will win plenty of races for Paul and Clare Rooney.

"We also have a horse here for Gigginstown called **Burren Life** and he could be worth following. He fell at the last in a point-to-point and he should win his bumper."

With two Wexford sand gallops and a woodchip gallop with an incline finish, two schooling grounds and now a new swimming pool installed, Elliott approaches the season with his best team of horses yet, together with even better facilities, but can he challenge Willie Mullins for the trainers' title in Ireland this year?

Dreams of becoming champion trainer

"I'm not stupid and I've been second behind Willie for the past five years now," he says.

"That's the way it's going to be for a while, but we'll keep nibbling away at him every year and maybe one day we'll get there.

"If I didn't dream of one day becoming champion then I shouldn't be training racehorses, because you need to be hungry in this game."

Interview by Brian Sheerin

SUPER STATS

☑ **A tally of 28 British winners last season saw Elliott earn more than £700,000, a record for him. And his 123 winners in Ireland last term was also a personal best**

☑ Elliott is renowned for his raids at Perth and his record since 2012-13 stands at 68-234 (29%, +£17.80)

☑ **Hurdlers return a profit at Cartmel (8-26, 31%, +£0.95) as do his rare runners over the small obstacles at Ascot (2-6, 33%, +£35)**

☑ Elliott has had his share of success at Cheltenham, where his hurdlers have returned a profit of £17.38 (5-45, 11%)

☑ **He has a superb record in handicaps in Britain. His runners over hurdles is 33-164, 20% (+£37.81) and chases 22-124, 18%) +£0.18**

☑ Tom Scudamore scored on two of his three rides in Britain for Elliott last season (67%, +£4.38)

Statistics cover the 2012-13 season onwards and are correct to September 9, 2016

Sprinter spearheads Seven Barrows team packed with quality

NICKY HENDERSON, who performed a minor miracle to return Sprinter Sacre to the top of the 2m chasing tree last season, hopes the popular ten-year-old will be able to maintain that form this term, but admits a formidable rival lies in wait in the shape of imposing Racing Post Arkle winner Douvan.

Henderson, who was champion trainer in 2013, earned plenty of plaudits for his handling of Caroline Mould's brilliant chaser, who brought the house down at Cheltenham in March when he regained the Champion Chase crown he won in 2013 before his career was threatened by heart problems.

The master of Seven Barrows, who has a crack team assembled for the coming months, says: "Cheltenham was everything and what happened that day was extraordinary. It was one of the most emotional days I can remember."

Sprinter Sacre's first main target is likely to be the Betfair Tingle Creek at Sandown in December, when he could clash with Douvan, who is odds-on in places for the Betway-backed Champion Chase.

"He's come back looking brilliant. He's as big as I've ever seen him – he weighs 630kg.

He's massive but looks fantastic. He's doing the same as everything else at the moment – they're all doing their build-up work – and if everything is 100 per cent with him off we go again.

"He was giving us very good vibes this time last year and into the Shloer Chase, but when I was looking for a reason not to run him at Sandown on the final day of the season he was so good and he told us that.

"I actually think he was a better horse at Sandown when he won the Celebration Chase than he was at Cheltenham and as long as he's in that mode we've got to keep going, but there's one little thing and it's called Douvan."

Henderson continues: "I'd imagine the Tingle Creek would be Sprinter's objective for the first part of the season and it's entirely possible he could run again in the Shloer at Cheltenham, but that's only three weeks before Sandown and this time he'd have the penalty he didn't have to carry last year.

"The race that matters is in March, and I suspect we all felt Kempton wasn't the ideal place for him last season and therefore the Desert Orchid Chase may not feature this year."

Sprinter Sacre is among the old guard at the stable and, while former favourite Bobs Worth has been retired, Henderson is optimistic **Simonsig** can continue to

'He's come back looking brilliant. He's as big as I've ever seen him – he's massive but looks fantastic'

DID YOU KNOW?

Nicky Henderson is a three-time champion trainer, but he had to wait a long time for his third title. He initially won it in 1986, taking over the mantle from his old boss Fred Winter, and again in 1987. It was 2013 before he did it again, although his biggest number of winners in a season was recorded the previous year when he had 167 victories.

perform with credit. He has had an interrupted career but thrilled Henderson with his third in Punchestown's Champion Chase in May before finishing down the field over hurdles on unsuitably soft ground in the Prix la Barka.

"He's purposely not had a very long break and we hope to be ready for an autumn campaign back over fences," says the trainer.

"There's no doubt he's retained a lot of his old ability and he showed us at home that he was very nearly as good as ever.

"Like Caroline with Sprinter, his owner Ronnie Bartlett has been amazing because it's taken a long time and he adores the horse."

Aintree again for Triolo

If there is one race Nicky Henderson would dearly love to add to his bulging CV it is the Grand National, and the trainer will be praying for a dry spring when **Triolo D'Alene** bids to make it third-time lucky in the sport's most famous jumps race.

The 2013 Topham winner's two efforts in the Aintree marathon – pulled up in 2014 and 14th in April – were affected by rain.

"We've encountered exceptionally soft ground, which is something he simply cannot cope with," says Henderson, whose best National finishes came with Zongalero and The Tsarevich, who were second in 1979 and 1987.

Aintree is also on the agenda for **Hadrian's Approach** and **Cocktails At Dawn**, who both prefer a sound surface, while **Vyta Du Roc** is another possible.

Henderson has won five Topham Chases over the National fences and says: "I seem to say the same every year in we can go round once, but can't seem to do it twice. We need to win the National.

"We have a good team of staying handicap chasers and some of those could be in the mix for Hennessys and all other Grand Nationals."

Other senior chasers expected to flourish over shorter trips are **Josses Hill**, **Vaniteux**, **L'Ami Serge** and **Full Shift**, who were involved at Cheltenham in March,

while Henderson would love to see **Close Touch** come back to what he's capable of.

Supreme ace heading over fences

Altior, whose five-race winning streak over hurdles last season culminated in a brilliant victory in the Supreme Novices' Hurdle, will spearhead Nicky Henderson's team of novice chasers this term.

"We'd always hoped he was a bit special and I'm glad to say hopes were realised last season," says Henderson, whose exciting gelding is a general 4-1 chance for the Racing Post Arkle.

"We've spent the summer deliberating whether we should stay over hurdles with a view to having a look at the Champion, or switch to fences and aim at the Arkle. After a lot of thought, discussion and at times a lot of indecision, we decided to take the novice chase route.

"He's now a six-year-old, rising seven, and if we don't go chasing now I suspect we might never. It was also very obvious he'd grown considerably through the summer and, although he was always a big horse, he now looks like a chaser. As much as it would be tempting to see if he was good enough for a Champion Hurdle, which I think he is, we've plumped for fences.

"We schooled him once in the spring to help us make this decision and he was absolutely excellent."

Buveur could also go chasing

Henderson's novice chase crew will be further strengthened if **Buveur D'Air** – third to Altior in the Supreme and a Grade 1 winner at Aintree – also makes the move to fences.

That decision has not yet been made but the five-year-old will be schooled over fences at home, possibly when new owner JP McManus's retained rider Barry Geraghty returns from injury.

"He has the size and scope to jump fences but could still be a very high-class hurdler," says Henderson.

"He's come back in looking bigger and

Sprinter Sacre (left) enjoying his summer break with Jenkins

stronger and has an enormous future whichever road we choose to take. Apart from Altior and possibly Buveur D'Air, we have a very big and talented squad of high-class hurdlers who are now due to switch to chasing.

Novice chase firepower

"**Days Of Heaven** has already won a novice chase and is heading for the American Grand National, but the likes of **Top Notch**, who isn't overly big, has already schooled very well, as have Graded hurdlers **Different Gravey**, **O O Seven** and **Brain Power**. **Whisper**, twice a winner of the Grade 1 Liverpool Stayers' Hurdle, could also join the party.

"Other talented performers **Laurium**, **Beware The Bear**, **Gold Present**, **Might Bite** and **Kilcrea Vale** are also set to make the transition, whereas **Theinval** and **Hammersly Lake** have already won their first novice chase."

Interestingly, four-year-olds **Fixe Le Kap** and **Protek Des Flos** are other possibles for the switch to fences.

Henderson added: "They're lovely, big horses, who love soft ground. These are smart juvenile hurdlers, but being precocious four-year-olds might as well get on with chasing now."

Breathing op for Peace

If Henderson produced the training performance of the campaign to get Sprinter Sacre back on track last term, he might have to go one better if **Peace And Co** is to return to the level that had connections dreaming he could be the next Seven Barrows superstar.

He led home a memorable 1-2-3 for the trainer in the Triumph Hurdle in 2015 but failed to fire last season when he was expected to develop into a Champion Hurdle horse.

The plan is to remain over hurdles this term, and Henderson says: "He clearly has a ton of talent but he can be his own worst enemy at times and we're going to continue to experiment and tinker with things at home with a view to getting him back to his best.

"He's had a wind procedure this summer and I sincerely hope we can manage to get the real Peace And Co back for his owners Simon Munir and Isaac Souede.

"Interestingly, his mark is now down to 149 so if we can get him back on song we may try to go for a big handicap."

Hargam, third behind Peace And Co in the Triumph, could be in line for a step up in trip over hurdles, while Henderson reckons **Cardinal Walter**, who has been running respectably on the Flat this summer, has "a good race in him".

Champion aim again

My Tent Or Yours also did Henderson proud when returning from nearly two years off to finish a fine second to Annie Power in the Champion Hurdle.

"He's come back from Martinstown looking in exceptionally good order," says Henderson.

"I don't think novice chasing is really on

NICKY HENDERSON

UPPER LAMBOURN, BERKS

	No. of Hrs	Races Run	1st	2nd	3rd	Unpl	Per cent	£1 Level Stake
NH Flat	40	65	8	10	9	38	12.3	-25.89
Hurdles	105	269	55	34	31	149	20.4	-59.88
Chases	28	84	20	10	9	45	23.8	-7.51
Totals	**152**	**418**	**83**	**54**	**49**	**232**	**19.9**	**-93.28**
14-15	157	499	127	91	62	219	25.5	-59.75
13-14	158	501	117	72	56	256	23.4	-42.81

BY MONTH

NH Flat	W-R	Per cent	£1 Level Stake	Hurdles	W-R	Per cent	£1 Level Stake
May	2-10	20.0	-2.00	May	8-27	29.6	-7.94
June	0-1	0.0	-1.00	June	0-3	0.0	-3.00
July	0-0	0.0	0.00	July	2-4	50.0	+0.35
August	0-1	0.0	-1.00	August	0-6	0.0	-6.00
September	0-1	0.0	-1.00	September	2-10	20.0	-3.17
October	1-4	25.0	-2.09	October	7-25	28.0	+7.13
November	0-6	0.0	-6.00	November	9-35	25.7	+6.82
December	1-2	50.0	+0.50	December	4-18	22.2	-9.14
January	0-4	0.0	-4.00	January	5-24	20.8	+12.73
February	1-13	7.7	-7.00	February	9-33	27.3	-6.43
March	1-12	8.3	-10.80	March	6-46	13.0	-21.98
April	2-11	18.2	+8.50	April	3-38	7.9	-29.27

Chases	W-R	Per cent	£1 Level Stake	Totals	W-R	Per cent	£1 Level Stake
May	2-5	40.0	+2.25	May	12-42	28.6	-7.69
June	0-1	0.0	-1.00	June	0-5	0.0	-5.00
July	0-0	0.0	0.00	July	2-4	50.0	+0.35
August	0-0	0.0	0.00	August	0-7	0.0	-7.00
September	0-1	0.0	1.00	September	2-12	16.7	-5.17
October	1-5	20.0	+2.00	October	9-34	26.5	+7.04
November	2-13	15.4	-8.40	November	11-54	20.4	-7.58
December	5-11	45.5	+2.79	December	10-31	32.3	-5.85
January	4-10	40.0	+3.85	January	9-38	23.7	+12.58
February	3-12	25.0	+1.41	February	13-58	22.4	-12.02
March	1-12	8.3	-6.00	March	8-70	11.4	-30.78
April	2-14	14.3	3.40	April	7-63	11.1	-24.17

DISTANCE

Hurdles	W-R	Per cent	£1 Level Stake	Chases	W-R	Per cent	Per£1 Level Stake
2m-2m3f	22-108	20.4	-17.56	2m-2m3f	9-19	47.4	+1.86
2m4f-2m7f	15-85	17.6	-21.97	2m4f-2m7f	6-29	20.7	+5.66
3m+	3-12	25.0	+0.88	3m+	1-19	5.3	-14.50

TYPE OF RACE

Non-Handicaps

	W-R	Per cent	£1 Level Stake
Nov Hrdls	25-69	36.2	-7.41
Hrdls	17-83	20.5	-4.30
Nov Chs	8-24	33.3	-2.12
Chases	7-17	41.2	+9.86
Sell/Claim	0-0	0.0	0.00

Handicaps

	W-R	Per cent	£1 Level Stake
Nov Hrdls	1-8	12.5	-3.50
Hrdls	12-109	11.0	-44.67
Nov Chs	2-8	25.0	+6.50
Chases	3-35	8.6	-21.75
Sell/Claim	0-0	0.0	0.00

RACE CLASS

	W-R	Per cent	£1 Level Stake
Class 1	15-112	13.4	-17.55
Class 2	15-74	20.3	+5.12
Class 3	13-71	18.3	-20.20
Class 4	29-87	33.3	-25.82
Class 5	8-39	20.5	-12.33
Class 6	3-35	8.6	-22.50

FIRST TIME OUT

	W-R	Per cent	£1 Level Stake
Bumpers	5-40	12.5	-19.59
Hurdles	20-87	23.0	-2.01
Chases	8-25	32.0	+5.47
Totals	33-152	21.7	-16.13

Statistics relate to runners in Britain from April 26, 2015 to April 23, 2016

Altior blasts to victory in the Supreme Novices' – he's now set for switch to fences

the agenda at this stage of his life and therefore we'll have to continue down the Champion Hurdle route. He's been a stalwart for so many years and I'm sure he retains his ability and enthusiasm."

Although Altior's win in the Supreme was Henderson's first in the race for 24 years, he is typically a force in the novice hurdling department and considers this autumn's crop to be a good squad of young horses.

The trainer says: "We had Altior last season and have got to find another one."

The obvious one

Jenkins, who won a bumper at Newbury before finishing second in the Land Rover edition at the Punchestown festival, is the "most obvious one", although Henderson plays down the significance of him sharing a field with Sprinter Sacre over the summer.

Baden, who also had solid form at Punchestown, is a novice from last term to note, as is **Consul De Thaix**, who ran in the Triumph, and **Khezerabad**, who was third in the Adonis.

Stowaway Magic did get off the mark over hurdles at Warwick in May but remains a novice the season, as does **Phobiaphiliac**, who struck at Southwell the same month.

The well-regarded and enthusiastic **Cultivator**, who runs in the Bobs Worth colours, also ran over hurdles in the spring, which Henderson believes he will have learned an "enormous amount" from, while **Rather Be**, not beaten far when ninth in the Champion Bumper at Cheltenham, is among a clutch of potential-packed youngsters ready to go hurdling.

They include **River Wylde**, **Jameson**, **Thomas Campbell**, **Fly Camp** and **Christmas In April**, who all created big impressions with wide-margin bumper victories.

Henderson is also looking forward to the return of **Gaitway** and **William Henry**, who have had time off, while **Minella Rebellion** and unrelated lookalikes **Lough Derg Farmer** and **Lough Derg Spirit** are point-to-point recruits to keep an eye on.

"You have a job telling them apart and they've got similar names," says the trainer. "They're likely types to appear shortly. Another point-to-pointer I like, but the commentators are going to hate, is **Claimantakinforgan**."

'She has everything'

Henderson usually has a strong squad of fillies and mares to go to war with and this season is no different.

Right at the top of the pecking order is French import **Kotkikova**, who has the Lambourn trainer purring.

Owned by JP McManus, the five-year-old has won 11 of her 14 starts including a Grade 1 over fences.

"She has absolutely everything," says Henderson. "She's the most gorgeous-looking mare, has a pedigree to die for and obviously a huge amount of talent. It's amazing what she's already achieved in such a short space of time.

"The plan at the moment would be to school her over British fences to see how she gets on and then make a decision as to which route, be it hurdling or chasing, that we take for this season. We're looking forward to her enormously."

Mares' aim for Mary

Bloody Mary, third in the inaugural running of the Grade 2 Trull House Stud

Racing Post iPad app

30-day free trial. On the App Store now.

Available on the **App Store**

Mares' Novices' Hurdle at the Cheltenham Festival, is another McManus mare Henderson "loves", and plans are a little clearer for her with a hurdling campaign in the spring on the agenda.

Henderson says: "She had a knee injury following that Cheltenham race and it required surgery, so she'll be back later in the season. I'm pretty sure she'll improve for the break and I hope she'll be up to contesting the mares' Grade 1 at the festival in March if Kotkikova, in the same ownership, goes elsewhere.

"Bloody Mary is a great jumper of hurdles but fences might be a bit too much for her, although she is just the most lovely character."

Henderson's hopes of winning the festival's newest race this season appear to rest with **Kayf Grace**, who won the Grade 2 mares' bumper at Aintree, and **Theatre Territory**, who was 11th in that race.

Spectacular

"Kayf Grace put up a spectacular performance to win really nicely at Aintree," he says. "We have to hope she could be top class in the mares' novice division, while Theatre Territory didn't run so well at Aintree but is talented."

Southwell bumper winner **Scorpio Queen** – "a lovely, big filly with great scope, spectacular cars and a great, honest look about her" – could also come into that category, while **Omessa Has**, who made the frame over fences at Auteuil last year before arriving in Britain for one run at Cheltenham in April, could go chasing.

"I think you'll see the real Omessa Has this time," the trainer says.

Interview by James Burn

☑ Since 2012-13, Henderson has a fine strike-rate at Huntingdon (25-63, 40%, +£6.16) but has recorded higher level-stake profits at Doncaster (28-76, 37%, +£36.67) and Kempton (60-203, 30%, +£57.48)

☑ He has a fine record in bumpers with most winners at Kempton (15-41, 37%, +£15.57) but runners are also well worth watching out for at Market Rasen (7-18, 39%, +£2.01) and Fakenham (4-5, 80%, +£1.93)

SUPER STATS

☒ Numbers were down at Seven Barrows last year with just 81 winners on the board – the first time Henderson failed to break the century barrier in eight seasons

☑ December is usually a good month for Henderson and that was when his strike-rate was at its highest last season (10-32, 31%, -£6.86) although he recorded a better level-stakes return in January (9-38, 24%, +£12.58)

Statistics cover the 2012-13 season onwards and are correct to September 9, 2016

THE LOWDOWN PHILIP HOBBS

Ton-up king out to beat handicapper for another big season

SUCCESS comes at a price in racing. The handicapper sees to that, but trainer Philip Hobbs is used to having to deal with this scenario annually as he sends out over 100 winners with regularity.

To reach such heights each year, his Sandhill stables near Minehead in Somerset nurtures young talent to rise to the occasion backed by the old guard manfully struggling against the handicapping tide.

The retirement of the likes of Captain Chris and Balthazar King leaves 11-year-old **Menorah** king of the Sandhill castle after his rousing hat-trick in the Oaksey Chase at Sandown's season-ending meeting in April.

The campaign saw Hobbs again top £1 million in prize-money and made it a 12th season with scores over 100, with 113 his best in a decade.

Unsurprisingly, Hobbs says: "The Oaksey is very much on the agenda again. Menorah doesn't want soft ground and will probably run in the Charlie Hall again or the 3m chase at Ascot on the same day."

Two achievers straining against the handicapper's leashes are Village Vic and Sternrubin, who ended their successful seasons struggling at the highest level.

Village Vic rocketed 30lb in the weights for his four consecutive wins including two around the turn of the year at Cheltenham including the Grade 3 Caspian Caviar Gold Cup when still eight. In the rarefied air of the 150-plus-rated chasers he found the Ryanair a flight too far.

Sternrubin is only rising six but has paid for winning the Gerry Feilden and dead-heating with Jolly's Cracked It in The Ladbroke at Ascot. Upped 20lb from his juvenile hurdling rating he found life tough in the County Hurdle at Cheltenham and the Scottish Champion Hurdle.

Hobbs said: "Both need to improve and with Sternrubin very high in the handicap over hurdles we might jump a fence with him."

It is a surprise if a big stable does not have a disappointment before the season gets into full swing and one such blow for Hobbs is the 2015 Swinton Hurdle winner War Sound missing the campaign. However, there are established performers and up-and-coming types in the yard.

Sausalito Sunrise was another top performer in the colours of long-time supporter Diana Whateley last season, and he could be even more high-profile this season with a possible big-race target next April.

He won the Grade 3 Murphy Group

'Last season saw Hobbs again top prize-money of £1 million, and he made it a 12th season with over 100 winners'

DID YOU KNOW?

Philip Hobbs recorded his first festival winner in 1990 with Moody Man in the County Hurdle. It was six years later before he had his next success at the meeting, Kibreet in the Grand Annual ridden by AP McCoy. Hobbs has had two dual festival winners – Rooster Booster who won the County Hurdle (2002) and the Champion Hurdle (2003) and Balthazar King, who has won two Cross Country Chases in 2012 and 2014. Philip's first major winner as a trainer was Joint Sovereignty in the 1989 Mackeson Gold Cup.

Handicap Chase at Cheltenham in November and a Listed chase at Ascot in February but the eight-year-old signed off with a very good run in the bet365 Gold Cup at Sandown.

"He could be a Grand National horse if he mans up a bit," says Hobbs. "He's just a bit soft and needs to get a view of his fences and he doesn't want soft ground."

The Aintree marathon turned out not to be to the liking of **Kruzhlinin** after his good fifth in the Ultima Handicap Chase at the Cheltenham Festival.

It will be back to the more conventional races over 3m on decent ground, with a hint the nine-year-old is better going left-handed.

Royal Regatta had a little bit of an in-and-out season as his trainer puts it, but managed a graduation chase win at Ascot in December before ending with a third to

Silviniaco Conti in the Ascot Chase.

Hobbs hopes there is more still to come from this eight-year-old, and says: "He's a very big horse and has taken time to mature. He has undoubted ability and doesn't want the ground too soft."

Haldon aim for Victoire

Two who climbed the novice chase ranks last year were Garde La Victoire and Onenightinvienna, although both found it an unequal struggle at the end of the season.

Garde La Victoire won three novice chases but then his season fell apart albeit at the highest level in Grade 1 races at Cheltenham and Aintree. He had made a mistake or two in winning his three races, but sharing favouritism with winner Black Hercules he was still travelling strongly and

Sandhill Stables is a hive of activity at this time of the year

seemingly poised to pounce when falling four out in the JLT Novice Chase at the festival.

His confidence looked affected at Aintree in the Manifesto Novices' Chase as he made mistakes before falling at the fourth-last.

"He's a very good horse," said Hobbs. "The Haldon Gold Cup is the obvious race for him as there are usually not many runners and the fences are not stiff. He might have a run over hurdles beforehand."

Onenightinvienna paid for chasing home subsequent RSA Chase winner Blaklion at Cheltenham in December three weeks after winning a novice chase at Exeter. While his mark has eased 5lb from its opening 151, the seven-year-old is another who will need to improve to match his tasks.

Hobbs says: "With his high rating we ran him in the Grand National which at the time we thought was a good idea but it was probably too much for the horse."

Novice chase team

As always, there is a new crop of novice chasers waiting in the wings and **Brother Tedd** will be one of the first to test the water with Hobbs looking to run him in October.

"He doesn't want the ground too soft and 2m4f is his trip," says the trainer.

Vieux Lille is another Hobbs hopes will step up over fences although the six-year-old paid his way as a novice hurdler with three wins and a third in the Rossington Main at Haydock.

"He had decent form but he's by Robin Des Champs and a 3m novice chase should be a better job for him."

Duke Des Champs is similarly a staying chaser in the making with Hobbs reporting: "He'll be going straight over fences and will end up in 3m races but will start over 2m4f to 2m6f. He's a big, strong horse who looks likely to be better over fences than he was over hurdles."

Braavos ended last season with a handicap hurdle win at Perth which saw his rating jump 10lb, and the five-year-old son of Presenting is earmarked for a switch to fences.

"He'll probably run in a hurdle race first and then go chasing. He doesn't want the ground too soft and will start off over 2m4f," says Hobbs.

Rock The Kasbah, winner of the Grade 3 Holloway's Hurdle at Ascot and beaten favourite in the Coral Cup at Cheltenham on the back of that, is an eyecatching convert to fences.

He is only six and brings a hurdle rating of 150 to the table which should ensure he gets respect in his early novice chases.

If In Doubt had his problems jumping fences and ended last season acquitting himself well back over hurdles, just a length off Pertemps Final success in third despite being hampered before running with credit at Aintree and Punchestown.

"Although he won chases he'll start back over hurdles," says Hobbs. "While he's gone up the handicap to 153 he wouldn't have to improve much to win 3m conditions hurdles."

Likely big improver

No Comment, like If In Doubt owned by JP McManus, already has a '1' against his name having won the 2m2f amateurs' bumper under Jamie Codd at Punchestown at the end of April. The five-year-old had previously shown his quality in finishing second in a bumper and novice hurdle.

"He's still a novice over hurdles for this season and could be a big improver with a bit of luck," says his trainer.

There has never been any hiding the high regard in which **Wait For Me** is held after

Rock The Kasbah: looks an interesting recruit to the novice chase ranks

PHILIP HOBBS
WITHYCOMBE, SOMERSET

	No. of Hrs	Races Run	1st	2nd	3rd	Unpl	Per cent	£1 Level Stake
NH Flat	36	60	15	11	9	25	25.0	-5.16
Hurdles	82	273	68	43	42	120	24.9	+7.20
Chases	55	199	33	29	32	105	16.6	-54.02
Totals	**146**	**532**	**116**	**83**	**83**	**250**	**21.8**	**-51.98**
14-15	137	548	100	92	76	280	18.2	-90.31
13-14	131	542	105	74	53	310	19.4	+17.62

BY MONTH

NH Flat	W-R	Per cent	£1 Level Stake	Hurdles	W-R	Per cent	£1 Level Stake
May	1-6	16.7	-2.00	May	4-11	36.4	+3.08
June	1-1	100.0	+5.00	June	0-7	0.0	-7.00
July	0-0	0.0	0.00	July	0-6	0.0	-6.00
August	0-0	0.0	0.00	August	0-4	0.0	-4.00
September	0-1	0.0	-1.00	September	2-6	33.3	+1.63
October	2-4	50.0	-0.25	October	9-21	42.9	+7.25
November	2-7	28.6	-0.63	November	13-48	27.1	+0.23
December	4-9	44.4	+7.78	December	12-35	34.3	+42.36
January	1-3	33.3	+2.00	January	9-31	29.0	-0.39
February	3-7	42.9	+1.93	February	3-23	13.0	-13.50
March	0-9	0.0	-9.00	March	6-34	17.6	-14.97
April	1-13	7.7	-9.00	April	10-47	21.3	-1.49

Chases	W-R	Per cent	£1 Level Stake	Totals	W-R	Per cent	£1 Level Stake
May	2-13	15.4	-2.75	May	7-30	23.3	-1.67
June	1-7	14.3	-4.25	June	2-15	13.3	-6.25
July	2-7	28.6	+2.12	July	2-13	15.4	-3.88
August	3-6	50.0	+4.88	August	3-10	30.0	+0.88
September	0-7	0.0	-7.00	September	2-14	14.3	-6.37
October	4-27	14.8	-10.40	October	15-52	28.8	-3.40
November	4-27	14.8	-11.09	November	19-82	23.2	-11.49
December	4-21	19.0	+9.75	December	20-65	30.8	+59.89
January	5-18	27.8	+1.17	January	15-52	28.8	+2.78
February	2-13	15.4	-7.56	February	8-43	18.6	-19.13
March	1-22	4.5	-19.50	March	7-65	10.8	-43.47
April	5-31	16.1	-9.38	April	16-91	17.6	-19.87

DISTANCE

Hurdles	W-R	Per cent	£1 Level Stake	Chases	W-R	Per cent	£1 Level Stake
2m-2m3f	34-131	26.0	-15.33	2m-2m3f	8-43	18.6	-13.25
2m4f-2m7f	14-65	21.5	-15.00	2m4f-2m7f	10-61	16.4	-4.63
3m+	2-13	15.4	-8.83	3m+	9-70	12.9	-31.06

TYPE OF RACE

Non-Handicaps	W-R	Per cent	£1 Level Stake	Handicaps	W-R	Per cent	£1 Level Stake
Nov Hrdls	24-94	25.5	-35.48	Nov Hrdls	1-6	16.7	+3.00
Hrdls	16-56	28.6	-5.44	Hrdls	27-115	23.5	+47.11
Nov Chs	5-17	29.4	-6.18	Nov Chs	1-15	6.7	-12.75
Chases	6-22	27.3	+1.79	Chases	20-143	14.0	-37.50
Sell/Claim	0-1	0.0	-1.00	Sell/Claim	0-0	0.0	0.00

RACE CLASS

	W-R	Per cent	£1 Level Stake	FIRST TIME OUT	W-R	Per cent	£1 Level Stake
Class 1	13-96	13.5	-20.34	Bumpers	8-36	22.2	4.22
Class 2	10-72	13.9	+17.38	Hurdles	17-66	25.8	+1.21
Class 3	22-106	20.8	-8.94	Chases	9-44	20.5	-12.27
Class 4	51-185	27.6	-27.07				
Class 5	8-35	22.9	-5.42	Totals	34-146	23.3	-15.28
Class 6	12-38	31.6	-5.59				

Statistics relate to runners in Britain from April 26, 2015 to April 23, 2016

his third in the Cheltenham Champion Bumper to Moon Racer two years ago.

After two confidence-building wins he was fourth in the County Hurdle before disappointing in the Swinton last season.

"He was a bit disappointing as he never got his jumping together. He's a decent horse if we can get him back to his best."

Perform was kept out of action by a minor injury after winning a maiden hurdle at Aintree last October but is raring to go again.

"That was a decent novice hurdle," says Hobbs. And scrutiny of the form confirms just that as Knockgraffon and American, who finished second and third, scored on their next start.

Another hurdler to look out for is **Roll The Dough**, who won both starts for Hobbs last October and November but missed the rest of the season.

"He had a minor fracture of his pelvis but is fine now and hopefully he can go the right way with races over 2m4f and he might want 3m."

Gala Ball has won three hurdles but his trainer says: "He's still improving mentally and is rated 145. He'll start over 2m as he's got plenty of pace but will get further."

Prince can improve a lot

There is no lack of talent in this season's novice hurdle department.

Westend Story won his two bumpers to earn his place in the Cheltenham Champion Bumper and was an unlucky fifth at the festival, so is one to watch out for now he goes novice hurdling with 2m4f races the plan.

Bridge Of Spies is an interesting new recruit having been bought privately in the summer out of Ireland.

Hobbs says: "He's only five and won his Irish point. He has plenty of scope and I'm happy with him."

Another five-year-old and also a winner of an Irish point, **Lisheen Prince** is one to note as he showed distinct promise last November in a Cheltenham Listed bumper won by subsequent festival winner Ballyandy.

"He ran very well looking to have a chance coming down the hill," said Hobbs. "He ran up light after that and we gave him the whole year off. He's better for it and can improve a lot."

With the increase in mares only races there are two who could boost the stable tally.

Copper Kay won a Listed bumper at

Cheltenham and ran with credit in other big bumpers at Aintree and Punchestown.

Hobbs says: "She'll be going for novice hurdles over 2m4f and I hope with her level of form she could do well in the mares races."

Ready to make hay

Tearsofclewbay was another useful bumper performer and is another mare who could make hay against her own sex in 2m4f hurdle races this season.

The five-year-old won her first two bumpers and was only a couple of lengths behind well regarded The Nipper in a Listed mares' bumper at Sandown in March before running better than the form suggests in the Punchestown festival Listed mares' bumper.

Once again Hobbs looks to have all departments covered and with over 20 winners on the board since the official start of the season another three-figure score beckons.

*Interview by
Bruce Jackson*

☑ Hobbs has enjoyed a resurgence in recent seasons and last season's tally of 113 was his best in 11 years

☑ He had an excellent record in handicap hurdles last season with 27-119 (23%, +£37.36)

☑ Since the 2012-13 season, Hobbs has recorded his highest level-stakes profit at Newbury (18-102, 18%, +£66.43)

☑ Hobbs has only had six jumps runners at Lingfield since 2012-13 but four of them have obliged (67%, +£4.82)

SUPER STATS

☑ James Best rides some decent-priced winners for the yard and seems to do best on the hurdlers. Last year he was 3-18 (17%, +£22.00)

☑ His partnership with Richard Johnson has been fruitful. Since 2012-13, their record reads 265-1186 (22%, +£78.93)

☑ His most impressive figures with chasers come at Stratford where his record stands at 15-42 (36%, +£35.43)

Statistics cover the 2012-13 season onwards and are correct to September 9, 2016

The Hobbs string heads back to base after work on the gallops

THE LOWDOWN ALAN KING

Smad Hennessy-bound with star Yanworth set to remain over hurdles

WITH well over 20 winners on the board so far this season, Alan King has made a fine start to 2016-17 and the signs are good as his stars return to Barbury Castle and gear up for the winter.

Last season King had no finer stalwart than the flying grey **Smad Place**. Winning over £200,000 in prize-money with three victories, including a 12-length romp in the Hennessy, the nine-year-old had his best season yet over fences, improving a stone in the ratings having thrived under more positive tactics – and King is planning some more shots at the big prizes with him.

"We'll probably get him out at the end of October and start him off in the Charlie Hall Chase at Wetherby," says the trainer. "The main aim for him in the first half of the season will be the Hennessy."

While Smad Place hit the headlines for King among the staying chasers last term, the horse who really caught everyone's attention was **Yanworth**.

The JP McManus-owned six-year-old won four out of five starts in his first season hurdling with his only defeat coming at the festival when he found the Willie Mullins-trained Yorkhill too good in the Neptune. Before that he had barely come off the bridle in his victories, two of which were achieved in Grade 2s.

Described by King in the past as frighteningly good and potentially very special, Yanworth will continue over hurdles for now.

"He could return at Ascot in the big 2m4f contest in November," says King. "We'll stick at around that trip for the time being and see how things pan out from there."

Another top novice hurdler for King last term was **Winter Escape**, who was unbeaten in all three starts, including the Grade 2 Dovecote at Kempton in February. Like Yanworth, King has described Winter Escape as "potentially very exciting" and he will continue over the smaller obstacles this season with a couple of valuable handicaps coming up being seen as potential targets.

"He could go to Ascot for the big handicap hurdle there at the end of October and then there's also the Greatwood at Cheltenham's Open meeting," says King.

Another JP star at Barbury Castle is **Uxizandre**. The 2015 Ryanair Chase hero – AP McCoy's final winner at the festival – missed last season but could return this term and is due back in in October according to the trainer.

Another big name who was not seen last

DID YOU KNOW?

Alan started his career in racing with trainer John Wilson in Scotland, where he looked after the 1985 Supreme Novices' Hurdle winner Harry Hastings. The following year he joined David Nicholson's outfit. When King took over from Nicholson his first big-race victory was with Relkeel, who landed a third straight Bula Hurdle. He seems to be making a habit of success with greys having landed his first festival victory with Fork Lightning and recorded one of his biggest victories last season when landing the Hennessy with Smad Place.

'The nine-year-old had his best season yet over fences, improving a stone having thrived under more positive tactics – and King is planning some more shots at the big prizes'

ALAN KING

BARBURY CASTLE, WILTS

	No. of Hrs	Races Run	1st	2nd	3rd	Unpl	Per cent	£1 Level Stake
NH Flat	29	53	9	9	5	30	17.0	-7.46
Hurdles	84	262	45	45	37	135	17.2	-102.83
Chases	27	86	14	5	11	56	16.3	-8.25
Totals	**122**	**401**	**68**	**59**	**53**	**221**	**17.0**	**-118.54**
14-15	122	455	77	78	45	254	16.9	-132.51
13-14	131	434	76	63	47	248	17.5	-21.10

BY MONTH

NH Flat	W-R	Per cent	£1 Level Stake	Hurdles	W-R	Per cent	£1 Level Stake
May	1-2	50.0	+0.50	May	0-12	0.0	-12.00
June	0-0	0.0	0.00	June	0-9	0.0	-9.00
July	0-0	0.0	0.00	July	0-7	0.0	-7.00
August	0-0	0.0	0.00	August	0-2	0.0	-2.00
September	0-1	0.0	-1.00	September	1-7	14.3	-5.67
October	1-5	20.0	0.00	October	7-28	25.0	-12.63
November	1-12	8.3	-9.13	November	7-40	17.5	-19.49
December	0-3	0.0	-3.00	December	13-40	32.5	+12.42
January	0-4	0.0	-4.00	January	9-26	34.6	+22.28
February	4-10	40.0	+9.67	February	6-31	19.4	-16.18
March	2-9	22.2	+6.50	March	0-33	0.0	-33.00
April	0-7	0.0	-7.00	April	2-27	7.4	-20.57

Chases	W-R	Per cent	£1 Level Stake	Totals	W-R	Per cent	£1 Level Stake
May	0-2	0.0	-2.00	May	1-16	6.3	-13.50
June	1-3	33.3	+0.75	June	1-12	8.3	-8.25
July	0-3	0.0	-3.00	July	0-10	0.0	-10.00
August	0-0	0.0	0.00	August	0-2	0.0	-2.00
September	1-1	100.0	+3.00	September	2-9	22.2	-3.67
October	0-6	0.0	-6.00	October	8-39	20.5	-18.63
November	3-19	15.8	+4.50	November	11-71	15.5	-24.12
December	2-17	11.8	-6.50	December	15-60	25.0	+2.92
January	3-12	25.0	+10.00	January	12-42	28.6	+28.28

DISTANCE

Hurdles	W-R	Per cent	£1 Level Stake	Chases	W-R	Per cent	£1 Level Stake
2m-2m3f	20-118	16.9	-58.39	2m-2m3f	1-6	16.7	-3.50
2m4f-2m7f	10-76	13.2	-29.79	2m4f-2m7f	5-30	16.7	+0.75
3m+	0-9	0.0	-9.00	3m+	7-34	20.6	+6.00

TYPE OF RACE

Non-Handicaps	W-R	Per cent	£1 Level Stake	Handicaps	W-R	Per cent	£1 Level Stake
Nov Hrdls	17-74	23.0	-29.78	Nov Hrdls	0-7	0.0	-7.00
Hrdls	22-78	28.2	-16.68	Hrdls	6-102	5.9	-48.38
Nov Chs	0-8	0.0	-8.00	Nov Chs	1-11	9.1	-7.25
Chases	2-5	40.0	+3.00	Chases	11-61	18.0	+5.00
Sell/Claim	0-0	0.0	0.00	Sell/Claim	0-0	0.0	0.00

RACE CLASS

	W-R	Per cent	£1 Level Stake
Class 1	11-73	15.1	-11.33
Class 2	7-39	17.9	-10.57
Class 3	11-78	14.1	-19.31
Class 4	26-145	17.9	-68.31
Class 5	7-36	19.4	+1.32
Class 6	6-30	20.0	-10.33

FIRST TIME OUT

	W-R	Per cent	£1 Level Stake
Bumpers	4-29	13.8	-9.83
Hurdles	12-71	16.9	-22.59
Chases	3-22	13.6	-2.75
Totals	19-122	15.6	-35.17

*Statistics relate to runners in Britain
from April 26, 2015 to April 23, 2016*

season was **Ordo Ab Chao**. A Grade 2 novice hurdle winner on Cheltenham's Trials Day last year, he has recovered from illness and is working his way back towards a return.

"He's back in work and the plan is to go chasing with him," says King, who is also pleased to have his talented eight-year-old **Carraig Mor** back in again following a year off. A Grade 2 winner over fences and always highly regarded, he has started cantering but nothing is set in stone for his return to the racetrack just yet.

Promising juvenile team

Always a force with his horses in the juvenile division, King had three around the 140 mark last season, all of whom ran in the Triumph Hurdle.

The one who fared best at the festival was **Gibralfaro**, who had been rated as high as 151 by the handicapper following two wins earlier in the season.

"We'll probably continue hurdling with him, although he's one of the younger ones I may consider sending over fences at some stage," says King.

"**Sceau Royal** will continue hurdling and we plan to start him off in October. There's a limited handicap at Chepstow and also a race we can look at at Cheltenham."

King will also be looking at handicap hurdles for **Who Dares Wins**, who has been racing on the Flat recently. The Henry Ponsonby-owned gelding was one of numerous winners during the summer for King, who enjoyed one of his best spells on the Flat yet in 2016, including a Royal Ascot success.

Another festival victory came at York's Ebor meeting with **Oceane**, who is one of the market leaders for the Cesarewitch at the time of writing. He is rated as high as 134 over hurdles at present and the four-year-old is likely to go back over the smaller obstacles at some stage.

"He must have good ground so we'll probably give him a mid-winter break before conditions improve," says King.

*Sceau Royal (3): set to
remain over hurdles*

Other fair Flat performers who could try their hand over the smaller obstacles are **Top Tug**, who could be set to go novice hurdling, while **Cosmeapolitan** and Melrose Stakes fourth **Master Blueyes** are set for the juvenile division.

Talented youngsters

Two youngsters King will have high hopes for in novice hurdles this season are **Messire Des Obeaux** and **Criq Rock**. The former performed well at the Cheltenham Festival last term when seventh in the Fred Winter, and King says: "As he remains a novice we'll continue down that route and he's one we're looking forward to. We'll be looking at a stiff two miles for Criq Rock and again he's exciting." The five-year-old won twice in bumpers last autumn and is clearly well regarded.

The novice chase team will be set to include **Label Des Obeaux**. "He'll be going over fences this term, probably staying at around two and a half miles. That'll also be the trip for **Big Chief Benny**, although he'll be staying over hurdles for now. He's a nice prospect. **William H Bonney** is similar. Only a five-year-old, he'll build on his experience from running in the Supreme Novices' last term and remain hurdling."

Messire Des Obeaux (4): promising type for novice hurdles

The only news of any delay comes with King's top mare **Katie Too**, who was good enough to win a Listed event at Cheltenham against her own sex in April.

"She's had a setback so is set to be out until the second half of the season," says King, who is hoping for a similar winter to last term which saw him win big races like the Paddy Power, Hennessy and Great Yorkshire. A few more prizes like those coming his way would be just the ticket.

Interview by James Hill

☑In terms of quantity, last season was no more than steady for King with just 68 winners on the board, but he enjoyed plenty of big-race success and broke the £1 million prize-money barrier for the fifth consecutive season

☑He can be followed with confidence at Bangor (12-42, 29%, +£18.09) and Towcester (10-31, 32%, +£7.49), while his rare visits to Hereford are always worth watching out for (3-6, 50%, +£16.33)

SUPER STATS

☑Over fences, King is best backed at Exeter (7-22, 32%, +£6.36) and Plumpton (5-10, 50%, +£4.08) while his chasers also return a profit at Cheltenham (7-55, 13%, +£3.63)

☑He has plenty of quality at his disposal, reflected by decent figures at Ascot (10-63, 16%, +£30.34)

☑January is often a good month for the yard and that proved the case last season with a record of 12-42 (29%, +£28.28)

Statistics cover the 2012-13 season onwards and are correct to September 9, 2016

Faugheen recovered, Annie looking fantastic – it's time for takeoff

WILLIE MULLINS' **stable stars have so much underneath the bonnet that the running joke between many of the staff working in Closutton is that their place of employment is more akin to an airport rather than a racehorse stable.**

Who could blame them? Horses seem to be jetting off to far flung places to run big races in the Melbourne Cup, Nakayama Grand Jump and even French Champion Hurdles.

Fresh from adding his first Classic success following Wicklow Brave's victory in the Irish St Leger, the man entrusted with playing air traffic controller in County Carlow admits the yard does resemble an airport, but for different reasons to what one may have expected.

"It's true that we do call some of the barns terminals but I think that was more a reflection on the fact that the horses went a little over budget and it wasn't necessarily anything to do with the machines that were in the boxes," Mullins jokes.

Keeping those machines purring nicely and mapping out plans for the season is at the top of a very long priority list for the champion trainer, and one such machine he is delighted to have back in his barn is **Faugheen**.

"He's good and strong and we hope to have a trouble-free year with him. He's made a full recovery from his injury and is back in full training," says Mullins.

"We're in a position most people wouldn't have been with previous Champion Hurdle winners in that we know he stays and jumps, so he could go novice chasing, because he's a point-to-point winner. At the moment, though, that isn't on the agenda. We saw last year how important it can be to have a bit of depth to the Champion Hurdle team, and he'll be an important member of that team."

Annie Power was one of those spares who filled the shoes of Faugheen to retain the Champion Hurdle for her owner Rich Ricci last season, and she could be back to defend her crown at Cheltenham in March.

"I'm delighted she did what she did last year. She's another who has the ability to go novice chasing but might stay down the hurdle route now. She has lots of different options from the Champion Hurdle, to the World Hurdle and even the Mares' Hurdle. The most important thing is that she's come back looking fantastic and we can't wait to get her going again."

Of the rest of his Champion Hurdle hand, **Arctic Fire** is most likely to be seen in the middle to late part of the season while **Apple's Jade** could improve enough to be considered good enough for the better 2m races.

'The most important thing is that she's come back looking fantastic and we can't wait to get her going again'

DID YOU KNOW?

Willie Mullins nearly became the first Irish trainer since Vincent O'Brien to win the British jumps trainers' title last season, but he was just pipped at the post by Paul Nicholls. Mullins had 27 winners in Britain, incredibly amassing well over £2 million in prize-money. In Ireland he won well over £3 million with a whopping 185 winners. But that's still short of his record tally in his homeland which was the 193 winners he accrued in 2012 13.

Punchestown Champion Hurdle scorer **Vroum Vroum Mag**, who is yet to taste defeat for Mullins, will have a multitude of options too.

"It was pleasing the way she adapted to jumping hurdles as quickly as she did, as we must remember most of her form was over fences," says Mullins.

"It makes her very versatile, so we can go a number of directions with her now, although we don't have any concrete plans for her just yet."

Yorkhill could stick to hurdles

One surprise nomination for the Champion Hurdle from Mullins is **Yorkhill**, who was the subject of a famous quote from Ruby Walsh after his win in last season's Neptune Novices' Hurdle at Cheltenham.

"Yes, Ruby did say he would win the Arkle, but you could look at Yorkhill and think if another owner had him, you might say he's a Champion Hurdle type. We probably said we were going to go chasing at the end of last season, but I wouldn't bet my life on it. I wouldn't be ruling anything out and he could have a very good career over hurdles."

Mullins insists he doesn't have favourites and concentrates on the team as opposed to individuals. One individual who looks to be en route to superstardom, and may even perhaps change Mullins' stance on having favourites in the yard, is the unbeaten **Douvan**.

"He's very good. He looks a natural and the Queen Mother Champion Chase over two miles looks like a good target for him."

It's unlikely **Nichols Canyon** will be campaigned over the minimum trip this season, with the World Hurdle at Cheltenham his ultimate aim. He could be joined there by **Shaneshill**, who was in the process of running a massive race before coming down at the last flight in the Grade 1 Stayers' Hurdle at Punchestown.

Mullins' possible Champion Hurdle hand is only rivalled for strength in depth for what he may be prepared to hurl into battle for the Gold Cup, one of the only major races the nine-time Irish Champion trainer has yet to win.

More to come from Djakadam

Djakadam has found just one too good in the last two Gold Cups, and Mullins believes the seven-year-old is still on the improve.

"He's going to be stronger again this year. I imagine we'll be going down the Gold Cup route, but if his running tells us during the season that he may benefit from dropping in trip, then we'll have to explore those other options. I think he can continue to improve and we mustn't forget he's still a young horse."

Vautour could go for gold

Perhaps one of the liveliest debates of last season revolved around **Vautour** and whether the three-time Cheltenham Festival winner would stay the Gold Cup trip – and Mullins looks like he will be providing us with plenty to talk about again this season.

"Vautour has come back in looking very well and I imagine he'll have a similar programme to last year," the trainer says.

"I can't see us changing much as regards his build-up to Cheltenham. There's a different school of thought regarding his ability to stay. He can be very difficult to train at times, but if we get a straighter run with him this year, he is Gold Cup material. He has lots of speed and can come back in trip to the Ryanair. I think he has huge ability."

Don Poli will also have a similar campaign to last season and will be aimed at the Lexus Chase as well as the Irish Gold Cup before another crack at the Cheltenham Gold Cup, while **Valseur Lido** is another exciting Gigginstown House Stud-owned staying chaser to go to war with.

There is no shortage of horses who could step up to the plate to have a major say in the Ryanair Chase, or even add to the stable's strong Gold Cup challenge. One is **Black Hercules**, who won every race he stood up in last season, culminating with a superb three-length success in the JLT Novices' Chase.

"He'll be sticking to middle distances and the Ryanair could be the ultimate aim for him. He was very good at Cheltenham and that was a late decision to run him in

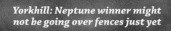
Yorkhill: Neptune winner might not be going over fences just yet

the JLT instead of the four-miler, which paid off."

'Hugely exciting prospect'

Killultagh Vic would have been many people's idea of the JLT winner before picking up an injury in the build-up to Cheltenham last year, but Mullins is quietly confident he can get the seven-year-old back to full fitness.

"He's going to come back into training a little late so we'll probably see him in the middle or the second half of the season. If we can get him back to his best he'll be a hugely exciting prospect as he has a lot of ability."

The search is always on for young horses capable of making the progression from the novice chase ranks into the senior chase brigade, but Mullins will feel he has unfinished business with Un De Sceaux and Champagne Fever, and perhaps now is the time for both of those to deliver on their ability.

Sceaux and Fever to mix it up

"**Un De Sceaux** looks as though he's maturing in his racing and that he may be able to get a longer trip now. He had a tough task at the end of the season when we asked him to run in the French Champion Hurdle. He'll win over the minimum trip, but we're probably thinking of running him over middle distance races as 2m4f looks like it's his optimum now. He could also go back over hurdles as well.

"As for **Champagne Fever**, he'll also mix it between hurdles and fences. He looks to be in good order at home so that's pleasing."

Novice chases for Min

Min arrived at Closutton from France with a big reputation and his only defeat under the care of Mullins came when finding Altior seven lengths too strong in the Supreme Novices' Hurdle.

"He'll go chasing. I thought the winner looked very good in the Supreme and we ran well enough to finish second. Maybe he was just beaten by a good horse in Altior, as if the winner wasn't in there, our fella would have looked good. I think Min will improve and he has more maturing to do still."

Up For Review and **Petit Mouchoir** are others for the novice chase notebook. Up For Review will be starting off over 2m4f to 3m and his main aim could be something like the four-miler at Cheltenham, while Petit Mouchoir is slowly maturing and getting the hang of racing.

With a maiden win over 1m5½f on the Flat in the French provinces, **Senewalk** is now with Mullins and, despite having yet to jump

W P MULLINS

CLOSUTTON, BAGENALSTOWN, COUNTY CARLOW

	Races Run	1st	2nd	3rd	Unpl	Per cent	£1 Level Stake
Non-hcp hurdles	295	110	56	32	97	37.3	+25.64
Handicap hurdle	100	8	7	10	75	8	-7.00
Non-hcp chases	176	56	35	20	65	31.8	-22.34
Handicap chases	58	3	6	1	48	5.2	-32.00
NH Flat	119	39	21	9	50	32.8	-5.10
TOTAL	**748**	**216**	**125**	**72**	**335**	**28.88**	**-40.80**

BY MONTH

	W-R	Per cent	£1 Level Stake
January	25-77	32.5	-29.70
February	24-67	35.8	+49.13
March	15-104	14.4	-58.64
April	25-102	24.5	+46.02
May	15-60	25	-15.35
June	2-21	9.5	-14.00
July	14-51	27.5	-16.22
August	15-39	38.5	+14.86
September	10-36	27.8	-7.97
October	10-33	30.3	+3.00
November	28-69	40.6	+0.35
December	33-89	37.1	-12.28

FAVOURITES

	W-R	Percent	£1 Level Stake
Non-hcp hurdles	85-148	57.4	+6.45
Handicap hurdles	0-14	0	-14.00
Non-hcp chases	44-76	57.9	+10.95
Handicap chases	0-6	0	-6.00
NH Flat	29-67	43.3	-8.49
TOTAL	**158-311**	**50.8**	**-11.09**

Statistics relate to runners in Ireland in 2015-16 season

Champagne Fever is in good order at home and will be mixing chasing with hurdling, while Killultagh Vic (above) is likely to return in the second half the season

a hurdle in public, already sits at the head of the betting for the Supreme Novices' next March. He has reportedly come back in from grass looking great and is doing all of the right things on the gallops.

Big future for Footpad

Asked to put forward some slightly darker horses, Mullins nominates the four-year-old Footpad, last season's Cheltenham Bumper fourth Castello Sforza and runaway Galway bumper winner Queen Deirdre.

"We'll certainly be looking at the French programme for **Footpad**, and you could even see him jump a fence this season or next. He has a big future.

Footpad: will be considered for forays to France, and could switch to fences

"**Castello Sforza** was very impressive when he won his first start at Fairyhouse two seasons back. He's had a few issues which held him up last year and he only ran once, when doing well in the Champion Bumper. We said we'd keep him as a novice for this year over hurdles. He has plenty of gears.

"You can't forget about **Queen Deirdre** either. It's a bit early for us to be talking about bumper horses, but she was very good at Galway, winning by 12 lengths. We'll keep her to her own sex for now and she could go to Gowran Park or even on to Navan next."

Mullins also outlines the mares' novice hurdle at Cheltenham for **Augusta Kate** and **Limini**.

Last season's bumper horses acquitted themselves well, with the highlight being **Blow By Blow** landing the Punchestown Champion Bumper under Katie Walsh.

"He should handle good ground being by Robin Des Champs, but he's massive and looks every inch a chaser. He'll be a lovely horse to contest staying novice hurdles this season. He improved with every run last year and showed us plenty at home so he's exciting."

Battleford was a narrow loser in the Cheltenham bumper, and Mullins believes he is another bumper horse from last season to keep a watchful eye on, along with Invitation Only and Bacardys.

"We're looking forward to **Battleford** and we think he'll be a nice staying novice, as well as **Invitation Only**. **Bacardys** has a nice turn of foot and goes well on good ground so we'll be keeping him to the minimum trip."

Title talk

Not only did Mullins dominate the Irish scene last season, and indeed every season since winning his first trainers' championship in 2007, but a first British trainers' championship almost went his way following his big-race exploits across the water.

Asked whether he will be targeting the British title this season Mullins says: "It's not something we're going to set out to do. If it happens, then so be it. You need a lot of luck. Last year lots of things went right for us and it was certainly achievable.

"We'll be preparing our horses the way we normally do and if the opportunities arise, then we will try and take them as they come."
Interview by Brian Sheerin

☑ Mullins recorded his best ever figures during a British jumps season last term. 27 winners accruing over £2.3 million saw him nearly land the trainers' championship

☑ **As you would expect, Ruby Walsh rode most of Mullins' British winners, but to a level-stake loss. Positive figures were returned on the Mullins runners ridden by Bryan Cooper (3-18, 17%, +£5.20) and Danny Mullins (2-6, 33%, +£1.83)**

SUPER STATS

☑ In Ireland Mullins can be relied on to supply a steady stream of winners at most tracks but his best level-stake figures are at Clonmel (34-85, 40%, +£17.50) and Gowran Park (46-118, 39%, +£16.58)

☑ **His Irish runners were best followed blind in February last season (23-58, 40%, +£56.54)**

☑ Since 2012-13, his runners in Irish bumpers have provided a steady level-stake profit (173-451, 38%, +£24.11)

Statistics cover the 2012-13 season onwards and are correct to September 9, 2016

THE LOWDOWN PAUL NICHOLLS

Overwhelming amount of talent suggests it's going to be epic again

DURING an epic campaign in which Paul Nicholls won the trainers' title on the final day of the season, his solitary Grade 1 win over fences came courtesy of Silviniaco Conti in the Ascot Chase. While the ten-year-old's best days may be behind him, he is still capable of high-class form and will bid for an eighth Grade 1 win over fences in the Champion Chase at Down Royal on November 5.

His trainer says: "Apart from when we had **Silviniaco Conti** right for Ascot, last season was an absolute nightmare. But he's looking a lot better physically than he did this time last year, so we'll get him spot-on for Down Royal and then form a plan for the rest of the season."

With Saphir Du Rheu failing to live up to the lofty hopes entertained for him this time last year and former champion chaser Dodging Bullets looking to have lost a bit of his speed, the spotlight is on the up-and-coming chasers and Nicholls is hopeful **Le Mercurey** could improve in his second season.

He says of the two-time Grade 2 winner:

"His first target is the Grade 2 chase at Down Royal on November 5, where the flat track should suit. He was getting a bit lazy last season – he virtually pulled himself up in front in the Reynoldstown – but we stuck the blinkers on at Ayr and he won impressively."

So what of **Saphir Du Rheu**? "After his Carlisle win last autumn I thought he had the chasing world at his feet, but things didn't go right after that," says Nicholls. "He was stopping abruptly in his races, so we gave him a soft-palate operation, and I hope a nice summer break will have helped. All I can say is I'll be disappointed if last season is as good as he is."

Dodging Bullets was not without his problems either, being forced to sit out the first half of the season with a splint.

"He ran no race in defence of his two-mile chase crown but his Celebration Chase third was more encouraging," says the trainer. "However, the speed he once had doesn't seem to be there any more, so we'll look to step him up in trip. There are no firm plans but I can see him getting a King George entry."

Haldon Gold Cup winner **Vibrato Valtat** went on to run well in Graded company but proved hard to place, and Nicholls says: "Life isn't easy for him, so we might try stepping him up in distance. He could start off back in the Haldon Gold Cup again."

Grand National hopes

A new handicap chasing star emerged in the spring in the shape of **Vicente**. Who could have foreseen, when he became the yard's first winner of last season in a beginners' chase at Newton Abbot in April, that almost a year later he'd be galloping to victory in the Scottish Grand National?

Nicholls describes it as "a fairytale" and adds a tilt at the Grand National could now be on the cards, although he warns life won't be so easy off a revised handicap mark.

A National entry could also be handed to the luckless **Virak**, who rarely ran a bad race last season but kept bumping into better-handicapped rivals.

The progressive **Vivaldi Collonges** is another to look out for in big long-distance handicap chases. He jumped his rivals ragged in three victories last season and the Becher Chase at Aintree is a possible big-race pre-Christmas target.

Another likely improver this winter is **Art Mauresque**. Despite a busy season he held his form well and Nicholls says: "Now he's learned to relax he's progressing all the time. He starts on quite a high mark, but we'll see how he gets on in the Old Roan Chase at Aintree."

We are warned not to rule out further chasing success for **Southfield Theatre**.

After struggling in the first half of last season, his fourth in the bet365 Gold Cup was far more like it and Nicholls says: "There's still a big race to be won with this horse."

The talented but luckless **Bouvreuil** should be competitive in handicaps. A runner-up at the last two Cheltenham Festivals, he travels well in his races and his assured jumping will stand him in good stead.

Sound Investment, who shot up the ratings on the back of a string of high-class efforts, has recovered from a small tendon injury, and another who has been on the sidelines is **Sametegal**. But he should be back later on and is one to look out for on good spring ground over 2m4f.

Exciting times

Nothing went right for **Aux Ptits Soins** last season. Plagued with sinus problems in the first half of the campaign that required several bouts of surgery, he finally came right but had to go to the World Hurdle without a prep, so in the circumstances he ran well before getting tired.

Nicholls says: "He took a long time to get over that, but has enjoyed a nice summer break and remains an exciting prospect for novice chases. He should be ready to debut in a beginners' chase towards the end of November."

Silviniaco Conti (front right) and Aux Ptits Soins wing their way up the steep gallop at Ditcheat

DID YOU KNOW?

The ten-time champion trainer has reached over £2 million in prize-money for 13 consecutive seasons. On four of those occasions he has surpassed the £3m barrier – in 2008, 2009, 2012 and 2015. His biggest winning tally was 155 winners in 2009, while his first big name to notch over £60,000 in prize-money for a season was See More Indians in 1993-94. It was See More Indians who also gave Nicholls his first Grade 1 success when winning the Feltham Novices' Chase at Kempton in 1993.

The six-year-old's owner John Hales has two other smart prospects in Politologue and Ibis Du Rheu. In a slightly up-and-down season, **Politologue** finished second in the Grade 1 Challow Hurdle but was over the top when down the field in the Coral Cup.

Nicholls predicts: "He's yet to fully develop and I've no doubt his best days are ahead of him over fences."

Ibis Du Rheu atoned for a narrow defeat in the Lanzarote Hurdle when landing the Martin Pipe Handicap Hurdle at Cheltenham. He too is still maturing physically and is taking a bit longer than the others to come to hand, but a switch to fences will be awaited with keen interest.

Guard in fantastic order

Nicholls does not attempt to hide his enthusiasm when talking about **Old Guard**. The five-year-old improved rapidly last autumn, winning the Greatwood and International Hurdle, but Nicholls says: "Things went wrong from then. I ran him too soon at Kempton and then he suffered a pelvic injury. But he's in fantastic order and I can't wait to see him jump a fence. He's Flat-bred but tough enough for chasing and I see him in the mould of Dodging Bullets."

Plans are fluid but there remains the possibility he might have one more outing over hurdles first.

Improving young hurdler **Le Prezien** was sold to JP McManus for £290,000 at the end of his novice campaign and big things are expected once he embarks on a chasing career.

"He was a star for us last season," says Nicholls, "ending with a career-best second behind Yorkhill. He's done very well over the summer and if he continues his improvement he could be a really good novice chaser for us this winter."

Fresh from a season that netted three victories, two in decent handicaps, **The Eaglehaslanded** now has his attentions turned to fences and his trainer predicts: "Three miles should bring out the best in him and I can see him developing into a good staying chaser."

The talented but frustrating **Arpege D'Alene** still has a bright future over fences according to his trainer, provided his jumping can be sorted out, and "a pair of cheekpieces might help".

The equally frustrating **As De Mee** can surely put his experience to good use in his second season over fences.

Nicholls says: "We'll start low down and work up. He's capable of landing a good handicap at some stage and will get an entry in the BetVictorGold Cup."

Once the ex-French **Mr Mix** got the hang of racing British-style he improved quite quickly over hurdles and he was still far from done with when falling in the conditional riders' handicap at the festival. Still lightly raced, he will probably switch to fences, but not before he has had a crack at Chepstow's Silver Trophy Hurdle.

The one-time frustrating **Emerging Talent** finally got his act together over hurdles last season and is regarded as a good chasing prospect "if he proves tough enough for the job".

Former festival winner **Qualando** found life harder in his second season, but once he fills his ever-expanding frame he is expected to show a useful level of form over fences.

Warriors Tale was an in-and-out performer last season but a summer breathing operation could lead to greater consistency.

Ptit Zig staying over hurdles

French Champion Hurdle winner **Ptit Zig** will head back across the Channel in November for a tilt at the country's other championship Grade 1, the Grand Prix d'Automne.

Although the seven-year-old boasts high-class form over fences, Nicholls says: "It's clear he's better over hurdles, so we'll stick to them now. After Auteuil he'll be aimed at the Long Walk."

The hurdling division is strengthened by a crack team of second-season four-year-olds. **Adrien Du Pont** became the yard's sole Grade 1 winner over hurdles last winter when landing the Finale at Chepstow.

Nicholls reckons there is further improvement to come and rates him a smart prospect, saying: "He'll get an entry for the four-year-olds' Champion Hurdle [Prix Renaud du Vivier] at Auteuil in November."

'He's got masses of improvement'

Another possible for that French Grade 1 is **Zubayr**. Winner of the Grade 2 Adonis on his debut, he found the Triumph coming too soon but showed his true colours when third to the smart Footpad in France.

Nicholls says: "There's no doubt in my mind he's got masses of improvement in him. We could go back to Auteuil in November or go for a decent handicap as he could be on an attractive mark [143]."

Rated 9lb lower than Adrien Du Pont on

Connetable (left): stepping up in trip and could be a decent stayer

138 is Fred Winter Handicap Hurdle winner **Diego Du Charmil**, and off that mark his trainer believes he could be competitive in something like the Greatwood Hurdle. Whatever this horse achieves this season – and four-year-olds often struggle in their second campaign – his size suggests he will come into his own over fences, although that is unlikely to be for another 12 months.

Considering chasing was always going to be **Clan Des Obeaux's** game, he did not fare badly when sixth in the Triumph Hurdle. Although four-year-olds get a much-reduced allowance over fences nowadays, this one is likely to make the switch and is clearly one of the trainer's favourites.

"He's one I really like and he's done so well physically," says Nicholls.

One place behind Clan Des Obeaux in the Triumph was **Tommy Silver**, a massive horse who can only progress as he strengthens up. "I hope there's lots of improvement to come from this one," his trainer said.

Connetable, winner of the Contenders Hurdle at Sandown on soft ground, later struggled on a quicker surface and Nicholls is planning a step up in trip.

More to come from Silsol

Among the older campaigners, none comes tougher or more consistent than seven-year-old **Silsol**, who reverted to hurdles after winning twice over fences and ended on a career-high mark after finishing third in Graded company at Aintree.

"There's more to come from him in staying hurdles," says the trainer.

Improving five-year-old **All Set To Go** is expected to continue his progress through the handicapping ranks having finished runner-up in the Swinton Hurdle in May.

Irving went off the boil after a valuable success at Haydock. The aim is to get this talented but frustrating performer back in A1 condition to add to his tally of four victories in Graded company. He is best in the first half of the season.

Capitaine tops novice hurdle list

The spotlight this winter will be on youth, with no fewer than 55 horses bound for juvenile or novice hurdles. One of the features of last season was a late flurry of bumper winners and a host of them are now

expected to do well over hurdles.

One of the best could be **Capitaine**, described by Nicholls as "the apple of my eye ever since he arrived from France".

A runaway Wincanton success in April, which has been followed by slick schooling, suggests the four-year-old could take high rank.

Visually even more impressive a few days earlier was **Brahms De Clermont**, a five-year-old from the family of Master Minded who put 16 lengths between himself and his Taunton rivals, despite running green.

The trainer says: "He gave Sean Bowen a great feel and looked as if he could go round again. His schooling since has been very good."

Either Brahms De Clermont or Capitaine could first take in the valuable bumper at the Cheltenham Open meeting.

Also successful at Wincanton was **Movewiththetimes**. The trainer says: "He'd been working just about as well as any of our bumper horses, so it was no surprise to see him win what could have been a warm contest. Tom George trained the runner-up in both divisions of that bumper and he fancied his pair, so the form could be okay. Movewiththetimes has progressed nicely since and jumps well."

Nicholls had a virtual monopoly on the spring bumpers at his local track and he had been successful in both divisions at the previous fixture with a promising pair owned by Trevor Hemmings. **Touch Kick**, a son of Presenting from the family of Big Buck's, gave the impression he'll be suited by further than 2m over hurdles, as should **Winningtry**, who may have another bumper run first.

Gibbes Bay was bought at last December's Cheltenham breeze-up sale as a future chaser, but judged on his Ayr bumper success on Scottish National day there are novice hurdles to be won with him first.

Packed with potential

There is no disguising the trainer's liking for **Capeland**, who won a Listed bumper at Cheltenham on New Year's Day on his only run last season.

Nicholls says: "We've looked after him with the future in mind and he's enjoyed an excellent summer. He has bags of potential and should be out in mid-October."

There is similar enthusiasm for **Give Me A**

PAUL NICHOLLS

DITCHEAT, SOMERSET

	No. of Hrs	Races Run	1st	2nd	3rd	Unpl	Per cent	£1 Level Stake
NH Flat	22	25	9	3	2	11	36.0	+12.63
Hurdles	92	273	64	43	40	126	23.4	-36.90
Chases	76	283	50	60	35	138	17.7	-46.95
Totals	**165**	**581**	**123**	**106**	**77**	**275**	**21.2**	**-71.22**
14-15	141	518	127	87	79	225	24.5	+50.54
13-14	164	562	112	102	65	283	19.9	-125.62

BY MONTH

NH Flat	W-R	Per cent	£1 Level Stake	Hurdles	W-R	Per cent	£1 Level Stake
May	0-1	0.0	-1.00	May	3-5	60.0	+4.11
June	0-0	0.0	0.00	June	0-3	0.0	-3.00
July	0-0	0.0	0.00	July	1-1	100.0	+1.50
August	0-0	0.0	0.00	August	0-0	0.0	0.00
September	0-0	0.0	0.00	September	0-1	0.0	-1.00
October	0-2	0.0	-2.00	October	9-23	39.1	+0.46
November	0-1	0.0	-1.00	November	8-39	20.5	-5.26
December	0-4	0.0	4.00	December	5-44	11.4	-25.63
January	1-1	100.0	+1.75	January	5-22	22.7	-7.83
February	1-1	100.0	+2.75	February	13-39	33.3	+15.89
March	0-1	0.0	1.00	March	7-42	16.7	+0.85
April	7-11	63.6	20.13	April	13-54	24.1	16.99

Chases	W-R	Per cent	£1 Level Stake	Totals	W-R	Per cent	£1 Level Stake
May	3-7	42.9	-1.58	May	6-13	46.2	+1.53
June	4-7	57.1	+4.58	June	4-10	40.0	+1.58
July	0-4	0.0	-4.00	July	1-5	20.0	-2.50
August	1-5	20.0	-2.00	August	1-5	20.0	-2.00
September	1-3	33.3	-0.13	September	1-4	25.0	-1.13
October	5-23	21.7	-0.72	October	14-48	29.2	-2.26
November	11-46	23.9	+4.50	November	19-89	21.3	-4.76
December	4-44	9.1	-28.63	December	9-92	9.8	-58.26
January	1-21	4.8	-16.50	January	7-44	15.9	-22.58
February	7-26	26.9	-5.93	February	21-66	31.8	+12.71
March	4-32	12.5	+10.75	March	11-75	14.7	+10.60
April	9-65	13.8	-7.30	April	29-130	22.3	-4.16

DISTANCE

Hurdles	W-R	Per cent	£1 Level Stake	Chases	W-R	Per cent	£1 Level Stake
2m-2m3f	32-124	25.8	-11.14	2m-2m3f	13-48	27.1	+20.29
2m4f-2m7f	13-71	18.3	-18.35	2m4f-2m7f	20-104	19.2	-40.67
3m+	2-15	13.3	-9.50	3m+	11-85	12.9	-11.87

TYPE OF RACE

Non-Handicaps	W-R	Per cent	£1 Level Stake	Handicaps	W-R	Per cent	£1 Level Stake
Nov Hrdls	27-94	28.7	-20.77	Nov Hrdls	0-6	0.0	-6.00
Hrdls	21-68	30.9	+1.41	Hrdls	15-104	14.4	-12.38
Nov Chs	24-71	33.8	+14.31	Nov Chs	6-32	18.8	-12.50
Chases	6-54	11.1	-37.89	Chases	14-125	11.2	-9.88
Sell/Claim	0-0	0.0	0.00	Sell/Claim	0-0	0.0	0.00

RACE CLASS

	W-R	Per cent	£1 Level Stake
Class 1	22-200	11.0	-41.91
Class 2	16-112	14.3	-25.86
Class 3	28-120	23.3	-16.04
Class 4	44-114	38.6	+3.09
Class 5	8-19	42.1	+4.04
Class 6	5-16	31.3	+6.25

FIRST TIME OUT

	W-R	Per cent	£1 Level Stake
Bumpers	8-22	36.4	+12.88
Hurdles	16-78	20.5	25.70
Chases	17-65	26.2	-8.12
Totals	41-165	24.8	-20.94

Far West (left): has the talent to land a decent race

Statistics relate to runners in Britain from April 26, 2015 to April 23, 2016

Copper, a £270,000 buy at the Goffs UK Aintree sale in April. This point-to-point and bumper winner has done plenty of work and should make his mark in staying novice hurdles.

Another to have reportedly done well is the ex-French **Cash Again**, second to the smart Jenkins at Newbury on his debut for the yard.

Nicholls says: "The form has been franked, he's summered well and I expect him to make a decent novice."

Summer stars

The vastly improved pair **El Bandit** and **Bagad Bihoue** carried all before them during the summer, unbeaten in their six outings, and both could take their chance in the Persian War Novices' Hurdle at Chepstow.

Coup De Pinceau has not been rushed, but there was a lot to like about his Ludlow debut success in April. "He's done very well physically and jumps nicely," says Nicholls.

Brio Conti has needed more time than some of the others but a Stratford bumper success in May suggests he is now ready to start repaying the patience.

Captain Buck's was also given time to mature. A heavy-ground winner at Taunton in February, he got caught out on a quicker surface back there in April and will be suited by 2m4f over hurdles.

Old favourites

It is welcome back to a host of well-known faces at Nicholls' Somerset yard, none more so than **Zarkandar**, one of the stable stars over the last few years who was forced to miss a year after being injured in the 2015 French Champion Hurdle.

"It's hard at this stage to tell if all the old ability is still there," says the trainer, "but he's been doing loads of work and showing all his usual enthusiasm. Provided he stays sound, the Long Distance Hurdle at Newbury is a possible starting point."

A tendon injury also halted the career of 2014 Cheltenham Festival winner **Lac Fontana**. He is due to go novice chasing and could be interesting.

The 2014 Paddy Power Gold Cup winner **Caid Du Berlais** has been off for 12 months with a leg problem. Only five at the time of his Cheltenham success, he had time to mature physically during his year off and he is a classy performer when on his A-game.

"He won't be easy to place and could begin in a 3m hurdle," says Nicholls.

Hopes are high that former classy novice chaser **Irish Saint** has retained all his ability after a layoff. "He could make up into a smart performer over staying distances, starting at the end of October," says the trainer.

The likeable **Far West**, a real favourite in the yard, is being primed to give his syndicate some more fun days out. If the old ability is still there he is tipped to pick up a decent prize over fences somewhere along the line.

Earthmoves was found to have injured a leg after disappointing on his return last October. The trainer says: "He's done well for a break, maturing physically, and remains a horse with potential over fences. He has a date over hurdles at Chepstow first, in the Silver Trophy."

Grade 3-placed hurdler **Great Try** always shaped as though he would improve for fences and now he has recovered from a tendon injury he will get the chance to prove it.

Persian Delight was not disgraced in a Grade 2 bumper at Aintree two seasons ago. He was given plenty of time to recover after a small hole was found in a tendon and is now expected to make up into a decent staying novice hurdler.

New blood

Expect **Dolos** to make his mark early. Third on his only run for Guillaume Macaire in the influential Prix Wild Monarch, he could go to the first Chepstow meeting.

Also expected out next month is **Divin Bere**, a maiden on the Flat after nine outings but much improved over hurdles, winning at Lyon and second twice at Auteuil in April.

Two other three-year-olds to note are

BEST ODDS GUARANTEED

Available in-shop for 2 hours each day

WHEN THE **FUN** STOPS **STOP**

gambleaware.co.uk

18+

Odds Guaranteed is available for a limited time period each day on all UK and Irish horse races in shops only. Single bets max stake £200 (Win or £200 EW). Multiple bets max bonus payout is £1000 per customer per total bet. Bets must on the day of the race to qualify. Bets placed outside the limited time period will not qualify for the offer. Ladbrokes reserves the right to withdraw this offer at any time and restrict bonuses to individual customers at its discretion. Ladbrokes y. See in-shop for full terms and conditions. PLEASE BET RESPONSIBLY. gambleaware.co.uk Need help? Call the National Helpline free on 0808 802 0133

Darling Maltaix, whose sharp turn of foot enabled him to win a bumper at Vichy on his only run in May, and **Wealth Des Mottes**. He impressed when making a successful hurdling debut at Clairefontaine in Deauville in July, although Paul Nicholls warns: "He may want a bit of time to grow up."

Among the new four-year-olds, **Casko D'Airy** "looks an old-fashioned chasing sort who will appreciate a trip", while **Contre Tous** was a bumper winner who has been placed over hurdles.

There is a good word for **Peak To Peak**, who is by Authorized, the same sire as Nicholls' smart young hurdler Zubayr. He joined the yard before last Christmas after winning on the Flat.

More a name to note for the future is **Cyrname**, a fine, big son of Nickname who bolted up at Pau and will come into his own when sent over fences.

'One of my favourites'

French bumper winner **Copain De Classe** has needed plenty of time to develop but is now progressing nicely and we should see a better horse over hurdles this season.

"As a physical model he'd be one of my favourites," says Nicholls.

Pilansberg came to Ditcheat with smart French Flat form but disappointed on his only run, which followed a busy campaign across the Channel. A gelding operation, plus a good summer break, has done him the world of good.

Brelan D'As ran a shocker on his only run in Britain but the word is: "You'll see a different animal this time". The same applies to **Crin Au Vent**, who did not fare any better on his sole outing, but Nicholls advises: "Put a line through it. He'll be a very different proposition now."

Clic Work had a breathing operation over the summer and his trainer reckons he could be fairly handicapped on 123, provided he learns to settle better.

Goffs purchase working well

The huge **Topofthegame** changed hands for £120,000 at the Goffs UK Aintree sale

First lot leaves the main yard on a typical morning at Manor Farm Stables

after making all to run out an impressive winner of an Irish maiden point-to-point in March. Despite his size, he has schooled well over hurdles according to his trainer.

Although early days, Nicholls is "very pleased" with **One More Hero**, who looked a real staying prospect when winning at Dromahane. He will relish a trip over hurdles.

The trainer appears equally sweet on Irish maiden point winner **Secret Investor**. "He has real presence and I'm thrilled with him, but we'll need to look after him and give him time to develop as he's a lovely prospect further down the line."

Blackwater Bramble, another winner at Dromahane, "will be ready early on to hopefully take advantage of some good ground".

A number of horses have come via Jack Barber's point-to-point academy at Seaborough in Dorset.

Rouge Devils was very green in a bumper for Nicholls last October, but a spell pointing led to him winning twice for Barber and he can continue to progress in staying novice hurdles on good ground.

Also on the green side up to now has been **The Happy Chappy**, but that did not stop him winning both starts. Other dual winners to note are **San Satiro**, who looked a thorough stayer when successful at Cotley and the Berkeley, and **Overland Flyer**, who has had a soft palate operation.

Bistouri D'Honore is a maiden in the pointing sphere but it was only by a whisker that he was beaten at the Berkeley and this fine, big son of Ballingarry looks the part.

Interview by Ben Newton

☑Nicholls' tally of 122 winners for last season and just under £2.5 million in prize-money weren't as good as his figures for the previous campaign, but it was just about enough for him to retain the trainer's championship, his tenth in the last 11 years

☑**It's best to follow his hurdlers in the West Country. They have returned level-stake profits at Exeter (20-59, 34%, +£7.81), Taunton (29-89, 33%, +£1.20) and Wincanton (44-122, 36%, +£5.72)**

SUPER STATS

☑Nicholls sent out five runners over fences at Fontwell last season, four of whom obliged (80%, +£2.98)

☑**His chasers can be backed with confidence at Haydock with a record of 11-24 over the larger obstacles at the Merseyside venue (46%, +£19.06)**

☑There are profits to be made by backing Nicholls' runners in the north – Ayr (+£27.75), Carlisle (+£5.95), Kelso (+£3.91) and Perth (+£5.16)

Statistics cover the 2012-13 season onwards and are correct to September 9, 2016

Minella Rocco leading charge to become next star at Jackdaws Castle

IT WAS far from Jonjo O'Neill's worst season but the head of Jackdaws Castle is keen to improve on his 2015-16 showing this time around.

O'Neill notched 81 winners last term, bringing in prize-money a shade shy of £850,000 but was left with a feeling of what might have been had his summer dreams of Holywell and More Of That come to life.

Instead, his stable stars could not hit the heights and his only Graded success came courtesy of Eastlake in the Topham Chase at Aintree in April.

"Last season was okay but we'd have liked to have done better," O'Neill says. "If your superstars don't perform or they aren't good enough, that's just the way it works out.

"That said, when you're looking at things you want to achieve, you'd want a winner at Cheltenham, a winner at Aintree, which we

'Everybody wants to get 100 winners and win £1 million in prize-money, but it's easier said than done. I've been in the game long enough to know it's up and down but I'm looking forward to a good year'

DID YOU KNOW?

Jonjo was a great jump jockey, amassing over 900 winners. His finest hour in the saddle came when he rode Dawn Run to victory in the 1986 Cheltenham Gold Cup, while he was twice champion jockey in 1978 and 1980. As a trainer he has won the Gold Cup and Grand National and is the only person to register a seasonal tally of 100 winners as a jockey and a trainer.

did last year, so that was good even though we didn't get the 100 winners.

"Everybody wants to get 100 winners and win £1 million in prize-money, but it's easier said than done. I've been in the game long enough to know it's up and down and I'm looking forward to a good year."

O'Neill's excitement as the autumn draws in is palpable, his passion for what lies ahead unmistakable.

"This is a great time of the year," he enthuses. "All the horses look great and the whole yard is excited. It's probably the best time because there are no disappointments yet."

One horse accounting for a good deal of that optimism is **Minella Rocco**, a strapping six-year-old for whom the sky appears to be the limit after an excellent victory in the National Hunt Chase at the Cheltenham Festival.

Colin Tizzard is already dreaming of the Gold Cup for Native River, who chased Minella Rocco home that day in March but O'Neill does not want to get carried away yet with a horse who could prove a leading Grand National contender in time.

"He's doing well," O'Neill says. "There's a few handicap chases he could go for to begin with, to see whether he's improved and how he's coping with things. He's rated 155, so he'd need to improve a bit before we can think about better races but I hope he's got that in him.

"He's a big baby of a horse, a massive thing at 17.1 and you'd hope he can improve. He's done very well to have done what he's done up to now, so hopefully with another summer on his back, he can come on again."

Holywell return delayed

O'Neill, who won the 2012 Gold Cup with Synchronised, will be hoping Minella Rocco could prove his latest contender for that great race, with **Holywell's** chances of elevating himself to that level now seemingly gone.

The nine-year-old finished fourth behind Coneygree in the 2015 Gold Cup and did not contest the race last season, instead finishing second in the Grade 3 Ultima Handicap Chase at the festival.

Holywell's season has already hit its first

More Of That (green): broke a blood vessel when finishing third in the RSA Chase

snag, O'Neill reveals, with the diminutive star having spent his summer overcoming colic that will delay his return to action.

"It took him a little while to get over but he's fine again now," says O'Neill. "We were hoping to get him out reasonably early but we're taking it easy with him now. He'll be out before Christmas but quite when, we don't know."

Wherever Holywell ends up racing, it will not be in the Grand National, in which he fell this year having not taken to the unique test.

"He's a great little horse but he didn't like Aintree at all," O'Neill explains. "They either love it or hate it and we weren't sure with him but he definitely hated it.

"He'll go for the long-distance chases but he's very high in the weights for a little horse, so he struggles to give it away. If we go for a Grade 1 he's probably not quite good enough, so we're in between the two."

Another wind op for RSA third

Another who ultimately failed to hit the heights expected of him last season was **More Of That** although he had excuses having bled when finishing third in the RSA Chase.

"He did nothing wrong at Cheltenham, he just bled. These things happen," says O'Neill, who stresses he has no thoughts of returning to hurdles with the 2014 World Hurdle winner.

"We think the bleeding may have been down to his wind, so he's had another wind operation. Hopefully, it's onwards and upwards for him now."

Taquin in good shape

The trainer hopes the same can be said for **Taquin Du Seuil**, who has struggled since winning the JLT Novices' Chase at the festival in 2014.

Now nine, this huge horse is set to be given the chance to prove himself outside of novice company once again, with the BetVictor Gold Cup a potential early opportunity.

"He's summered well and we might have a go at something like the BetVictor," O'Neill

says. "He just didn't have the best season last year but you often get that in the novice years. He's a grand horse."

Should he end up heading to Cheltenham's early-season showpiece, Taquin Du Seuil could find himself, of course, up against stablemate **Johns Spirit**.

It is becoming hard to imagine racing at the famous old venue without the nine-year-old and while O'Neill is aware the seven-time winner is not getting any younger, he is hopeful there are more big days in the popular bay yet.

"He's another one for the BetVictor, I'd imagine," says the trainer. "We've tried him at three miles but he doesn't seem to get it, so we'll have to go back to those good handicaps again.

"The problem is he's getting a bit older now, so whether he still has the fire in his belly I don't know. He looks great though."

One to emerge from the 2015-16 campaign on more of a positive note was **Eastlake**, not the most straightforward horse in training but a talented one nonetheless and one who opened up options available with his victory in the Topham.

O'Neill says: "We're going to go back to the Becher. He'd never won any further than two miles until he won the Topham, so we'll give him a try and see how we get on."

If Eastlake can prove himself a contender for the big staying handicaps, he will be joining a host of stablemates whose seasons are set to revolve around these sorts of races – some well established names and others emerging on the scene.

It won't be third time lucky

Perhaps the best known of them is **Shutthefrontdoor**, who has finished in the top ten in the last two Grand Nationals but is unlikely to have another go, with O'Neill not convinced the marathon trip is to his liking.

JONJO O'NEILL

CHELTENHAM, GLOUCS

	No. of Hrs	Races Run	1st	2nd	3rd	Unpl	Per cent	£1 Level Stake
NH Flat	22	31	7	6	2	15	22.6	-1.75
Hurdles	100	304	39	41	24	200	12.8	-84.22
Chases	62	230	34	26	19	151	14.8	-38.08
Totals	**152**	**565**	**80**	**73**	**45**	**366**	**14.2**	**-124.05**
14-15	165	631	105	85	69	371	16.6	-179.71
13-14	188	803	133	105	90	474	16.6	-176.99

MONTH

NH Flat	W-R	Per cent	£1 Level Stake	Hurdles	W-R	Per cent	£1 Level Stake
May	1-8	12.5	-2.50	May	5-31	16.1	-5.20
June	1-1	100.0	+2.75	June	5-17	29.4	+18.00
July	0-1	0.0	-1.00	July	3-21	14.3	-6.00
August	0-0	0.0	0.00	August	4-17	23.5	+0.88
September	0-1	0.0	-1.00	September	1-18	5.6	-9.00
October	1-1	100.0	+5.00	October	6-25	24.0	8.49
November	1-7	14.3	-4.75	November	5-31	16.1	5.08
December	3-3	100.0	+8.75	December	3-36	8.3	-21.17
January	0-0	0.00	0.00	January	0-13	0.0	-13.00
February	0-2	0.0	-2.00	February	0-28	0.0	-28.00
March	0-5	0.0	-5.00	March	1-27	3.7	-24.90
April	0-2	0.0	-2.00	April	6-40	15.0	+17.75

Chases	W-R	Per cent	£1 Level Stake	Totals	W-R	Per cent	£1 Level Stake
May	4-25	16.0	-9.29	May	10-64	15.6	-16.99
June	2-13	15.4	+2.50	June	8-31	25.8	+23.25
July	4-12	33.3	+7.38	July	7-34	20.6	+0.38
August	3-12	25.0	+2.00	August	7-29	24.1	+2.88
September	2-13	15.4	-1.75	September	3-32	9.4	-11.75
October	2-24	8.3	-9.50	October	9-50	18.0	-12.99
November	5-33	15.2	-4.13	November	11-71	15.5	-13.96
December	1-28	3.6	-26.67	December	7-67	10.4	-39.09
January	0-12		-12.00	January	0-25	0.0	-25.00
February	4-14	28.6	+1.88	February	4-44	9.1	-28.12
March	2-23	8.7	8.50	March	3-55	5.5	38.40
April	5-21	23.8	+20.00	April	11-63	17.5	+35.75

DISTANCE

Hurdles	W-R	Per cent	£1 Level Stake	Chases	W-R	Per cent	£1 Level Stake
2m-2m3f	10-88	11.4	-32.62	2m-2m3f	4-34	11.8	-14.17
2m4f-2m7f	15-114	13.2	-19.93	2m4f-2m7f	16-88	18.2	+17.33
3m+	6-28	21.4	+4.38	3m+	7-65	10.8	-26.75

TYPE OF RACE

Non-Handicaps	W-R	Per cent	£1 Level Stake	Handicaps	W-R	Per cent	£1 Level Stake
Nov Hrdls	9-72	12.5	-39.53	Nov Hrdls	1-10	10.0	-5.00
Hrdls	5-35	14.3	+2.00	Hrdls	22-185	11.9	-43.58
Nov Chs	5-23	21.7	-4.17	Nov Chs	8-41	19.5	+0.38
Chases	0-10	0.0	-10.00	Chases	21-153	13.7	-21.29
Sell/Claim	2-2	100.0	+1.90	Sell/Claim	0-0	0.0	0.00

RACE CLASS

	W-R	Per cent	£1 Level Stake
Class 1	2-63	3.2	31.00
Class 2	8-59	13.6	-10.54
Class 3	19-142	13.4	34.88
Class 4	34-221	15.4	52.41
Class 5	10-56	17.9	+0.52
Class 6	7-24	29.2	+5.25

FIRST TIME OUT

	W-R	Per cent	£1 Level Stake
Bumpers	7-22	31.8	+7.25
Hurdles	8-80	10.0	-41.33
Chases	9-50	18.0	-8.92
Totals	24-152	15.8	-43.00

Statistics relate to runners in Britain from April 26, 2015 to April 23, 2016

Shutthefrontdoor (6): his trainer is reluctant to have a third crack at the Grand National

"He ran a great race in the National but for me, he doesn't quite get the trip," he says. "He'll be going for those long-distance races again but maybe not quite as long as that."

Shutthefrontdoor has an Irish Grand National victory on his CV, and **Another Hero** could be campaigned to have a second shot at emulating his stablemate, having fallen at Fairyhouse at his first shot.

"He's back in again but I'm not sure if there's much improvement in him," says O'Neill. "He'll be going for the same sort of races again and he's done nothing wrong."

In the Scottish National, O'Neill was represented last season by **Spookydooky**, who had never finished outside the first five until pulling up in the race won by Vicente at Ayr last April.

O'Neill says: "He had a long season but he'd be another for a race like the Welsh National and other long-distance chases.

"The handicapper looks to have him in his grasp now though, so it will maybe be tougher for him."

'Very strong and powerful'

The Welsh National could also be on the agenda for arguably one of the most promising horses at Jackdaws, **Beg To Differ**, who was last seen unseating Aidan Coleman in the Ultima Handicap Chase but retains a great deal of potential at only six.

O'Neill is clearly fond of the son of Flemensfirth and says: "We're looking forward to him. He was pretty raw in his jumping as a novice last year at times but he's come back in very good order, he looks very strong and powerful."

Upswing contested last season's Welsh National and was pulled up, but could it be Aintree this time around for the eight-year-old?

His trainer is now of the opinion he could be a spring horse and will therefore not be rushing him for any early season targets.

"He's a nice horse but I don't really know what he'll go for at this point," says the trainer. "He improved as the season went on last year and I'm starting to think he maybe isn't an early season horse. He seems to come to life more as you go along, so we wouldn't be in a hurry with him."

Champagne could sparkle

Of those about to embark on their chasing careers, the pick would appear to be **Champagne At Tara**, who gave a hint at his ability when second in a Grade 3 handicap hurdle over 2m4f in April, leaving him rated 135 over the smaller obstacles.

"He's had a few problems along the way but he seems like he might have grown up now and got over them, so hopefully he can show his true ability," says O'Neill. "If he does jump, you'd certainly be looking forward to him."

A return to the larger obstacles also beckons for **Join The Clan**, whose only experience of chasing saw him bump into an extremely talented sort in Bristol De Mai at Leicester last December.

Three times a winner over hurdles, the seven-year-old continues to please in his schooling at home and O'Neill remains

Champagne At Tara: could make his mark as a novice chaser this season

optimistic about his chasing prospects, saying: "He's not the biggest but he's very honest and a grand horse to have. We've schooled him over fences and he jumps away grand at home."

If there are question marks over Join The Clan, mystery surrounds **Forthefunofit**, who has run only eight times during his seven years but has managed to achieve a mark of 132 over hurdles in that time.

Connections are keeping the faith despite the string of soundness issues that have plagued his career and he could well be a horse to keep an eye on.

"He has ability but he's hard to train," says O'Neill. "He's back in training now and looks great – he's another I'd expect to go chasing. He's got potential but the problem is keeping him together."

Another for the notebook is the Paul and Clare Rooney-owned **Go Conquer**, also a lightly raced seven-year-old but one who has been with O'Neill only since last November.

His three runs in that time concluded with a win at Wincanton and O'Neill is cautiously optimistic that he may have found the key to the son of Arcadio.

O'Neill explained: "We got a bit lost with him when he first came – it took us a while to get to know him but I'm hopeful there's more improvement in him this year. He could be a nice horse."

The dual-purpose performer **Matorico** is another who could be set to see a fence in the near future, while **Capard King** will be competitively campaigned, albeit despite O'Neill's concern that he may be in the grip of the handicapper.

Interview by Mark Scully

☑ Since the 2012-13 season, O'Neill's most profitable track has been Huntingdon (23-83, 28%, +£14.87), closely followed by Stratford (20-107, 19%, +£13.44)

☑ O'Neill's yard always has a quiet spell at some stage during the winter and that was the case in January last term with a record 0-25. However, he normally compensates for this by hitting form in the spring and his runners in April returned a healthy level-stake profit (11-56, 20%, +£42.75)

SUPER STATS

☑ Since the 2012-13 season, the best jockey to follow for the yard has been Aidan Coleman (20-97, 21%, +£23.18)

☑ O'Neill dropped two hurdlers into selling company last season and both obliged (+£1.90). And his runners in maiden hurdles returned a level-stake profit of £6.00

☑ Richard Johnson rode most winners for the yard last season, for a profit of £9.38

Statistics cover the 2012-13 season onwards and are correct to September 9, 2016

Festival aces Temps and Racer lead a promising team from Pond House

A KEY measure of how the season has gone for the bigger yards is how they did at Cheltenham, and for David Pipe, with so much festival history behind his Pond House operation, success over those four days in March is all the more important.

The pressure was soon off for Pipe last season, for having sat out the first two races of Tuesday's card he scored with **Un Temps Pour Tout** in race three, the Ultima Handicap Chase. Un Temps Pour Tout did not just win either – he bolted up from well-handicapped Holywell in what looked a two-horse race from a fair way out.

There was no second winner, but others from the stable ran well and Pipe's tenth season – yes tenth, although it does not seem that long – ended with a very respectable 80 winners and well over £1 million in prize-money in Britain, those figures not including Un Temps Pour Tout's highly prestigious win in the previous June's Grande Course de Haies d'Auteuil, which is to all intents and purposes the French Champion Hurdle and is worth £129,000 to the winner.

Pipe has high hopes of Un Temps Pour Tout once again and says: "People think it's a bad season if you don't have a Cheltenham winner. It's not, but the meeting is our shop window and I was very glad to get a winner in so early.

"Un Temps Pour Tout will be going for the better 3m-plus chases, handicaps and conditions races, and he'll probably have an entry in the Hennessy, which I think will suit him well.

"He's a very good horse, and on his day he's very hard to get past. The first half of the season didn't go to plan, but it all came right at the festival, albeit in the Ultima rather than the RSA Chase, which was where we thought we would end up."

Moon Racer, who won the Weatherby's Champion Bumper at the 2015 festival, is another big name to look out for after a frustrating second season in which he raced only once.

Pipe says: "He did very well to be second in the Punchestown bumper considering he'd been off so long and the race didn't really pan out for him. We'd hoped to get him ready for the Supreme Novices', but we ran out of time. He's well forward this time. Hopefully he can go to the top of the division in 2m novice hurdles."

Pipe is delighted that **Red Sherlock**, another who has been on the sidelines, is back, saying: "We tried to get him back last season,

WINNERS IN LAST FIVE SEASONS 80, 116, 90, 104, 101

and we did get close. Fingers crossed we'll manage it now, as he's obviously very talented and has been beaten just the once in seven starts, when he got a tendon injury against Faugheen in the Neptune two years ago."

Doctor Harper, another for the Johnson family, was strongly fancied for the Kim Muir at Cheltenham in March, but the writing was on the wall at an early stage. Pipe says: "He made a mistake at the first and could never really get into a rhythm after that. He disappointed at Haydock afterwards, but the ground was quick.

"He has to bounce back, but he's had a good break and hopefully he will. Unusually for a Presenting, his best form seems to be on soft ground."

Veterans back for more

Still also very much part of the set-up are **Ballynagour**, who has Graded wins to his name in the 2014 Byrne Group Plate over fences and in the 2015 Prix la Barka over hurdles, and **Dynaste**, who has struggled to get his head in front since the 2014 Ryanair Chase. They are both ten now, but both are back for more and Dynaste, in particular, is not acting his age.

Pipe says: "Dynaste is full of beans and has loads of enthusiasm still. He's got to go in Graded races or the better handicaps, and although he's still very good he's slightly on the downgrade. His mark is down to 153 now though, and if it drops to 150 he qualifies for veteran chases.

Ballynagour is rated slightly higher, having been second in good summer handicap chases off 152 and 157. Pipe adds: "Everyone knows Ballynagour isn't the easiest to predict, and we've probably seen the best of him, but he's a strong traveller and on his day he's still pretty good. He fell in the National, but may well have another try."

Aintree the target again

Vieux Lion Rouge is another Aintree possible, and the trainer says: "He had a good season and won at Haydock before running a great race at Cheltenham in the National

Vieux Lion Rouge (leading): long-distance handicap chaser heading back to Aintree

Hunt Chase. He then ran well when finishing seventh in the National, and that will be a target again. He could well go for the Becher Chase first."

Broadway Buffalo is another long-distance chaser to look forward to when he returns, hopefully in the second half of the season from the leg injury he picked up on his last appearance. There is more to come from him and he too could be Aintree bound.

Fellow handicap chaser **Katkeau**, an out-and-out stayer who loves the mud, is high in the ratings but will qualify for veteran chases in the second half of the season.

Gevrey Chambertin, who is "talented but quirky" and has not scaled the heights once hoped for him, is still at Pond House. He

did well last season, winning twice, and is likely to have another go over fences. When tried before he has never jumped as well in public as he had done at home, where he is "brilliant".

Dell' Arca is another who is not easy to predict, but the handicapper has given him a chance and Pipe hopes he might pop up again one day in a decent handicap, either over hurdles or fences.

Novice chase aspirations

The pick of the novice chasers include two well known names, Champers On Ice and Starchitect.

Champers On Ice, who finished third to Unowhatimeanharry in the Albert Bartlett, is an obvious candidate for top honours. Pipe reports the six-year-old has had a good break and summered well, and he adds: "He's got that relentless gallop and we're hoping he can take high rank, with the RSA Chase an obvious target.

"He wore cheekpieces at Cheltenham, but I don't think he'll be starting off over fences in them. They were just to help him go Cheltenham pace on that better ground."

Betfair Hurdle runner-up **Starchitect**, a Flat winner during the summer, is another who is likely to go novice chasing. Pipe says: "He competed in all the best handicaps and ran with great credit, finally getting his head in front at Newton Abbot on his last run over hurdles.

"He'd have run at Royal Ascot if he'd made the cut. He's staying better now, and anything

DID YOU KNOW?

When David Pipe took over from his father Martin he began his training career in the perfect style, with a double at Kelso in May 2006. By the end of the 2006-07 season, Pipe's tally of winners stood at 134, more than any other trainer. Since then Pipe has surpassed the 1,000-winner mark. David is named after his grandfather, who began the legend of Pond House in 1973 when he sold his bookmaking chain to William Hill and bought a derelict pig farm, from where his son Martin would begin his record-breaking training career.

DAVID PIPE
NICHOLASHAYNE, DEVON

	No. of Hrs	Races Run	1st	2nd	3rd	Unpl	Per cent	£1 Level Stake
NH Flat	22	32	2	3	7	20	6.3	-15.00
Hurdles	98	361	44	47	33	237	12.2	-97.83
Chases	46	181	34	27	28	92	18.8	-2.09
Totals	**126**	**574**	**80**	**77**	**68**	**349**	**13.9**	**-114.92**
14-15	*136*	*579*	*116*	*71*	*67*	*325*	*20.0*	*-47.46*
13-14	*155*	*594*	*91*	*65*	*58*	*380*	*15.3*	*-85.26*

BY MONTH

NH Flat	W-R	Per cent	£1 Level Stake	Hurdles	W-R	Per cent	£1 Level Stake
May	1-6	16.7	+2.00	May	5-27	18.5	+0.50
June	0-4	0.0	-4.00	June	2-25	8.0	-16.50
July	0-3	0.0	-3.00	July	0-20	0.0	-20.00
August	0-2	0.0	-2.00	August	4-20	20.0	-6.52
September	0-4	0.0	-4.00	September	6-24	25.0	-0.59
October	0-2	0.0	-2.00	October	2-30	6.7	-23.75
November	0-1	0.0	-1.00	November	2-40	5.0	-25.00
December	0-1	0.0	-1.00	December	3-37	8.1	-4.88
January	0-0	0.0	0.00	January	4-28	14.3	+10.00
February	0-3	0.0	-3.00	February	6-37	16.2	-14.21
March	1-2	50.0	+7.00	March	6-40	15.0	+11.25
April	0-4	0.0	-4.00	April	4-33	12.1	-8.13

Chases	W-R	Per cent	£1 Level Stake	Totals	W-R	Per cent	£1 Level Stake
May	3-10	30.0	-5.04	May	9-43	20.9	-2.54
June	1-8	12.5	-6.67	June	3-37	8.1	-27.17
July	1-7	14.3	-5.27	July	1-30	3.3	-28.27
August	2-4	50.0	+9.00	August	6-26	23.1	+0.48
September	3-6	50.0	+10.25	September	9-34	26.5	+5.66
October	2-19	10.5	-14.13	October	4-51	7.8	-39.88
November	5-29	17.2	+1.50	November	7-70	10.0	-24.50
December	4-21	19.0	-2.75	December	7-59	11.9	-8.63
January	2-12	16.7	-2.27	January	6-40	15.0	+7.73
February	2-20	10.0	-8.38	February	8-60	13.3	-25.59
March	9-27	33.3	+39.66	March	16-69	23.2	+57.91
April	0-18	0.0	-18.00	April	4-55	7.3	-30.13

DISTANCE

Hurdles	W-R	Per cent	£1 Level Stake	Chases	W-R	Per cent	£1 Level Stake
2m-2m3f	14-121	11.6	-40.99	2m-2m3f	6-33	18.2	-4.42
2m4f-2m7f	20-122	16.4	-14.01	2m4f-2m7f	13-56	23.2	-2.47
3m+	5-31	16.1	+6.57	3m+	10-67	14.9	+2.45

TYPE OF RACE

Non-Handicaps	W-R	Per cent	£1 Level Stake	Handicaps	W-R	Per cent	£1 Level Stake
Nov Hrdls	5-47	10.6	-25.65	Nov Hrdls	2-18	11.1	-11.13
Hrdls	5-47	10.6	-33.02	Hrdls	30-246	12.2	-28.94
Nov Chs	10-20	35.7	-3.50	Nov Chs	6-24	25.0	+10.41
Chases	0-10	0.0	-10.00	Chases	18-116	15.5	+4.00
Sell/Claim	2-2	100.0	+1.91	Sell/Claim	0-1	0.0	-1.00

RACE CLASS / FIRST TIME OUT

	W-R	Per cent	£1 Level Stake		W-R	Per cent	£1 Level Stake
Class 1	2-65	3.1	-46.00	Bumpers	2-22	9.1	-5.00
Class 2	8-94	8.5	+2.00	Hurdles	7-77	9.1	-42.00
Class 3	30-155	19.4	+7.99	Chases	7-27	25.9	-2.66
Class 4	31-174	17.8	-26.59				
Class 5	8-60	13.3	-34.31	Totals	16-126	12.7	-49.66
Class 6	1-26	3.8	-18.00				

Statistics relate to runners in Britain from April 26, 2015 to April 23, 2016

Champers On Ice (below): could go to the top in staying novice chases

*The Pipe team gears up
for action at Pond House*

over 2m4f looks like his distance.

A novice hurdler to make a note of is **Mr Big Shot**, who surprised the team when he made a winning debut in a bumper at Uttoxeter. "The penny didn't drop until the last two furlongs, but he won well," says the trainer. "It was a decent bumper and he's a massive horse who looks a nice prospect."

Promising new recruits

As usual at this time of the year there are new recruits to watch out for. Among them is **Magie Du Ma**, who could prove a top juvenile.

"She's one to look forward to," says Pipe. "She has good form in France, where she's already a winner and has run well against some of their best three-year-olds. I think she'll be rated around 140, but is eligible for juvenile hurdles."

Pipe bought **King's Socks** at the same sale and says: "He's a four-year-old who has some very good form in France over fences and hurdles. He's a handicapper under both codes, rated around the 150 mark so will hopefully be competing at a decent level."

Shaama Grise, a handicap hurdler and novice chaser, with recent form at Auteuil, and **Dauphine Ereine**, a four-year-old half-sister to Dynaste who has already won three chases, also came from France, as did **Full**, who has been placed over hurdles at Auteuil and has novice handicaps as an option.

☑ Numbers were down at Nicholashayne last season with just 80 winners on the board, Pipe's lowest total in five seasons although a return of more than £1.1 million in prize-money was a good effort in the circumstances

☑ **September is when the yard starts to get going and it was profitable for Pipe last season (+£5.66) but he earned his best level-stake profit during March last term (16-69, 23%, +£57.91)**

SUPER STATS

☑ Pipe is renowned for giving chances to conditionals, and Michael Heard enjoyed a good run last term (8-48, 17%, +£11.82) while Conor O'Farrell also rode well for the stable last season following the loss of his claim (7-65, 11%, +£11.00)

☑ **Pipe did better over fences last season – his record in handicaps was 24-142 (17%, +£12.41) while his runners in novice races was 14-51 (27%, +£2.68)**

Statistics cover the 2012-13 season onwards and are correct to September 9, 2016

Several others have been bought from the point-to-point field. The first Pipe mentions is **It's Obvious**, an Irish pointer bought at Aintree, described as "a big horse who hopefully has a nice future".

Ramses De Teillee, "a racy type who won his second point-to-point and could start in a bumper", and **Orchard Thieves**, a tall angular gelding who was second in an Irish point-to-point, are also dark horses who could be anything.

Even though numbers might be down a shade on last season, there is clearly plenty to look forward to from the Pond House team.

Interview by Graham Dench

THE LOWDOWN DAN SKELTON

Progress looks nailed on as quest for success at top table continues

AFTER nine years as assistant to Paul Nicholls, Dan Skelton left Ditcheat not only with an appetite for success and also an appetite to dine at the same top table as the ten times champion jumps trainer.

Having trained superstar jumpers like Kauto Star, Big Buck's and Master Minded, Nicholls set the bar very high but, after just three seasons with a licence, his student is on the right path establishing his state of the art Lodge Hill in Shelfield Green, Warwickshire among the best in Britain.

Last term Skelton recorded his first century, ending what was only his third campaign with a licence with 104 winners who collected total prize-money of £1.2 million on top of which came a first Cheltenham Festival winner when Superb Story landed the County Hurdle.

Skelton finished only 18 winners behind his mentor but more than £1m short in prize-money, the only numbers that matter in trainers' championships.

Nevertheless, with brother Harry as stable jockey, Skelton believes there is scope for the yard's fortunes to improve yet again. There has been investment in new blood among a string of around 120 horses but also in the infrastructure of the yard including the completion of a new accommodation block for stable staff.

"It's not a secret what our objective is," says Skelton. "There is a massive gap in prize-money between me and Paul. I think we have the quality to step up again this year but after going from £700,000 to £1.2m the percentage gains are going to be smaller. That's not to say we won't still be looking for them.

"The main change is we've put in an accommodation block for the staff with 14 rooms and two flats. We know how important it is to have good staff. They now have a big block with a gym, living room, dining room, all en suite bedrooms which will hopefully pay dividends. We've also put in a new sand ring, a new jumping lane and installed more infrared lights in stables."

Superb Story's festival triumph was an exercise in patience by Skelton who kept him off the track after the Greatwood Hurdle in November to deliver a headline victory for the team in March. He will be given a similar preparation this season.

"It was great that he gave us our first Cheltenham Festival winner," says the trainer. "If I had my time again I wouldn't have gone to Galway afterwards but it was worth so much money, he likes decent ground and he hasn't been over-raced, but

WINNERS IN LAST THREE SEASONS 104, 73, 27

'I think we have the quality to step up again this year but after going from £700,000 to £1.2 million the percentage gains are going to be smaller. That's not to say we won't still be looking for them'

everything that could go wrong on the day did and he pulled up.

"He's out in the field and will get all of September off and we'll look to resume and build up to March. I still think he's progressive and there's scope within his handicap mark so he'll stick to hurdling for a while yet."

More to come from Scottish ace

With no intention on the trainer's part, Skelton has been labelled a 2m hurdle specialist and the horse who delivered his richest win last season was **Ch'Tibello**, who took the Scottish Champion Hurdle either side of place finishes in the Gerry Feilden and Swinton Hurdles.

"I'm not deliberately leaning towards those races, it's where we ended up," he says. "Ch'Tibello won the Scottish Champion Hurdle but in the autumn had a frustrating time as he kept bumping into all the best novices. He delivered when we really wanted him to at Ayr. It was probably a run too many at Haydock.

"I think there's scope for him to do more over hurdles and he'll either go to Ascot for a Listed race or Wincanton for the Elite. He'll end up being a chaser one day."

One more season for Al

Skelton's most notable success over fences came from one of the sport's old guard as **Al Ferof**, formerly with Nicholls, captured the Peterborough Chase. The 11-year-old is due back in training but this could be his final season.

"We took the approach that if he's okay we'll creep on," says Skelton. "The idea is he'll come back to me during September and we'll work towards the Peterborough again. If he won that we might call it a day with him. He's such a good horse he doesn't owe anyone anything."

Promising young brigade

Success this season will depend on the younger brigade being able to step up, and Skelton is not short of candidates including Virgilio, Its'afreebee, Welsh Shadow and Mister Miyagi.

Virgilio won his first three starts for Skelton until pulling up in the Relkeel Hurdle in January but got off the mark over fences in May. Its'afreebee won the Rossington Main and finished third in the Neptune Investment Management Novices' Hurdle with stablemate Welsh Shadow in fifth. Mister Miyagi suffered his only defeat over hurdles in the Supreme.

"**Virgilio** is a lovely horse," says Skelton. "He was really good at Warwick on his chasing debut. He was a disaster when I ran him on bad ground at Cheltenham over new year so I've got to keep him away from that. Hopefully he'll run at the October Cheltenham meeting then go on to the Rising Stars at Wincanton.

"**Its'afreebee** has been amazing. We bought him last year. He's a bit unconventional looking but he's such a willing partner. He really tries hard. He won a Grade 2 having improved beyond all recognition. I think there's more to come. He always keeps pulling out a little bit. We'll go straight over fences, start him off in a beginners' chase and work him up from there.

"**Welsh Shadow** is very talented and from a great family. He improved from bumpers to win a Listed novice hurdle but he'll go chasing now after winning a decent match race at Ayr at the end of last season. He'll start over two miles and in time he'll be a 3m chaser.

"**Mister Miyagi** had a good season. I always thought he was going to be pretty smart and I'm glad he went the way he did as he could have got lost on the bad ground over the winter. The owners were keen to let me keep him away from it and he picked up really well at the end of the season over 2m4f. That opens up new avenues for him. He's not one of those horses we've got to the bottom of so he'll carry on over hurdles."

A real improver

Two Taffs was one of five winners for Skelton at Ayr last season and is earmarked for better things along with Kasakh Noir.

"He's a real improver. He's getting stronger all the time and the type to make a very good chaser. He's not ready for that mentally yet. I'll probably aim him at the Persian War at Chepstow and then look to go to the Fixed Brush Hurdle at Haydock. He might improve for another season over hurdles.

"**Kasakh Noir** probably got made to look exceptional on his first start at Newbury

Its'afreebee (right): set to kick off his season in a beginners' chase

where they went very fast, not many got home and he came from the back and won as he liked. He's a decent horse and a chaser for the future but not one ready to go and do it just yet. We'll probably look at the Elite or Gerry Feilden Hurdle before making plans."

Harvey has more to give

North Hill Harvey has registered just one victory but was seen in the best company running second to Barters Hill last season and finishing fourth to Buveur D'Air at Aintree.

"He works like a stayer at home but on the track is a strong-staying two-miler," says Skelton.

"I tried him over two and a half against Barters Hill and he ran creditably but was never going to beat him.

"He won at Cheltenham in December and I think barring a mistake two out in the Supreme he could have finished second. He wasn't at his absolute best at Aintree.

"I don't think we're done with him yet over hurdles but will be schooling him over fences before we make a decision. How high he can go I don't know."

Value At Risk began a novice chase campaign but by March was winning a Grade 2 hurdle at Fairyhouse.

"He got it together in the end last season but who was to blame is debatable," Skelton says. "I probably shouldn't have sent him straight into a Grade 2 at Newbury but if you'd seen him at home you'd have no problem running him anywhere.

"It took a couple of runs over hurdles before we got the wheels back on but it all came together well at Fairyhouse. We'll start over fences early autumn and give it our best shot. He's obviously very good. He just needs all the chips to fall right for him."

Value At Risk: heading back over fences this autumn

DAN SKELTON

SHELFIELD GREEN, WARWICKSHIRE

	No. of Hrs	Races Run	1st	2nd	3rd	Unpl	Per cent	£1 Level Stake
NH Flat	35	45	7	7	7	24	15.6	-14.84
Hurdles	112	349	70	54	51	174	20.1	-112.21
Chases	41	137	27	27	12	71	19.7	-31.29
Totals	**148**	**531**	**104**	**88**	**70**	**269**	**19.6**	**-158.34**
14-15	*108*	*378*	*74*	*48*	*44*	*212*	*19.6*	*-58.19*
13-14	*54*	*167*	*26*	*25*	*22*	*94*	*15.6*	*-20.16*

BY MONTH

NH Flat	W-R	Per cent	£1 Level Stake	Hurdles	W-R	Per cent	£1 Level Stake
May	0-0	0.0	0.00	May	6-20	30.0	+1.34
June	0-0	0.0	0.00	June	5-16	31.3	-1.65
July	0-2	0.0	-2.00	July	1-14	7.1	-11.75
August	0-2	0.0	-2.00	August	0-3	0.0	-3.00
September	0-2	0.0	-2.00	September	1-5	20.0	+0.50
October	2-8	25.0	+2.38	October	7-40	17.5	-16.52
November	0-8	0.0	-8.00	November	13-58	22.4	-5.16
December	0-1	0.0	-1.00	December	7-39	17.9	-18.57
January	0-1	0.0	-1.00	January	5-29	17.2	-8.50
February	2-7	28.6	-1.96	February	11-45	24.4	-23.68
March	1-6	16.7	2.25	March	4-40	10.0	-23.36
April	2-8	25.0	+3.00	April	10-40	25.0	-1.86

Chases	W-R	Per cent	£1 Level Stake	Totals	W-R	Per cent	£1 Level Stake
May	5-12	41.7	+1.36	May	11-32	34.4	+2.70
June	4-8	50.0	+2.73	June	9-24	37.5	+1.08
July	1-10	10.0	-8.17	July	2-26	7.7	-21.92
August	0-9	0.0	-9.00	August	0-14	0.0	-14.00
September	0-0	0.0	0.00	September	1-7	14.3	-1.50
October	3-17	17.6	-3.00	October	12-65	18.5	17.14
November	5-23	21.7	+5.13	November	18-89	20.2	-8.03
December	3-17	17.6	+2.13	December	10-57	17.5	-17.44
January	0-6	0.0	-6.00	January	5-36	13.9	-15.50
February	3-10	30.0	-4.16	February	16-62	25.8	-29.80
March	1-15	6.7	-13.80	March	6-61	9.8	-38.41
April	2-10	20.0	+1.50	April	14-58	24.1	+2.04

DISTANCE

Hurdles	W-R	Per cent	£1 Level Stake	Chases	W-R	Per cent	£1 Level Stake
2m-2m3f	31-158	19.6	-53.95	2m-2m3f	9-40	22.5	-10.23
2m4f-2m7f	23-87	26.4	-5.81	2m4f-2m7f	8-42	19.0	-6.97
3m+	2-14	14.3	-8.27	3m+	4-21	19.0	-1.68

TYPE OF RACE

Non-Handicaps	W-R	Per cent	£1 Level Stake	Handicaps	W-R	Per cent	£1 Level Stake
Nov Hrdls	38-133	28.6	-23.92	Nov Hrdls	1-11	9.1	-8.25
Hrdls	15-73	20.5	-27.76	Hrdls	16-128	12.5	-48.27
Nov Chs	8-25	32.0	-6.27	Nov Chs	4-21	19.0	+4.13
Chases	2-8	25.0	+0.25	Chases	13-80	16.3	-26.40
Sell/Claim	0-4	0.0	-4.00	Sell/Claim	0-0	0.0	0.00

RACE CLASS / FIRST TIME OUT

RACE CLASS	W-R	Per cent	£1 Level Stake	FIRST TIME OUT	W-R	Per cent	£1 Level Stake
Class 1	7-85	8.2	-39.75	Bumpers	6-35	17.1	-8.59
Class 2	8-64	12.5	-30.13	Hurdles	22-86	25.6	-2.73
Class 3	16-93	17.2	-22.45	Chases	8-27	29.6	-1.02
Class 4	56-214	26.2	-51.53				
Class 5	10-39	25.6	-8.65	Totals	36-148	24.3	-12.34
Class 6	7-36	19.4	-5.84				

Statistics relate to runners in Britain from April 26, 2015 to April 23, 2016

DID YOU KNOW?

Dan and brother Harry are the sons of Olympic gold medallist Nick Skelton, and it's fair to say Harry has much more of his father's riding genes, although Dan did used to be an amateur rider and rode a winner. Skelton has already made a super start to his training career, amassing 27 winners in his first full season training and over 100 last term.

Meet The Legend has demonstrated in three starts for Skelton he could be a candidate for the big handicap hurdles.

"He came to us midway through last season and won a decent novices hurdle at Newbury. It means he's not a novice this season, but a fast-run race will suit him and I might take him straight to the Greatwood Hurdle. I think there's improvement in him."

Patience can start to pay off

Of his second-season chasers Skelton expects to get more out of Three Musketeers, who won a Grade 2 novice chase from Activial before finishing fourth in the JLT. And there is more to come from Pain Au Chocolat and Long House Haul, who has won the Summer Plate at Market Rasen.

"I've always trained **Three Musketeers** knowing there's the potential for massive improvement," the trainer says.

"We've protected him so he needs to repay our patience with him and I think he's well able to do that now now.

"**Pain Au Chocolat** is such an honest horse who would probably win a moderate novice chase as well as he would a good one. He's always full bore and is a bit like that in training. In work we're trying to protect him from himself.

"He's eligible for graduation chases and that's the way he'll go. He's talented. He fell in the Future Champions Novices' Chase at Ayr when I felt 2m4f would help and he was over the top when he went to France. A graduation chase over the same trip round Kempton could be ideal for him.

Old Roan aim

"**Long House Hall** might get an entry in the Old Roan Chase at Aintree or he could go to Down Royal for a Grade 2. I wouldn't want to run him on bad ground through the winter. If we wanted to go back over hurdles we could

try the Coral Cup again but really we are sticking to chasing now."

There are lesser-known stable members and those new to the yard this season who should also go in the notebook, according to Skelton.

"**Captain Forez** is a novice hurdler for this year who will take time," he said. "He's a big horse who will make a chaser.

"**Betameche** won two bumpers and is a novice hurdler who could be one to follow.

"The same goes for **Asum**, who was third in his first bumper but met all sorts of trouble in running. **Mont Lachaux**, who we won the first three-year-old hurdle in Enghien with in March is a brother to Whisper and could go back to France for Graded races."

Interview by Jon Lees

☑ Last season was groundbreaking for Skelton, going beyond the century barrier for the first time with 104 winners and amassing more than £1.2 million in prize-money

☑ **Skelton's visits to Lingfield are rare but he often makes the trip pay with a record of 5-9 (56%, +£16.00)**

☑ **Follow his runners in the north. His records at Ayr (6-19, 32%, +£3.99) and Wetherby (9-25, 36%, +£4.08) stand out**

SUPER STATS

☑ **Skelton's hurdlers are best followed at Ludlow (7-29, 24%, +£2.85), Sedgefield (5-11, 45%, +£0.49) and Southwell (11-34, 32%, +£8.50)**

☑ His stable is usually at its busiest between November and December as this period provides him with the bulk of his winners. However, his best level-stake profit last season was recorded in April (13-55, 24%, +£4.39)

Statistics cover the 2012-13 season onwards and are correct to September 9, 2016

Three Musketeers: can start to repay his trainer's faith in him

THE LOWDOWN COLIN TIZZARD

'Last year was our best – we're excited by what we can achieve now'

WHEN Colin Tizzard started training a handful of point-to-pointers from Venn Farm in 1995 he surely couldn't have imagined the extent to which his fledgling operation would flourish over the next two decades.

The Dorset-based handler, whose twin passions are dairy farming and horses, goes into the new jumps season on the back of a record-breaking 2015-16 campaign blessed with one of the strongest equine teams in Britain, and it is by no means inconceivable he could be triply represented in the sport's most prestigious race, the Cheltenham Gold Cup, with Thistlecrack, Cue Card and Native River.

Last term's win and place prize-money total of £1,442,082 – boosted considerably by the Grade 1 exploits of World Hurdle hero Thistlecrack, arguably the most exciting jumps horse in training at present, and Cue Card's trio of triumphs at the highest level – saw Team Tizzard gatecrash the top four in the British jump trainers' championship for the first time.

Only the mighty battalions of multiple champion Paul Nicholls, Irish maestro Willie Mullins and Lambourn legend Nicky Henderson finished above the Sherborne stable.

West Country big guns Philip Hobbs and David Pipe, plus the likes of Alan King and Jonjo O'Neill were below Tizzard.

Tizzard's son and assistant Joe is fiercely proud of the achievement, but prefers to look to the future rather than dwell in the past.

"It was another big step forward for the stable," he says. "It was our best year by a long way, and we're all very excited about what we can achieve over the next few seasons.

"We've got the most beautiful bunch of horses. The babies we've looked after for a couple of seasons are coming through now to join the more established names.

"We have a team of around 70 horses, and there are some very promising individuals among them. We can't wait for the season proper to start."

A record number of over 2,000 people visited Venn Farm for the stable's annual open day on August Bank Holiday Monday, confirmation the Tizzards are now established among the elite trainers.

"It was an incredible turnout," Tizzard recalls. "We were overwhelmed by the number of people here. Many, of course, came to see Thistlecrack and Cue Card. They are public horses after all they have achieved,

WINNERS IN LAST FIVE SEASONS 50, 38, 26, 43, 46

'We've got the most beautiful bunch of horses. The babies we've looked after for a couple of seasons are coming through now to join the more established names' and people love to see them."

Thistlecrack's progress last season was nothing short of sensational, the eight-year-old winning all five of his starts, including the World Hurdle, in seemingly effortless fashion. His cruising speed had to be seen to be believed, and somehow he managed to go through an entire season without coming off the bridle.

His official rating soared from 150 to 174 during the course of the campaign, and he will now pursue a novice chasing path which connections hope will lead to the Gold Cup.

"Thistlecrack is set to go down the novice chasing route, perhaps beginning at Chepstow over 2m4f in early October and, if all goes well, he could run in the Gold Cup next spring along with Cue Card and Native River," Tizzard explains.

"We'll take it step by step with him, but there's no reason why he can't end up in the Gold Cup in his first season over fences.

"He's the most exciting horse we've ever had at Venn Farm and possesses so much class. It's quite frightening really when you consider we haven't got to the bottom of him.

"His owners, the Snooks, are very keen on him going chasing this season, and the Gold Cup is the natural target for a horse of his calibre and potential.

"If things didn't pan out as we would hope, Thistlecrack can always go back over hurdles and defend his World Hurdle crown. There are plenty of options for him."

Card to take familiar path

The wonderfully talented ten-year-old **Cue Card**, denied a £1m triple crown bonus when taking a costly fall at the third-last in last season's Gold Cup won by Don Cossack, is expected to prove as good as ever this time.

"He's some horse, and has come back in looking an absolute picture," Tizzard reveals. "We'll go the same route with him as last year, taking in the Charlie Hall Chase, Betfair Chase, King George, Gold Cup and Betfred Bowl at Aintree.

"He was in the form of his life last season, winning four of those races after benefiting from an operation on a trapped epiglottis.

"He had an amazing season, and it was just a shame what happened in the Gold Cup. We'll never know if he'd have won had he stood up. It was the first time he had fallen, but that's championship racing for you."

Cue Card may be approaching the twilight

Thistlecrack: sensational season ended in World Hurdle victory in March. Now he'll embark on a novice chase campaign

of his illustrious career, but Tizzard cannot see any sign of age taking its toll.

"He's showing no sign of age whatsoever," he says. "The horse certainly looks as good as ever and we're very excited about the new season with him."

'He's looking a million dollars'

Hopes are high that the less-exposed six-year-old Native River could also make sufficient progress to take his place in the Gold Cup.

Currently rated 154 following an impressive, strong-staying success in a Grade 1 novice chase over 3m1f at Aintree in April, the son of Indian River is being carefully laid out for the Hennessy Gold Cup in late November.

"He's come back in looking a million dollars and really could be anything at this stage," Tizzard says. "He's grown again over the summer, and is a big, strong horse now. We're aiming him at the Hennessy, and I'm not sure as yet whether we'll give him a run beforehand. After all, I'd hate to see him touched off at Newbury under a penalty.

"The Gold Cup would be entirely possible if he went and won the Hennessy in style. He stays particularly well – he ran a blinder to finish second to Minella Rocco in the four-miler at Cheltenham – but showed plenty of class to win at

Cue Card: heading back to the Gold Cup, where he could meet up to two stablemates

COLIN TIZZARD
MILBORNE PORT, DORSET

	No. of Hrs	Races Run	1st	2nd	3rd	Unpl	Per cent	£1 Level Stake
NH Flat	16	31	0	1	4	26	0.0	-31.00
Hurdles	36	130	22	6	19	83	16.9	-13.14
Chases	28	164	29	32	30	73	17.7	-1.60
Totals	**58**	**325**	**51**	**39**	**53**	**182**	**15.7**	**-45.74**
14-15	61	292	37	34	40	181	12.7	-79.21
13-14	68	314	26	31	44	213	8.3	-153.81

BY MONTH

NH Flat	W-R	Per cent	£1 Level Stake	Hurdles	W-R	Per cent	£1 Level Stake
May	0-4	0.0	-4.00	May	0-4	0.0	-4.00
June	0-1	0.0	-1.00	June	0-1	0.0	-1.00
July	0-0	0.0	0.00	July	0-1	0.0	-1.00
August	0-0	0.0	0.00	August	0-0	0.0	0.00
September	0-0	0.0	0.00	September	0-1	0.0	-1.00
October	0-2	0.0	-2.00	October	4-13	30.8	+21.39
November	0-7	0.0	-7.00	November	2-13	15.4	-1.50
December	0-2	0.0	-2.00	December	1-15	6.7	-12.00
January	0-1	0.0	-1.00	January	2-17	11.8	-12.32
February	0-6	0.0	-6.00	February	3-13	23.1	-1.50
March	0-2	0.0	-2.00	March	5-26	19.2	+5.00
April	0-6	0.0	-6.00	April	5-26	19.2	-5.21

Chases	W-R	Per cent	£1 Level Stake	Totals	W-R	Per cent	£1 Level Stake
May	0-1	0.0	-1.00	May	0-9	0.0	-9.00
June	0-1	0.0	-1.00	June	0-3	0.0	-3.00
July	0-1	0.0	-1.00	July	0-2	0.0	-2.00
August	0-0	0.0	0.00	August	0-0	0.0	0.00
September	0-0	0.0	0.00	September	0-1	0.0	-1.00
October	2-14	14.3	-5.25	October	6-29	20.7	+14.14
November	7-35	20.0	+0.53	November	9-55	16.4	-7.97
December	4-27	14.8	+3.08	December	5-44	11.4	-10.92
January	3-19	15.8	+13.50	January	5-37	13.5	+0.18
February	7-22	31.8	+11.08	February	10-41	24.4	+3.58
March	3-23	13.0	-12.50	March	8-51	15.7	-9.50
April	3-21	14.3	-9.05	April	8-53	15.1	20.26

DISTANCE

Hurdles	W-R	Per cent	£1 Level Stake	Chases	W-R	Per cent	£1 Level Stake
2m-2m3f	4-46	8.7	-27.75	2m-2m3f	5-31	16.1	-9.59
2m4f-2m7f	6-38	15.8	-16.58	2m4f-2m7f	7-50	14.0	+1.75
3m+	4-9	44.4	+6.79	3m+	13-56	23.2	+14.66

TYPE OF RACE

Non-Handicaps	W-R	Per cent	£1 Level Stake	Handicaps	W-R	Per cent	£1 Level Stake
Nov Hrdls	2-37	5.4	-33.77	Nov Hrdls	3-11	27.3	+22.88
Hrdls	8-25	32.0	-0.75	Hrdls	9-57	15.8	-1.50
Nov Chs	3-18	16.7	-0.13	Nov Chs	5-35	14.3	-1.34
Chases	4-17	23.5	-2.80	Chases	16-93	17.2	-4.83
Sell/Claim	0-0	0.00	0.00	Sell/Claim	0-0	0.0	0.00

RACE CLASS

	W-R	Per cent	£1 Level Stake
Class 1	13-47	27.7	+9.29
Class 2	4-37	10.8	-20.38
Class 3	18-93	19.4	-22.74
Class 4	13-102	12.7	-21.56
Class 5	3-21	14.3	-10.83
Class 6	0-25	0.0	-25.00

FIRST TIME OUT

	W-R	Per cent	£1 Level Stake
Bumpers	0-16	0.0	-16.00
Hurdles	5-21	23.8	-0.11
Chases	3-21	14.3	3.25
Totals	8-58	13.8	-19.36

Statistics relate to runners in Britain from April 26, 2015 to April 23, 2016

DID YOU KNOW?

Ian Botham was skittled out by Colin Tizzard when the pair played cricket together in their schooldays. Botham was captain and Tizzard vice-captain for Yeovil area schoolboys. Botham was just a batsman back then, but one day he decided to have a bowl after a quick consultation with Tizzard. It turned out he was rather good at it.

Aintree, a track that doesn't necessarily put a premium on stamina. He's a very exciting, progressive horse to have in the yard, and we're more than hopeful the best is yet to come."

Wind op for Theatre Guide

The Grand National is likely to be on the radar for several Tizzard chasers, including **Masters Hill**, **Theatre Guide**, **Theatrical Star** and **Third Intention**.

Perhaps it is Theatre Guide of that quartet who appears the most interesting with the 4m2½f Aintree marathon in mind.

Runner-up to Smad Place in the Hennessy last year, Theatre Guide progressed to land Kempton's BetBright Chase by ten lengths from Opening Batsman, and looks the type who could take to the demands of Aintree's National course.

"He's just had a wind op, and we feel it could make a big difference to him," Tizzard reveals. "The plan is to start him off in the 2m4f Listed chase he finished third in at Wetherby last October before having another crack at the Hennessy. Later on I could see him taking his chance in the Grand National."

Every progressive stable needs young, unexposed, exciting fresh talent to make the breakthrough each year, and there seems to be plenty of that type of horse lurking in the Venn Farm shadows.

West Approach, a half-brother to Thistlecrack, is one. "We purposely saved his novice status for this season," Tizzard says.

"He's going the right way, and will be aimed at a couple of the big novice races. He could even progress up to World Hurdle class in due course. He goes well at home, and we think an awful lot of him."

Cheltenham class

Quiz Master, an unraced four-year-old gelding, is another. "He got a bruised foot and missed all of last season which was a shame as we've always considered him a Cheltenham horse," Tizzard says.

"He'll start off in a bumper and, if he progresses in the way we hope he will, the Champion Bumper at the festival will be his target. He's a gorgeous horse owned by Brocade Racing, and is one to keep an eye out for."

Theatre Guide: could head to Aintree for the National

Elegant Escape, a four-year-old Dubai Destination gelding, is another for the notebook. "We paid decent money for him at Goffs in April after he finished second in a maiden point-to-point," Tizzard says.

"We turned him away over the summer, and are very pleased with him. He's a big horse who will start over hurdles, and looks to have a bright future. He's one of the more unexposed horses in the yard, but hopefully you'll be hearing plenty more about him in the coming years."

Another potential star

Murrayana, **Robinsfirth** and **Kings Walk** are others who receive favourable mentions, but it's clear from Tizzard's voice that the apple of his eye is **Royal Vacation**, a six-year-old King's Theatre gelding who has the potential to take high rank over fences this campaign.

"He goes novice chasing this season and we think he has the potential to be a star over fences," Tizzard enthuses. "We're very excited about his future. He won three times last term and we're going to tweak his wind ahead of aiming him at the top events between 2m4f to 3m. He's a lovely horse. We've been patient with him, and he's definitely one to follow. I really like him."

Team Tizzard have come a long way in 21 years, but the journey is far from over. Further heroics from Thistlecrack and Cue Card this season plus the emergence into Graded company of some of the younger, highly regarded brigade could well push them up another rung towards the top of the ladder.

Interview by Richard Birch

☑ Although Tizzard doesn't possess anything like the number of horses that other top trainers do, he still has plenty of quality in his yard which earned him more than £1.4 million in prize-money last season. That was easily a personal best, as was his tally of 50 winners

☑ **He doesn't send many runners to Newcastle (4-7, 57%, +£30.00) and Wetherby (4-7, 50%, +£16.98) but his record at the tracks speaks for itself**

SUPER STATS

☑ Thanks to the quality in his yard, Tizzard is able to maintain decent strike-rates and level-stake profits at Aintree (6-28, 21%, +£33.49) and Ascot (7-42, 17%, +£5.21)

☑ **Chasers form the backbone of his team and they return level-stake profits at Exeter (12-54, 22%, +£4.71), Newton Abbot (8-51, 16%, +£6.00) and Wincanton (12-63, 19%, +£0.83), all tracks relatively close to his base in Dorset**

Statistics cover the 2012-13 season onwards and are correct to September 9, 2016

VIEW FROM IRELAND RICHARD FORRISTAL

It's going to be a hard act to follow after last season's heroics

AS a rule, the conclusion that there isn't much room for improvement in something or other would infer negative connotations.

That is possibly no less true in relation to the collective exploits of Irish jump racing's leading performers, but it is also indicative of the dizzy heights that were scaled throughout the 2015-2016 season.

Below the surface the industry continues to contract alarmingly, but those in the elite echelon have combined to set the bar ridiculously high.

The retrospective promotion of **Josies Orders** in the cross-country race meant Irish-trained runners outscored the locals at the 2016 Cheltenham Festival for the first time in history. In March, the addition of the mares' novices' hurdle saw 28 races run across the four-day Cotswolds bonanza. By the close of play the raiders had equalled the previous best of 14 to share the honours, and subsequent events saw them set that new benchmark.

It was a hollow victory announced to little fanfare, but it is a reflection of the unprecedented prowess with which the heavyweight Irish prize fighters are being campaigned over jumps right now.

Don Cossack secured Gordon Elliott a famous Gold Cup success at Prestbury Park, three days after **Annie Power** carved her own little piece of history by emulating Dawn Run with a devastating Champion Hurdle triumph. By setting a record time, her performance left many to muse that she only got to compete in the 2m decider as a result of the respective defections of reigning title-holder Faugheen and Arctic Fire.

However, apart from being a consequence of the bloated big-race programme, that is a symptom of Willie Mullins' continued omnipotence. The incredible champion trainer again departed Cheltenham with a mind-boggling seven winners, and he went on to push Paul Nicholls all the way to the wire in the British trainers' championship.

Mullins exerts a startling level of dominance and, while he is unlikely to play it up, there must be a chance he will have another go at wresting away Nicholls' crown.

Getting chinned at Sandown will have left a mark that the competitive instinct in him will surely want to repair.

Mouse Morris also masterminded Grand National glory with **Rule The World**, having secured the Irish version with **Rogue Angel** 11 days earlier. When you factor in the emergence of Joseph O'Brien, it is clear that Irish trainers will continue to flex their muscles at the highest level for a time to come.

SENIOR CHASERS

For the second year in a row, Don Cossack was crowned king of the staying chasing ranks by the official handicappers. This time, though, that distinction was complemented by a glorious Gold Cup victory, when he capitalised on Cue Card's dramatic exit to lead home a stunning one-two-three-four for the raiders.

Djakadam filled the runner-up berth again and may well be campaigned over slightly shorter trips this term, although there aren't many better than him in the staying ranks. **Don Poli**, on the other hand, confirmed his status as a quality slogger with a laboured third at Cheltenham. He and the fourth **Carlingford Lough** could well win more Grade 1s, but you would expect them to again come up short in the Prestbury Park showpiece.

Gordon Elliott, who lost the exciting No More Heroes at Cheltenham, remains optimistic he will get Don Cossack back following his tendon strain in time for a prep run ahead of the Gold Cup, with the Kinloch Brae at Thurles already pencilled in. Horses like **Road To Riches**, **Un De Sceaux**, **Killultagh Vic** and **Black Hercules** are classy, trip-versatile individuals who will all add depth to the chasing ranks.

Douvan and **Vautour** are the two who will likely cause Willie Mullins and pundits the greatest reason for procrastination. Vautour seemed to confirm he isn't a two-miler at Punchestown, and many would relish the prospect of seeing the runaway Ryanair winner and narrow King George runner-up tackle the Gold Cup. The mighty Douvan will surely lead the two-mile charge. He was a sensational novice who will prove a formidable prospect if he matures, but could Mullins be tempted to see if he is the horse to break his Gold Cup hoodoo? Don't discount that possibility.

Gold glory: Don Cossack lands the festival showpiece

SENIOR HURDLERS

Annie Power reigned supreme in Faugheen's absence last March. She is by some way the best mare we have seen since Dawn Run, and, should she and **Faugheen** perform to their respective optimum levels, Mullins is going to have some big calls to make. Good luck to anyone second-guessing how it will play out.

Faugheen produced a career-best turn in the Irish Champion Hurdle before succumbing to injury. Should Mullins and Rich Ricci ever decide to pit them against each other, it would constitute a showdown on a par with those epic Kauto Star-Denman duels. Fascinatingly, elsewhere in these pages, Mullins has mooted the possibility of **Yorkhill** going down the Champion Hurdle route although at this stage it seems unlikely.

The likes of **Vroum Vroum Mag**, **Apple's Jade** and **Nichols Canyon** will have options over a range of distances for the champion trainer, while **Ivanovich Gorbatov**, **Jer's Girl** and the returning **Jezki** are others who have the scope to make a big impact. There is real depth across the entire spectrum of Irish hurdlers.

NOVICES

Over fences, it is hard not to get excited about the prospect of seeing Yorkhill strut his stuff; he has all the attributes of a horse who could go right to the top. His talented but unfurnished stablemate **Min** might be better suited to chasing, while **Identity Thief** is another who could be interesting over the bigger obstacles for Henry de Bromhead.

We are even more precariously in the realm of conjecture with the hurdlers. Mullins will go to war with the likes of **Blow By Blow**, **Bacardys**, **Battleford**, **Avenir D'Une Vie** and **Augusta Kate**, while O'Brien's JP McManus-owned **Aspen Colorado** could be a real player.

There is also Mullins' now annual mysterious Supreme Novices' ante-post favourite **Senewalk**. A Flat-winning son of Walk In The Park, he could be anything – quite literally.

Min: could be back at Cheltenham in March as a novice chaser

The big races could all go to Ireland – but there is still value to be found

CHAMPION HURDLE

If someone had told you this time last year that Willie Mullins would win the 2016 Champion Hurdle no-one would have been surprised. The name of the horse might have been surprising though as it wasn't Faugheen who won, but the reinvented former World Hurdle second and mares' hurdle winner Annie Power.

She turned into the ultimate supersub, winning at Cheltenham easily, and is deservedly right up in the market for a repeat this season, perched alongside Faugheen with many layers at around 5-2.

How Mullins shuffles his pack this season will have a big bearing on this race as Faugheen and Annie Power are unlikely to run together, and out of the two it might be Faugheen who is asked to stretch out again and tackle longer distances.

After all, he is a former winner of the Neptune at Cheltenham, and has a Graded win to his name over three miles too.

Could there be a third Mullins contender to trump both of them, though? Quite possibly. **Apple's Jade** is owned by Gigginstown so could easily be given licence to attack either of the Rich Ricci-owned duo who go for the Champion.

Her second in the Triumph Hurdle might have hinted that she had limitations, but it was her first outing since Christmas and since then she has been devastating.

To win two Grade 1 events by an aggregate margin of 50 lengths is barely credible yet that is what she did. She thrashed her Triumph conqueror Ivanovich Gorbatov both times, at Aintree and Punchestown, and she must now have forced her way into the Champion Hurdle reckoning.

To see her beating up inferior mares all season would be disappointing and boring so let's hope Michael O'Leary and his team are intent on going for the top 2m contests, ending up in the fourth race on the first day of Cheltenham.

CHAMPION CHASE

The 2m chasing crown might well end up going back to Closutton too with last season's Arkle winner **Douvan** looking nigh-on invincible.

His transition to chasing was faultless – six wins from six starts including five Grade 1s – and the closest any horse got to him was when Sizing John ran him to seven lengths at Cheltenham.

He is already odds-on in some places and, while there is always plenty of conjecture about where and how a Mullins horse may be campaigned during the season, it would be a surprise if Douvan was asked to go up in trip.

Mullins has never won the Champion

Chase and he would surely never have a better chance of doing so.

Sprinter Sacre's renaissance last season was a fantastic story and it was great to see. A fall for Un De Sceaux on his comeback and a couple of good wins for Sprinter in the first half of the campaign had people believing again, and he produced in glorious style at the festival, having the race won by the last fence.

It won't get any easier for him next year as an 11-year-old and facing a horse of Douvan's calibre, but his work is done. His legacy is secure and, while it is hard to see him locking horns with the younger Douvan and coming off best, he could still be placed at Cheltenham.

There is scarce little else to get excited about in this market. Vautour has always threatened to be effective over 2m as a chaser, but fluffed his lines at Punchestown during the spring meaning the experiment is only likely to be rekindled if something untoward happens to Douvan.

Traffic Fluide could get involved and did run well in the Clarence House on his only start of the previous campaign when third to Un De Sceaux. He would need to improve on that but he is only six and has run only ten times in his life so it is perfectly possible. Although, should Douvan prove to be unstoppable in the first half of the season, you may well see trainers with fringe candidates in this sphere looking elsewhere.

WORLD HURDLE

There is some good value to be had in this market with the first four in the betting not all likely to turn up.

Faugheen could come for this but easily might not. Thistlecrack goes chasing, Annie Power always gets quoted for this but doesn't stay and won the Champion Hurdle last season, while Vroum Vroum Mag might go the mares route again, or go chasing.

Therefore, **Jezki** at 16-1 looks fantastic value if he is fully recovered from the injury that kept him off the track last season. This is

Jezki (right): the 2014 Champion Hurdle winner has proved he stays 3m and can be a big player in this season's World Hurdle

a horse who has won eight Grade 1s including the Champion Hurdle, and on his latest start defeated Hurricane Fly at Punchestown over three miles, thereby proving conclusively he stays the World Hurdle trip.

His season-ending injury, picked up last autumn, was a surprise as he had previously stood up to some rigorous campaigns without a blemish. However, it was caught early, he has had ample time to recover, and it could have been for the best as Thistlecrack was unbeatable in this division in his absence.

Jezki will be nine by the time of the next festival, but that is not old in staying terms and he could easily have a big say in the destination of the World Hurdle.

The other interesting one here is Shaneshill, who has festival form figures of 222. He ran a cracker in the RSA Chase last season when second to Blaklion and then reverted to hurdles where he might have won a Grade 1 at Punchestown (the same race Jezki won in 2015) but for falling at the last. He was last seen in America in the Iroquois Hurdle, finishing second to Rawnaq, so don't be surprised if he isn't out too early this time as he had a hard spring.

CHELTENHAM GOLD CUP

The Gold Cup is baffling hence why it is 7-1 the field. How will Thistlecrack get on chasing? Will Don Cossack return? Will Vautour stay and will he even go for it? Can Cue Card possibly be as good as he was? Will Coneygree be as good as he was?

With all these unknowns it may be best to stick to the tried and trusted **Djakadam**. He has finished second in the previous two renewals and has achieved a lot for a young horse. He will only be eight next season yet has already won a Thyestes, a John Durkan and been placed numerous times at the top level.

As a lightly raced sort, there may well be some improvement left in him and he obviously acts well round Cheltenham so the 16-1 currently available looks tempting.

Of those at the top end of the market,

Thistlecrack could easily be the most dangerous. Yes he will be a novice and he will be nine next year, but such was the class he showed over hurdles last season (rated 174) that if he took to the job he might blitz all of these. Things are rarely that easy in racing, but Colin Tizzard has good reason to hope he can do what Cue Card failed to do last season and win the Gold Cup.

KING GEORGE

Cue Card did win the King George, just touching off Vautour, and that pair are sure to be back at Kempton again on Boxing Day.

Of the two, Vautour might come off best this time as he was only a slow jump away from winning last year. However, he is already favourite, and if you wanted a speculative bet then **Tea For Two** fits the bill.

His season ended after he finished third to Bristol De Mai in February and he needs to improve from his current rating of 153. However, he does love Kempton, he has course form at the track of 111 including a Lanzarote and a Feltham, and he is 33-1.

GRAND NATIONAL

The 2016 Grand National was remarkable for a few reasons. It was won by a novice in Rule The World and it was almost won by a 13-year-old in Vics Canvas. The latter wasn't the first to excel over the National fences as an oldie as Hello Bud and Oscar Time have both won races there as teenagers.

Therefore, **Alvarado**, a young buck at the age of 12 should be given due consideration. He has finished fourth in the race twice and was a great second in the Scottish National on his last start behind Vicente. Hopefully that will put him high enough in the handicap to get a run – something he missed out on last season. He still has more to offer.

Alvarado: has National form and could yet land the big one

Five to follow from the Post's speed figures and ratings experts . . . .

ON THE FIGURES

Ballyoptic (Nigel Twiston-Davies) His RPR of 154 is upwards of a stone below the level of a typical World Hurdle winner, but the staying hurdle division has a very open look to it and this lightly raced six-year-old remains open to plenty of improvement.

Bristol De Mai (Nigel Twiston-Davies) A Grade 1-winning juvenile hurdler, he repeated the feat over fences as a novice last season. He should develop into a 165+ chaser this season and a current official mark of 154 gives him the option of tackling some of the better handicaps.

Ch'Tibello (Dan Skelton) His current official mark of 144 is a fair reflection of his form, but he can rate a fair bit higher and Cheltenham's Greatwood Hurdle looks a logical early season target.

Henri Parry Morgan (Peter Bowen) Unseated his rider when favourite for the bet365 Gold Cup at Sandown, but he has a mark of 150 and looks an ideal type for the big staying handicap chases.

Vintage Vinnie (Rebecca Curtis) Scored over hurdles in September and an official chase mark of 129 looks ripe for exploitation now stable is back in better form.

[Steve Mason, Racing Post Ratings]

ON THE CLOCK

Altior (Nicky Henderson) Unbeaten in five starts over hurdles, he clocked a time that stacked up well against the Champion Hurdle when slamming a smart field in the Supreme Novices' and can take high rank among this season's novice chasers.

Coneygree (Mark Bradstock) Sidelined with a hock injury for most of last season, he left an indelible impression when lifting the 2015 Gold Cup and can confirm he is still the best staying chaser around.

Definitly Red (Brian Ellison) Runner-up to subsequent festival winners at Warwick and Wetherby, the four-miler at Cheltenham proved too much, but he could still be well treated.

Taper Tantrum (Michael Bell) An 80-rated handicapper on the Flat, he made a fine start to the hurdling by winning at Newton Abbot and earned a decent figure when following up at Stratford. He can make his mark in much better grade.

Yanworth (Alan King) Looked the real deal when routing his rivals on Cheltenham Trials day in January but could not match strides with Yorkhill in a moderately paced Neptune. Keep the faith.

[Dave Edwards, Topspeed]

I'm sticking with mighty Don – but backing him at 25s for National glory

SIX months have passed since that hugely expensive day, but I still can't get Don Poli out of my mind as the 2016-17 jumps season proper dawns.

I spent nearly all of last season utterly convinced that the stamina-packed 2015 RSA Chase hero was tailor-made for the demands of the Gold Cup and backed him accordingly.

Don Poli performed well to finish third in chasing's blue riband after being settled well off the pace, but the overwhelming feeling when he crossed the line was one of disappointment.

A subsequent Aintree second to Cue Card, where he was given a far more attacking ride, tends to confirm popular belief the seven-year-old is just below the very best chasers in the land, but I am still adamant he possesses the raw ability to bulldoze his way up the Cheltenham hill to win a Gold Cup if the ground comes up soft or heavy.

That rarely happens, though, so it is time to focus on perhaps a more realistic Plan B, and invest plenty of cash on him winning the Grand National instead.

As I have said so many times before, Don Poli is all about stamina. He jumps well and is just the type to get into a good rhythm over those Aintree fences which are considerably less challenging than they used to be.

With so much potential Gold Cup ammunition to fire, it would come as no surprise if his trainer Willie Mullins earmarked the National as 161-rated Don Poli's principal target for this campaign, and the general 25-1 is simply too big to resist at this stage.

Another horse who I am particularly looking forward to seeing this winter is 107-rated hurdler **Arty Campbell**.

Bernard Llewellyn's stayer was in cracking form on the Flat during the summer, winning 2m handicaps at Chepstow and Kempton before finishing an excellent Goodwood third to Sir Mark Prescott's hugely progressive three-year-old St Michel.

It doesn't take a genius to work out that Arty Campbell, who boasts an official Flat rating of 84, is potentially thrown in over jumps, and last November's narrow Kempton second to Thunder Sheik stands the closest of inspection.

Best on good ground, there will doubtless be a plan for Arty Campbell which could revolve around a valuable handicap or two next spring, and he is emphatically one to follow, particularly when stepped up to 2m4f.

Baywing became a great personal favourite of mine last season, winning four heavy-ground handicap hurdles in the style of a rapidly progressive stayer.

His trainer Nicky Richards places this type of horse particularly well, and Baywing's confidence was sky-high when he stepped up in grade to win a Class 3 event at Haydock in January.

Whatever Baywing *(right)* did over hurdles was always going to be a bonus because, in the longer term, connections believe he is destined for marathon chases such as the Welsh National.

I have no doubt it will pay to follow Baywing once again in his novice chase campaign, bearing in mind he needs testing conditions to excel.

It will be great to see the better horses out again in late autumn and early winter because the overall quality of summer jumping this year seemed poorer than in recent seasons. One reason could be the retirement of John Ferguson, who tended to send out a string of winners during May to September, and he will also be missed this winter.

TRAINERS

Most people expect Dan Skelton to take another significant step forward, including his mentor Paul Nicholls, and it would be no surprise to see him break into racing's top four, joining Nicholls, Mullins and Nicky Henderson.

Colin Tizzard's stable, blessed with two of jump racing's most popular performers, Thistlecrack and Cue Card, should enjoy another wonderful season, while Nigel Twiston-Davies also has the ammunition to do well once again.

JOCKEYS

The latter's son Sam flourished in his role as stable jockey to Nicholls in the second half of last season, and bagged three Cheltenham Festival winners plus a Scottish National via Vicente.

He took that confidence into the start of the new season, and even led Richard Johnson at one point.

Twiston-Davies and his friend Aidan Coleman both have the talent and drive to put Johnson under far more pressure than he experienced during last year's runaway title romp, while further progress from an even younger gun Sean Bowen is also anticipated.

Craig Nichol, unquestionably the most promising rider in the north, should do well once again, while David Noonan and Harry Cobden will both be looking to build on excellent campaigns which suggest they have very bright futures indeed.

The leaves are beginning to fall off the trees and the nights are getting longer. That can only mean the likes of Sprinter Sacre, Annie Power, Vautour, Vroum Vroum Mag, Faugheen and Don Poli, of course, will soon be back in action. I can't wait.

Three who can make their mark in the saddle this season (from top): Aidan Coleman, Craig Nichol and David Noonan

Fire can burn bright to give Mullins another player for the big days

BRAHMS DE CLERMONT Paul Nicholls

Towards the backend of last season champion trainer Nicholls unleashed a flurry of bumper winners. Among them was this French-bred five-year-old, who created an outstanding impression when serving up a demolition job on his debut at Taunton. He powered clear to score despite being green and looked well suited by the good ground. From the same family as the yard's brilliant Master Minded, his novice hurdle campaign should be fruitful.

BABENY BRIDGE Nick Williams

Once considered a smart prospect by the Williams family, Babeny Bridge has had his problems since recording a fifth point-to-point success in 2014. However, his return from a layoff, in a novice hurdle over 3m at Worcester in May, showed the engine remains and he is considered to be attractively treated. He stays very well, is versatile regards underfoot conditions, and is one to be with when switched to regulation fences.

COUP DE PINCEAU Paul Nicholls

He shot clear once the penny dropped on his debut at Ludlow in April. He is related to very useful hurdler/chaser Une Artiste and out of a dam who scored over fences at up to 3m6f. With that in mind it will be interesting to see what distance he kicks off at once sent hurdling. No doubt connections will have the spring festivals firmly in mind for him.

FIRE IN SOUL Willie Mullins

Despite costing €200,000 and hailing from top connections, Fire In Soul was allowed to go off at odds of 9-2 on his hurdling bow at Clonmel last season. The five-year-old comfortably completed the task, looking better the further he went over the minimum distance on deep ground. He failed to fire upped to Grade 2 company next time at Fairyhouse, but bounced back in no uncertain terms when slamming an interesting field at Ballinrobe in May. The runner-up came out and won a Flat maiden next time, and Mullins has yet another exciting prospect in his care.

GIBBES BAY Paul Nicholls

A 90,000gns purchase at the Cheltenham sales, this grey son of Al Namix was sent for a prestigious bumper at Ayr's Scottish National meeting for his racecourse debut. He came home a workmanlike winner, from a reliable sort in second, but the market suggested he might need the experience and he is very much a work in progress. Jumping fences will be his game in due course, but he has got a lot of scope and ought to win his share of hurdle races beforehand.

HOKE COLBURN Harry Whittington

An eyecatcher on his debut in a Warwick bumper in March, Hoke Colburn was well backed on his next outing at Southwell and didn't disappoint. He pulled clear with a promising mare, proving himself versatile regards ground, and will go under the radar somewhat when kicking off his novice hurdle campaign. He is a half-brother to a 3m winner and looks nailed on to improve.

LE BREUIL Ben Pauling

Created a deep impression when taking a bumper on his debut at Warwick in May by ten lengths. There was some ease in the ground that day and there was plenty to like about the way he went about his business, scoring under a confident ride. His young trainer can't wait to get him going over hurdles, and he is bred to make his mark in that sphere, although Pauling hasn't ruled out taking in another bumper under a penalty first. He could well be Graded class in time.

LE VAGABOND Edward O'Grady

This talented ex-French performer is proving a versatile acquisition for his Irish trainer. An unlucky run on the Flat at Galway during the summer was followed by an emphatic display when showing his true colours in decent company over 1m6f at Killarney. A switch back to hurdles beckons this season and he is expected to prove very well treated off a mark around 120. He looks just the sort his wily handler can get to the big spring festivals for some valuable handicaps.

PERFORM Philip Hobbs

An imposing horse, Perform strongly appeals as one to rise through the ranks this season. He was too keen on his Uttoxeter debut in March 2015 and showed vast improvement when winning back from a break at Aintree last October over 2m4f. He missed out the rest of last season, but is reportedly ready to show his true colours again and is in the right hands. Chasing will be on his agenda at some

stage, but off a mark in the mid-130s there is surely more to come over hurdles first.

QUEEN DEIRDRE Willie Mullins

More and more each year Ireland's champion trainer uses the Galway festival to unleash new and exciting prospects. This time around he took the final event on the Saturday when the highly promising Queen Deirdre bolted up on her bumper debut. Mullins was worried about her immaturity, being a four-year-old against more experienced elders, but she could hardly have won more impressively. She is bred to be high class over hurdles, being a half-sister to Identity Thief, who landed the Fighting Fifth last term. It will be very interesting to see if she is sent jumping or kept for a high-profile bumper campaign.

TOLETHORPE Harry Whittington

Whittington has made a name for himself over the past few seasons and this young chestnut gelding is expected to provide the trainer with another exciting novice hurdler. He overcame inexperience in fine style when shooting clear to win his bumper debut at Huntingdon in March on soft ground, and was immediately put away for the autumn. His half-sister Balmusette won a Listed event over jumps and, boasting a neat turn of foot, Graded races beckon if he matures along the right lines.

WOOLSTONE ONE Harry Whittington

This four-year-old filly really impressed when winning her first two junior bumpers for Whittington last term. Her trainer couldn't resist the temptation of then sending her for a Listed bumper at Sandown for her final outing, having previously said he would like to put her away, and it backfired as she trailed home last of the 13-strong field. That was just too bad to be true, but she can achieve her potential over hurdles. She has plenty of speed, winter ground holds no fears, and it will be fascinating to chart her progress.

Le Vagabond (2): could turn out to be very well treated over hurdles

A dozen names I can't wait to see as excitement is starting to build

IT IS hard not to be bursting with excitement for the start of the jumps season proper, but has there ever been a stranger market for the Cheltenham Gold Cup?

Favourite Thistlecrack has yet to jump a fence in public, second favourite Vautour ducked the gig last year, third favourite Don Cossack is injured, fourth favourite Cue Card will be 11 in March and no winner has been older than ten since 1969, fifth favourite Douvan is evens for the Champion Chase and sixth favourite Coneygree has raced just five times in the last 44 months.

We can expect as many market upheavals in that race as any other this season and I've had my stab at a left-field contender in the list below.

This list is not necessarily a list of horses likely to be challenging for top honours this season, but simply one of horses I am looking forward to seeing step up.

There are a lot of obvious star contenders missed out, but you know all about those anyway.

ALTIOR Nicky Henderson

One of the big surprises at the end of last season was the decision by connections of the Supreme Novices' Hurdle winner to swerve a potential follow-up at Aintree and school him over fences. Altior had demonstrated some change of gear when winning over hurdles at Christmas and did so again when slamming Min at Cheltenham. Wherever he ends up going, he is one of the stars in Britain and should continue to do well.

AUGUSTA KATE Willie Mullins

The strength in depth possessed by Mullins can be seen by looking at the markets for the Cheltenham novice hurdles – and he even has eight of the top ten in the betting for the novice mares' event. Any of the French imports could be something special, but the one thing we know about Augusta Kate is that she is very tough. The winner of her first two bumpers, she went on to run with credit in the Champion Bumper at Cheltenham, finishing seventh, and was then second in the Aintree mares' bumper before going on to win the mares' event at Punchestown. She

wasn't far off the best in that sphere, and should develop into a really good hurdler, possibly over further than 2m.

BRISTOL DE MAI Nigel Twiston-Davies

There is every hope this front-running grey can go to the top. Connections originally thought he was a two-miler, but he was a heavy-ground winner of the Finale Junior Hurdle at Chepstow two seasons ago and winners of that tend to stay well, and Bristol De Mai strikes as one who is going to get 3m. We have to remember he is only a five-year-old and that, according to Racing Post Ratings, he was the best chaser of his age group in Britain or Ireland last season by 10lb. Indeed, he was the first horse for five years to break a chase RPR of 160 (he ran 161 twice) in the spring of his five-year-old campaign. His Jewson second came on good ground, so he does handle the surface but, assuming he improves again (and he has run

only 15 times, finishing in the first two on 11 of them) he will move further up the pecking order on very soft ground this season.

CAPITAINE Paul Nicholls

Very well regarded by Nicholls, Capitaine was nonetheless defeated on his debut at Taunton in December. However, it might have been a decent race because the winner was sent to Ireland to run in a Grade 2 on his hurdles debut (no show) and the third is now already rated 138 over hurdles. Capitaine certainly made no mistake next time when sauntering clear at Wincanton to win by 13 lengths and 18 lengths in what looked a strongly run contest. He can take high rank among the British novice hurdlers this season.

CH'TIBELLO Dan Skelton

Skelton's patience with this five-year-old paid off when he returned from a near five-month break to win the Scottish Champion

Bristol De Mai: can make giant strides in the top staying chases

Hurdle, and he may well have followed up in the Swinton had they gone faster earlier. The problem for Skelton is that he is going to have to be patient again as Ch'Tibello apparently can't go a yard on soft ground. That might change as he matures, but the five-year-old who ran Altior to a length and a quarter at Ascot last November, still looks nicely enough treated on a mark of 144.

DJAKADAM Willie Mullins

There are much darker horses in the Mullins camp than this dual Gold Cup runner-up, but I'm not prepared to guess about those I've never seen and I still think this is one of the most likely Gold Cup winners this season. He already has the course form to win an average Gold Cup and, while on paper next year's race may be anything but, we are used to horses falling by the wayside. He was the only horse able to live with Don Cossack and Cue Card in last season's Gold Cup and, while he would probably have finished third if the latter had remained on his feet, it was still a top effort. Djakadam, still only seven, ought to be at his absolute peak this season.

IDENTITY THIEF Henry de Bromhead

De Bromhead could do with a change of luck after losing all the Potts horses, but this one is likely to take the yard to all the top meetings. He might not have quite made the grade over hurdles last season, having gone off at just 8-1 for the Champion Hurdle, but it is worth remembering that was only his second season and he began rated just 137. He ended the campaign 22lb higher, so was clearly very much going the right way and he is an exciting prospect for fences this season. There are plenty of horses ahead of him in the betting for the Arkle and JLT, but his hurdles form is as good if not better than any of them and he has just as much potential.

MINELLA ROCCO Jonjo O'Neill

With Don Cossack far from certain to bounce back from injury, Cue Card soon to be turning 11 and Vautour probably odds-on to go for a penalty kick again, there is plenty of potential for some Gold Cup contenders to emerge and a slightly left-field one could be Minella Rocco. O'Neill's six-year-old looked very exciting as a novice hurdler and was expected to make a big splash as a novice chaser last season. Things did not go according to plan in the first half of the campaign with some sloppy jumping halting his progress, but he finally got his act together when second in the Reynoldstown at Ascot and then won the four-miler at the Cheltenham Festival. As he continues to become more accomplished at his fences, the six-year-old will surely have a lot more to give.

TOMMY SILVER Paul Nicholls

Nicholls had his fair share of juvenile hurdlers just below the top bracket last season and, of those, Tommy Silver was probably the most backward. He still showed plenty, though, finishing seventh in the Triumph Hurdle and a close third on the final day of the season. A big horse with plenty of scope, his future may lie over fences, but it will be a surprise if a handicap mark of 139 over hurdles is not left well behind.

TRAFFIC FLUIDE Gary Moore

If there is a trainer who deserves some luck in the 2016-17 jumps season it is Gary Moore, who suffered plenty of disappointment in the run-up to Cheltenham last season with the injuries to Ar Mad and Traffic Fluide. It is to be hoped both horses find their way back to full health this season and either could develop into a Champion Chase contender. Douvan will be in their way, but there will be big prizes to be won when the Mullins wonderhorse is not around and Traffic Fluide could pick up plenty of prize-money if returning fit and well. Still only a six-year-old and with just six British runs behind him, he will have more to come.

WAIT FOR ME Philip Hobbs

This six-year-old was a slow learner last season and he remains a horse with a huge amount of potential. Third to Moon Racer in the Champion Bumper two seasons ago, he began the last campaign by getting thrashed by Buveur D'Air at Newbury, when pulling far too hard, and his keen-going tendencies have so far held him back. A first-time hood almost did the trick at Cheltenham, where he was fourth in the County Hurdle, looking as though he wanted to go further if anything, but he was back to his hard-pulling ways in the Swinton next time. If and when he grows up and consents to race more professionally, he will be one of the best handicapped hurdlers around.

YANWORTH Alan King

A second in the Neptune to Yorkhill is a fair bit of form to have on your CV, but I think there is a chance we didn't quite see the best of Alan King's six-year-old when it mattered in March. King had his string in rude health throughout the winter and had 40 winners from 152 runners from December to February, but was just five from 94 in March and April. That Neptune second was no bad run, but Yanworth had earlier looked a potential superstar when taking apart his field in the trials meeting at Cheltenham in January and, having never been seriously tested over hurdles before then, is worth another chance to prove he is the real deal. King said he seemed to have got quicker last season despite seeing out the 2m5f trip really well, and it will be interesting to see what route is decided upon.

Djakadam: has already finished second in two Gold Cups and could be at the peak of his powers this season

WEEKENDER
EDITOR
DYLAN HILL'S
KEY HORSES

Form figures are up to September 1, 2016

A Good Skin (Ire)

7 b g Presenting - Trixskin (Buckskin)

Tom George   Power Panels Electrical Systems Ltd

PLACINGS: 531/24472211/53922P-   RPR **143**c

Starts	1st	2nd	3rd	4th	Win & Pl
14	2	5	1	2	£40,666

130	4/15	Chel	3m1¹/₂f Cls3 Nov 115-134 Ch Hcap good	£6,256
125	4/15	Ludl	3m Cls3 122-129 Ch Hcap soft	£8,447

Knocking on the door in good handicaps all last season, producing his best effort when second in the Kim Muir on good ground (best win as a novice had also come on a similar surface at Cheltenham); still going the right way.

A Hare Breath (Ire)

8 b g Alkaadhem - Lady Willmurt (Mandalus)

Ben Pauling   Mrs S N J Embiricos

PLACINGS: P/P1/24/141P-   RPR **138**+h

Starts	1st	2nd	3rd	4th	Win & Pl
6	2	1	-	2	£13,629

	1/16	Kemp	2m5f Cls4 Nov Hdl soft	£3,249
120	11/15	Chel	2m⁷/₂f Cls3 Nov 110-125 Hdl Hcap good	£7,507

Out for nearly two years before returning last season but quickly made up for lost time when winning at Cheltenham and Kempton; balloted out of the County Hurdle but could be one for similarly valuable 2m handicaps.

A Toi Phil (Fr)

6 b g Day Flight - Lucidrile (Beyssac)

Willie Mullins (Ir)   Gigginstown House Stud

PLACINGS: 2/O117-P   RPR **152**+h

Starts	1st	2nd	3rd	4th	Win & Pl
6	2	1	-	-	£37,575

	1/16	Leop	2m4f Nov Gd2 Hdl soft	£18,529
	12/15	Leop	2m2f Mdn Hdl heavy	£6,953

Very impressive in both wins in novice hurdles last season but cut out very quickly when stepped up in grade at Cheltenham and Punchestown having also run out at Clonmel; has plenty to prove and far from straightforward but clearly talented.

Abbyssial (Ire)

6 ch g Beneficial - Mega D'Estruval (Garde Royale)

Willie Mullins (Ir)   Mrs Violet O'Leary

PLACINGS: 3111F/16F0/   RPR **161**h

Starts	1st	2nd	3rd	4th	Win & Pl
9	4	-	-	-	£100,899

	5/14	Punc	2m Gd1 Hdl 4yo gd-yld	£51,667
	2/14	Fair	2m Gd2 Hdl 4yo sft-hvy	£20,313
	1/14	Gowr	2m Hdl 4yo soft	£11,375
	12/13	Fair	2m Mdn Hdl 3yo gd-yld	£4,207

Plagued by injuries since winning a Grade 1 four-year-old hurdle at Punchestown in 2014 and hasn't run since finishing last in the 2015 World Hurdle; looked a likely winner of the Red Mills Trial Hurdle that year when falling two out.

Acapella Bourgeois (Fr)

6 ch g Network - Jasmine (Valanjou I)

Sandra Hughes (Ir)   Slaneyville Syndicate

PLACINGS: 70/1/31211-4   RPR **145**h

Starts	1st	2nd	3rd	4th	Win & Pl
9	4	1	1	1	£59,515

	3/16	Fair	2m4f Nov Gd2 Hdl yield	£19,522
	2/16	Thur	2m4f Nov Gd2 Hdl soft	£19,522
	12/15	Leop	2m4f Mdn Hdl heavy	£6,953
	10/14	Rcpp	1m4f NHF 4-5yo gd-sft	£4,167

Progressed throughout last season and won Grade 2 novice hurdles at Thurles and Fairyhouse; beaten only five lengths when stepped up to Grade 1 level at Punchestown despite jumping errors; looks a good chasing prospect.

Activial (Fr)

6 gr g Lord Du Sud - Kissmirial (Smadoun)

Neil Mulholland   Potensis Bloodstock Limited

PLACINGS: 1218/333/49213-   RPR **154**+c

Starts	1st	2nd	3rd	4th	Win & Pl
12	3	2	4	1	£88,673

	1/16	Extr	2m3f Cls4 Ch heavy	£3,899
	2/14	Kemp	2m Cls1 Gd2 Hdl 4yo soft	£15,661
	9/13	Sliga	1m4f NHF 3yo	£4,878

Restricted to just three runs over fences last season, winning well second time out at Exeter before failing to stay when beaten at odds-on at Newbury (second disappointment in two runs beyond 2m5f); sold out of Harry Fry's yard for £80,000 in August.

Adrien Du Pont (Fr)

4 b g Califet - Santariyka (Saint Des Saints)

Paul Nicholls   Mrs Johnny De La Hey

PLACINGS: 1/1211-   RPR **145**+h

Starts	1st	2nd	3rd	4th	Win & Pl
5	4	1	-	-	£79,069

139	4/16	Asct	1m7¹/₂f Cls2 116-139 Hdl 4yo Hcap gd-sft	£25,024
	1/16	Chep	2m Cls1 Gd1 Hdl 4yo heavy	£28,475
	10/15	Chep	2m Cls4 Hdl 3yo good	£3,899
	4/15	Engh	2m1¹/₂f Hdl 3yo v soft	£17,860

Kept away from the big spring festivals last season but still proved himself a very smart juvenile, winning the Grade 1 Finale Hurdle and adding a competitive handicap at Ascot; versatile regarding ground and should stay further.

Affaire D'Honneur (Fr)

5 ch g Shirocco - Affaire De Moeurs (Kaldounevees)

Harry Whittington   Holt, Robinson, Kronbauer, Macnabb & O'Connor

PLACINGS: 23244-   RPR **133**+h

Starts	1st	2nd	3rd	4th	Win & Pl
5	-	2	1	2	£29,948

Ran with promise in some good handicaps last

season, going close at Kempton on his British debut before running on well into fourth in the Betfair Hurdle having badly missed the break; slightly disappointing when only filling same spot in the Imperial Cup.

Agrapart (Fr)

5 b/br g Martaline - Afragha (Darshaan)

Nick Williams		The Gascoigne Brookes Partnership III		
PLACINGS: 521316-				RPR **151+h**
Starts	1st	2nd	3rd	4th	Win & Pl
6	2	1	1	-	£101,623
137	2/16	Newb	2m¹/₂f Cls1 Gd3 128-153 Hdl Hcap heavy............£88,273
	12/15	Aint	2m1f Cls3 Nov Hdl soft......................................£6,279

Suited by heavy ground and galloped to a stunning success in last season's Betfair Hurdle, although flattered by rise to 150 (very few in contention after a botched start and main rival blundered at the last); modest sixth next time at Aintree.

Al Ferof (Fr)

11 gr g Dom Alco - Maralta (Altayan)

Dan Skelton				J Hales	
PLACINGS: 3/1/1325/1352/1342-6					RPR **171+c**
Starts	1st	2nd	3rd	4th	Win & Pl
28	11	4	7	2	£510,856
	12/15	Hntg	2m4f Cls1 Gd2 Ch gd-sft............................£38,753
	11/14	Asct	2m3f Cls1 Gd2 Ch soft...............................£28,609
	11/13	Asct	2m3f Cls1 Gd2 Ch gd-sft............................£28,475
159	11/12	Chel	2m4¹/₂f Cls1 Gd3 137-163 Ch Hcap soft.........£91,120
	12/11	Sand	1m7¹/₂f Cls1 Nov Gd1 Ch gd-sft....................£20,787
	11/11	Chel	2m Cls1 Nov Gd2 Ch gd-sft..........................£13,668
	3/11	Chel	2m¹/₂f Cls1 Nov Gd1 Hdl good......................£57,010
	2/11	Newb	2m¹/₂f Cls3 Nov Hdl gd-sft............................£5,204
	1/11	Tntn	2m3f Cls4 Nov Hdl 4-7yo gd-sft......................£3,426
	2/10	Newb	2m¹/₂f Cls1 Gd2 NHF 4-6yo gd-sft.................£10,832
	12/09	Fair	2m NHF 4yo heavy.....................................£6,038

Veteran chaser who has an outstanding record first time out but has often failed to follow up; again returned with a bang in last season's Peterborough Chase and was kept fresh for the Ryanair Chase when running an honourable race in fourth.

Alisier D'Irlande (Fr)

6 b/br g Kapgarde - Isati'S (Chamberlin)

Henry De Bromhead (Ir)				R S Brookhouse	
PLACINGS: 1/361/F115-					RPR **151+c**
Starts	1st	2nd	3rd	4th	Win & Pl
7	3	-	1	-	£25,042
	2/16	Leop	2m1f Nov Ch soft.......................................£9,496
	2/16	Naas	2m Ch soft...£6,331
	3/15	Thur	2m Mdn Hdl yld-sft......................................£5,349

Exciting front-running chaser who would have won his first three chases last season but for falling when well clear on his debut; finished very tired when taking on Douvan at Aintree but open to significant progress and could thrive at a slightly lower level.

All Set To Go (Ire)

5 gr g Verglas - Firecrest (Darshaan)

Paul Nicholls				C G Roach	
PLACINGS: 4/14011-2					RPR **140h**
Starts	1st	2nd	3rd	4th	Win & Pl
7	3	1	-	2	£26,871
	4/16	Tntn	2m¹/₂f Cls4 Nov Hdl good.............................£4,874
	3/16	Tntn	2m¹/₂f Cls4 Nov Hdl good.............................£3,899
	12/15	Sthl	1m7¹/₂f Cls5 Mdn Hdl soft............................£3,249

Rated 105 when third in a Group 3 Derby trial in 2014 and steadily found his feet last season over hurdles, winning twice at Taunton in the spring before a good second to Gwafa in the Swinton.

Allblak Des Places (Fr)

4 b/br g Full Of Gold - Amiraute (Septieme Ciel)

Willie Mullins (Ir)				George Creighton	
PLACINGS: 32/12-					RPR **139h**
Starts	1st	2nd	3rd	4th	Win & Pl
4	1	2	1	-	£28,479
	12/15	Fair	2m Mdn Hdl 3yo heavy................................£5,349

Twice placed in France before getting off the mark on first run for new connections at Fairyhouse, taking advantage of runner-up Outspoken's final-flight blunder; stepped up again when second to Footpad in a Grade 1 at Leopardstown next time.

Aloomomo (Fr)

6 b g Tirwanako - Kayola (Royal Charter)

Warren Greatrex				The Large G & T Partnership	
PLACINGS: 71F66/5P66646/11136-					RPR **144c**
Starts	1st	2nd	3rd	4th	Win & Pl
17	4	-	1	1	£43,420
129	11/15	Newb	2m6¹/₂f Cls3 122-140 Ch Hcap soft................£25,024
115	11/15	Wwck	2m4f Cls4 98-117 Ch Hcap gd-sft...................£3,899
108	10/15	Uttx	2m4f Cls4 94-120 Ch Hcap soft......................£3,798
	10/13	Nant	1m4f NHF 3yo heavy..................................£6,098

3-1 for the novice handicap chase at last season's Cheltenham Festival having won three times over fences and enjoyed a good prep run over hurdles but could manage only sixth; capable of better.

Alpha Des Obeaux (Fr)

6 b g Saddler Maker - Omega Des Obeaux (Saint Preuil)

Mouse Morris (Ir)				Gigginstown House Stud	
PLACINGS: 1/2122F/22212-3					RPR **170h**
Starts	1st	2nd	3rd	4th	Win & Pl
11	2	7	1	-	£153,246
	1/16	Gowr	3m Gd2 Hdl heavy....................................£18,750
	11/14	Punc	2m4f Mdn Hdl 4yo yield...............................£5,750

Progressive staying hurdler last season, running away with the Galmoy Hurdle and doing much the best of the rest when second to Thistlecrack in the World Hurdle; has always looked a chaser in the making and could be a very exciting novice.

Altior (Ire)
6 b g High Chaparral - Monte Solaro (Key Of Luck)

Nicky Henderson — Mrs Patricia Pugh

PLACINGS: 13/611111-   RPR **163+h**

Starts	1st	2nd	3rd	4th	Win & Pl
8	6	-	1	-	£113,454

3/16	Chel	2m1½f Cls1 Nov Gd1 Hdl gd-sft	£68,340
12/15	Kemp	2m Cls2 Nov Hdl gd-sft	£11,696
11/15	Chel	2m1½f Cls1 Nov Gd2 Hdl gd-sft	£17,286
10/15	Asct	1m7½f Cls3 Nov Hdl good	£7,798
10/15	Chep	2m Cls4 Nov Hdl good	£3,899
5/14	MRas	2m1½f Cls6 NHF 4-6yo good	£1,560

Hugely impressive winner of the Supreme Novices' Hurdle last season, stretching unbeaten run over hurdles to five; had looked a Champion Hurdle contender but set to head over fences and should prove a force in the 2m novice division.

Always On The Run (Ire)
6 br g Robin Des Pres - Kerrys Cottage (Leading Counsel)

Tom George — Paul & Clare Rooney

PLACINGS: P/1d5/4122411U-1   RPR **142+c**

Starts	1st	2nd	3rd	4th	Win & Pl
10	4	2		2	£26,746

133	5/16	Kels	2m1f Cls3 115-133 Ch Hcap good	£8,123
129	3/16	Kemp	2m Cls3 Nov 116-135 Ch Hcap good	£8,133
120	2/16	Kemp	2m Cls4 Nov 101-120 Ch Hcap soft	£3,899
	6/15	Worc	2m4f Cls4 Mdn Hdl gd-fm	£3,899

Sharply progressive novice chaser last season and made it three wins out of four (unseated his rider at the first in other race) at Kelso in May; jumped right that day and may do even better back on a right-handed track (two previous wins at Kempton).

Amore Alato
7 b g Winged Love - Sardegna (Medaaly)

Johnny Farrelly — Mrs Sarah Faulks

PLACINGS: 1/411320/250/42U249-   RPR **150c**

Starts	1st	2nd	3rd	4th	Win & Pl
17	3	4	1	3	£56,249

12/13	Kemp	2m Cls2 Nov Hdl soft	£9,384
11/13	Winc	1m7½f Cls3 Nov Hdl 4-6yo gd sft	£6,498
4/13	Chep	2m Cls6 NHF 4-6yo gd-fm	£1,560

Failed to win last season but looked likely to land a Grade 2 novice chase at Ascot in December when unseating his rider at the last; fair fourth back there in the Ascot Chase but well beaten at Cheltenham; should win decent novice chases.

ON THE FIGURES

Alpha Des Obeaux Finished over 20 lengths clear of the rest when chasing home Thistlecrack in the World Hurdle. Heads over fences and should develop into a top staying novice. *[Steve Mason, Racing Post Ratings]*

Anibale Fly (Fr)
6 b g Assessor - Nouba Fly (Chamberlin)

Tony Martin (Ir) — John P McManus

PLACINGS: 211/1346-1   RPR **149+h**

Starts	1st	2nd	3rd	4th	Win & Pl
8	4	1	1	1	£70,956

135	4/16	Punc	2m4f 125-149 Hdl Hcap yield	£43,382
	12/15	Navn	2m Mdn Hdl heavy	£7,488
	4/15	Fair	2m NHF 4-7yo soft	£7,221
	3/15	Navn	2m NHF 5-7yo heavy	£4,814

Realised early potential when winning a good handicap hurdle at Punchestown in May; had won two bumpers and a maiden hurdle before beaten twice as favourite (big eyecatcher when never-nearer fourth at Leopardstown); should continue to progress.

Annacotty (Ire)
8 b g Beneficial - Mini Moo Min (Ardross)

Alan King — Mrs Peter Prowting

PLACINGS: 55162128/3P10F/1610-   RPR **159c**

Starts	1st	2nd	3rd	4th	Win & Pl
21	7	2	2	1	£219,646

151	1/16	Chel	2m5f Cls3 Gd3 137-154 Ch Hcap heavy	£34,170
147	11/15	Chel	2m4½f Cls1 Gd3 140-159 Ch Hcap gd-sft	£91,120
144	1/15	Chel	2m5f Cls3 Gd3 130-148 Ch Hcap soft	£28,475
	12/13	Kemp	3m Cls1 Nov Gd1 Ch soft	£39,865
123	11/13	Kemp	3m Cls3 Nov 111-134 Ch Hcap gd-sft	£6,657
	3/13	Hayd	2m4f Cls4 Nov Hdl gd-sft	£3,899
	2/13	Chep	2m3½f Cls4 Mdn Hdl gd sft	£3,899

Has gained his last three victories at Cheltenham, most notably in the Paddy Power Gold Cup last season; starts this term 9lb higher after another success there later in the campaign but could find improvement stepped up in trip (has won twice over 3m at Kempton).

Annie Power (Ire)
8 ch m Shirocco - Anno Luce (Old Vic)

Willie Mullins (Ir) — Mrs S Ricci

PLACINGS: 111111/1112/1F/1111-   RPR **170+h**

Starts	1st	2nd	3rd	4th	Win & Pl
17	15	1	-	-	£715,232

4/16	Aint	2m4f Cls1 Gd1 Hdl soft	£113,072
3/16	Chel	2m1½f Cls1 Gd1 Hdl gd-sft	£248,302
2/16	Punc	2m4f Hdl heavy	£9,044
5/15	Punc	2m2f Gd1 Hdl soft	£46,512
5/14	Punc	2m2f Gd1 Hdl gd-yld	£51,667
1/14	Donc	2m1½f Cls1 Gd2 Hdl gd-sft	£21,031
1/14	Asct	2m4½f Cls1 Cls2 Hdl soft	£15,640
11/13	Asct	2m3½f Cls1 Gd2 Hdl gd-sft	£52,233
3/13	Fair	2m4f Nov Gd1 Hdl soft	£47,561
2/13	Naas	2m Nov Gd2 Hdl sft-hvy	£21,931
2/13	Clon	2m1½f Hdl heavy	£5,610
11/12	Thur	2m Mdn Hdl soft	£4,313
9/12	List	2m NHF 4-7yo heavy	£8,050
8/12	WxfR	2m NHF 4-7yo soft	£5,750
8/12	Gway	2m NHF 4-7yo sft-hvy	£5,750

Finally allowed to show her full potential last season when drafted in to replace the same connections' Faugheen in the Champion Hurdle, winning easily and following up in the Aintree Hurdle; a brilliant mare but hard to know how she'll be campaigned.

Another Hero (Ire)

7 b g Kalanisi - Storm Front (Strong Gale)

Jonjo O'Neill   **John P McManus**

PLACINGS: 111122182/11F-   RPR **140+c**

Starts		1st	2nd	3rd	4th	Win & Pl
12		7	3	-	-	£35,341
131	2/16	Ludl	3m Cls3 Nov 116-135 Ch Hcap soft			£6,498
125	11/15	Asct	3m Cls3 Nov 120-130 Ch Hcap gd-sft			£7,148
	11/13	Sedg	2m1f Cls4 Nov Hdl 4-6yo gd-sft			£3,444
	7/13	Worc	2m4f Cls5 Nov Hdl good			£3,249
	7/13	NAbb	2m2¹/₂f Cls5 Mdn Hdl gd-fm			£2,464
	6/13	Strf	2m¹/₂f Cls6 NHF 4-6yo gd-fm			£1,560
	6/13	Worc	2m Cls6 NHF 4-6yo good			£1,560

Made a terrific return from more than 18 months out last season, winning 3m novice handicap chases at Ascot and Ludlow; fell around halfway when well fancied for Irish Grand National; likely contender for similar staying handicaps.

Apache Stronghold (Ire)

8 b g Milan - First Battle (Un Desperado)

Noel Meade (Ir)   **Mrs Patricia Hunt**

PLACINGS: 133/114/212212F/3-   RPR **162c**

Starts		1st	2nd	3rd	4th	Win & Pl
14		5	4	3	1	£157,461
	2/15	Leop	2m5f Nov Gd1 Ch yield			£39,535
	10/14	DRoy	2m4f Ch yield			£7,188
	11/13	Navn	2m4f Nov Gd2 Hdl gd-yld			£19,817
	10/13	Punc	2m4f Mdn Hdl good			£5,610
	11/12	DRoy	2m NHF 4-7yo yld-sft			£7,475

High-class novice chaser two seasons ago, winning a Grade 1 at Leopardstown over 2m5f and finishing second to Vautour in the JLT at Cheltenham; off the track through injury since finishing third to Valseur Lido at Punchestown that April.

Apple's Jade (Fr)

4 b f Saddler Maker - Apple's For Ever (Nikos)

Willie Mullins (Ir)   **Gigginstown House Stud**

PLACINGS: 1121-1   RPR **164+h**

Starts		1st	2nd	3rd	4th	Win & Pl
5		4	1	-	-	£154,691
	4/16	Punc	2m Gd1 Hdl 4yo yield			£43,382
	4/16	Aint	2m1f Cls1 Gd1 Hdl 4yo soft			£56,437
	12/15	Leop	2m Gd2 Hdl 3yo heavy			£21,415
	5/15	Vich	2m¹/₂f Hdl 3yo soft			£7,814

By far last season's leading juvenile hurdler despite narrow defeat in the Triumph Hurdle, comprehensively reversing that form with Ivanovich Gorbatov at Aintree and Punchestown; fascinating Champion Hurdle contender with lots more to come.

Ar Mad (Fr)

6 b g Tiger Groom - Omelia (April Night)

Gary Moore   **Ashley Head**

PLACINGS: 4032541/61111-   RPR **164+c**

Starts		1st	2nd	3rd	4th	Win & Pl
12		5	2	3	2	£68,139
155	2/16	Plum	2m3¹/₂f Cls3 Nov 136-155 Ch Hcap heavy			£6,498
	12/15	Kemp	2m Cls1 Nov Gd2 Ch gd-sft			£19,933
	12/15	Sand	1m7¹/₂f Cls1 Nov Gd1 Ch gd-sft			£25,748
	11/15	Sand	1m7¹/₂f Cls3 Ch gd-sft			£6,975
	4/15	Plum	2m4¹/₂f Cls4 Nov Hdl good			£4,224

Developed into an exciting front-running novice chaser last season, beating Bristol De Mai and Vaniteux in impressive wins at Sandown and Kempton; looked the main Arkle threat to Douvan before ruled out by injury despite doubts over effectiveness racing left-handed.

Arctic Fire (Ger)

7 b g Soldier Hollow - Adelma (Sternkoenig)

Willie Mullins (Ir) **Wicklow Bloodstock (Ireland)**

PLACINGS: 1S342/123322F/21142- RPR **161**h

Starts	1st	2nd	3rd	4th	Win & Pl
17	4	6	3	2	£275,129
	11/15	Fair	2m4f Gd1 Hdl soft		£39,535
	11/15	Navn	2m4f Gd2 Hdl yld-sft		£20,155
	5/14	Punc	2m Nov Hdl gd-yld		£12,188
	10/13	Tipp	2m Mdn Hdl 4-5yo good		£4,207

Top-class hurdler who has been unlucky to bump into stablemate Faugheen on several occasions, though he gained an overdue Grade 1 in last season's Hatton's Grace Hurdle; looked a patent non-stayer when tried over 3m subsequently.

Aristo Du Plessis (Fr)

6 b g Voix Du Nord - J'Aime (Royal Charter)

James Ewart **Mrs J M Dodd**

PLACINGS: 6351/04432111/F1116- RPR **148+**h

Starts	1st	2nd	3rd	4th	Win & Pl
17	7	1	2	2	£70,836
145	1/16	Muss	1m7½f Cls2 119-145 Hdl Hcap gd-sft		£25,992
132	11/15	Muss	1m7½f Cls3 125-132 Hdl Hcap good		£8,447
126	10/15	Ayr	2m Cls2 123-149 Hdl Hcap gd-sft		£12,996
120	4/15	Ayr	2m Cls3 103-129 Hdl Hcap good		£7,798
	3/15	Weth	2m Cls4 Nov Cond Hdl good		£3,249
	2/15	Catt	1m7½f Cls5 Mdn Hdl soft		£2,599
	9/13	Clun	1m4f NHF 3yo soft		£4,878

Has gone from strength to strength since breaking his duck over hurdles in February 2015, winning six out of seven (fell when well clear on only other run) before managing only sixth in the Scottish County Hurdle; may do better back on good ground.

Arpege D'Alene (Fr)

6 gr g Dom Alco - Joliette D'Alene (Garde Royale)

Paul Nicholls

Mr & Mrs P K Barber & Potensis Bloodstock Ltd

PLACINGS: 151/2P129- RPR **151+**h

Starts	1st	2nd	3rd	4th	Win & Pl
8	3	2	-	-	£60,877
140	2/16	Chep	2m7½f Cls2 125-151 Hdl Hcap soft		£12,512
	2/15	Asct	2m3½f Cls2 Nov Hdl soft		£15,640
	11/14	Asct	2m3½f Cls3 Mdn Hdl gd-sft		£5,630

Needed a wind operation after being pulled up on his second run last season, putting his chasing career on hold, but did well back over hurdles and finished second in the Pertemps Final; should do well back over fences.

Art Mauresque (Fr)

6 b g Policy Maker - Modeva (Valanour)

Paul Nicholls **Mrs Johnny De La Hey**

PLACINGS: 1273/P151/131677P2-1 RPR **154+**c

Starts	1st	2nd	3rd	4th	Win & Pl
19	8	2	2	-	£109,130
144	5/16	NAbb	2m5f Cls2 126-144 Ch Hcap good		£15,640
	10/15	Chel	2m4f Cls2 Nov Ch good		£12,628
	5/15	Kemp	2m Cls3 Nov Ch good		£6,498
	4/15	Tntn	2m Cls4 Nov Ch gd-fm		£4,549
135	3/15	Kemp	2m Cls3 Nov 122-135 Ch Hcap good		£9,747
	8/13	Claf	2m1f Hdl 3yo v soft		£13,268
	6/13	Nanc	2m1f Hdl 3yo good		£7,024
	6/13	Stra	2m Hdl 3yo heavy		£7,024

Has gained all five wins over fences on good ground or quicker, with just one defeat in such conditions when pulled up at last season's Cheltenham Festival; not beaten far in the Paddy Power Gold Cup and could win similar races on good ground.

Apache Stronghold (right): set to return from injury this season

Arthur's Oak

8 b g Kayf Tara - Myumi (Charmer)

Venetia Williams   **Mrs J K Burt**

PLACINGS: 32413/4431/12110-   RPR **154**+c

Starts	1st	2nd	3rd	4th	Win & Pl
14	5	2	3	3	£70,424

148	2/16	Chep	2m Cls2 130-153 Ch Hcap soft	£25,554
144	2/16	Sand	1m7½f Cls2 139-144 Ch Hcap gd-sft	£15,640
124	12/15	Hayd	1m7½f Cls3 116-134 Ch Hcap heavy	£9,747
117	4/15	Hntg	2m4f Cls3 99-125 Ch Hcap gd-sft	£6,498
	2/14	Extr	2m2½f Cls4 Nov Hdl heavy	£4,549

Progressive in 2m handicap chases last season, winning three times including off 148 at Chepstow in February; less effective on good ground when below best in Grand Annual; stays further having won over 2m4f as a novice in 2015.

As De Mee (Fr)

6 b/br g Kapgarde - Koeur De Mee (Video Rock)

Paul Nicholls   **The Stewart Family & Judi Dench**

PLACINGS: 12/3217116/223F2579-   RPR **153**c

Starts	1st	2nd	3rd	4th	Win & Pl
18	4	6	2	-	£91,582

130	3/15	Sand	2m4f Cls1 Nov Gd3 117-134 Hdl 4-7yo Hcap gd-sft	£34,170
	1/15	Leic	2m4½f Cls3 Nov Hdl 4-7yo heavy	£6,498
118	12/14	Sand	2m Cls4 Nov 110-119 Hdl Hcap soft	£6,498
	9/13	Agtn	1m4½f NHF 3yo soft	£6,098

Failed to get off the mark in eight attempts over fences last season but was very highly tried and ran several fine races in defeat (twice placed at Grade 1 level); retains novice status and could do better in that sphere as well as being interesting in handicaps.

Aso (Fr)

6 b/br g Goldneyev - Odyssee Du Cellier (Dear Doctor)

Venetia Williams   **The Bellamy Partnership**

PLACINGS: 12/3131100/22213561-   RPR **154**+c

Starts	1st	2nd	3rd	4th	Win & Pl
17	6	4	3	-	£72,733

4/16	NAbb	2m5f Cls3 Nov Ch soft	£7,280
1/16	MRas	2m5½f Cls2 Ch soft	£12,777
1/15	Hayd	2m Cls1 Nov Gd2 Hdl heavy	£15,661
12/14	Tntn	2m3f Cls4 Nov Hdl soft	£3,574
11/14	Wwck	2m Cls4 Nov Hdl soft	£3,899
7/13	Gran	1m4f NHF 3yo gd-fm	£4,065

Has won five times in novice company (hurdles and fences) over the last two seasons, all on soft or heavy ground; twice came up short in top company, although both times on ground quicker than ideal; could be interesting back on soft ground.

Aubusson (Fr)

7 b/br g Ballingarry - Katioucha (Mansonnien)

Nick Williams   **Mrs Jane Williams**

PLACINGS: 7113/21390/721P-54   RPR **150**h

Starts	1st	2nd	3rd	4th	Win & Pl
15	4	2	2	1	£178,108

141	12/15	Uttx	3m Cls4 Nov Ch heavy	£4,089
	11/14	Hayd	2m7f Cls1 Gd3 129-149 Hdl Hcap soft	£45,560
	1/14	Chel	2m4½f Cls3 Nov Hdl soft	£6,256
	12/13	Chep	2m3½f Cls4 Nov Hdl gd-sft	£3,119

Impressed on his chasing debut at Uttoxeter last season but ran only once more in that sphere when pulled up at Cheltenham; smart hurdler (won the Fixed Brush Hurdle in 2014 and beaten a nose in a French Grade 1 last season) and could yet be even better over fences.

Arthur's Oak (right): should do well in handicap chases this season

Augusta Kate

5 b m Yeats - Feathard Lady (Accordion)

Willie Mullins (Ir)   **The Masters Syndicate**

PLACINGS: 1172-1   RPR **130+b**

Starts	1st	2nd	3rd	4th	Win & Pl
5	3	1	-	-	£52,406
	4/16	Punc	2m List NHF 4-7yo gd-yld		£17,353
	11/15	Navn	2m List NHF 4-7yo soft		£20,155
	9/15	List	2m NHF 4-7yo yld-sft		£6,419

Favourite for last season's Champion Bumper at Cheltenham after two impressive wins but could manage only seventh; did better back in mares' company when second to Kayf Grace at Aintree before landing second Listed success at Punchestown; should do well over hurdles.

Aux Ptits Soins (Fr)

6 gr g Saint Des Saints - Reflexion Faite (Turgeon)

Paul Nicholls   **J Hales**

PLACINGS: 1/311/5-   RPR **141h**

Starts	1st	2nd	3rd	4th	Win & Pl
5	3		1	-	£94,250
139	3/15	Chel	2m5f Cls1 Gd3 138-158 Hdl Hcap good		£45,560
	9/14	Autl	2m1½f Hdl 4yo v soft		£19,200
	3/14	Autl	2m1½f Hdl 4yo heavy		£19,200

Famously won the Coral Cup in 2015 on his British debut but has run only once since then having been held up by injury, running well for a long way before fading into fifth in last season's World Hurdle; looks a top chasing prospect.

Avant Tout (Fr)

6 ch g Agent Bleu - Quiwfty (Dark Moondancer)

Willie Mullins (Ir)
     Supreme Horse Racing Club & Brett T Graham

PLACINGS: 114P/112F91-1   RPR **156 l c**

Starts	1st	2nd	3rd	4th	Win & Pl
11	6	1	-	1	£94,905
145	4/16	Punc	2m5f Nov 126-145 Ch Hcap yield		£43,382
	4/16	Limk	3m Nov Gd2 Ch heavy		£18,438
	5/15	Tram	2m Ch yield		£5,884
129	4/15	Punc	3m 111 130 Hdl Hcap yield		£11,337
	1/15	Tram	2m Mdn Hdl heavy		£4,814
	5/14	Vire	1m5f NHF 4yo		£4,167

Had his progress over fences held up by a fall at Thurles in January but enjoyed a successful spring, notably when winning a novice handicap at Punchestown at the end of April; lightly raced and seen as a Hennessy type by his trainer.

Azzuri

4 b g Azamour - Folly Lodge (Grand Lodge)

Dan Skelton   **The Blind Squirrels**

PLACINGS: 523-   RPR **134h**

Starts	1st	2nd	3rd	4th	Win & Pl
3	-	1	1	-	£17,718

Highly tried in just three runs over hurdles

last season, finishing second to Zubayr in the Adonis Hurdle at Kempton before a distant but creditable third to Apple's Jade in a Grade 1 at Aintree; still a novice and could win good races.

Bacardys (Fr)

5 b g Coastal Path - Oasice (Robin Des Champs)

Willie Mullins (Ir)   **Shanakiel Racing Syndicate**

PLACINGS: F1/131-3   RPR **136b**

Starts	1st	2nd	3rd	4th	Win & Pl
4	2		2	-	£41,964
	4/16	Aint	2m1f Cls1 Gd2 NHF 4-6yo soft		£22,508
	12/15	Leop	2m NHF 4yo heavy		£5,349

Third in last season's Champion Bumper at Cheltenham before improving on a softer surface at Aintree, reversing form with Ballyandy and Battleford; finished strongly both times and looks a top prospect for novice hurdles on soft ground.

Bachasson (Fr)

5 gr g Voix Du Nord - Belledonne (Shafoun)

Willie Mullins (Ir)   **Edward O'Connell**

PLACINGS: 611/111128U-   RPR **148+h**

Starts	1st	2nd	3rd	4th	Win & Pl
10	6	1	-	-	£62,005
	10/15	Tipp	2m Nov Gd3 Hdl good		£15,116
	9/15	Gway	2m2f Nov Hdl good		£9,093
	7/15	Gway	2m Nov Hdl 4yo good		£10,078
	7/15	Slig	2m Mdn Hdl 4yo good		£5,616
	9/14	Stra	1m4f NHF 3yo v good		£5,000
	7/14	Vitt	1m4f NHF 3yo gd-sft		£4,583

Won his first four races over hurdles last year before a narrow defeat in the Grade 1 Royal Bond; didn't cope with heavy ground next time but was running a big race when departing at the last when stepped up to 3m in the Albert Bartlett.

Ball D'Arc (Fr)

5 b g Network - Pretty Moon (Moon Madness)

Gordon Elliott (Ir)   **Gigginstown House Stud**

PLACINGS: 15/012U13117-6   RPR **144h**

Starts	1st	2nd	3rd	4th	Win & Pl
11	4	1	2	-	£51,509
	2/16	Naas	2m Nov Gd2 Hdl sft-hvy		£20,173
	1/16	Punc	2m Nov List Hdl sft-hvy		£14,338
	12/15	Limk	2m Mdn Hdl 4yo heavy		£6,686
	11/15	Thur	2m NHF 4-7yo yield		£4,814

Won three novice hurdles last season, all on soft or heavy ground, though connections felt he would improve on a better surface; failed to prove the point at Aintree and Punchestown but remains a ueful chasing prospect.

'Winner of the 2015 Coral Cup looks a top chasing prospect this season'

Ballyalton (Ire)
9 b g Pierre - Almilto (Mandalus)

Ian Williams John Westwood

PLACINGS: **111/2/11142/U62F15-** RPR **153+c**

Starts	1st	2nd	3rd	4th	Win & Pl
14	6	3		1	£92,881

140	3/16	Chel	2m4¹/₂f Cls1 Nov List 136-140 Ch Hcap gd-sft..... £37,018
	12/13	Chel	2m1f Cls3 Nov Hdl 4-6yo good........................... £7,507
	11/13	Newc	2m6f Cls2 Nov Hdl good £9,384
	10/13	Uttx	2m Cls5 Mdn Hdl good...................................... £2,209
	2/12	Donc	2m1¹/₂f Cls6 NHF 4-6yo good £1,625
	1/12	Wwck	2m Cls6 NHF 5-6yo gd-sft.................................. £1,437

Off the mark over fences in the novice handicap chase at last season's Cheltenham Festival; suspicion that race wasn't up to its usual standard (very condensed handicap with several top candidates balloted out) and something to prove after being well beaten at Aintree.

Ballyandy
5 b g Kayf Tara - Megalex (Karinga Bay)

Nigel Twiston-Davies Options O Syndicate

PLACINGS: **112114-** RPR **137+b**

Starts	1st	2nd	3rd	4th	Win & Pl
6	4	1		1	£72,735

	3/16	Chel	2m¹/₂f Cls1 Gd1 NHF 4-6yo good......................... £39,865
	2/16	Newb	2m4¹/₂f Cls1 List NHF 4-6yo heavy £11,390
	11/15	Chel	2m¹/₂f Cls1 List NHF 4-6yo gd-sft £11,390
	10/15	Worc	2m Cls6 NHF 3-5yo gd-sft................................. £1,560

Classy and consistent in top bumpers last season and did remarkably well to win the Champion Bumper at Cheltenham having badly lost his place (stuck behind a weakening rival) down the hill; should make a fine novice hurdler.

Ballybolley (Ire)
7 b g Kayf Tara - Gales Hill (Beau Sher)

Nigel Twiston-Davies Simon Munir & Isaac Souede

PLACINGS: **11/2213015/37433314-** RPR **148+c**

Starts	1st	2nd	3rd	4th	Win & Pl
18	6	2	5	2	£80,358

129	3/16	Hayd	2m4f Cls2 110-136 Ch Hcap good..................... £30,970
	2/15	Kels	2m Cls4 Nov Hdl gd-sft.................................. £3,249
	12/14	Aint	2m1f Cls3 Nov Hdl gd-sft £7,507
	4/14	Aint	2m1f Cls1 Gd2 NHF 4-6yo gd-sft...................... £17,085
	3/14	Towc	2m Cls6 NHF 4-6yo gd-sft............................... £1,560
	12/13	Sthl	1m7¹/₂f Cls6 NHF 4-6yo good £1,643

Struggled on soft ground for much of last season but came good on better ground in the spring, winning well at Haydock; no match for Douvan next time but could do well back in handicaps.

Ballycasey (Ire)
9 gr g Presenting - Pink Mist (Montelimar)

Willie Mullins (Ir) Mrs S Ricci

PLACINGS: **4F/2173PB/4935U6-F31** RPR **159+c**

Starts	1st	2nd	3rd	4th	Win & Pl
23	7	1	4	2	£169,694

150	8/16	Klny	2m4¹/₂f 122-150 Ch Hcap soft........................... £21,691
	11/14	Gowr	2m4f Ch heavy £10,833
	2/14	Leop	2m5f Nov Gd1 Ch sft-hvy £43,438
	11/13	Navn	2m1f Ch gd-yld.. £8,415
	1/13	Thur	2m6f Nov Hdl heavy £7,854
	12/12	Clon	2m4f Mdn Hdl heavy..................................... £4,313
	12/11	Leop	2m4f Nov 4-7yo gd-yld £5,948

Hasn't hit the heights expected when beating Don Cossack in a Grade 1 novice chase at Leopardstown in 2014; dropped to a good mark last season, though, and looked much better when third in the Galway Plate in July.

Ballynagour (Ire)

10 b g Shantou - Simply Deep (Simply Great)

David Pipe   Allan Stennett

PLACINGS: 13/2P2/F1535PP7U-722   RPR **162**c

Starts		1st	2nd	3rd	4th	Win & Pl
30		5	6	2	1	£347,594
	5/15	Autl	2m5½f Gd2 Hdl v soft			£61,047
140	3/14	Chel	2m4f Cls1 Gd3 131-157 Ch Hcap good			£51,255
123	2/13	Wwck	2m4½f Cls2 123-149 Ch Hcap soft			£18,768
	4/12	Engh	2m1½f Hdl v soft			£19,200
	6/11	Autl	2m5½f Ch 5yo v soft			£22,345

Placed three times at Grade 1 level from 2m to 3m, including when beaten a head in the 2015 Betfred Bowl; well below that form last season but much better during the summer when second in Summer Cup at Uttoxeter and Summer Plate at Market Rasen.

Ballyoptic (Ire)

6 b g Old Vic - Lambourne Lace (Un Desperado)

Nigel Twiston-Davles   Mills & Mason Partnership

PLACINGS: 31F/225111-   RPR **154**+h

Starts		1st	2nd	3rd	4th	Win & Pl
4		3	-	-	-	£65,882
	4/16	Aint	3m1½f Cls1 Nov Gd1 Hdl soft			£56,270
	3/16	Uttx	2m4f Cls4 Nov Hdl soft			£5,064
	2/16	Ffos	2m4f Cls4 Nov Hdl 4-7yo heavy			£4,549

Beaten in point-to-points and a bumper last autumn but proved a revelation when sent over hurdles during the spring, completing a quickfire hat-trick in the Grade 1 Sefton at Aintree; will be given a chance in top staying hurdles, although long-term future lies over fences.

Baltimore Rock (Ire)

7 b g Tiger Hill - La Vita E Bella (Definite Article)

Neil Mulholland   R S Brookhouse

PLACINGS: 124/312114/073/12F-4   RPR **149**c

Starts		1st	2nd	3rd	4th	Win & Pl
16		5	3	2	3	£74,629
139	12/15	Donc	2m1½f Cls3 Nov 122-139 Ch Hcap gd-sft			£6,279
125	3/14	Sand	2m Cls3 Gd3 118-139 Hdl Hcap soft			£39,865
116	2/14	Ludl	2m Cls3 104-125 Hdl Hcap heavy			£9,495
	1/14	Winc	1m7½f Cls4 Nov Hdl heavy			£3,899
	11/12	Bang	2m1½f Cls6 NHF 3-5yo gd-sft			£1,437

Won the Imperial Cup for David Pipe in 2014 and lightly raced since then; won well on his chasing debut last season and highly tried subsequently, twice taking on Douvan and running well until falling two out in the Arkle.

Bamako Moriviere (Fr)

5 b g Califet - Halladine (Passing Sale)

Willie Mullins (Ir)   Mrs S Ricci

PLACINGS: 131/3P0-461101   RPR **156**+h

Starts		1st	2nd	3rd	4th	Win & Pl
12		5	-	2	1	£45,902
	8/16	Cork	2m Hdl 4-5yo good			£6,783
	7/16	Bell	2m4f Hdl yield			£5,879
133	6/16	Punc	2m 110-135 Hdl Hcap good			£10,853
	1/15	Pau	2m1½f Hdl 4yo heavy			£11,907
	10/14	Pmnl	1m4f NHF 3yo gd-sft			£4,167

Became slightly disappointing last season but did much better on quicker ground this summer, winning twice before finding the Galway Hurdle too much under a big weight; big chasing type who should do well over fences, especially when allowed to dominate.

Ballycasey (left): could yet reach heights over fences his early performances promised

Barney Dwan (Ire)

6 b g Vinnie Roe - Kapricia Speed (Vertical Speed)

Fergal O'Brien   **Paul & Clare Rooney**

PLACINGS: 52/5311413-   RPR **142+h**

Starts	1st	2nd	3rd	4th	Win & Pl
7	3	-	2	1	£44,645
129	3/16	Sand	2m4f Cls1 Nov Gd3 120-135 Hdl 4-7yo Hcap soft	£34,170
	12/15	Sedg	2m1f Cls4 Nov Hdl heavy	£3,769
	11/15	MRas	2m2½f Cls4 Nov Hdl gd-sft	£3,899

Three-time winner in novice hurdles last season, most notably the EBF Final at Sandown when relishing a stiff test of stamina; expected by connections to improve on better ground but well beaten by Up For Review on good at Perth next time.

Barters Hill (Ire)

6 b g Kalanisi - Circle The Wagons (Commanche Run)

Ben Pauling   **Circle Of Friends**

PLACINGS: 1111/1114-   RPR **153+h**

Starts	1st	2nd	3rd	4th	Win & Pl
8	7	-	-	1	£81,630
	1/16	Donc	3m1½f Cls1 Nov Gd2 Hdl good	£17,165
	12/15	Newb	2m4½f Cls1 Nov Gd1 Hdl soft	£22,780
	11/15	Hntg	2m3½f Cls4 Nov Hdl gd-sft	£3,899
	4/15	Aint	2m1f Cls1 Gd2 NHF 4-6yo gd-sft	£16,881
	2/15	Newb	2m1½f Cls1 List NHF 4-6yo soft	£11,390
	12/14	Wwck	2m Cls6 NHF 4-6yo soft	£1,560
	11/14	Hntg	2m Cls6 NHF 4-6yo gd-sft	£1,560

Hugely exciting stayer who won first seven races under rules, most notably the Challow Hurdle,

before a creditable fourth in the Albert Bartlett at Cheltenham (paid price for going too hard up front); has the scope to make a top chaser.

Battleford

5 b g Midnight Legend - Well Maid (Saddlers' Hall)

Willie Mullins (Ir)   **Andrea & Graham Wylie**

PLACINGS: F/122-   RPR **136b**

Starts	1st	2nd	3rd	4th	Win & Pl
3	1	2	-	-	£28,005
	1/16	Punc	2m NHF 5-7yo sft-hvy	£4,566

High-class bumper performer last season when just touched off in top races at Cheltenham and Aintree, probably doing best on quicker ground at the festival but proving his versatility regarding conditions; should make a good novice hurdler.

Baywing (Ire)

7 br g Winged Love - Cerise De Totes (Champ Libre)

Nicky Richards   **David & Nicky Robinson**

PLACINGS: 5065/1111P-   RPR **135+h**

Starts	1st	2nd	3rd	4th	Win & Pl
9	4	-	-	-	£16,764
125	1/16	Hayd	2m7f Cls3 124-137 Hdl Hcap heavy	£6,498
112	12/15	Uttx	2m7½f Cls4 105-112 Hdl Hcap heavy	£3,509
104	12/15	Uttx	2m4f Cls4 104-119 Hdl Hcap heavy	£3,509
89	11/15	Carl	2m4f Cls4 Nov 89-110 Hdl Hcap heavy	£3,249

Improved out of all recognition last season, easily winning four handicaps off marks from 89 to 125

Barters Hill: exciting chase prospect

(all on heavy ground); thoroughly merited step up to Grade 2 level at Haydock but ran too badly to be true when pulled up.

Beat That (Ire)

8 b g Milan - Knotted Midge (Presenting)

Nicky Henderson   Michael Buckley

PLACINGS: 26/121/16/   RPR **159**h

Starts		1st	2nd	3rd	4th	Win & Pl
7		3	2	-	-	£115,246
	4/14	Punc	3m Nov Gd1 Hdl gd-yld			£46,500
	4/14	Aint	3m¹/₂f Cls1 Nov Gd1 Hdl gd-sft			£56,270
	11/13	Asct	2m3¹/₂f Cls3 Mdn Hdl gd-sft			£5,630

Form of Grade 1 double at Aintree (over Cole Harden) and Punchestown (over Don Poli) in novice hurdles in 2014 repeatedly franked since but has been seen only once subsequently; still hugely exciting if top trainer can work his magic.

Beg To Differ (Ire)

6 ch g Flemensfirth - Blossom Trix (Saddlers' Hall)

Jonjo O'Neill   Mrs John Magnier, D Smith & M Tabor

PLACINGS: 783111/3321U-   RPR **147**+c

Starts		1st	2nd	3rd	4th	Win & Pl
11		4	1	3		£31,242
133	2/16	Sand	3m Cls3 113-134 Ch Hcap soft			£7,798
128	3/15	Uttx	2m4f Cls3 114-135 Hdl Hcap soft			£10,260
119	2/15	Carl	2m1f Cls4 97-120 Hdl Hcap soft			£3,899
	1/15	Weth	2m Cls4 Nov Hdl soft			£3,736

Finished two seasons ago with three successive wins over hurdles and got better with practice over fences last term, winning a good handicap chase at Sandown on his fourth run; unlucky to stumble and unseat his rider at Cheltenham last time.

Bello Conti (Fr)

5 b g Coastal Path - Posterite (Video Rock)

Willie Mullins (Ir)   Gigginstown House Stud

PLACINGS: 3/144-2   RPR **141**h

Starts		1st	2nd	3rd	4th	Win & Pl
5		1	1	1	2	£21,691
	12/15	Clon	2m1/₂f Mdn Hdl heavy			£5,349

Terrific fourth in last season's Neptune Hurdle and probably not at that level despite finishing closer to Yorkhill at Aintree (raced too keenly);

Bellshill (Ire)

6 b g King's Theatre - Fairy Native (Be My Native)

Willie Mullins (Ir)   Andrea & Graham Wylie

PLACINGS: 2/1202/1111302-1   RPR **155**+h

Starts		1st	2nd	3rd	4th	Win & Pl
12		6	3	1	-	£194,212
	4/16	Punc	3m Nov Gd1 Hdl gd-yld			£43,382
	1/16	Naas	2m4f Nov Gd1 Hdl heavy			£39,706
	12/15	Navn	2m4f Nov Gd2 Hdl heavy			£20,155
	11/15	Cork	2m Mdn Hdl heavy			£7,488
	4/15	Punc	2m Gd1 NHF 4-7yo gd-yld			£44,186
	11/14	Thur	2m NHF 4-7yo soft			£4,313

Often let down by his jumping last season but still proved prolific and was unlucky not to win three times at Grade 1 level (just pipped after a dreadful late blunder at Aintree); could go for the World Hurdle or go novice chasing; clearly has a huge engine.

Bigmartre (Fr)

5 b g Montmartre - Oh La Miss (Le Balafre)

Harry Whittington   P J Dixon

PLACINGS: F8PO2/121433-   RPR **134**+h

Starts		1st	2nd	3rd	4th	Win & Pl
11		2	2	2	1	£20,529
	12/15	Hayd	1m7¹/₂f Cls4 Nov Hdl 4-6yo heavy			£3,899
	10/15	Font	2m1¹/₂f Cls4 Nov Hdl good			£5,198

Won at 20-1 on his British debut in a novice hurdle at Fontwell last season and proved that was no fluke, winning on very different ground at Haydock and running well in good handicaps; has already finished second over fences in France.

Bishops Road (Ire)

8 b g Heron Island - Nice Resemblance (Shernazar)

Kerry Lee   Alan Halsall

PLACINGS: 11/62153/86F30311UF-   RPR **157**c

Starts		1st	2nd	3rd	4th	Win & Pl
17		5	1	3	-	£77,968
144	2/16	Hayd	3m4¹/₂f Cls1 Gd3 125-149 Ch Hcap heavy			£45,050
130	1/16	Sand	2m4f Cls3 116-130 Ch Hcap heavy			£9,384
123	1/15	Leop	2m5f 100-123 Ch Hcap yld-sft			£8,023
	10/13	Gowr	2m Mdn Hdl soft			£5,610
	5/13	Klny	2m1f NHF 5-7yo soft			£3,927

Improved massively for a change in yard last

IT'S YOUR PAPER WITHOUT THE PAPER

IF YOU'RE ON HOLIDAY OR JUST TOO BUSY TO GET TO YOUR NEWSAGENT, THE RACING POST DIGITAL NEWSPAPER IS AT HAND

View every page on your computer, tablet or smartphone, with rather clever features including language translation, downloadable editions and bookmarking. It'll even read articles OUT LOUD.

Buy single editions (from £2.10/€2.60) or save with a discounted subscription.

RACINGPOST.com/digitalnewspaper

winter, immediately scoring at Sandown and Haydock (in the Grand National Trial); out of luck during the spring (missed the cut in the Grand National and departed at the first in the Topham and bet365 Gold Cup).

Blaklion: Cheltenham ace won the RSA Chase last season and can continue to progress

Black Hercules (Ire)

7 b g Heron Island - Annalecky (Bob's Return)

Willie Mullins (Ir)　　　　　**Andrea & Graham Wylie**

PLACINGS: 1/114/0117/11F1-　　　RPR **164**+c

Starts	1st	2nd	3rd	4th	Win & Pl
11	7	-	-	1	£134,186

3/16	Chel	2m4f Cls1 Nov Gd1 Ch good	£74,035
1/16	Wwck	3m Cls1 Nov List Ch heavy	£13,253
12/15	Navn	2m4f Ch heavy	£6,953
12/14	Cork	3m Nov Gd3 Hdl heavy	£17,604
11/14	Cork	2m Mdn Hdl heavy	£6,900
1/14	Gowr	2m NHF 5-7yo soft	£7,475
12/13	Punc	2m NHF 4yo gd-yld	£4,768

Good winner of last season's JLT Novices' Chase at Cheltenham; had been seen as more of a stayer until failing to settle well enough at Navan on his previous start (would still have won but for falling at the last) and should have plenty of options from 2m4f to 3m+.

Blaklion

7 b g Kayf Tara - Franciscaine (Legend Of France)

Nigel Twiston-Davies — S Such & Cg Paletta

PLACINGS: **11/112132P4/4F12113-** — RPR **162 + c**

Starts	1st	2nd	3rd	4th	Win & Pl
17	8	3	2	2	£199,901

3/16	Chel	3m1½f Cls1 Gd1 Ch good		£85,425
2/16	Weth	3m Cls1 Nov Gd2 Ch heavy		£19,221
12/15	Chel	3m1½f Cls2 Nov Ch soft		£14,442
12/14	Chel	3m Cls1 Nov Gd2 Hdl gd-sft		£17,085
10/14	Chep	2m3½f Cls1 Nov Gd2 Hdl soft		£17,085
9/14	Prth	2m4f Cls4 Nov Hdl good		£3,119
4/14	Hayd	1m7½f Cls5 NHF 4-6yo good		£1,949
3/14	Ffos	2m Cls6 NHF 4-5yo soft		£1,625

Game winner of last season's RSA Chase; form is questionable with main rivals not performing but hasn't been hit hard by the handicapper; loves Cheltenham (three-time winner there in all) so shouldn't be underestimated in March.

Blazer (Fr)

5 ch g Network - Juppelongue (Trebrook)

Willie Mullins (Ir) — John P McManus

PLACINGS: **F1/391947-** — RPR **144h**

Starts	1st	2nd	3rd	4th	Win & Pl
126	2		1	1	£28,483

2/16	Leop	2m 109-133 Hdl Hcap heavy		£10,853
2/15	Bord	2m2½f Hdl 4yo soft		£11,907

Beaten over fences on first two runs following move from France last season but flourished back over hurdles, winning at Leopardstown and finishing fourth in the Coral Cup, albeit twice disappointing as well; probably best at 2m4f.

Bleu Et Rouge (Fr)

5 gr g Charming Groom - Lady Du Renom (Art Francais)

Willie Mullins (Ir) — John P McManus

PLACINGS: **22/141F5-** — RPR **151 + h**

Starts	1st	2nd	3rd	4th	Win & Pl
7	2	2		1	£54,267

2/16	Leop	2m2f Nov Gd1 Hdl sft-hvy		£39,044
11/15	Cork	2m Mdn Hdl 4yo heavy		£6,419

Looked all about stamina when winning the Grade 1 Deloitte at Leopardstown last season and still in touch when falling five out in the Albert Bartlett at Cheltenham; surprisingly dropped to 2m for his final run at Aintree when outpaced in fifth behind Buveur D'Air.

Bloody Mary (Fr)

5 gr m Fragrant Mix - Sacade (Robin Des Champs)

Nicky Henderson — **John P McManus**

PLACINGS: **01/1111113-** RPR **139+h**

Starts	1st	2nd	3rd	4th	Win & Pl
9	7	-	1	-	£49,939
	2/16 Tntn	2m1/2f Cls4 Nov Hdl heavy			£3,899
	9/15 Autl	2m2f Hdl 4-5yo v soft			£17,860
	8/15 Le L	1m3/2f NHF 4yo good			£4,651
	6/15 Morl	1m5f NHF 4-5yo gd-sft			£3,876
	5/15 Seno	1m3/2f NHF 4yo gd-sft			£3,876
	5/15 Morl	1m5f NHF 4yo			£3,876
	4/15 Vire	1m5f NHF 4yo soft			£3,876

Six-time winner in France (five bumpers) who won again on debut for new connections at Taunton in February; no match for Limini in mares' novice hurdle at Cheltenham but still ran well to finish third under a penalty; seems sure to improve.

Blow By Blow (Ire)

5 ch g Robin Des Champs - Shean Rose (Roselier)

Willie Mullins (Ir) — **Gigginstown House Stud**

PLACINGS: **211-1** RPR **136+b**

Starts	1st	2nd	3rd	4th	Win & Pl
4	3	1	-	-	£54,509
	4/16 Punc	2m Gd1 NHF 4-7yo gd-yld			£43,382
	3/16 Fair	2m NHF 4-7yo yld-sft			£5,879
	2/16 Navn	2m NHF 5-7yo heavy			£4,070

Top-class bumper performer last season and completed a quickfire hat-trick when winning the Grade 1 bumper at Punchestown in April, claiming a notable scalp in Moon Racer; versatile regarding ground conditions and should be a smart novice hurdler.

Blue Hell (Fr)

6 b g Russian Blue - Art Fair (Fairy King)

Alan Fleming (Ir) — **Barry Connell**

PLACINGS: **11243/359/10-** RPR **140+h**

Starts	1st	2nd	3rd	4th	Win & Pl
10	3	2	1	1	£44,457
124	11/15 Fair	2m 115-133 Hdl Hcap sft-hvy			£23,256
	9/13 Nant	2m1/2f Hdl 3yo soft			£7,024
	9/13 Agtn	2m1f Hdl 3yo good			£5,073

Took time to find his feet after move from France but looked much improved first time out last season when beating subsequent Coral Cup

winner Diamond King; laid out for the County Hurdle but reported to have bled from the nose.

Blue Heron (Ire)

8 b g Heron Island - American Chick (Lord Americo)

Dan Skelton — **Horwood Harriers Partnership**

PLACINGS: **21315/14314/** RPR **155h**

Starts	1st	2nd	3rd	4th	Win & Pl
10	4	1	2	2	£79,751
	2/15 Winc	1m71/2f Cls1 Gd2 Hdl soft			£34,170
	10/14 Kemp	2m Cls1 Nov List Hdl gd-sft			£11,591
	3/14 Chep	2m Cls5 Mdn Hdl soft			£1,949
	12/13 Ludl	1m6f Cls4 NHF 4-5yo gd-sft			£3,249

Developed into a smart hurdler two seasons ago when winning the Kingwell Hurdle in between finishing third and fourth at Grade 1 level; missed last season through injury but remains a good prospect for novice chases.

Boondooma (Ire)

9 b g Westerner - Kissantell (Broken Hearted)

Dr Richard Newland — **P Jenkins & C E Stedman**

PLACINGS: **4/51346115/15421/1P-** RPR **156+c**

Starts	1st	2nd	3rd	4th	Win & Pl
20	6	2	2	4	£71,063
147	10/15 Chel	2m Cls2 125-151 Ch Hcap good			£31,280
	12/14 Hayd	1m7 1/2f Cls2 Nov Ch heavy			£12,001
123	10/14 Chep	2m3 1/2f Cls3 110-134 Hdl Hcap gd-sft			£9,747
	3/14 Newc	2m4 1/2f Cls4 Nov Hdl soft			£3,119
	3/14 Fknm	2m Cls4 Cond Mdn Hdl good			£3,119
	12/13 Limk	2m NHF 4-7yo heavy			£4,488

Restricted to just five runs over fences due to injuries last season but won well on return at Cheltenham last season before suffering a pelvis fracture when pulled up in Paddy Power Gold Cup; being aimed at same race for return.

Born Survivor (Ire)

5 b g King's Theatre - Bob's Flame (Bob Back)

Dan Skelton — **Mrs G Widdowson & Mrs R Kelvin-Hughes**

PLACINGS: **1/141-** RPR **140+h**

Starts	1st	2nd	3rd	4th	Win & Pl
3	2	-	-	1	£8,177
	2/16 Weth	2m3 1/2f Cls4 Nov Hdl soft			£3,249
	12/15 Wwck	2m5f Cls4 Mdn Hdl soft			£3,249

Looked a terrific prospect when winning novice hurdles at Warwick and Wetherby last season, though he fluffed his lines when stepped up in

Racing Post iPad app
30-day free trial. On the App Store now.
MIND-BLOWING
Available on the App Store

grade in between; should still make an exciting novice chaser, though he may need soft ground.

Bouvreuil (Fr)

5 b g Saddler Maker - Madame Lys (Sheyrann)

Paul Nicholls   **Chris Giles & Potensis Bloodstock Ltd**

PLACINGS: 73/339213427/051524-   RPR **151**c

Starts	1st	2nd	3rd	4th	Win & Pl
17	2	3	4	2	£75,910
	1/16	Donc	2m3f Cls4 Nov Ch soft		£3,899
	11/14	Engh	2m1½f Hdl 3yo heavy		£19,200

Has finished second at the last two Cheltenham Festivals in the Fred Winter Hurdle and novice handicap chase; 8lb rise for latest near miss looks harsh, though, and was well beaten for the fourth time at Grade 1 or 2 level next time at Aintree.

Brain Power (Ire)

5 b g Kalanisi - Blonde Ambition (Old Vic)

Nicky Henderson   **Michael Buckley**

PLACINGS: 10/121-3   RPR **144**h

Starts	1st	2nd	3rd	4th	Win & Pl
6	3	1	1	-	£19,575
	3/16	Kemp	2m Cls4 Nov Hdl good		£3,249
	11/15	Kemp	2m Cls4 Nov Hdl 4-6yo gd-sft		£3,899
	2/15	Newc	2m1½f Cls6 NHF 4-6yo gd-sft		£1,560

Won two novice hurdles at Kempton last season and acquitted himself well at a higher level (second to Charbel at Musselburgh and third in a Grade 1 at Punchestown) despite still being very

---

green; grand chasing type who should do much better this season.

Briar Hill (Ire)

8 b g Shantou - Backaway (Bob Back)

Willie Mullins (Ir)   **Andrea & Graham Wylie**

PLACINGS: P111/111F/84F/4-21   RPR **134+**c

Starts	1st	2nd	3rd	4th	Win & Pl
12	6	1	-	2	£108,772
	8/16	Klny	2m4½f Ch soft		£5,200
	1/14	Naas	2m4f Nov Gd2 Hdl soft		£20,313
	12/13	Navn	2m4f Nov Gd1 Hdl yld-sft		£36,992
	11/13	WxfR	2m2f Mdn Hdl soft		£4,207
	3/13	Chel	2m1½f Cls1 Gd1 NHF 4-6yo gd-sft		£34,170
	1/13	Thur	2m NHF 5-7yo sft-hvy		£3,927

Former Champion Bumper winner who failed to fulfil potential in three seasons over hurdles, with confidence badly affected by a couple of falls; began novice chasing this summer and still young enough to make up for lost time.

Briery Belle

7 b m King's Theatre - Briery Ann (Anshan)

Henry Daly   Mrs H Plumbly, J Trafford, K Deane & S Holme

PLACINGS: 7G224P/83121   RPR **140+**h

Starts	1st	2nd	3rd	4th	Win & Pl
11	2	3	1	1	£28,492
129	4/16	Chel	2m4½f Cls1 List 117-132 Hdl Hcap good		£12,529
	1/16	Hntg	2m4½f Cls4 Mdn Hdl soft		£3,249

Progressed well over hurdles last season and won two of her last three races, including a

Blue Heron: smart novice chase prospect

Listed handicap at Cheltenham, with a second to top prospect The Organist in between; should make a good staying novice chaser.

Bristol De Mai (Fr)

5 gr g Saddler Maker - La Bole Night (April Night)

Nigel Twiston-Davies   **Simon Munir & Isaac Souede**

PLACINGS: **4611323/21211122-**   RPR **161+c**

Starts	1st	2nd	3rd	4th	Win & Pl
15	6	5	2	1	£169,241
	2/16	Sand	2m4f Cls1 Nov Gd1 Ch gd-sft.....................£25,628
	1/16	Hayd	2m4f Cls1 Nov Gd2 Ch heavy.......................£18,438
	12/15	Leic	2m4f Cls3 Nov Ch soft...................................£6,330
	11/15	Wwck	2m Cls3 Nov Ch 4-5yo gd-sft.......................£9,384
	12/14	Chep	2m Cls1 Gd1 Hdl 3yo heavy........................£19,933
	9/14	Autl	2m2f Hdl 3yo v soft..................................£19,200

Did really well over fences last season, especially when stepped up in trip to win the Scilly Isles Novices' Chase and finish second in the JLT (may have won but for a few mistakes); over the top when beaten at Ayr next time; looks ready to go up to 3m.

Broadway Buffalo (Ire)

8 ch g Broadway Flyer - Benbradagh Vard (Le Bavard)

David Pipe   **Mrs Jo Tracey**

PLACINGS: **4588/12343515F26/52-**   RPR **148c**

Starts	1st	2nd	3rd	4th	Win & Pl
24	7	3	2	3	£114,485
129	12/14	Hayd	2m7f Cls2 118-144 Ch Hcap heavy............£18,768
135	5/14	Hayd	2m7f Cls2 125-149 Hdl Hcap soft................£18,768
	3/13	Plum	2m4¹/₂f Cls4 Nov Hdl soft.............................£3,422
	2/13	Wwck	2m3f Cls4 Nov Hdl 4-7yo soft........................£3,899
	2/13	Newc	2m¹/₂f Cls4 Mdn Hdl heavy..........................£3,119
	10/12	Aint	2m1f Cls6 NHF 4-6yo soft.............................£1,949
	5/12	Worc	2m Cls6 NHF 4-6yo good..............................£1,437

Enjoyed a busy and productive novice chase campaign two seasons ago, winning the Tommy Whittle at Haydock and finishing second in the National Hunt Chase; much quieter last term but ran another cracker on his only run over fences when second in the Haydock Grand National Trial.

Brother Tedd

7 gr g Kayf Tara - Neltina (Neltino)

Philip Hobbs   **Scrase Farms**

PLACINGS: **15/F116421/1347-5**   RPR **152h**

Starts	1st	2nd	3rd	4th	Win & Pl
14	5	1	1	2	£54,548
144	11/15	Kemp	2m5f Cls2 135-157 Hdl Hcap good...............£12,346
135	4/15	Sand	2m4f Cls2 114-137 Hdl Hcap gd-sft..............£18,768
	11/14	Kemp	2m5f Cls4 Nov Hdl soft................................£3,119
	11/14	Kemp	2m5f Cls4 Nov Hdl gd-sft..............................£3,899
	12/13	Hntg	2m Cls6 NHF 4-6yo gd-sft.............................£1,560

Steadily progressive over hurdles over the last two seasons, though he seemed to reach the limit of his ability after winning at Kempton on his return last term and was well held in the Ascot Hurdle and good handicaps subsequently; should make a good novice chaser.

Buveur D'Air (Fr)

5 b g Crillon - History (Alesso)

Nicky Henderson   **Potensis Bloodstock Ltd & Chris Giles**

PLACINGS: **1124/1131-**   RPR **154+h**

Starts	1st	2nd	3rd	4th	Win & Pl
8	5	1	1	1	£81,070
	4/16	Aint	2m¹/₂f Cls1 Nov Gd1 Hdl soft.....................£42,203
	1/16	Hntg	2m Cls4 Nov Hdl gd-sft................................£3,249
	11/15	Newb	2m¹/₂f Cls3 Mdn Hdl soft..............................£6,498
	10/14	Nant	1m4f NHF 3yo gd-sft...................................£6,250
	8/14	Sjdm	1m5f NHF 3yo...£4,167

Very smart novice hurdler last season, winning three out of four with sole defeat coming when a fine third in the Supreme Novices' Hurdle; confirmed that form when a gutsy winner at Aintree next time; should stay further and seems effective on any going.

Buywise (Ire)

9 b g Tikkanen - Greenogue Princess (Rainbows For Life)

Evan Williams   **T Hywel Jones**

PLACINGS: **5811151/15145/32430-**   RPR **158c**

Starts	1st	2nd	3rd	4th	Win & Pl
18	6	1	2	2	£124,907
	2/15	Ffos	2m6f Cls4 Nov Hdl soft................................£3,899
	10/14	Ludl	2m Cls4 Nov Hdl good.................................£3,899
134	4/14	Chel	2m5f Cls1 Gd2 129-146 Ch Hcap good.........£28,475
120	2/14	Ludl	2m4f Cls3 107-133 Ch Hcap heavy..............£12,660
109	1/14	Tntn	2m7f Cls4 Nov 85-110 Ch Hcap heavy............£4,660
102	1/14	Ludl	2m4f Cls4 Nov 88-110 Ch Hcap heavy............£4,549

Has been knocking on the door in top handicaps for more than two seasons and amazing to think he hasn't won a big one, often staying on just too late after jumping errors; came closest in last season's Paddy Power Gold Cup and starts this season just 2lb higher.

Campeador (Fr)

4 gr g Gris De Gris - Royale Video (Video Rock)

Gordon Elliott (Ir)   **John P McManus**

PLACINGS: **2/14F-**   RPR **143+h**

Starts	1st	2nd	3rd	4th	Win & Pl
4	1	1	-	1	£17,732
	6/15	Claf	2m1f Hdl 3yo v soft..................................£12,651

French hurdle winner who was running a big race in the Fred Winter at Cheltenham on her second start for current connections when falling at the last; looks a likely contender for more good 2m handicaps.

'He did really well over fences last season and looks ready to go up to 3m now'

Camping Ground (Fr)

6 b g Goldneyev - Camomille (Pennekamp)

Robert Walford　　　　　　　　　　　　　　**G L Porter**

PLACINGS: 1123611/14/U1595-　　　　　　RPR **163+h**

Starts		1st	2nd	3rd	4th	Win & Pl
14		6	1	1	1	£139,909
	1/16	Chel	2m4½f Cls1 Gd2 Hdl heavy			£22,780
145	2/15	Wwck	2m4½f Cls2 124-145 Ch Hcap soft			£18,768
	3/14	Autl	2m2f Hdl 4yo v soft			£28,000
	11/13	Autl	2m1½f Ch 3yo heavy			£22,634
	5/13	Chat	2m1f Hdl 3yo soft			£8,585
	5/13	Nant	1m7½f Hdl 3yo gd-sft			£6,634

Ploughed through the mud to an impressive win in last season's Relkeel Hurdle but looked a non-stayer over 3m in the Cleeve Hurdle and suspicion those hard races left a mark when disappointing in the spring; capable of better over hurdles and fences.

Carlingford Lough (Ire)

10 b g King's Theatre - Baden (Furry Glen)

John Kiely (Ir)　　　　　　　　　　　　**John P McManus**

PLACINGS: /21221U6/1519/4614-1　　　　RPR **170+c**

Starts		1st	2nd	3rd	4th	Win & Pl
29		10	3	2	3	£528,614
	4/16	Punc	3m1f Gd1 Ch gd-yld			£86,765
	2/16	Leop	3m1½f Gd1 Ch heavy			£62,316
	2/15	Leop	3m Gd1 Ch yield			£66,860
	4/14	Punc	3m1f Nov Gd1 Ch good			£46,500
	12/13	Leop	3m Nuv Gd1 Ch yld-sft			£39,634
133	7/13	Gway	2m6½f 133-147 Ch Hcap soft			£97,866
129	8/12	Gway	2m5½f 114-142 Hdl Hcap sft-hvy			£21,667
119	7/12	Bell	2m4f 116-135 Hdl Hcap soft			£12,729
109	7/11	Gway	2m 95-116 Hdl Hcap good			£8,625
	7/11	Rosc	2m Mdn Hdl 4-5yo good			£4,461

Thorough stayer whose stamina brought a couple more Grade I successes last season, getting on top late in the Irish Gold Cup and the Punchestown Gold Cup to take his top-flight tally to five; has twice flopped in the Gold Cup at Cheltenham.

Carole's Destrier

8 b g Kayf Tara - Barton May (Midnight Legend)

Neil Mulholland　　　　　　　　　　**Mrs C Skipworth**

PLACINGS: F21710/21P4115/51P0-　　　RPR **152+c**

Starts		1st	2nd	3rd	4th	Win & Pl
20		6	4	-	1	£102,319
146	12/15	Sand	3m5f Cls2 122-148 Ch Hcap gd-sft			£25,024
	3/15	Weth	3m1f Cls4 Nov Ch good			£5,198
142	2/15	Asct	3m Cls1 List 132-152 Ch Hcap soft			£25,748
	11/14	Extr	3m Cls2 Nov Ch gd-sft			£12,628
129	3/14	Kemp	2m5f Cls2 121-135 Hdl Hcap gd-sft			£21,896
	1/14	Hntg	2m4½f Cls5 Mdn Hdl heavy			£1,949

Useful staying chaser who enjoyed the step up to a marathon trip when winning the London National at Sandown last season; better than he showed when twice disappointing in the spring and should be a contender for good staying handicaps.

Castello Sforza (Ire)

5 b g Milan - Young Elodie (Freedom Cry)

Willie Mullins (Ir)　　　　　　　　　**John P McManus**

PLACINGS: 1/4-　　　　　　　　　　　　RPR **130+b**

Starts		1st	2nd	3rd	4th	Win & Pl
2		1	-	-	1	£49,467
	4/15	Fair	2m NHF 4-5yo soft			£45,736

Did well to finish fourth in last season's

Camping Ground: capable of scoring again over hurdles and fences

Champion Bumper at Cheltenham on only his second run (and first in nearly a year); still very green that day and seems sure to progress over hurdles, especially when stepping up in trip.

Cause Of Causes (USA)

8 b g Dynaformer - Angel In My Heart (Rainbow Quest)

Gordon Elliott (Ir)   **John P McManus**

PLACINGS: 03372220/7518/0051P-   RPR **156**+c

Starts	1st	2nd	3rd	4th	Win & Pl
33	7	6	3	1	£311,314
142	3/16	Chel	3m2f Cls2 134-145 Am Ch Hcap good		£38,974
	3/15	Chel	4m Cls1 Nov List Am Ch gd-sft		£50,966
	1/13	Navn	2m Hdl heavy		£10,569
142	12/12	Asct	1m7¹/₂f Cls1 List 130-155 Hdl Hcap heavy		£84,405
	11/12	Fair	2m Hdl soft		£5,750
	7/12	Dpat	2m2f Hdl good		£5,750
	5/12	Kbgn	2m3f Mdn Hdl 4yo good		£4,313

Has won at the last two Cheltenham Festivals, running away with the Kim Muir last season by 12 lengths; has failed to win in 15 runs over fences otherwise, though, including when well fancied for several major staying handicaps.

Ch'Tibello (Fr)

5 b g Sageburg - Neicha (Neverneyev)

Dan Skelton   **The Can't Say No Partnership**

PLACINGS: 1/2231-3   RPR **145**+h

Starts	1st	2nd	3rd	4th	Win & Pl
6	2	2	2	-	£80,565
135	4/16	Ayr	2m Cls1 Gd2 133-147 Hdl Hcap gd-sft		£57,520
	4/15	Comp	2m1f Hdl 4yo heavy		£8,186

Won last season's Scottish Champion Hurdle having been put away for a big spring handicap; ran another good race when third in the Swinton and should make a decent chaser, although set to stay over hurdles for now.

Champagne Fever (Ire)

9 gr g Stowaway - Forever Bubbles (Roselier)

Willie Mullins (Ir)   **Mrs S Ricci**

PLACINGS: 123113/132/614F14/5-   RPR **166**c

Starts	1st	2nd	3rd	4th	Win & Pl
20	9	3	3	2	£333,066
	2/15	Gowr	2m4f Gd2 Ch sft-hvy		£21,415
	11/14	Clon	2m4f Gd2 Ch heavy		£24,375
	11/13	Punc	2m4f Ch yield		£6,732
	3/13	Chel	2m¹/₂f Cls1 Nov Gd1 Hdl soft		£68,340
	2/13	Leop	2m2f Nov Gd1 Hdl soft		£42,276
	11/12	Cork	2m Mdn Hdl soft		£7,763
	4/12	Punc	2m Gd1 NHF 4-7yo heavy		£40,625
	3/12	Chel	2m¹/₂f Cls1 Gd1 NHF 4-6yo good		£31,323
	1/12	Fair	2m NHF 4-7yo soft		£4,600

Came within a head of winning at a third successive Cheltenham Festival in 2014 when touched off in the Arkle and also finished second in the King George that year; disappointing the following spring and missed last season through injury; will mix hurdling and chasing this time.

Champagne West (Ire)

8 b g Westerner - Wyndham Sweetmarie (Mister Lord)

Philip Hobbs   **R S Brookhouse**

PLACINGS: 12/921114/112F/2PFP-   RPR **162**+c

Starts	1st	2nd	3rd	4th	Win & Pl
15	5	4		1	£83,869
	12/14	Chel	2m5f Cls2 Nov Ch gd-sft		£13,436
	11/14	Chel	2m4¹/₂f Cls2 Nov Ch soft		£12,512
	1/14	Asct	2m5¹/₂f Cls3 Nov Hdl 4-7yo heavy		£5,630
123	12/13	Winc	2m5¹/₂f Cls2 121-147 Hdl Hcap heavy		£11,711
	12/13	Wwck	2m5f Cls4 Mdn Hdl gd-sft		£3,769

Unfulfilled talent having had his novice campaign cut short by injury and then lost his way due to jumping issues last season; had run a huge race when second to Village Vic on his comeback at Cheltenham and remains capable of winning a big handicap.

Champers On Ice (Ire)

6 gr g Robin Des Champs - Miss Nova (Ra Nova)

David Pipe   **Professor Caroline Tisdall & Bryan Drew**

PLACINGS: U1/121133-   RPR **147**+h

Starts	1st	2nd	3rd	4th	Win & Pl
6	3	1	2	-	£41,098
	1/16	Chel	2m4¹/₂f Cls3 Nov Hdl heavy		£6,256
	11/15	Newb	2m4¹/₂f Cls3 Nov Hdl soft		£6,498
	4/15	Punc	2m2f NHF 5-7yo gd-yld		£5,884

Terrific third in last season's Albert Bartlett at Cheltenham, getting the better of a duel with Barters Hill up front before being mugged late; had also won twice in more testing conditions at Cheltenham and Newbury; looks a fine chasing prospect.

Charbel (Ire)

5 b g Iffraaj - Eoz (Sadler's Wells)

Kim Bailey   **Mrs Julie Martin & David R Martin**

PLACINGS: 11/412215-5   RPR **150**h

Starts	1st	2nd	3rd	4th	Win & Pl
9	4	2	-	1	£53,284
	2/16	Muss	1m7¹/₂f Cls2 Nov Hdl gd-sft		£14,389
	10/15	Strf	2m¹/₂f Cls3 Nov Hdl 4-6yo soft		£6,498
	3/15	Limk	2m List NHF 4yo heavy		£12,597
	2/15	Leop	2m NHF 4yo soft		£5,349

Steadily progressive in novice hurdles last season, producing his best performances when winning easily at Musselburgh and then finishing fifth in a strong Supreme Novices' Hurdle; over the top when well beaten at Punchestown; should stay further.

ON THE CLOCK

Clan Des Obeaux Wide-margin winner on his hurdling bow and sixth in the Triumph. Soft ground, a longer trip and a chasing career could bring out the best in the the four-year-old. *[Dave Edwards, Topspeed]*

Charmix (Fr)

6 b/br g Laveron - Open Up (Fabulous Don)

Harry Fry   Nicholas Cooper

PLACINGS: 1/0121P-   RPR **144+h**

Starts	1st	2nd	3rd	4th	Win & Pl
5	2	1	-	-	£11,163

12/15	Newb	2m3f Cls4 Nov Hdl 4-6yo soft	£3,899
10/15	Weth	2m Cls3 Nov Hdl soft	£5,393

Won two novice hurdles on soft ground and particularly impressive when stepped up to 2m3f at Newbury, winning by 17 lengths; should stay further but bitterly disappointing when raised in class and trip at Cheltenham last time.

Clan Des Obeaux (Fr)

4 b/br g Kapgarde - Nausicaa Des Obeaux (April Night)

Paul Nicholls   Mr & Mrs P K Barber & Potensis Bloodstock Ltd

PLACINGS: 1/126-   RPR **139h**

Starts	1st	2nd	3rd	4th	Win & Pl
4	2	1	-	-	£15,143

12/15	Newb	2m¹/₂f Cls4 Hdl 3yo soft	£3,249
4/15	Lrsy	1m4f NHF 3yo	£3,876

Terrific long-term chasing prospect who made a hugely impressive British debut at Newbury last season; slightly disappointing he couldn't build on that but looked unlucky in a messy race next time before staying on after getting outpaced in the Triumph.

Clarcam (Fr)

6 b g Califet - Rose Beryl (Lost World)

Gordon Elliott (Ir)   Gigginstown House Stud

PLACINGS: 211281/325483-511252   RPR **157c**

Starts	1st	2nd	3rd	4th	Win & Pl
28	7	10	3	2	£245,638

6/16	DRoy	2m4f Hdl good	£7,962
5/16	Klny	2m4¹/₂f Gd3 Ch good	£17,353
4/15	Aint	2m4f Cls1 Nov Gd1 Ch gd-sft	£50,882
12/14	Leop	2m1f Nov Gd1 Ch soft	£46,042
12/14	Navn	2m1f Nov Ch yld-sft	£10,833
10/14	Limk	2m2f Hdl 4yo good	£10,833
10/13	Thur	2m Mdn Hdl 3yo good	£4,207

Out of sorts for much of last season, failing to build on a stellar novice campaign when winning Grade 1 races at Leopardstown and Aintree; finally showed more promise in the spring and summer, winning twice and finishing fifth in the Galway Plate.

Cloudy Dream (Ire)

6 gr g Cloudings - Run Away Dream (Acceglio)

Malcolm Jefferson   Trevor Hemmings

PLACINGS: 31/13112-   RPR **140+h**

Starts	1st	2nd	3rd	4th	Win & Pl
7	4	2	-	-	£38,825

122	3/16	MRas	2m2¹/₂f Cls3 115-129 Hdl Hcap soft	£9,384
	11/15	Donc	2m3¹/₂f Cls4 Nov Hdl 4-6yo good	£3,899
	10/15	Carl	2m1f Cls6 NHF 4-6yo good	£1,560
	4/15	Hexm	2m Cls6 NHF 4-5yo good	£1,711

Prolific over the last 18 months, winning two

Charbel: remains open to improvement

bumpers and a novice and handicap over hurdles; ran a cracker when stepped up in class for the Scottish Champion Hurdle, finishing strongly in second having been ninth at the last; should do better over further.

Cocktails At Dawn

8 b g Fair Mix - Fond Farewell (Phardante)

Nicky Henderson　　　　**R J H Geffen & Sir John Ritblat**

PLACINGS: F/4/3012/2F491/10F-P					RPR **155+c**
Starts	1st	2nd	3rd	4th	Win & Pl
14	3		1	2	£43,313
	10/15	Chep	2m3¹/₂f Cls2 Nov Ch good		£12,996
133	4/15	Sand	2m4f Cls2 124-141 Ch Hcap good		£18,768
119	4/14	Kemp	2m5f Cls3 110-130 Hdl Hcap good		£5,848

Plagued by jumping problems over fences and failed to build on rich promise of reappearance win at Chepstow last October in competitive handicaps; talented enough to win good races if jumping better and could go back over hurdles.

Cogry

7 b g King's Theatre - Wyldello (Supreme Leader)

Nigel Twiston-Davies　　　　**Graham & Alison Jelley**

PLACINGS: 163118F/F1216F/4P33-					RPR **139c**
Starts	1st	2nd	3rd	4th	Win & Pl
17	5	1	3	1	£53,188
	2/15	Wwck	3m2f Cls3 Nov Ch soft		£9,384
128	12/14	Chep	2m7¹/₂f Cls3 Nov 120-137 Ch Hcap heavy		£6,498
	2/14	Wwck	2m3f Cls4 Nov Hdl 4-7yo soft		£3,899
	1/14	Leic	2m4¹/₂f Cls4 Nov Hdl heavy		£3,899
	10/13	Sthl	1m7¹/₂f Cls6 Mdn NHF 4-6yo gd-sft		£1,560

Knocking on the door in good staying handicaps since a couple of wins as a novice two seasons

ago; pulled up when favourite for last season's Welsh National but remains a likely sort for that race having already won at the course.

Cold March (Fr)

6 b/br g Early March - Tumultueuse (Bering)

Venetia Williams　　　　**A Brooks**

PLACINGS: P54F/115F322P/13605-					RPR **153c**
Starts	1st	2nd	3rd	4th	Win & Pl
20	3	4	2	1	£114,930
140	10/15	Asct	2m1f Cls1 List 130-148 Ch Hcap good		£34,170
	6/14	Autl	2m1¹/₂f Ch 4yo soft		£22,000
	5/14	Sbri	2m2f Ch 4yo good		£6,800

French chase winner who got off the mark in Britain in a Listed handicap over 2m1f at Ascot last October; good third at the same course next time and remains unexposed over further having run out (still in touch going well) when stepped up to 2m5f.

Cole Harden (Ire)

7 b g Westerner - Nosie Betty (Alphabatim)

Warren Greatrex　　　　**Mrs Jill Eynon & Robin Eynon**

PLACINGS: /1411272/123412/334-					RPR **158h**
Starts	1st	2nd	3rd	4th	Win & Pl
17	6	4	3	3	£292,478
	3/15	Chel	3m Cls1 Gd1 Hdl good		£170,850
	11/14	Weth	3m1¹/₂f Cls1 Gd2 Hdl good		£21,072
	1/14	Newb	2m3f Cls4 Nov Hdl soft		£3,574
	11/13	Font	2m3f Cls4 Mdn Hdl heavy		£3,119
	8/13	Worc	2m Cls6 NHF 4-6yo good		£1,560
	3/13	Sedg	2m1f Cls6 NHF 4-6yo heavy		£1,560

Surprise winner of the World Hurdle in 2015 when transformed by a breathing operation;

Cogry (right): remains an ideal type for the Welsh National

trained for a repeat last season (short of fitness in both prep runs on unsuitable ground) but disappointed in a distant fourth; could go novice chasing.

Colms Dream (Ire)

7 ch g Beneficial - African Waters (Be My Native)

Karl Thornton   **Colm's Dream Syndicate**

PLACINGS: 146/2156335111FF11-2   RPR **145c**

Starts		1st	2nd	3rd	4th	Win & Pl
27		7	3	3	1	£76,000
94	3/16	DRoy	3m¹/₂f 80-109 Hdl Hcap soft			£5,426
125	2/16	Leop	2m5¹/₂f 114-137 Ch Hcap soft			£21,691
112	10/15	Punc	2m4f 98-112 Ch Hcap yield			£5,884
104	10/15	Punc	2m4f 96-121 Ch Hcap good			£8,558
95	9/15	Rosc	2m5f 86-114 Ch Hcap good			£6,151
88	6/15	Clon	2m4f 80-95 Hdl Hcap good			£4,279
80	3/15	DRoy	2m4f 80-93 Hdl Hcap yld-sft			£5,616

Hugely progressive chaser whose second to Irish Cavalier at Punchestown at the end of April was his first defeat in last five completed starts over fences (also won over hurdles during that run); effective from 2m4f to 3m.

Coney Island (Ire)

5 b g Flemensfirth - Millys Gesture (Milan)

Edward Harty (Ir)   **John P McManus**

PLACINGS: 32151-2   RPR **148+h**

Starts		1st	2nd	3rd	4th	Win & Pl
6		2	2	1	-	£48,495
130	3/16	Fair	3m Nov 109-131 Hdl Hcap yield			£23,860
	12/15	Leop	2m Mdn Hdl 4yo heavy			£6,953

Steady improver last season who flourished in the spring, winning a novice handicap at Fairyhouse and pushing Bellshill close in a Grade 1 at Punchestown; very much a chaser in the making and should have lots more to offer.

Coneygree

9 b g Karinga Bay - Plaid Maid (Executive Perk)

Mark Bradstock   **The Max Partnership**

PLACINGS: 18/1113/1111/1-   RPR **175+c**

Starts		1st	2nd	3rd	4th	Win & Pl
11		9	-	1	-	£454,599
	11/15	Sand	2m Cls1 List Ch gd-sft			£17,085
	3/15	Chel	3m2¹/₂f Cls1 Gd1 Ch soft			£313,225
	2/15	Newb	2m7¹/₂f Cls1 Gd2 Ch soft			£28,475
	12/14	Kemp	3m Cls1 Nov Gd1 Ch gd-sft			£42,047
	11/14	Newb	2m4f Cls1 Nov Gd2 Ch soft			£18,184
	12/12	Chel	3m Cls1 Nov Gd2 Hdl heavy			£14,238
	11/12	Chel	2m5f Cls1 Nov Gd2 Hdl soft			£14,238
	11/12	Uttx	2m4f Cls4 Nov Hdl soft			£2,534
	11/11	Uttx	2m Cls6 NHF 4-6yo gd-sft			£1,365

Became the first novice to win the Gold Cup in more than 40 years with a sensational all-the-way triumph in 2015; injury problems resurfaced last season when running just once at Sandown (won by 25 lengths); should again be a force in top staying chases.

Connetable (Fr)

4 b g Saint Des Saints - Montbresia (Video Rock)

Paul Nicholls   **Chris Giles & Dan Macdonald**

PLACINGS: 41/32100-   RPR **135h**

Starts		1st	2nd	3rd	4th	Win & Pl
7		2	1	1	1	£30,316
	2/16	Sand	2m Cls1 List Hdl soft			£14,238
	4/15	Comp	2m Hdl 3yo v soft			£8,186

Achieved a tremendous feat for a juvenile when winning an open Listed hurdle at Sandown on his second run for current connections from Rayvin Black; has to prove he wasn't flattered by that after disappointing at Cheltenham and Ayr.

Consul De Thaix (Fr)

4 b g Loxias - Mange De Thaix (Mont Basile)

Nicky Henderson   **John P McManus**

PLACINGS: 230-   RPR **131h**

Starts		1st	2nd	3rd	4th	Win & Pl
3		-	1	1	-	£12,140

Ran only twice for current connections last season but telling that his trainer thought him worthy of a place in the Triumph Hurdle (finished tenth) after a fair third in a Grade 2 at Cheltenham; retains novice status and looks the type to improve with time.

Coo Star Sivola (Fr)

4 b g Assessor - Santorine (Della Francesca)

Nick Williams   **Babbit Racing**

PLACINGS: 67/233-   RPR **133h**

Starts		1st	2nd	3rd	4th	Win & Pl
5		-	1	2	-	£19,786

Ran three fine races in top company last season, most notably when beaten less than a length into third in the Fred Winter at Cheltenham; should win novice hurdles and capable of running well in more good handicaps.

Coologue (Ire)

7 b g Helissio - Scolboa (Bob's Return)

Charlie Longsdon   **The New Club Partnership**

PLACINGS: 2/2214P/13222P-   RPR **145+c**

Starts		1st	2nd	3rd	4th	Win & Pl
11		2	5	1	1	£38,394
	10/15	Bang	2m4¹/₂f Cls4 Nov Ch good			£5,198
	12/14	Bang	2m4f Cls4 Mdn Hdl gd-sft			£3,119

Unable to add to successful chasing debut at Bangor last season but ran several good races in defeat, most notably when second in the Sky Bet Chase at Doncaster; seems best on good ground and remains open to further progress.

Court Minstrel (Ire)

9 b g Court Cave - Theatral (Orchestra)

Evan Williams   **Mrs Janet Davies**

PLACINGS: **7412/114546/9011246-**   RPR **155+h**

Starts		1st	2nd	3rd	4th	Win & Pl
28		10	3	2	6	£216,519
149	10/15	Chep	2m3¹/₂f Cls1 Gd3 130-149 Hdl Hcap good			£28,475
145	8/15	Prth	2m Cls2 131-151 Hdl Hcap good			£12,512
	10/14	Chel	2m Cls2 Nov Ch good			£12,558
	9/14	NAbb	2m¹/₂f Cls4 Nov Ch good			£3,899
147	4/14	Aint	2m¹/₂f Cls2 146-147 Cond Am Hdl Hcap gd-sft			£25,024
141	4/13	Ayr	2m Cls1 Gd2 133-153 Hdl Hcap good			£34,170
131	3/13	Plum	2m Cls2 123-149 Hdl Hcap gd-sft			£16,245
	10/12	Chel	2m¹/₂f Cls3 Mdn Hdl gd-sft			£6,256
	3/12	Ludl	2m Cls5 NHF 4-6yo good			£1,949
	11/11	Ludl	2m Cls5 Mdn NHF 4-6yo good			£1,949

Smart hurdler when able to come late off a strong pace and has won several good handicaps over the years off seemingly stiff marks judged on more modest efforts in Graded company; showed similar form over fences as a novice two seasons ago.

Cue Card

10 b g King's Theatre - Wicked Crack (King's Ride)

Colin Tizzard   **Mrs Jean R Bishop**

PLACINGS: **12/312/4452/4111F1-4**   RPR **180+c**

Starts		1st	2nd	3rd	4th	Win & Pl
31		14	7	1	5	£1,079,753
	4/16	Aint	3m1f Cls1 Gd1 Ch gd-sft			£84,655
	12/15	Kemp	3m Cls1 Gd1 Ch gd-sft			£114,436
	11/15	Hayd	3m Cls1 Gd1 Ch soft			£112,540
	10/15	Weth	3m Cls1 Gd2 Ch soft			£56,950
	11/13	Hayd	3m Cls1 Gd1 Ch soft			£112,637
	3/13	Chel	2m5f Cls1 Gd1 Ch gd-sft			£156,613
	2/13	Asct	2m¹/₂f Cls1 Gd1 Ch soft			£84,405
157	11/12	Extr	2m1¹/₂f Cls1 Gd2 140-160 Ch Hcap gd-sft			£35,594
	12/11	Newb	2m2¹/₂f Cls3 Nov Ch soft			£7,323
	10/11	Chep	2m3¹/₂f Cls3 Nov Ch good			£7,148
	11/10	Chel	2m¹/₂f Cls1 Nov Gd2 Hdl good			£14,253
	10/10	Aint	2m4f Cls3 Nov Hdl 4-6yo gd-sft			£4,554
	3/10	Chel	2m¹/₂f Cls1 Gd1 NHF 4-6yo good			£34,206
	1/10	Font	1m5¹/₂f Cls6 NHF 4-6yo soft			£1,431

Hugely popular chaser who bounced back to his best last season with a hat-trick of Grade 1 wins, most memorably nailing Vautour close home to win the King George at his fourth attempt; going well when fell three out in the Gold Cup; will take in the major 3m contests en route to another crack at the big one, starting out in the Charlie Hall at Wetherby, which he won last season.

Cup Final (Ire)

7 ch g Presenting - Asian Maze (Anshan)

Nicky Henderson   **John P McManus**

PLACINGS: **4/230/31/1P-1**   RPR **146+h**

Starts		1st	2nd	3rd	4th	Win & Pl
9		3	1	2	1	£49,511
137	4/16	Punc	3m 119-144 Hdl Hcap yield			£17,353
132	2/16	Muss	3m2f Cls2 128-154 Hdl Hcap soft			£12,996
127	12/14	Sand	2m6f Cls2 116-133 Hdl Hcap soft			£12,512

Smart stayer who has been held up by injury over

---

the last few seasons but won three of his last four across that period, with sole defeat coming in last season's Pertemps Final; got back on track when landing a gritty success at Punchestown.

Cyrus Darius

7 b g Overbury - Barton Belle (Barathea)

Malcolm Jefferson   **Mr & Mrs G Calder & P M Warren**

PLACINGS: **4/3111/1-**   RPR **130+c**

Starts		1st	2nd	3rd	4th	Win & Pl
6		4	-	1	1	£47,417
	9/15	Prth	2m4f Cls3 Nov Ch gd-sft			£6,882
	4/15	Aint	2m¹/₂f Cls1 Nov Gd2 Hdl gd-sft			£33,762
	3/15	Hexm	2m Cls4 Nov Hdl gd-sft			£3,285
	3/15	Newc	2m¹/₂f Cls4 Nov Hdl good			£3,249

Won three out of three over hurdles two seasons ago, all by wide margins including a ten-length victory in a Grade 2 novice at Aintree; set to return after suffering a tendon injury following a successful chasing debut last September.

Dandridge

7 ch g Doyen - Arantxa (Sharpo)

Arthur Moore (Ir)   **R A Bartlett**

PLACINGS: **152043/0451F216122-9**   RPR **147+c**

Starts		1st	2nd	3rd	4th	Win & Pl
21		4	6	1	2	£108,714
125	1/16	Donc	2m¹/₂f Cls2 124-149 Ch Hcap good			£31,280
114	10/15	Wxfd	2m4f 104-132 Ch Hcap yield			£12,597
	8/15	Tram	2m Ch gd-fm			£6,419
	9/14	Gway	2m Mdn Hdl good			£5,750

Progressed throughout last season when sent chasing, winning handicaps at Wexford and Doncaster before finishing second in the Grand Annual at Cheltenham and Red Rum at Aintree; should continue to run well in good 2m handicaps.

Definitly Red (Ire)

7 ch g Definite Article - The Red Wench (Aahsaylad)

Brian Ellison   **P J Martin**

PLACINGS: **P/1117/1211P/2122F1-**   RPR **150c**

Starts		1st	2nd	3rd	4th	Win & Pl
14		7	4	-		£111,440
137	4/16	Ayr	2m4¹/₂f Cls1 List 132-148 Ch Hcap soft			£25,628
	1/16	Catt	3m1f Cls4 Nov Ch soft			£7,148
	2/15	Hayd	2m7f Cls1 Nov Gd2 Hdl soft			£15,735
	1/15	Catt	2m3¹/₂f Cls4 Nov Hdl gd-sft			£4,874
	11/14	Chel	2m¹/₂f Cls1 List NHF 4-6yo soft			£11,390
	2/14	Newb	2m¹/₂f Cls1 List NHF 4-6yo heavy			£11,390
	12/13	Uttx	2m Cls6 Mdn NHF 4-6yo heavy			£1,949

Showed very smart form over fences last season, winning twice and finishing second to Cheltenham winners Black Hercules and Blaklion; out on his feet when falling two out in the National Hunt Chase and better suited by trips just short of 3m.

Devils Bride (Ire)

9 b g Helissio - Rigorous (Generous)

Willie Mullins (Ir)   Gigginstown House Stud

PLACINGS: 141P/11/2P811611-241   RPR **165+c**

Starts		1st	2nd	3rd	4th	Win & Pl
18		10	2		2	£112,947
150	7/16	Gway	2m2f 122-150 Ch Hcap good			£14,697
	11/15	Naas	2m Gd3 Ch yield			£15,116
	10/15	Limk	2m3¹/₂f Ch yield			£12,597
	9/15	List	2m4f Ch soft			£15,116
134	9/15	Gway	2m2f 112-139 Ch Hcap good			£13,857
	7/14	Limk	2m3¹/₂f Nov Ch yield			£9,488
	6/14	Rosc	2m5f Ch good			£5,175
	10/13	Limk	2m Mdn Hdl good			£5,610
	7/13	Tipp	2m NHF 4-7yo gd-fm			£5,890
	6/13	Rosc	2m NHF 4-7yo soft			£3,528

Lightly raced for his age and has gone from strength to strength over the last couple of seasons; won four times over fences last autumn and returned from a break even better this summer, winning off 150 at Galway after coming fourth in the Galway Plate.

Diakali (Fr)

7 gr g Sinndar - Diasilixa (Linamix)

Willie Mullins (Ir)   Wicklow Bloodstock (Ireland) Ltd

PLACINGS: 11241/211343/34/10-   RPR **165h**

Starts		1st	2nd	3rd	4th	Win & Pl
15		6	2	3	3	£324,814
	7/15	Tipp	2m Gd3 Hdl good			£31,492
	11/13	Naas	2m Gd3 Hdl 4yo yld-sft			£14,533
	6/13	Autl	2m3¹/₂f Gd1 Hdl 4yo v soft			£98,780
	4/13	Punc	2m Gd1 Hdl 4yo heavy			£40,375
	1/13	Punc	2m Gd3 Hdl 4yo heavy			£14,533
	11/12	Gowr	2m Mdn Hdl 3yo heavy			£5,750

Very lightly raced due to injury, running just

Diamond King (Ire)

8 b g King's Theatre - Georgia On My Mind (Belmez)

Gordon Elliott (Ir)   Mrs Diana L Whateley

PLACINGS: 11/131/7P/4211-4   RPR **154+h**

Starts		1st	2nd	3rd	4th	Win & Pl
12		6	1	1	2	£83,900
149	3/16	Chel	2m5f Cls1 Gd3 139-158 Hdl Hcap good			£51,255
	1/16	Punc	2m4f Hdl heavy			£8,118
	1/14	Donc	2m¹/₂f Cls4 Nov Hdl gd-sft			£3,119
	11/13	Weth	2m Cls4 Nov Hdl gd-sft			£3,422
	4/13	Bang	2m¹/₂f Cls6 Am NHF 4-6yo good			£1,643
	2/13	Weth	2m Cls6 NHF 4-5yo soft			£1,643

Held in high regard by former trainer Donald McCain and finally began to fulfil his potential after a switch last season, most notably when winning the Coral Cup; only fourth in a 3m Grade 1 at Punchestown but may be up to that level in time.

Dicosimo (Fr)

5 b g Laveron - Coralisse Royule (Tip Moss)

Willie Mullins (Ir)   Mrs S Ricci

PLACINGS: F1184/1FF-P   RPR **150+h**

Starts		1st	2nd	3rd	4th	Win & Pl
9		3	-	-	1	£43,614
	12/15	Limk	2m List Hdl 4yo heavy			£13,101
	1/15	Gowr	2m Hdl 4yo sft-hvy			£10,581
	10/14	Autl	2m1¹/₂f Hdl 3yo heavy			£19,200

Wide-margin winner of a Listed hurdle first time out last season but failed to get away

twice in the last two years; had developed into a smart hurdler prior to that, winning two Grade 1 races as a four-year-old and just touched off by The New One in the Aintree Hurdle in 2014.

Dicosimo: could make an impact over fences

with free-going tendencies in big handicaps, twice falling and pulled up after going too fast at Punchestown; imposing type who could do better over fences.

Diego Du Charmil (Fr)

4 b g Ballingarry - Daramour (Anabaa Blue)

Paul Nicholls   **Mrs Johnny De La Hey**

PLACINGS: **32214-**   RPR **135+h**

Starts	1st	2nd	3rd	4th	Win & Pl
5	1	2	1	1	£63,295
133	3/16	**Chel**	2m¹/₂f Cls1 Gd3 128-142 Hdl 4yo Hcap good £42,713

Won last season's Fred Winter Hurdle at Cheltenham on his first run for new connections

having been placed three times in France; may have been lucky (two rivals fell at the last and just held on by a nose) but could have more to come off just 5lb higher.

Different Gravey (Ire)

6 b g High Chaparral - Newtown Dancer (Danehill Dancer)

Nicky Henderson   **Mr & Mrs Kelvin Hughes**

PLACINGS: **1/1411/15-**   RPR **164+h**

Starts	1st	2nd	3rd	4th	Win & Pl
6	4	-	-	1	£59,865
149	2/16	Asct	2m3¹/₂f Cls2 126-149 Hdl Hcap soft £28,152
	4/15	Ayr	2m4¹/₂f Cls3 Nov Hdl good £6,498
	2/15	Hntg	2m3¹/₂f Cls1 Nov List Hdl soft £14,266
	11/14	Newb	2m¹/₂f Cls3 Mdn Hdl soft £6,498

Ran only twice last season but showed he was

Different Gravey: quality prospect for novice chases

still progressing rapidly as he built on a light but successful novice campaign by running away with a handicap at Ascot; disappointing over further at Aintree but remains a top novice chasing prospect.

Disko (Fr)

5 gr g Martaline - Nikos Royale (Nikos)

Noel Meade (Ir)   Gigginstown House Stud

PLACINGS: 1/221-6   **RPR 134+h**

Starts	1st	2nd	3rd	4th	Win & Pl
5	2	2	-	-	£27,839
	11/15	Naas	2m4f Mdn Hdl soft		£6,686
	2/15	Punc	2m NHF 4yo yield		£4,814

Looks an exciting prospect on the evidence of wide-margin bumper/maiden hurdles wins in 2015 (also second in a Grade 1 bumper in between); pulled muscles last season and off for nearly six months before disappointing at Punchestown.

Djakadam (Fr)

7 b g Saint Des Saints - Rainbow Crest (Baryshnikov)

Willie Mullins (Ir)   Mrs S Ricci

PLACINGS: 1124/11F/812/21F23-2   **RPR 177c**

Starts	1st	2nd	3rd	4th	Win & Pl
18	6	6	1	1	£452,918
145	12/15	Punc	2m4f Gd1 Ch heavy		£39,535
	1/15	Gowr	3m1f 117-145 Ch heavy		£46,512
	1/14	Leop	2m5f Nov Gd2 Ch soft		£21,667
	12/13	Leop	2m3f Ch yld-sft		£7,293
	3/13	Limk	2m Hdl 4yo heavy		£7,293
	2/13	Gowr	2m Mdn Hdl 4yo heavy		£5,890

Has finished second in each of the last two Gold Cups, proving himself a tough and strong stayer; beaten twice more subsequently but may not have been at his best after Cheltenham; also looked very smart over 2m4f when winning the John Durkan.

Doctor Harper (Ire)

8 b g Presenting - Supreme Dreamer (Supreme Leader)

David Pipe   The Johnson Family

PLACINGS: 110/115131/9221U-P   **RPR 145+c**

Starts	1st	2nd	3rd	4th	Win & Pl
15	7	2	1	-	£64,924
138	1/16	Leic	2m Cls3 Nov Hdl soft		£6,498
	4/14	Aint	3m1½f Cls1 Gd3 135-147 Hdl Hcap good		£28,475
	2/14	Fknm	2m4f Cls3 Nov Hdl 4-7yo heavy		£5,848
	11/13	Extr	2m1f Cls4 Nov Hdl good		£3,249
	11/13	Extr	2m1f Cls3 Nov Hdl gd-sft		£5,523
	2/13	Sand	2m Cls5 NHF 4-6yo gd-sft		£2,599
	12/12	Tntn	2m1½f Cls5 NHF 3-5yo soft		£2,060

Sent off just 4-1 for last season's Kim Muir having caught the eye in novice chases but well beaten when unseating his rider there and pulled up next time; had won a Grade 3 handicap hurdle at Aintree on good ground but may now need softer after subsequent leg trouble.

Dodging Bullets

8 b g Dubawi - Nova Cyngi (Kris S)

Paul Nicholls   Martin Broughton & Friends

PLACINGS: 397/111245/3111/273-   **RPR 162c**

Starts	1st	2nd	3rd	4th	Win & Pl
21	8	3	3	2	£503,998
	3/15	Chel	2m Cls1 Gd1 Ch good		£199,325
	1/15	Asct	2m1f Cls1 Gd1 Ch soft		£70,338
	12/14	Sand	1m7½f Cls1 Gd1 Ch soft		£85,425
	12/13	Kemp	2m Cls1 Nov Gd2 Ch soft		£20,167
	11/13	Chel	2m1f Cls1 Nov Gd2 Ch good		£18,224
	10/13	Kemp	2m Cls4 Ch good		£4,549
	11/12	Chel	2m1½f Cls1 Nov Gd2 Hdl gd-sft		£14,238
	10/12	Chel	2m1½f Cls2 Hdl 4yo gd-sft		£18,768

Dominated an admittedly weak 2m division two seasons ago, culminating with victory in the Champion Chase; held up by injury last term and not at his best in three runs, though he stayed on well in third at Sandown last time; likely to step up in trip.

Don Cossack (Ger)

9 br g Sholokhov - Depeche Toi (Konigsstuhl)

Gordon Elliott (Ir)   Gigginstown House Stud

PLACINGS: 12F2/4111131/111F11-   **RPR 182+c**

Starts	1st	2nd	3rd	4th	Win & Pl
27	16	4	2	1	£907,364
	3/16	Chel	3m2²/₃f Cls1 Gd1 Ch good		£327,463
	1/16	Thur	2m4f Gd2 Ch soft		£18,750
	10/15	DRoy	3m Gd1 Ch yld-sft		£65,116
	10/15	Punc	2m4f Gd3 Ch good		£16,124
	4/15	Punc	3m1f Gd1 Ch gd-yld		£93,023
	4/15	Aint	2m4f Cls1 Gd1 Ch good		£112,637
	1/15	Thur	2m4f Gd2 Ch sft-hvy		£20,155
	12/14	Punc	2m4f Gd1 Ch gd-yld		£40,000
	11/14	DRny	2m4f Gd2 Ch yield		£27,083
	10/14	Punc	2m7f Gd3 Ch gd-fm		£17,333
	12/13	Fair	2m4f Nov Gd1 Ch gd-yld		£39,634
	10/13	Gway	2m6½f Ch heavy		£9,537
	11/12	Navn	2m Mdn Hdl heavy		£7,763
	4/12	Fair	2m NHF 4-7yo soft		£7,479
	12/11	Navn	2m Gd2 NHF 4-7yo sft-hvy		£15,409
	10/11	Naas	2m3f NHF 4-7yo heavy		£5,056

Brilliant staying chaser who has won ton of his last 11 completed starts, culminating in a seventh Grade 1 success in last season's Cheltenham Gold Cup; touch and go whether he returns this season after sustaining a tendon injury in April.

Don Poli (Ire)

7 b g Poliglote - Dalamine (Sillery)

Willie Mullins (Ir)   Gigginstown House Stud

PLACINGS: 2/2111/2111/51132-3   **RPR 168c**

Starts	1st	2nd	3rd	4th	Win & Pl
15	8	4	2	-	£415,089
	12/15	Leop	3m Gd1 Ch heavy		£69,767
	12/15	Aint	3m1f Cls1 List Ch soft		£22,780
	3/15	Chel	3m1½f Cls1 Gd1 Ch good		£85,425
	12/14	Leop	3m Nov Gd1 Ch sft-hvy		£40,625
	11/14	Gowr	2m4f Ch heavy		£8,625
143	3/14	Chel	2m4¹/₂f Cls2 133-146 Cond Hdl Hcap good		£31,280
	2/14	Clon	3m Nov Gd3 Hdl heavy		£17,063
	1/14	Thur	2m6f Mdn Hdl sft-hvy		£6,325

Seemed to have his limitations exposed last spring when coming up short at Cheltenham,

Aintree and Punchestown; had still managed to win the Lexus and might have gone closer in the Gold Cup under a more forceful ride; still open to improvement.

Don't Touch It (Ire)

6 b g Scorpion - Shandora (Supreme Leader)

Jessica Harrington (Ir)					John P McManus
PLACINGS: 42/212213-1					RPR **149+h**

Starts	1st	2nd	3rd	4th	Win & Pl
9	3	4	2	1	£63,481
	4/16	Punc	2m Nov Gd1 Hdl gd-yld		£43,382
	1/16	Leop	2m Mdn Hdl soft		£6,596
	10/15	Punc	2m NHF 5-7yo yield		£4,814

Took advantage of what was probably a soft Grade I opening when beating Petit Mouchoir at Punchestown at the end of April; still much improved on better ground that day having reportedly got bogged down when well beaten at Naas previously.

Double Shuffle (Ire)

6 b g Milan - Fiddlers Bar (Un Desperado)

Tom George					Crossed Fingers Partnership
PLACINGS: 3/5611/24135-					RPR **145c**

Starts	1st	2nd	3rd	4th	Win & Pl
9	3	1	1	1	£31,402
134	12/15	Ludl	2m4f Cls3 Nov 120-134 Ch Hcap soft		£11,372
	3/15	Newb	2m¹/₂f Cls4 Nov Hdl gd-sft		£3,422
	2/15	Donc	2m¹/₂f Cls4 Nov Hdl 4-7yo good		£3,574

Won last two novice hurdles two seasons ago and continued to progress over fences last season, winning at the third attempt before a good third in the novice handicap chase at the Cheltenham Festival; only six so may well improve again.

Douvan (Fr)

6 b g Walk In The Park - Star Face (Saint Des Saints)

Willie Mullins (Ir)					Mrs S Ricci
PLACINGS: 21111/111111-1					RPR **176+c**

Starts	1st	2nd	3rd	4th	Win & Pl
12	11	1	-	-	£435,964
	4/16	Punc	2m Nov Gd1 Ch yield		£49,890
	4/16	Aint	2m Cls1 Nov Gd1 Ch gd-sft		£56,270
	3/16	Chel	2m Cls1 Gd1 Ch gd-sft		£85,827
	1/16	Leop	2m1f Nov Gd1 Ch soft		£39,706
	12/15	Leop	2m1f Nov Gd1 Ch heavy		£42,558
	11/15	Navn	2m1f Ch soft		£8,558
	4/15	Punc	2m Nov Gd1 Hdl gd-yld		£44,186
	3/15	Chel	2m¹/₂f Cls1 Nov Gd1 Hdl gd-sft		£68,340
	1/15	Punc	2m Nov Gd2 Hdl soft		£20,155
	11/14	Gowr	2m Nov Hdl 4yo heavy		£7,475
	6/14	Comp	2m1f Hdl 4yo v soft		£8,800

Unbeaten in ten races since joining Willie Mullins from France, including six wide-margin victories over fences; effortlessly landed the Arkle at Cheltenham and looked even more impressive at Aintree and Punchestown; seems sure to stay beyond 2m.

Drop Out Joe

8 ch g Generous - La Feuillarde (Nikos)

Charlie Longsdon					The Jesters
PLACINGS: 6232P/13429/411570-1					RPR **155+c**

Starts	1st	2nd	3rd	4th	Win & Pl
21	6	3	2	2	£127,234
144	6/16	Uttx	3m2f Cls1 List 138-164 Ch Hcap good		£45,016
143	11/15	Winc	3m1f Cls1 List 123-149 Ch Hcap soft		£34,170
133	10/15	Chep	2m7¹/₂f Cls2 125-150 Ch Hcap good		£16,245
	10/14	Carl	2m4f Cls4 Nov Ch soft		£4,224
	10/13	Carl	2m4f Cls4 Nov Hdl good		£3,249
	9/13	Uttx	2m4f Cls5 Mdn Hdl good		£2,209

Progressive staying chaser who won at Chepstow and Wincanton (in the Badger Ales Trophy) last season before bouncing back from some moderate efforts in the spring to add the Summer Cup at Uttoxeter; likely to be aimed at the Grand National.

Drumacoo (Ire)

7 b g Oscar - My Native (Be My Native)

Ben Pauling					Mrs Robin Birley
PLACINGS: F202/4111/14-					RPR **155+c**

Starts	1st	2nd	3rd	4th	Win & Pl
8	4	1	1	2	£24,902
	1/16	Hntg	2m7¹/₂f Cls4 Nov Ch soft		£3,834
	11/14	Thur	2m6¹/₂f Nov Hdl soft		£6,900
	10/14	Punc	2m6f Mdn Hdl good		£5,750
	10/14	Dpat	2m2f NHF 4-7yo yield		£4,313

Made a remarkable return from more than a year out when making all and destroying a small field on his chasing debut at Huntingdon last season; hard to assess the form but was sent off favourite for the Reynoldstown next time and surely better than he showed there.

Duke Des Champs (Ire)

6 b g Robin Des Champs - Ballycowan Lady (Accordion)

Philip Hobbs					Diana Whateley & Tim Syder
PLACINGS: 18/212136-					RPR **142+h**

Starts	1st	2nd	3rd	4th	Win & Pl
8	3	2	1	-	£20,598
	1/16	Asct	2m5¹/₂f Cls3 Nov Hdl 4-7yo soft		£6,498
	12/15	MRas	2m2¹/₂f Cls4 Nov Hdl heavy		£3,899
	10/14	Chep	2m Cls5 NHF 4-6yo gd-sft		£1,949

Looked a potential star when winning his second novice hurdle last season by 14 lengths at Ascot; failed to build on that in stronger company,

ON THE FIGURES

Douvan His stable boasts a glut of talented chasers, but this six-year-old is potentially the best of the lot and RPRs in excess of 180 should prove within his compass. *[Steve Mason, Racing Post Ratings]*

though still a fair sixth in a Grade 1 at Aintree; should make a good staying chaser.

Dynaste (Fr)

10 gr g Martalina - Bellissima De Mai (Pistolet Bleu)

David Pipe | A J White

PLACINGS: 1/2512/323/92382749-   RPR **161**c

Starts	1st	2nd	3rd	4th	Win & Pl
31	7	8	4	4	£588,608
	3/14	Chel	2m5f Cls1 Gd1 Ch good	£156,613
	4/13	Aint	3m1f Cls1 Nov Gd2 Ch good	£42,914
	12/12	Kemp	3m Cls1 Nov Gd1 Ch heavy	£22,780
	11/12	Newb	2m4f Cls1 Nov Gd2 Ch gd-sft	£13,732
	11/12	Chel	2m4¹/₂f Cls2 Nov Ch gd-sft	£12,628
141	11/11	Hayd	2m7f Cls1 Gd3 131-151 Hdl Hcap gd-sft	£42,713
130	12/10	Tntn	2m3f Cls2 122-147 Cond Hdl Hcap gd-sft	£12,674

Without a win since the 2014 Ryanair Chase and looked out of sorts early last season but showed more promise following a wind operation; hinted at a future in handicaps when running well for a long way in the bet365 Gold Cup last time.

Eastlake (Ire)

10 b g Beneficial - Guigone (Esprit Du Nord)

Jonjo O'Neill | John P McManus

PLACINGS: /131463/5P32P/P5P91-   RPR **151**+c

Starts	1st	2nd	3rd	4th	Win & Pl
36	11	4	4	2	£200,650
142	4/16	Aint	2m5f Cls1 Gd3 131-157 Ch Hcap soft	£67,356
140	12/13	Chel	2m1¹/₂f Cls2 126-152 Ch Hcap good	£18,768
135	10/13	Aint	2m3f Cls2 122-139 Ch Hcap good	£13,763
132	3/13	NAbb	2m¹/₂f Cls2 124-146 Ch Hcap soft	£15,784
125	2/13	Sand	1m7¹/₂f Cls2 122-149 Ch Hcap heavy	£15,640
118	12/12	Asct	2m1f Cls4 Nov 104 120 Ch Hcap heavy	£6,882
	5/12	Weth	1m7f Cls4 Nov Ch good	£2,599
	5/12	Uttx	2m Cls5 Ch soft	£2,339
	8/11	Hrfd	2m1f Cls4 Nov Hdl gd-fm	£2,014
	4/11	Hrfd	2m1f Cls5 Mdn Hdl good	£1,399
	10/10	Worc	2m Cls6 NHF 4-6yo gd-sft	£1,370

Finally nailed a big handicap when winning last season's Topham having finished third in the race two years earlier and second in the Grand Annual in 2015; has the Becher Chase as an early aim this time.

Eduard (Ire)

8 b g Morozov - Dinny Kenn (Phardante)

Nicky Richards | Eddie Melville

PLACINGS: 1/213124/2111/224/   RPR **165**c

Starts	1st	2nd	3rd	4th	Win & Pl
14	6	5	1	2	£94,116
	4/14	Ayr	2m4f Cls1 Nov Gd2 Ch gd-sft	£26,748
	3/14	Ayr	1m7¹/₂f Cls4 Nov Ch heavy	£4,549
	12/13	Carl	2m Cls3 Nov Ch gd-sft	£7,148
	2/13	Carl	2m1f Cls4 Nov Hdl soft	£3,119
	11/12	Newc	2m1¹/₂f Cls4 Nov Hdl gd-sft	£2,859
	3/12	Kels	2m Cls6 NHF 4-6yo good	£1,300

Looked a very smart prospect three seasons ago when winning three out of four novice chases but just came up short in top company the following campaign; out through injury since finishing fourth in the 2015 Ryanair Chase.

Emerging Force (Ire)

6 b g Milan - Danette (Exit To Nowhere)

Harry Whittington | Webb Holt Carpenter Tucker

PLACINGS: 63/3131U-P   RPR **148**h

Starts	1st	2nd	3rd	4th	Win & Pl
5	2	-	1	-	£13,568
128	2/16	Donc	3m1¹/₂f Cls3 105-130 Hdl Hcap gd-sft	£9,747
	11/15	Font	2m3f Cls4 Mdn Hdl soft	£3,249

Much improved when stepped up to 3m last season, winning at Doncaster and set to follow up in a valuable staying hurdle final at Haydock when unseating his rider at the last; disappointed next time at Punchestown but should resume progress over fences.

Emerging Talent (Ire)

7 b g Golan - Elviria (Insan)

Paul Nicholls | Mr & Mrs Paul Barber

PLACINGS: 1/221 2/41211-   RPR **140**+h

Starts	1st	2nd	3rd	4th	Win & Pl
10	4	4		1	£30,658
	4/16	Winc	2m4f Cls4 Nov Hdl gd-sft	£3,574
	4/16	Tntn	2m3f Cls4 Nov Hdl good	£4,544
	1/16	Extr	2m1f Cls5 Mdn Hdl heavy	£2,599
	3/14	Naas	2m NHF 4 6yo yld-sft	£4,600

Benefited from a drop in grade last season following fourth at odds-on in Persian War Novices' Hurdle (fourth time beaten as favourite in first five runs over hurdles), winning three times albeit all at odds-on again; likely to go novice chasing.

Empire Of Dirt (Ire)

9 b g Westerner - Rose Of Inchiquin (Roselier)

Colm Murphy (Ir) | Gigginstown House Stud

PLACINGS: 02415/4F32F1F/F2P11-   RPR **154**+c

Starts	1st	2nd	3rd	4th	Win & Pl
21	5	4	1	2	£156,488
142	3/16	Chel	2m5f Cls1 Gd3 135-157 Ch Hcap good	£56,950
133	1/16	Leop	2m5f Cls3 153 Ch Hcap soft	£44,118
125	2/15	Naas	2m4f Nov 119-134 Ch Hcap sft-hvy	£25,194
	3/14	Naas	2m Nov List Hdl yld-sft	£13,542
	10/13	Punc	2m Mdn Hdl yld-sft	£5,610

Progress over fences hampered by jumping problems (fell in four of first eight chases) but got his act together last season and soon made up for lost time, winning the Brown Advisory & Merriebelle Stable Plate at Cheltenham; open to further improvement.

'Looked a potential star in a novice hurdle last season and should make a good staying chaser'

Fagan

6 ro g Fair Mix - Northwood May (Teenoso)

Gordon Elliott (Ir) — R A Bartlett

PLACINGS: U/234111/111224- — RPR **147h**

Starts	1st	2nd	3rd	4th	Win & Pl
7	3	2	1	1	£38,688

12/15	Muss	1m7¹/₂f Cls4 Nov Hdl 4-6yo soft	£3,899
10/15	Ayr	2m Cls6 NHF 4-6yo good	£1,711
9/15	Prth	2m Cls6 NHF 4-6yo gd-sft	£2,053

Very lightly raced under rules and ran a huge race on only his third run over hurdles when second in the Albert Bartlett at Cheltenham; won three point-to-points in the spring of 2015 and looks a fine prospect for staying novice chases.

Faugheen (Ire)

8 b g Germany - Miss Pickering (Accordion)

Willie Mullins (Ir) — Mrs S Ricci

PLACINGS: 1/11111/1111/1211- — RPR **177+h**

Starts	1st	2nd	3rd	4th	Win & Pl
13	12	1	-	-	£695,657

1/16	Leop	2m Gd1 Hdl soft	£48,529
12/15	Kemp	2m Cls1 Gd1 Hdl gd-sft	£56,950
5/15	Punc	2m Gd1 Hdl gd-yld	£93,023
3/15	Chel	2m¹/₂f Cls1 Gd1 Hdl gd-sft	£227,800
12/14	Kemp	2m Cls1 Gd1 Hdl gd-sft	£57,218
11/14	Asct	2m3¹/₂f Cls1 Hdl soft	£50,643
4/14	Punc	2m Nov Gd1 Hdl gd-yld	£46,500
3/14	Chel	2m5f Cls1 Nov Gd1 Hdl good	£68,340
12/13	Limk	3m Nov Gd3 Hdl heavy	£15,061
12/13	Navn	2m4f Nov Hdl gd-yld	£7,293
11/13	Punc	2m6f Mdn Hdl yield	£7,293
5/13	Punc	2m NHF 5yo yield	£4,488

Brilliant winner of the 2015 Champion Hurdle and robbed of the chance to defend his title by injury last spring; had looked as good as ever when running away with the Irish Champion Hurdle; likely to go over fences at some point but expected to stay hurdling for now and should again be tough to beat in all the top 2m contests.

Felix Yonger (Ire)

10 b g Oscar - Marble Sound (Be My Native)

Willie Mullins (Ir) — Andrea & Graham Wylie

PLACINGS: /111224/42111/1311P- — RPR **165c**

Starts	1st	2nd	3rd	4th	Win & Pl
24	12	6	1	2	£323,391

1/16	Punc	2m Gd2 Ch sft-hvy	£18,750
12/15	Navn	2m1f Gd2 Ch heavy	£23,934
4/15	Punc	2m Gd1 Ch gd-yld	£93,023
3/15	Navn	2m4f Gd2 Ch heavy	£20,155
2/15	Leop	2m2f Hdl soft	£10,078
12/14	Cork	2m Gd2 Ch heavy	£24,375
12/13	Navn	2m1f Nov Ch gd-yld	£10,569
11/13	Punc	2m Nov Gd2 Ch yield	£20,874
5/13	Punc	2m4f Ch yield	£6,732
2/12	Naas	2m Nov Gd2 Hdl soft	£22,479
12/11	Dpat	2m2f Mdn Hdl 4-5yo sft-hvy	£6,841
1/11	Muss	1m7¹/₂f Cls6 NHF 4-6yo good	£1,626

Prolific chaser who has won six of his nine races since his novice campaign, including a Grade 1 at Punchestown in 2015 and two Grade 2 contests last season (all from 2m to 2m1f); still has it to

prove against the very best and pulled up in the Champion Chase.

Fethard Player (Ire)

9 b g King's Theatre - Sly Empress (Supreme Leader)

William Treacy (Ir) — W F Treacy

PLACINGS: /3521U4396122d/8212-4 — RPR **155+h**

Starts	1st	2nd	3rd	4th	Win & Pl
26	4	4	4	2	£87,537

137	10/15	DRoy	2m 109-137 Hdl Hcap yld-sft	£20,155
121	10/14	Tipp	2m 106-130 Hdl Hcap gd-yld	£9,056
110	6/14	Baln	2m4f 102-120 Hdl Hcap good	£8,913
	2/14	Thur	2m6f Mdn Hdl heavy	£4,600

Very lightly raced over the last couple of years and ran a stormer on his return from a winter break when second in the County Hurdle at Cheltenham; did well when fourth behind Vroum Vroum Mag at Punchestown, though still has a bit to find at that level.

Fine Rightly (Ire)

8 b g Alflora - Bealtaine (Zaffaran)

Stuart Crawford (Ir) — Miss Patricia Duffin

PLACINGS: 3/11215/2211/014311- — RPR **150+c**

Starts	1st	2nd	3rd	4th	Win & Pl
18	9	4	2	1	£101,903

	3/16	Cork	2m Gd3 Ch heavy	£14,697
	3/16	DRoy	3m2f Ch soft	£7,914
140	12/15	Navn	2m4f 121-140 Ch Hcap heavy	£15,116
	3/15	Naas	2m4f Nov Gd3 Ch soft	£15,116
132	1/15	Ayr	2m4¹/₂f Cls3 Nov 124-132 Ch Hcap heavy	£6,498
	2/14	Weth	2m4f Cls4 Nov Hdl heavy	£3,119
	1/14	Ayr	2m Cls4 Nov Hdl 4-7yo heavy	£3,899
	12/13	Navn	2m Gd2 NHF 4-7yo yld-sft	£14,533
	1/13	Ayr	2m Cls6 NHF 4-6yo heavy	£1,643

Has gone from strength to strength in winning five of his last seven races over fences, only defeats coming when a close fourth in a big handicap and third in the Irish Gold Cup; could be competitive at Grade 1 level on soft ground if he keeps progressing.

Firebird Flyer (Ire)

9 b g Winged Love - Kiora Lady (King's Ride)

Evan Williams — R E R Williams

PLACINGS: 04213/3F141U47/P321- — RPR **144c**

Starts	1st	2nd	3rd	4th	Win & Pl
37	8	5	4	7	£172,102

138	3/16	Uttx	4m1¹/₂f Cls1 List 129-145 Ch Hcap soft	£73,757
131	1/15	Ludl	3m Cls3 112-134 Am Ch Hcap soft	£9,982
125	11/14	Ffos	2m6f Cls3 120-125 Hdl Hcap heavy	£5,525
121	2/14	Ludl	3m Cls3 121-135 Ch Hcap soft	£12,660
119	3/13	Ffos	3m Cls4 99-119 Ch Hcap soft	£3,769
119	12/12	Ffos	3m Cls4 96-119 Hdl Hcap heavy	£3,249
117	11/12	Ludl	3m Cls4 94-120 Ch Hcap good	£6,330
	1/12	Tram	2m5f Mdn Hdl heavy	£4,744

Thorough stayer who took his form to a new level last season, finishing second in the Welsh National to Mountainous before winning the Midlands National at Uttoxeter (took advantage of final-fence fall); raised just 3lb so still on a feasible mark.

Fixe Le Kap (Fr)

4 gr g Kapgarde - Lady Fix (Turgeon)

Nicky Henderson | Simon Munir & Isaac Souede

PLACINGS: 52/41128- RPR **142+h**

Starts	1st	2nd	3rd	4th	Win & Pl
7	2	1	-	1	£29,130
	1/16	Wwck	2m Cls4 Hdl 4yo soft		£3,899
	12/15	Newb	2m¹/₂f Cls3 Hdl 3yo soft		£6,498

Very impressive winner of first two starts for current connections last season (both on soft ground) but proved disappointing after when beaten at 1-4 at Haydock and only eighth in the Fred Winter; may appreciate stepping up in trip.

Fletchers Flyer (Ire)

8 b g Winged Love - Crystal Chord (Accordion)

Harry Fry | Masterson Holdings Limited

PLACINGS: 1/2/13112/P232-1 RPR **154+c**

Starts	1st	2nd	3rd	4th	Win & Pl
11	4	4	2	-	£48,232
138	4/16	Punc	3m6f 116-144 Ch Hcap gd-yld		£13,566
	1/15	Winc	2m5¹/₂f Cls4 Nov Hdl heavy		£3,249
	11/14	Asct	2m5¹/₂f Cls2 Nov Hdl soft		£12,558
	4/14	Punc	2m2f NHF 5-7yo gd-yld		£5,750

Slightly disappointing when initially sent chasing last season but came good in terrific fashion when winning a handicap at Punchestown at the end of April; retains his novice status in Britain and could be one for top staying handicaps by the spring.

Flying Angel (Ire)

5 gr g Arcadio - Gypsy Kelly (Roselier)

Nigel Twiston-Davies | R J Rexton

PLACINGS: 12353123- RPR **145+h**

Starts	1st	2nd	3rd	4th	Win & Pl
8	2	2	3		£81,417
133	3/16	Sand	2m Cls1 Gd3 123-149 Hdl Hcap soft		£39,865
	10/15	Worc	2m4f Cls4 Nov Hdl good		£3,249

Progressed throughout last season and flourished in the spring, winning the Imperial Cup and finishing second in the Martin Pipe Hurdle under a 5lb penalty; just came up short in a soft Grade 1 at Aintree but could make a smart chaser.

Footpad (Fr)

4 b g Creachadoir - Willamina (Sadler's Wells)

Willie Mullins (Ir) | Simon Munir & Isaac Souede

PLACINGS: 7213113F-11 RPR **145h**

Starts	1st	2nd	3rd	4th	Win & Pl
10	5	2	2	-	£212,073
	6/16	Autl	2m3¹/₂f Gd1 Hdl 4yo soft		£89,338
	5/16	Autl	2m3¹/₂f Gd3 Hdl 4yo v soft		£44,669
	2/16	Leop	2m Gd1 Hdl 4yo sft-hvy		£36,875
	1/16	Gowr	2m Hdl 4yo heavy		£10,037
	11/15	Gowr	2m Mdn Hdl 3yo soft		£6,419

Has won Grade 1 four-year-old hurdles at Leopardstown and Auteuil, relishing a stamina test both times having looked short of pace in stronger company at Cheltenham and Aintree; should get further and could be a smart staying hurdler.

Fox Norton (Fr)

6 b g Lando - Natt Musik (Kendor)

Neil Mulholland | B Dunn

PLACINGS: 1/4216/381/11233331- RPR **152c**

Starts	1st	2nd	3rd	4th	Win & Pl
16	6	2	5	1	£117,132
	4/16	Chel	2m¹/₂f Cls2 Nov Ch good		£12,512
	10/15	MRas	2m1f Cls3 Nov Ch good		£7,798
	5/15	Hntg	2m¹/₂f Cls4 Nov Ch good		£3,769
140	2/15	Tntn	2m¹/₂f Cls2 129-145 Hdl Hcap soft		£11,078
	12/13	Donc	2m¹/₂f Cls1 Gd2 Hdl 3yo good		£15,876
	4/13	Fntb	2m Hdl 3yo soft		£8,585

Very highly tried in top novice chases last season and won all three runs below Grade 2 level; showed his best form at Cheltenham (second to Garde La Victoire and third to Douvan in the Arkle before signing off with a win) and could be interesting in good 2m handicaps there.

Foxrock (Ire)

8 b g Flemensfirth - Midnight Light (Roselier)

Ted Walsh (Ir) | Barry Connell

PLACINGS: 13119/532120/86343-5 RPR **162c**

Starts	1st	2nd	3rd	4th	Win & Pl
22	5	4	5	1	£185,300
149	1/15	Leop	2m5f 123-151 Ch Hcap soft		£46,512
	2/14	Navn	3m Nov Gd2 Ch soft		£20,313
	1/14	Naas	3m Nov Gd2 Ch sft-hvy		£21,667
	11/13	Fair	2m7¹/₂f Ch gd-yld		£6,732
	3/13	Naas	3m Mdn Hdl soft		£5,610

Sharply progressive two seasons ago and went close to winning the Irish Gold Cup; failed to kick on last term, though he wasn't beaten far in the Lexus; connections could try to exploit falling handicap mark and have considered cross-country chases.

Free Expression (Ire)

7 b g Germany - Create A Storm (Bob Back)

Gordon Elliott (Ir) | John P McManus

PLACINGS: 11/113/233- RPR **146+c**

Starts	1st	2nd	3rd	4th	Win & Pl
7	3	1	3	-	£66,908
	11/14	Navn	2m4f Nov Gd2 Hdl soft		£20,313
	11/14	Naas	2m Mdn Hdl soft		£5,750
	4/14	Fair	2m2f NHF 4-6yo gd-yld		£24,792

Failed to win in three runs over fences last season but ran to a good level of form when placed behind No More Heroes and Outlander; expected to do better on quicker ground and certainly capable of winning good novice chases.

Frodon (Fr)
4 b g Nickname - Miss Country (Country Reel)

Paul Nicholls   Ian Fogg & Potensis Bloodstock Ltd

PLACINGS: 1/3F543185-					RPR **136**h
Starts	1st	2nd	3rd	4th	Win & Pl
9	2	-	2	1	£61,537
2/16	Hayd	1m7¹/₂f Cls2 Hdl 4yo heavy			£9,747
4/15	Autl	1m7f Hdl 3yo heavy			£20,465

Tough juvenile hurdler last season, running well in a couple of open handicaps as well as winning at Haydock on heavy ground and finishing eighth in the Triumph Hurdle on good; should improve as he steps up in trip.

Gala Ball (Ire)
6 b g Flemensfirth - Nuit Des Chartreux (Villez)

Philip Hobbs   Robert & Janet Gibbs

PLACINGS: 5323/F621112-					RPR **146**+h
Starts	1st	2nd	3rd	4th	Win & Pl
11	3	3	2		£25,378
133	3/16	Newb	2m1¹/₂f Cls3 119-140 Hdl Hcap soft		£12,512
2/16	Winc	1m7¹/₂f Cls4 Nov Hdl soft			£3,899
1/16	Winc	1m7¹/₂f Cls4 Nov Hdl soft			£3,249

Progressed rapidly over hurdles last season, winning two novice races at Wincanton before completing a hat-trick on handicap debut at Newbury (all on soft ground); possibly unsuited by quicker conditions when second off 10lb higher in April.

Gallant Oscar (Ire)
10 b g Oscar - Park Wave (Supreme Leader)

Tony Martin (Ir)   John P McManus

PLACINGS: 1F/411U/12243/1U75U-					RPR **146**c
Starts	1st	2nd	3rd	4th	Win & Pl
23	5	2	1	4	£88,552
135	5/15	Punc	3m1f 122-150 Ch Hcap soft		£25,194
104	11/14	Navn	2m7f 80-107 Ch Hcap yld-sft		£5,750
119	3/14	Naas	3m 114-142 Ch Hcap soft		£27,083
93	1/14	Navn	2m4f 80-109 Ch Hcap soft		£5,750
3/13	Clon	2m4f Ch soft			£4,488

Laid out for the Grand National last season and was going notably well at Aintree when unseating his rider, albeit early on the second circuit; had run away with a good handicap at Punchestown in May 2015 and capable of winning more races, perhaps even the National.

Gangster (Fr)
6 ch g Green Tune - Dahlia's Krissy (Kris S)

Willie Mullins (Ir)   Gigginstown House Stud

PLACINGS: 42/15117P-5					RPR **147**+h
Starts	1st	2nd	3rd	4th	Win & Pl
9	3	1		1	£44,882
12/15	Fair	3m Nov Gd3 Hdl heavy			£16,376
9/15	List	2m Nov Hdl yld-sft			£10,078
6/15	Rosc	2m4¹/₂f Mdn Hdl good			£5,616

Disappointing towards end of last season but

had shown abundant promise when winning three of his first four novice hurdles and running well for a long way in the Albert Bartlett before fading to seventh; may well bounce back.

Garde La Victoire (Fr)
7 b g Kapgarde - Next Victory (Akarad)

Philip Hobbs   Mrs Diana L Whateley

PLACINGS: 1124011/31541/111FF-					RPR **157**+c
Starts	1st	2nd	3rd	4th	Win & Pl
18	10	1	1	2	£138,103
1/16	Ludl	2m Cls3 Nov Ch heavy			£6,657
11/15	Chel	2m Cls1 Nov Gd2 Ch gd-sft			£18,224
10/15	Uttx	2m Cls4 Ch soft			£3,833
1/15	Sand	2m Cls1 List Hdl soft			£14,238
144	11/14	Chel	2m¹/₂f Cls3 121-147 Hdl Hcap soft		£56,950
4/14	Chel	2m4¹/₂f Cls2 Nov Hdl good			£10,010
4/14	Tntn	2m3f Cls4 Nov Hdl good			£4,106
11/13	Wwck	2m Cls4 Nov Hdl gd-sft			£3,899
10/13	Aint	2m¹/₂f Cls4 Mdn Hdl gd-sft			£4,549
10/12	Extr	1m5f Cls6 NHF 3yo gd-sft			£1,365

Let down by his jumping last spring, falling four out at Cheltenham and Aintree when still in contention; had won three out of three over fences prior to that, stepping up on some solid hurdles form; could be a smart handicapper if jumping improves.

Gilgamboa (Ire)
8 b g Westerner - Hi Native (Be My Native)

Enda Bolger (Ir)   John P McManus

PLACINGS: 13110/11321/34554-					RPR **165**c
Starts	1st	2nd	3rd	4th	Win & Pl
15	6	1	3	2	£226,774
4/15	Fair	2m4f Nov Gd1 Ch soft			£46,512
12/14	Limk	2m3¹/₂f Nov Gd2 Ch sft-hvy			£21,125
11/14	Navn	2m Ch yld-sft			£8,625
128	1/14	Leop	2m 115-142 Hdl Hcap soft		£50,000
120	12/13	Punc	2m4f 106-128 Hdl Hcap heavy		£8,134
10/13	Gway	2m Mdn Hdl 5yo heavy			£6,171

Ran a remarkable race for a dubious stayer in the Grand National, finishing fourth when the only horse carrying more than 11st in the first 15; previous best had been a fine fifth in the Ryanair over 2m5f and should have lots more to come over at least 3m.

God's Own (Ire)
8 b g Oscar - Dantes Term (Phardante)

Tom George   Crossed Fingers Partnership

PLACINGS: 10242/117322F/3241-1					RPR **170**+c
Starts	1st	2nd	3rd	4th	Win & Pl
23	7	6	4	2	£412,344
4/16	Punc	2m Gd1 Ch gd-yld			£86,765
4/16	Aint	2m4f Cls1 Gd1 Ch gd-sft			£112,788
155	11/14	Extr	2m1¹/₂f Cls1 Gd2 152-172 Ch Hcap gd-sft		£35,594
5/14	Punc	2m Nov Gd1 Ch yield			£56,833
129	11/13	Kemp	2m5f Cls2 129-155 Hdl Hcap gd-sft		£11,574
2/13	Muss	2m3¹/₂f Cls4 Nov Hdl good			£3,899
11/12	Donc	2m1¹/₂f Cls4 Nov Hdl soft			£3,899

Did exceptionally well to win two Grade 1 races last spring, capitalising on Vautour's fall to win the Melling Chase and then following up at Punchestown; may still come up short against the very best but clearly not to be underrated on preferred good ground.

Goonyella (Ire)

9 br g Presenting - Miss Fresher (Pampabird)

Jim Dreaper (Ir) **Ann & Alan Potts Partnership**

PLACINGS: /25827/2U7312/39425- **RPR 152c**

Starts		1st	2nd	3rd	4th	Win & Pl
22		3	5	2	1	£180,406
136	3/15	Uttx	4m1½f Cls1 List 127-147 Ch Hcap soft			£56,950
127	4/13	Punc	3m6f 116-144 Ch Hcap heavy			£13,211
	12/12	Limk	2m6f Mdn Hunt Ch heavy			£4,888

Has run some fine races in top staying handicaps in recent seasons, winning the Midlands National in 2015 and since finishing second in the Scottish and Leinster Nationals; yet to show his best in three runs at Aintree, though he plugged on for fifth in the Grand National in April.

Great Field (Fr)

5 h g Great Pretender - Eaton Lass (Definite Article)

Willie Mullins (Ir) **John P McManus**

PLACINGS: 2/11/1P- **RPR 148+h**

Starts		1st	2nd	3rd	4th	Win & Pl
5		3	1	-	-	£29,896
	2/16	Leop	2m2½f Hdl soft			£9,496
	11/16	Pari	2m1f Hdl 3yo gd-sft			£8,400
	9/14	Pari	2m1f Hdl 3yo gd-sft			£8,000

Dual winner in France who also made a successful debut for new connections last season at Leopardstown despite racing keenly; again pulled hard when failing to get home in the County Hurdle; clearly has a big engine if learning to settle better.

Grey Gold (Ire)

11 gr g Strategic Choice - Grouse-N-Heather (Grey Desire)

Kerry Lee **Mrs M A Boden**

PLACINGS: /33212/15524/P1P236- **RPR 155c**

Starts		1st	2nd	3rd	4th	Win & Pl
28		7	4	4	6	£123,041
147	11/15	Newb	2m1½f Cls2 121-147 Ch Hcap soft			£21,896
148	10/14	Chep	2m Cls2 132-152 Ch Hcap soft			£25,320
138	2/14	Sand	1m7½f Cls2 135-148 Ch Hcap heavy			£15,640
	4/13	Punc	2m2f Nov Ch heavy			£9,817
	3/13	Carl	2m Cls3 Nov Ch heavy			£7,148
124	11/11	Bang	2m½f Cls3 116-130 Hdl Hcap gd-sft			£5,697
	1/11	Hrfd	2m1f Cls4 Nov Hdl heavy			£2,017

As good as ever last season despite advancing years and showed plenty of courage to battle to victory at Newbury in November; good second two starts later at Chepstow and could benefit from handicapper's leniency with older horses; loves soft ground.

Gwafa (Ire)

5 gr g Tamayuz - Atalina (Linamix)

Paul Webber **Saleh Al Homaizi & Imad Al Sagar**

PLACINGS: 611U-13 **RPR 145h**

Starts		1st	2nd	3rd	4th	Win & Pl
6		3	-	1	-	£46,362
137	5/16	Hayd	1m7½f Cls1 Gd3 132-149 Hdl Hcap good			£34,170
	2/16	Hntg	2m Cls4 Nov Hdl gd-sft			£3,249
	1/16	Fknm	2m Cls4 Mdn Hdl soft			£5,198

Has flourished in 2016, winning two novice hurdles before adding the Swinton in May and running another big race when third under top-weight in the Summer Hurdle; versatile regarding ground and should continue to be a force in top handicap hurdles.

That winning feeling: the God's Own team after victory at Punchestown

Gwencily Berbas (Fr)

5 b g Nickname - Lesorial (Lesotho)

Alan Fleming (Ir)				Barry Connell
PLACINGS: R3119/136-				RPR **147**h

Starts	1st	2nd	3rd	4th	Win & Pl
8	3	-	2	-	£68,710

	11/15	Naas	2m Gd3 Hdl 4yo soft	£16,376
	2/15	Fair	2m Gd2 Hdl 4yo soft	£21,163
	10/14	Autl	2m1¹/₂f Hdl 3yo heavy	£19,200

Has run just five times since moving to Ireland from France but looked a potential star when running away with a Grade 3 at Fairyhouse last season and ran well when third in the Hatton's Grace; always marking time before going chasing this term.

Hargam (Fr)

5 gr g Sinndar - Horasana (Galileo)

Nicky Henderson				John P McManus
PLACINGS: 21136/4330-				RPR **159**h

Starts	1st	2nd	3rd	4th	Win & Pl
9	2	1	3	1	£73,557

	2/15	Muss	1m7¹/₂f Cls1 List Hdl 4yo good	£14,238
	12/14	Chel	2m1f Cls2 Hdl 3yo gd-sft	£12,512

Without a win in more than 18 months but has proved himself a smart 2m hurdler in that time, finishing third in the Triumph Hurdle in 2015 and the International and Christmas Hurdles last season; capable of winning good races, especially on preferred good ground.

Harry Topper

9 b g Sir Harry Lewis - Indeed To Goodness (Welsh Term)

Kim Bailey				A N Solomons
PLACINGS: 1127/111UB/1331P/P5/				RPR **170**c

Starts	1st	2nd	3rd	4th	Win & Pl
18	8	1	2	-	£143,065

	2/14	Newb	2m7¹/₂f Cls1 Gd2 Ch heavy	£28,810
	11/13	Weth	3m1f Cls1 Gd2 Ch gd-sft	£57,218
	2/13	Extr	3m Cls2 Ch heavy	£12,512
	11/12	Newb	2m7¹/₂f Cls1 Nov Gd2 Ch soft	£13,732
	10/12	Extr	3m Cls4 Ch soft	£3,899
	1/12	Winc	2m5¹/₂f Cls4 Nov Hdl soft	£3,249
	12/11	Uttx	2m4f Cls5 Mdn Hdl soft	£1,689
	4/11	Hrfd	2m1f Cls6 NHF 4-6yo good	£1,431

Three-time Grade 2 winner over fences, most impressively when winning the 2014 Denman Chase on heavy ground, though he also won the Charlie Hall that season on good to soft; missed last season through injury.

Hell's Kitchen

5 b g Robin Des Champs - Mille Et Une (Trempolino)

Harry Fry				John P McManus
PLACINGS: 312-				RPR **139+**h

Starts	1st	2nd	3rd	4th	Win & Pl
3	1	1	1	-	£6,742

	3/16	Newb	2m4¹/₂f Cls4 Nov Hdl soft	£4,549

Made a big impression when stepped up in trip and winning easily at Newbury in March; not in the same form when beaten at 1-3 next time having jumped poorly; big, imposing type who remains a fine prospect for novice chasing.

Henri Parry Morgan

8 b g Brian Boru - Queen Of Thedaises (Over The River)

Peter Bowen				Ednyfed & Elizabeth Morgan
PLACINGS: /352P56/321464U112U-				RPR **160**c

Starts	1st	2nd	3rd	4th	Win & Pl
23	5	4	2	2	£62,082

135	3/16	Uttx	3m Cls2 Nov 120-139 Ch Hcap soft	£18,838
122	2/16	Chep	2m7¹/₂f Cls3 Nov 107-123 Ch Hcap soft	£6,498
118	6/15	Sthl	3m Cls3 114-140 Hdl Hcap good	£5,523
	5/13	Uttx	3m Cls5 Mdn Hdl gd-fm	£2,209
	8/12	Worc	2m Cls6 NHF 4-6yo good	£1,437

Rapidly progressive over fences last season, showing little prior to wide-margin wins at Chepstow and Uttoxeter and a Grade 1 second behind Native River at Aintree; much better than he showed when a disappointing favourite in the bet365 Gold Cup.

Henryville

8 b g Generous - Aquavita (Kalaglow)

Harry Fry				R P B Michaelson & E M Thornton
PLACINGS: 1227/2112445/121-48B				RPR **150+**c

Starts	1st	2nd	3rd	4th	Win & Pl
23	6	7	1	3	£84,173

	3/16	Extr	2m3f Cls3 Nov Ch good	£6,498
	10/15	Font	2m5f Cls4 Nov Ch good	£6,725
138	10/14	Font	2m3f Cls2 119-138 Hdl Hcap good	£9,812
130	8/14	NAbb	2m5¹/₂f Cls2 121-147 Hdl Hcap good	£22,378
118	3/14	Font	2m3f Cls4 101-120 Hdl Hcap gd-sft	£3,119
	3/13	Plum	2m4¹/₂f Cls4 Nov Hdl gd-sft	£4,874

Progressed into a very smart staying hurdler (fourth off 152 in 2015 Pertemps Final) but has just fallen short of that level over fences; has a lower chase mark, though, and would have gone close in the Summer Plate but for being brought down at the last.

IT'S YOUR PAPER WITHOUT THE PAPER

RACING POST

IF YOU'RE ON HOLIDAY OR JUST TOO BUSY TO GET TO YOUR NEWSAGENT, THE RACING POST DIGITAL NEWSPAPER IS AT HAND

View every page on your computer, tablet or smartphone, with rather clever features including language translation, downloadable editions and bookmarking. It'll even read articles OUT LOUD.

Buy single editions (from £2.10/€2.60) or save with a discounted subscription.

RACING POST.com/digitalnewspaper

Highland Lodge (Ire)

10 b g Flemensfirth - Supreme Von Pres (Presenting)

James Moffatt   **Bowes Lodge Stables**

PLACINGS: **1356/24P68/584/721P-**   RPR **140+c**

Starts	1st	2nd	3rd	4th	Win & Pl
21	5	2	2	3	£126,983

132	12/15	Aint	3m2f Cls1 Gd3 132-158 Ch Hcap soft	£78,598
	12/12	Chel	3m1½f Cls2 Nov Ch heavy	£12,512
	11/12	Towc	3m½f Cls3 Ch gd-sft	£5,507
	12/11	Hayd	2m3f Cls4 Nov Hdl heavy	£4,874
	11/11	Extr	2m5½f Cls4 Nov Hdl gd-sft	£2,274

Formerly smart novice chaser who finally exploited a falling handicap mark when winning last season's Becher Chase despite being 7lb out of the weights; balloted out of the Grand National and remains interesting over the big fences.

Holywell (Ire)

9 b g Gold Well - Hillcrest (Thatching)

Jonjo O'Neill   **Mrs Gay Smith**

PLACINGS: **32U1111/3U143/54P2F-**   RPR **164+c**

Starts	1st	2nd	3rd	4th	Win & Pl
26	7	7	4	3	£311,565

145	2/15	Kels	3m2f Cls2 Ch gd-sft	£12,512
	4/14	Aint	3m1f Cls1 Nov Gd1 Ch good	£50,643
	3/14	Chel	3m½f Cls1 Gd3 129-151 Ch Hcap gd-sft	£51,255
	2/14	Donc	3m Cls4 Nov Ch gd-sft	£3,769
	1/14	Catt	2m3f Cls4 Ch soft	£4,660
140	3/13	Chel	3m Cls1 List 135-148 Hdl Hcap gd-sft	£45,560
	2/12	Chep	2m3½f Cls4 Mdn Hdl soft	£2,274

Well below the form he had shown when fourth in the 2015 Gold Cup for much of last season but bounced back with a fine second in the 3m handicap chase at Cheltenham in March; not the

first time he had run badly over the winter but will remain a threat come the spring.

Houblon Des Obeaux (Fr)

9 b g Panoramic - Harkosa (Nikos)

Venetia Williams   **Mrs Julian Blackwell**

PLACINGS: **14396U/2220F/99841P-**   RPR **164+c**

Starts	1st	2nd	3rd	4th	Win & Pl
45	8	8	5	5	£297,684

	2/16	Newb	2m7½f Cls1 Gd2 Ch soft	£28,978
152	12/13	Asct	3m Cls1 List 132-152 Ch Hcap soft	£24,525
144	11/13	Asct	3m Cls1 Gd3 133-153 Ch Hcap gd-sft	£56,270
	11/12	Winc	2m5f Cls1 Nov Gd2 Ch gd-sft	£14,238
	10/12	Worc	2m7f Cls4 Nov Ch gd-sft	£3,054
135	1/12	Chel	3m Cls2 134-160 Hdl Hcap gd-sft	£12,512
	2/11	Hayd	2m Cls2 Hdl 4yo heavy	£6,895
	5/10	Seno	1m7f Hdl 3yo good	£5,522

Has run many fine races in top staying handicaps but struggled off high marks after second in 2014 Hennessy Gold Cup, with only win last season in a soft Grade 2 at Newbury; back on a feasible mark now (just 1lb higher than 2013 Silver Cup win).

Ibis Du Rheu (Fr)

5 b g Blue Bresil - Dona Du Rheu (Dom Pasquini)

Paul Nicholls   **J Hales**

PLACINGS: **21/64/23518-**   RPR **146h**

Starts	1st	2nd	3rd	4th	Win & Pl
9	2	2	1	1	£74,759

139	3/16	Chel	2m4½f Cls2 135-142 Cond Hdl Hcap good	£37,536
	4/14	Engh	2m1½f Hdl 3yo v soft	£19,200

Won last season's Martin Pipe Hurdle at Cheltenham having long looked a likely type

Houblon Des Obeaux: could be well treated

for a big handicap (given too much to do in the Lanzarote and failed to stay 2m6f on soft ground at Sandown); should make a good novice chaser.

Identity Thief (Ire)

6 b g Kayf Tara - Miss Arteea (Flemensfirth)

Henry de Bromhead (Ir) **Gigginstown House Stud**

PLACINGS: 11P2/31126-2 RPR **164**h

Starts	1st	2nd	3rd	4th	Win & Pl
10	4	3	1	-	£154,107

11/15	Newc	2m¹/₂f Cls1 Gd1 Hdl soft	£63,585
10/15	DRoy	2m Gd2 Hdl yld-sft	£23,256
12/14	Leop	2m4f Mdn Hdl 4yo soft	£6,325
11/14	Fair	2m NHF 4yo yield	£4,600

Much-improved hurdler last season, winning the Fighting Fifth Hurdle and continuing to run well at the top level with seconds behind Nichols

Canyon and Vroum Vroum Mag; may well progress again and has the size to jump fences.

If In Doubt (Ire)

8 b g Heron Island - Catchers Day (Catcher In The Rye)

Philip Hobbs **John P McManus**

PLACINGS: 3/1229/U2115P/P132-5 RPR **155+**h

Starts	1st	2nd	3rd	4th	Win & Pl
20	5	6	2	-	£114,304

140	12/15	Winc	2m5¹/₂f Cls2 123-146 Hdl Hcap soft	£11,574
139	1/15	Donc	3m Cls1 List 129-154 Ch Hcap gd-sft	£42,713
	12/14	Catt	3m1f Cls3 Ch gd-sft	£7,988
124	11/13	Towc	2m3f Cls3 102-124 Hdl Hcap gd-sft	£5,254
	1/13	Towc	2m Cls4 Nov Hdl heavy	£3,119

Desperately unlucky not to win the Pertemps Final at Cheltenham (repeatedly blocked in the straight) and came close to making amends when

If In Doubt: unlucky in last season's Pertemps but could make amends

second at Aintree; may well have a big staying handicap in him over hurdles or back over fences (former Sky Bet Chase winner).

Irish Cavalier (Ire)

7 rg g Aussie Rules - Tracker (Bustino)

Rebecca Curtis   **A McIver**

PLACINGS: 417/3231F/42155P5F-1   RPR **164+c**

Starts 21	1st 7	2nd 2	3rd 2	4th 2	Win & Pl £159,791
153	4/16	Punc	2m4f 125-153 Ch Hcap gd-yld		£43,382
	10/15	NAbb	2m5f Cls2 Ch gd-sft		£18,838
137	3/15	Chel	2m4¹/₂f Cls1 Nov List 134-140 Ch Hcap gd-sft		£34,170
	3/14	Bang	2m¹/₂f Cls4 Nov Hdl gd-sft		£3,249
	11/13	Bang	2m¹/₂f Cls4 Nov Hdl soft		£3,249
	10/13	Strf	2m¹/₂f Cls3 Nov Hdl 4-6yo soft		£6,330
	5/13	Worc	2m Cls6 NHF 4-6yo good		£1,560

Inconsistent during a busy campaign last season but signed off with an excellent win in a handicap at Punchestown in April, belatedly fulfilling promise of his fifth in the Paddy Power Gold Cup (led at the last); yet to win beyond 2m5f.

Irish Saint (Fr)

7 b/br g Saint Des Saints - Minirose (Mansonnien)

Paul Nicholls   **Mrs Johnny De La Hey**

PLACINGS: 11213/F0136/1312143/   RPR **160c**

Starts 17	1st 7	2nd 3	3rd 2	4th 1	Win & Pl £184,393
	2/15	Kemp	2m4¹/₂f Cls1 Nov Gd2 Ch soft		£18,224
	12/14	Asct	2m5f Cls2 Ch gd-sft		£15,784
	11/14	Sand	1m7¹/₂f Cls2 Nov Ch gd-sft		£12,904
140	1/14	Asct	2m3¹/₂f Cls1 Gd2 125-145 Hdl Hcap heavy		£22,780
	2/13	Kemp	2m Cls1 Gd2 Hdl 4yo good		£15,661
	12/12	Kemp	2m Cls3 Hdl 3yo heavy		£5,848
	9/12	Autl	2m2f List Hdl 3yo v soft		£26,000

Useful novice chaser two seasons ago but just came up short in four runs at Grade 1 level; promising third at Aintree on first attempt at 3m when last seen and could do better on a right-handed track (all six wins in Britain going that way); missed last season through injury.

Irving

8 b g Singspiel - Indigo Girl (Sternkoenig)

Paul Nicholls   **Axom XLIX**

PLACINGS: 11119/F1P2P/1164-   RPR **158+h**

Starts 14	1st 7	2nd 1	3rd -	4th 1	Win & Pl £215,640
	11/15	Hayd	2m Cls2 Hdl soft		£61,900
154	11/15	Winc	1m7¹/₂f Cls1 Gd2 134-154 Hdl Hcap soft		£34,170
	11/14	Newc	2m¹/₂f Cls1 Gd1 Hdl soft		£56,270
	2/14	Kemp	2m Cls1 Nov Gd2 Hdl soft		£15,661
	12/13	Asct	1m7¹/₂f Cls1 Nov Gd2 Hdl soft		£17,387
	11/13	Asct	2m¹/₂f Cls3 Hdl gd-sft		£6,882
	11/13	Tntn	2m¹/₂f Cls3 Nov Hdl good		£5,848

Plagued by breathing problems in the last couple of seasons, giving his profile a rather inconsistent look, but won the Fighting Fifth Hurdle in 2014 plus good races at Wincanton and Haydock early last season; a smart two-miler on his day.

Its'afreebee (Ire)

6 b g Danroad - Aphra Benn (In The Wings)

Dan Skelton   **Rebel Jumping**

PLACINGS: 3/543121113-   RPR **146h**

Starts 8	1st 4	2nd 1	3rd 2	4th 1	Win & Pl £44,673
	1/16	Hayd	1m7¹/₂f Cls1 Nov Gd2 Hdl heavy		£17,085
	12/15	Hayd	2m3f Cls4 Nov Hdl 4-7yo heavy		£3,899
	11/15	Bang	2m¹/₂f Cls4 Nov Hdl soft		£3,249
	8/15	Bell	2m1f NHF 4-7yo yld-sft		£5,081

Won his first three races over hurdles last season, all on soft or heavy ground including a Grade 2 at Haydock, but coped with quicker conditions better than expected when a terrific 33-1 third in the Neptune; may do better back at 2m.

Ivan Grozny (Fr)

6 b g Turtle Bowl - Behnesa (Suave Dancer)

Willie Mullins (Ir)   **Andrea & Graham Wylie**

PLACINGS: 21401/00815-1   RPR **158+h**

Starts 11	1st 4	2nd 1	3rd -	4th 1	Win & Pl £86,248
	7/16	Tipp	2m Gd3 Hdl yield		£27,114
141	4/16	Aint	2m¹/₂f Cls2 124-141 Cond Am Hdl Hcap soft		£30,950
	4/14	Fair	2m Gd3 Hdl 4yo gd-yld		£16,250
	1/14	Naas	2m Mdn Hdl 4yo sft-hvy		£5,750

Took a long time to build on initial juvenile promise but flourished in the last six months; gained wide-margin victories over hurdles at Aintree and Tipperary before winning so well on the Flat at Galway that he was favourite for the Ebor until going lame.

Ivanovich Gorbatov (Ire)

4 b g Montjeu - Northern Gulch (Gulch)

Joseph O'Brien (Ir)   **John P McManus**

PLACINGS: 1412-3   RPR **152+h**

Starts 5	1st 2	2nd 1	3rd 1	4th 1	Win & Pl £106,312
	3/16	Chel	2m1f Cls1 Gd1 Hdl 4yo good		£68,340
	12/15	Leop	2m Mdn Hdl 3yo heavy		£7,488

Very smart Flat recruit who took well to hurdles last season and won the Triumph Hurdle at Cheltenham with a terrific turn of foot; much less effective in a couple of runs on softer ground and put in his place by Triumph second Apple's Jade at Punchestown.

'Desperately unlucky not to win the Pertemps Final and may well have a big staying handicap in him'

Jer's Girl (Ire)

4 b f Jeremy - African Scene (Scenic)

Gavin Cromwell (Ir)   John P McManus

PLACINGS: 11251-1   RPR **143+h**

Starts	1st	2nd	3rd	4th	Win & Pl
6	4	1	-	-	£112,152

4/16	Punc	2m4f Nov Gd1 Hdl yield	£43,382
3/16	Fair	2m4f Nov Gd1 Hdl yield	£43,382
12/15	Aint	2m1f Cls1 List Hdl 3yo soft	£12,529
11/15	Limk	2m Mdn Hdl 3yo soft	£5,349

One of the success stories of last season and completed a Grade 1 double at Punchestown, stepping out of mares' company to win by ten lengths over 2m4f; should stay further and will have plenty of opportunities in mares' races.

Jessber's Dream (Ire)

6 b m Milan - Maddy's Supreme (Supreme Leader)

Paul Nicholls   Chris Giles & Potensis Bloodstock Ltd

PLACINGS: 1/4112212-   RPR **143+h**

Starts	1st	2nd	3rd	4th	Win & Pl
7	3	3	-	1	£47,690

2/16	Sand	2m4f Cls1 Nov Gd2 Hdl heavy	£17,085
12/15	Extr	2m2½f Cls4 Nov Hdl heavy	£3,249
11/15	Ling	2m3½f Cls4 Mdn Hdl heavy	£3,899

Progressive last season and peaked with an eight-length win in a Grade 2 mares' novice hurdle at Sandown on heavy ground; easily shaken off by Jer's Girl in a Grade 1 at Punchestown next time but still finished a fair second; sold out of Harry Fry's yard for £190,000 in August.

Jezki (Ire)

8 b g Milan - La Noire (Phardante)

Jessica Harrington (Ir)   John P McManus

PLACINGS: 1131/11241/122341/1-   RPR **168h**

Starts	1st	2nd	3rd	4th	Win & Pl
21	13	3	2	2	£856,656

4/15	Punc	3m Gd1 Hdl yield	£93,023
4/15	Aint	2m4f Cls1 Gd1 Hdl gd-sft	£113,072
5/14	Punc	2m Gd1 Hdl gd-yld	£100,000
3/14	Chel	2m1½f Cls1 Gd1 Hdl gd-sft	£238,051
12/13	Fair	2m4f Gd1 Hdl gd-yld	£42,276
11/13	DRoy	2m Gd2 Hdl gd-yld	£26,423
4/13	Punc	2m Nov Gd1 Hdl soft	£40,325
12/12	Leop	2m Nov Gd1 Hdl soft	£43,333
12/12	Fair	2m Nov Gd1 Hdl soft	£40,625
11/12	Naas	2m Gd3 Hdl 4yo sft-hvy	£14,896
10/12	Naas	2m Mdn Hdl 4yo soft	£5,750
3/12	Leop	2m NHF 4yo good	£5,750
1/12	Leop	2m NHF 4yo yield	£4,600

Won the Champion Hurdle in 2014 and stepped up in trip successfully the following year, winning the 3m Grade 1 hurdle at Punchestown (eighth victory at the top level); missed last season through injury having been favourite for the World Hurdle.

Jolly's Cracked It (Fr)

7 b g Astarabad - Jolly Harbour (Rudimentary)

Harry Fry   **GDM Partnership**

PLACINGS: 42/1/112596/31-   RPR **147h**

Starts	1st	2nd	3rd	4th	Win & Pl
11	4	2	1	1	£99,084

141	12/15	Asct	1m7¹/₂f Cls1 Gd3 131-150 Hdl Hcap gd-sft.........£58,740
	11/14	Asct	1m7¹/₂f Cls3 Hdl soft £6,882
	11/14	Asct	1m7¹/₂f Cls3 Nov Hdl good £10,635
	1/14	Winc	1m7¹/₂f Cls6 NHF 4-6yo heavy £1,625

Ran well in several top handicaps after winning his first two runs over hurdles in 2014 and just about gained his reward when dead-heating in the Ladbroke at Ascot last season; likely to go novice chasing and may again be one for top 2m handicaps in the spring.

Jollyallan

7 b g Rocamadour - Life Line (Exit To Nowhere)

Harry Fry   **John P McManus**

PLACINGS: 1/611128/   RPR **151h**

Starts	1st	2nd	3rd	4th	Win & Pl
7	4	1	-	-	£28,165

	12/14	Kemp	2m Cls2 Nov Hdl gd-sft £9,419
	11/14	Newb	2m¹/₂f Cls3 Nov Hdl soft £6,256
	11/14	Extr	2m1f Cls3 Nov Hdl gd-sft £5,523
	4/14	Winc	1m7¹/₂f Cls6 NHF 4-6yo gd-sft £1,625

Very promising novice hurdler two seasons ago, winning three times before near miss against more experienced Garde La Victoire at Sandown; came back wrong after disappointing run in the Supreme (suffered heat exhaustion) and missed last season.

Jonniesofa (Ire)

6 b g Well Made - Lucky Sarah (Aahsaylad)

Rose Dobbin   **R & Mrs A Houghton & A Houghton**

PLACINGS: 22321221/3121219-   RPR **140h**

Starts	1st	2nd	3rd	4th	Win & Pl
7	3	2	1		£28,966

	2/16	Hayd	2m7f Cls1 Nov Gd2 Hdl heavy £17,138
	12/15	Newc	2m6f Cls4 Nov Hdl heavy £3,249
	11/15	Kels	2m6¹/₂f Cls4 Nov Hdl soft £3,249

Won three times over hurdles last season, most notably when outstaying Vintage Clouds in a Grade 2 at Haydock on heavy ground; ran well to two out in the Albert Bartlett; dual Irish point winner and should do well over fences.

Jolly's Cracked It (below): could do well in 2m novice chases this season

Josies Orders (Ire)

8 b g Milan - Silent Orders (Bob Back)

Enda Bolger (Ir)					John P McManus
PLACINGS: 11008/688P6/U181191-				RPR	**153+c**

Starts	1st	2nd	3rd	4th	Win & Pl
24	7	1	1	-	£104,046
	3/16	Chel	3m6f Cls2 Ch good		£37,140
	12/15	Chel	3m6f Cls2 Ch gd-sft		£21,896
129	11/15	Chel	3m6f Cls2 127-153 Ch Hcap good		£15,640
	5/15	Punc	3m Ch yield		£5,349
122	1/14	Hntg	3m1f Cls2 122-135 Hdl Hcap heavy		£11,574
114	12/13	Asct	2m7¹/₂f Cls4 Nov 95-120 Hdl Hcap soft		£6,256
107	10/13	Aint	3m¹/₂f Cls4 Nov 94-117 Hdl Hcap gd-sft		£4,549

Transformed by a switch to cross-country chases last season and was twice successful at Cheltenham before being awarded the festival contest over that course on the disqualification of Any Currency; should again set the standard in that sphere.

Josses Hill (Ire)

8 b g Winged Love - Credora Storm (Glacial Storm)

Nicky Henderson					A D Spence
PLACINGS: 211221/21234/F18-				RPR	**160+c**

Starts	1st	2nd	3rd	4th	Win & Pl
14	5	5	1	1	£122,111
	2/16	Kemp	2m4¹/₂f Cls2 Ch soft		£12,996
	1/15	Donc	2m¹/₂f Cls4 Nov Ch good		£3,899
	4/14	Aint	2m¹/₂f Cls1 Nov Gd2 Hdl gd-sft		£34,170
	12/13	Newb	2m¹/₂f Cls4 Mdn Hdl soft		£3,899
	11/13	Asct	1m7¹/₂f Cls5 NHF 4-6yo gd-sft		£2,283

Hugely talented horse (Grade I winner and Supreme runner-up over hurdles) who looks built for chasing but has been slow to get his act together in two seasons over fences; showed more promise in an impressive win at Kempton last term and should have more to come.

Junction Fourteen (Ire)

7 b g King's Theatre - Chevet Girl (Roselier)

Emma Lavelle				Martin St Quinton & Tim Syder	
PLACINGS: 5/311F0/02450/1151-0				RPR	**151+c**

Starts	1st	2nd	3rd	4th	Win & Pl
16	5	1	1	1	£63,589
	4/16	Sand	2m4f Cls2 Nov 122-145 Ch Hcap good		£18,768
	11/15	Winc	2m4f Cls1 Nov Gd2 Ch soft		£18,310
135	10/15	Uttx	2m6¹/₂f Cls3 Nov 121-135 Ch Hcap good		£6,330
121	12/13	Kemp	2m5f Cls3 113-130 Hdl Hcap soft		£9,747
	11/13	Font	2m3f Cls4 Nov Hdl gd-sft		£3,899

Took well to chasing last season when winning

three out of four, including a Grade 2 at Wincanton and a competitive novice handicap at Sandown on his final start; disappointing when well fancied for the Galway Plate in July.

Just A Par (Ire)

9 b g Island House - Thebrownhen (Henbit)

Paul Nicholls				C G Roach & Paul K Barber	
PLACINGS: 21476/5P42031/09202-				RPR	**156c**

Starts	1st	2nd	3rd	4th	Win & Pl
20	3	6	1	2	£180,749
140	4/15	Sand	3m5f Cls1 Gd3 137-163 Ch Hcap good		£85,425
	11/13	Newb	2m7¹/₂f Cls1 Nov Gd2 Ch gd-sft		£18,184
	11/12	Punc	2m4f Mdn Hdl heavy		£5,750

Won the bet365 Gold Cup in 2015 and ran even better in the same race last season to finish a short-head second off an 8lb higher mark; well suited by an extreme test of stamina on good ground but yet to show the same level of form on softer.

Kalkir (Fr)

5 gr g Montmartre - Kakira (Cadoudal)

Willie Mullins (Ir)					Mrs S Ricci
PLACINGS: 4/122P/26-				RPR	**146h**

Starts	1st	2nd	3rd	4th	Win & Pl
7	1	3		1	£55,504
	11/14	Fair	2m Gd3 Hdl 3yo yield		£16,250

Became slightly disappointing as a juvenile two seasons ago but improved last term to finish second in a valuable handicap at Leopardstown first time out; eyecatching sixth in the Betfair Hurdle next time and well fancied for the Coral Cup before suffering a setback.

Karezak (Ire)

5 b g Azamour - Karawana (King's Best)

Alan King					McNeill Family
PLACINGS: 1222203/2224-				RPR	**147h**

Starts	1st	2nd	3rd	4th	Win & Pl
11	1	7	1	1	£45,595
	10/14	Chep	2m Cls4 Hdl 3yo gd-sft		£3,899

Without a win since his hurdling debut in 2014 but has run a string of fine races in defeat (second seven times); promising first run over 3m when

Picture Perfect
Moments made into memories
ORDER NOW *RACING POST*.com/photos

fourth in last season's Long Walk Hurdle (ground softer than ideal) and being trained for the World Hurdle when ruled out by injury.

Kasakh Noir (Fr)

4 ch g Redback - Vale Of Honor (Singspiel)

Dan Skelton   **T P Radford**

PLACINGS: 1316-   RPR **134+h**

Starts	1st	2nd	3rd	4th	Win & Pl
4	2	-	1	-	£11,706
	2/16	MRas	2m¹/₂f Cls3 Hdl 4yo heavy		£3,249
	11/15	Newb	2m¹/₂f Cls3 Hdl 3yo soft		£6,498

Didn't quite fulfil promise of runaway win at Newbury on his debut for new connections last season but managed to win again at Market Rasen and better than bare form of Fred Winter sixth (hampered at the last); has plenty of scope.

Katachenko (Ire)

7 b g Kutub - Karalee (Arokar)

Donald McCain   **Trevor Hemmings**

PLACINGS: 1433112/4/212231-   RPR **139+c**

Starts	1st	2nd	3rd	4th	Win & Pl
13	4	4	4	3	£76,886
133	4/16	Aint	2m Cls3 Gd3 128-150 Ch Hcap gd-sft		£56,270
128	10/15	Weth	1m7f Cls3 Nov 120-132 Ch Hcap soft		£6,657
	4/14	Kels	2m4f Cls4 Nov Hdl soft		£3,249
	2/14	Muss	2m3¹/₂f Cls5 Mdn Hdl soft		£2,599

Balloted out of the novice handicap chase at the Cheltenham Festival having been laid out for the race all season but made amends by winning the Red Rum at Aintree; jumped badly left when beaten at odds-on at Carlisle and likely to be kept to left-handed tracks.

Katie Too (Ire)

5 b m King's Theatre - Shivermetimber (Arctic Lord)

Alan King   **Mr & Mrs Christopher Harris**

PLACINGS: 17/1121-   RPR **132h**

Starts	1st	2nd	3rd	4th	Win & Pl
6	4	1	-	-	£26,771
	4/16	Chel	2m4¹/₂f Cls1 Nov List Hdl good		£11,390
	12/15	Wwck	2m5f Cls4 Nov Hdl heavy		£3,899
	12/15	Font	2m4f Cls4 Nov Hdl heavy		£3,249
	2/15	Newb	2m¹/₂f Cls6 NHF 4-6yo soft		£1,625

Won three out of four over hurdles last season, with sole defeat when second to Jessber's Dream; lucky to win a Listed mares' novice at Cheltenham after The Organist's fall but was short of work after a setback and may well improve again.

ON THE CLOCK ⏱

Katachenko was a model of consistency last term and could pick up a decent purse this winter. [Dave Edwards, Topspeed]

Katkeau (Fr)

9 b g Kotky Bleu - Levine (Luynes)

David Pipe   **Prof C Tisdall, J A Gent & R C Wilkin**

PLACINGS: 1742/15P20/35113P-1P   RPR **154+c**

Starts	1st	2nd	3rd	4th	Win & Pl
23	5	4	4	1	£118,789
143	4/16	Uttx	3m Cls2 127-148 Ch Hcap soft		£18,768
139	12/15	Ludl	3m Cls3 122-139 Ch Hcap soft		£16,245
	11/15	Fknm	3m Cls3 Ch gd-sft		£7,798
124	11/14	Chel	3m1¹/₂f Cls1 List 120-143 Hdl Hcap soft		£15,377
0	6/12	Autl	2m3¹/₂f Hdl 5yo Hcap heavy		£20,000

Won his first two chases last season and bounced back when returned to 3m in a handicap chase at Uttoxeter at the end of April; unsuited by a drop to 2m4f and then failed to stay in the Midlands National in between; still prone to the odd blunder.

Kayf Grace

6 b m Kayf Tara - Potter's Gale (Strong Gale)

Nicky Henderson   **James & Jean Potter**

PLACINGS: 33/211-   RPR **128+b**

Starts	1st	2nd	3rd	4th	Win & Pl
5	2	1	2	-	£27,517
	4/16	Aint	2m1f Cls1 Gd2 NHF 4-6yo soft		£22,508
	3/16	Fknm	2m Cls4 Mdn NHF 4-6yo soft		£3,422

Beaten in first three runs but found her form during the spring, following a runaway win at Fakenham by wearing down Augusta Kate in the mares' bumper at Aintree in April; out of a half-sister to Denman and should thrive over jumps.

Khezerabad (Fr)

4 ch g Dalakhani - Khelwa (Traditionally)

Nicky Henderson   **Simon Munir & Isaac Souede**

PLACINGS: 3P-   RPR **133+h**

Starts	1st	2nd	3rd	4th	Win & Pl
2	-	-	1	-	£3,210

Smart Flat horse (fourth when joint-favourite for a French Listed race in 2015 having won at Saint-Cloud) who was highly tried in two runs last season, doing best when third in the Adonis at Kempton; could make a good novice hurdler.

Kilcooley (Ire)

7 b g Stowaway - Bealaha Essie (Denel)

Charlie Longsdon   **J H & S M Wall**

PLACINGS: 2/21110/5721P17/1P-   RPR **167+h**

Starts	1st	2nd	3rd	4th	Win & Pl
14	6	2	-	-	£87,312
	10/15	Weth	3m Cls1 Gd2 Hdl soft		£22,780
	2/15	Font	2m3f Cls1 Gd2 Hdl heavy		£28,810
137	12/14	Hayd	2m3f Cls2 113-139 Hdl Hcap heavy		£12,512
	3/14	MRas	2m¹/₂f Cls4 Nov Hdl gd-sft		£3,249
	2/14	MRas	2m¹/₂f Cls3 Nov Hdl soft		£5,697
	11/13	MRas	2m¹/₂f Cls6 NHF 4-6yo soft		£1,643

Injury curtailed initial promise last season and

was seen only once (pulled up in the World Hurdle) after running away with a Grade 2 hurdle at Wetherby; possibly unsuited by good ground at Cheltenham with all his best form coming on much softer.

Kilcrea Vale (Ire)

6 b g Beneficial - Inflation (Port Etienne)

Nicky Henderson   A D Spence

PLACINGS: 11/F69-   RPR 142h

Starts	1st	2nd	3rd	4th	Win & Pl
4	1	-	-	-	£3,919
1/15	MRas	2m2¹/₂f Cls4 Nov Hdl gd-sft.............£3,249

Hugely impressive winner of his only novice hurdle two seasons ago and looked set to make a winning return back at Ascot last term when falling two out; twice slightly disappointing in handicaps but always likely to make a better chaser.

Killultagh Vic (Ire)

7 b g Old Vic - Killultagh Dawn (Phardante)

Willie Mullins (Ir)

Rose Boyd, B Anderson & Mrs M Armstrong

PLACINGS: 3/2116/51231/111-   RPR 156+c

Starts	1st	2nd	3rd	4th	Win & Pl
12	7	2	1	-	£132,787
	1/16	Leop	2m3f Nov Gd2 Ch soft...............£18,529
	12/15	Fair	2m Ch heavy...............£7,488
	4/15	Punc	3m Nov Gd1 Hdl gd-yld...............£44,186
135	3/15	Chel	2m4¹/₂f Cls2 135-144 Cond Hdl Hcap soft...........£31,280
	11/14	Clon	2m4f Mdn Hdl heavy...............£6,325
	2/14	Naas	2m NHF 4-7yo sft-hvy...............£7,763
	1/14	Naas	2m3f NHF 5-7yo sft-hvy...............£4,600

Missed the second half of last season with injury having looked a leading contender for top novice chases when winning two out of two over fences (in remarkable circumstances after final-fence blunder on second occasion); Grade 1 winner over hurdles and could reach similar heights as a chaser.

King's Odyssey (Ire)

7 b g King's Theatre - Ma Furie (Balleroy)

Evan Williams   Mr & Mrs William Rucker

PLACINGS: 2/2421/311-   RPR 155+c

Starts	1st	2nd	3rd	4th	Win & Pl
8	3	3	1	1	£29,094
139	1/16	Chel	2m5f Cls2 Nov 126-152 Ch Hcap heavy...............£15,640
	12/15	Winc	2m4f Cls3 Nov Ch vsft...............£6,657
	3/15	Wwck	2m5f Cls4 Mdn Hdl heavy...............£3,249

Much improved for switch to fences last season, winning two out of three including a strong novice handicap at Cheltenham in January; relished heavy ground that day and missed spring targets on quicker; likely contender for top soft-ground handicaps.

Kitten Rock (Fr)

6 b g Laverock - The Cat Eater (Tagel)

Edward O'Grady (Ir)   John P McManus

PLACINGS: 112/411116/13-   RPR 131+c

Starts	1st	2nd	3rd	4th	Win & Pl
11	7	1	1	1	£102,647
11/15	Navn	2m Ch yld-sft...............£8,558
2/15	Gowr	2m Gd2 Hdl soft...............£21,415
1/15	Naas	2m3f Gd3 Hdl soft...............£15,116
12/14	Limk	2m List Hdl 4yo heavy...............£14,083
11/14	Naas	2m Gd3 Hdl 4yo soft...............£16,250
3/14	Limk	2m Hdl 4yo heavy...............£7,475
3/14	Navn	2m Mdn Hdl 4yo sft-hvy...............£5,750

Developed into a high-class hurdler two seasons ago, winning four in a row before being beaten less than ten lengths by Faugheen in the Champion Hurdle; didn't look a natural over fences last season, though found to be lame after his only defeat.

Koshari (Fr)

4 br g Walk In The Park - Honor May (Balleroy)

Willie Mullins (Ir)   Mrs S Ricci

PLACINGS: 51-1   RPR 131+h

Starts	1st	2nd	3rd	4th	Win & Pl
3	2	-	-	-	£24,398
4/16	Punc	2m Nov Hdl yield...............£11,305
12/15	Cagn	2m1¹/₂f Hdl 3yo v soft...............£11,907

Made a most impressive debut for new connections when winning at Punchestown at the end of April from stablemate Bello Conti; has plenty of size but reportedly likely to stick to hurdles and looks a terrific prospect.

Kruzhlinin (Ger)

9 ch g Sholokhov - Karuma (Surumu)

Philip Hobbs   Paul & Clare Rooney

PLACINGS: 41P2/4411730/72/15P-   RPR 153+c

Starts	1st	2nd	3rd	4th	Win & Pl
24	7	5	2	3	£70,291
138	1/16	Kemp	3m Cls2 132-147 Ch Hcap soft...............£12,021
138	12/13	Kels	2m7¹/₂f Cls2 121-138 Ch Hcap gd-sft...............£12,027
130	11/13	Kels	2m7¹/₂f Cls3 125-138 Ch Hcap gd-sft...............£7,148
	2/13	Kels	2m1f Cls3 Nov Ch heavy...............£6,498
	11/12	Carl	2m Cls3 Ch heavy...............£5,653
115	5/12	Prth	2m1¹/₂f Cls3 Nov 97-123 Hdl Hcap good...........£4,791
	4/12	Prth	2m4f Cls4 Mdn Hdl gd-sft...............£3,249

Laid out for the Grand National last season and went into many notebooks with a reappearance win at Kempton but struggled for the third time over the Aintree fences; capable of better but has shown all his best form in small fields.

MIND-BLOWING

iPad Daily Edition
£99 for 5 months.

To claim this offer visit
Racingpost.com/ipad5months

App Store

Kylemore Lough

7 b g Revoque - One Of The Last (Supreme Leader)

Kerry Lee   **M J McMahon & Denis Gallagher**

PLACINGS: 5311113PP/311111-   RPR **162+c**

Starts	1st	2nd	3rd	4th	Win & Pl
12	8	-	2	-	£91,487
	3/16	Fair	2m4f Nov Gd1 Ch yield....................................£43,382		
151	3/16	Sand	1m7¹/₂f Cls3 Nov 132-151 Ch Hcap soft £6,498		
147	2/16	Hayd	2m4f Cls3 Nov 128-147 Ch Hcap heavy....................£8,123		
	12/15	Extr	2m1¹/₂f Cls2 Ch heavy...................................£12,820		
132	11/15	Uttx	2m4f Cls3 Nov 117-132 Ch Hcap soft.....................£6,343		
	1/15	Weth	2m5¹/₂f Cls4 Nov Hdl soft...............................£3,249		
	1/15	Weth	2m3¹/₂f Cls4 Nov Hdl 4-7yo gd-sft.......................£3,769		
	12/14	Wwck	2m5f Cls4 Mdn Hdl soft.................................£3,249		

Went from strength to strength last season and won five in a row, including the Grade 1 Ryanair Gold Cup at Fairyhouse from Outlander; more needed this term starting from a mark of 156 but capable of winning good races at around 2m4f on soft ground.

L'Ami Serge (Ire)

6 h g King's Theatre - La Zingarella (Phardante)

Nicky Henderson   **Simon Munir & Isaac Souede**

PLACINGS: 323622/1114/11232-   RPR **159c**

Starts	1st	2nd	3rd	4th	Win & Pl
15	5	5	3	1	£182,748
	1/16	Weth	2m3¹/₂f Cls4 Nov Ch heavy..............................£3,899		
	1/16	Plum	2m1f Cls3 Nov Ch heavy.................................£6,498		
	1/15	Sand	2m Cls1 Nov Gd1 Hdl soft..............................£23,491		
	12/14	Asct	1m7¹/₂f Cls1 Nov Gd2 Hdl soft.........................£18,690		
132	11/14	Newb	2m¹/₂f Cls1 List 129-149 Hdl Hcap soft................£22,780		

Won the Tolworth in 2015 and unlucky not to strike at the top level last season over fences, especially when looking a non-stayer when third in the JLT Novices' Chase (also let down by jumping badly left); definitely capable of better, possibly back at 2m.

La Bague Au Roi (Fr)

5 b m Doctor Dino - Alliance Royale (Turgeon)

Warren Greatrex   **Mrs Julien Turner & Andrew Merriam**

PLACINGS: 1/117-   RPR **126+b**

Starts	1st	2nd	3rd	4th	Win & Pl
4	3	-	-	-	£16,614
	12/15	Hntg	2m Cls1 List NHF 4-6yo gd-sft.........................£11,390		
	10/15	Aint	2m1f Cls4 NHF 4-6yo good...............................£3,249		
	4/15	NAbb	2m1f Cls6 NHF 4-6yo good...............................£1,711		

Completed a hat-trick in a Listed bumper at Huntingdon last season and described in glowing terms by her trainer afterwards; disappointing when 2-1 for the mares' bumper at Aintree in April but likely to prove much better than that.

Last Goodbye (Ire)

5 b g Millenary - Welsh Ana (Welsh Term)

Elizabeth Doyle (Ir)   **Last Goodbye Syndicate**

PLACINGS: 81111-0   RPR **143+h**

Starts	1st	2nd	3rd	4th	Win & Pl
6	4	-	-	-	£32,114
130	3/16	Cork	2m3f 107-131 Hdl Hcap heavy..........................£13,566		
	1/16	Navn	2m4f Nov Hdl sft-hvy...................................£8,118		
	10/15	Wxfd	2m Mdn Hdl 4yo soft....................................£5,616		
	9/15	Rosc	2m NHF 4yo good..£4,814		

Won four in a row last season, starting with a bumper and completing a hat-trick over hurdles on handicap debut at Cork; never a threat in a more competitive race at Punchestown but may well resume progress back on soft/heavy ground.

Le Mercurey (Fr)

6 b g Nickname - Feroe (Bulington)

Paul Nicholls   **Colm Donlon & Chris Giles**

PLACINGS: 1F1/737/113P381-   RPR **160+c**

Starts	1st	2nd	3rd	4th	Win & Pl
13	5	3	-	-	£113,682
	4/16	Ayr	2m4¹/₂f Cls1 Nov Gd2 Ch gd-sft........................£26,283		
	12/15	Asct	2m5f Cls1 Nov Gd2 Ch soft.............................£18,310		
	11/15	Plum	2m3¹/₂f Hdl Ch soft....................................£7,148		
	11/13	Autl	2m1¹/₂f Hdl 3yo heavy.................................£27,317		
	10/13	Autl	2m2f Hdl 3yo v soft...................................£21,463		

Possibly flattered to win three times last season (owed plenty to a final fence faller and a below-par favourite), though overall record is solid discounting three moderate efforts at Cheltenham (prefers flat tracks); may be hard to place off tough mark.

Le Reve (Ire)

6 b g Milan - Open Cry (Montelimar)

Lucy Wadham   **P H Betts**

PLACINGS: 4P2/1P3123/P026150P-   RPR **154+c**

Starts	1st	2nd	3rd	4th	Win & Pl
27	6	3	4	2	£151,487
144	2/16	Sand	3m Cls2 130-152 Ch Hcap gd-sft.......................£31,280		
139	1/15	Sand	3m Cls2 127-152 Ch Hcap gd-sft.......................£31,396		
128	11/14	Sand	3m Cls3 122-129 Ch Hcap gd-sft.......................£12,558		
	11/13	Hntg	2m4f Cls4 Nov Ch gd-sft................................£5,198		
	4/13	Kemp	2m5f Cls4 Nov Hdl gd-sft...............................£3,899		
	2/13	MRas	2m2¹/₂f Cls3 Nov Hdl 4-7yo soft........................£5,848		

Very useful staying chaser who has a fine record on right-handed tracks, winning three times at Sandown (plus a third in the bet365 Gold Cup) and twice second at Kempton in the last two seasons; should win more good races.

'Missed second half of last season with injury having looked a contender for top novice chases. Grade 1 hurdle winner and could hit similar heights as a chaser'

Let's Dance (Fr)
4 b f Poliglote - Baraka Du Berlais (Bonnet Rouge)

Willie Mullins (Ir)   **Mrs S Ricci**

PLACINGS: 2/234-21   RPR **132+h**

Starts	1st	2nd	3rd	4th	Win & Pl
6	1	3	1	1	£36,343
	5/16	Slig	2m Mdn Hdl 4yo gd-yld		£4,522

Among last season's leading juvenile hurdlers when making the first four in three Grade 1 races, including the Triumph Hurdle at Cheltenham; easily off the mark at Sligo in May and retains novice status this season.

Lil Rockerfeller (USA)
5 ch g Hard Spun - Layounne (Mt. Livermore)

Neil King   **Davies Smith Govier & Brown**

PLACINGS: 332411/3312317-   RPR **156+h**

Starts	1st	2nd	3rd	4th	Win & Pl
13	4	2	5	1	£160,684
	2/16	Font	2m3f Cls1 Gd2 Hdl gd-sft		£45,560
146	12/15	Sand	2m Cls1 List 125-147 Hdl Hcap soft		£34,170
133	4/15	Sand	2m Cls2 111-137 Hdl 4yo Hcap gd-sft		£31,280
125	3/15	Asct	1m7¹/₂f Cls2 120-142 Hdl 4yo Hcap gd-sft		£25,962

Tough hurdler who punched above his weight throughout last season, winning a Listed handicap at Sandown under a big weight and the National Spirit Hurdle; fair seventh in the Champion Hurdle but could find more opportunities if staying 3m.

Limini (Ire)
5 ch m Peintre Celebre - Her Grace (Spectrum)

Willie Mullins (Ir)   **Mrs S Ricci**

PLACINGS: 1113-2   RPR **148+h**

Starts	1st	2nd	3rd	4th	Win & Pl
5	3	1	1	-	£87,787
	3/16	Chel	2m1f Cls1 Nov Gd2 Hdl good		£42,713
	1/16	Fair	2m2f Nov Gd3 Hdl heavy		£16,728
	5/15	Punc	2m Mdn Hdl good		£6,419

Much hyped last season and delivered at odds-on in the inaugural mares' novice hurdle at the Cheltenham Festival; failed to live up to expectations when a beaten favourite at Aintree and Punchestown, albeit at Grade 1 level; should still win good races.

Listen Dear (Ire)
6 b m Robin Des Champs - Crescendor (Lavirco)

Willie Mullins (Ir)   **Supreme Horse Racing Club**

PLACINGS: 254/12211-1   RPR **138+h**

Starts	1st	2nd	3rd	4th	Win & Pl
8	4	2	-	1	£38,502
	6/16	DRoy	2m Hdl good		£7,914
	10/15	DRoy	2m Nov Gd3 Hdl yld-sft		£17,636
	9/15	Clon	2m1/₂f Mdn Hdl 4-5yo good		£5,349
	6/15	Dpat	2m2f NHF 5-7yo good		£4,814

Missed most of last season but had looked a smart prospect when switched to front-running tactics, winning her last two including a Grade 3 at Down Royal; returned with a win at the same track in June; likely contender for good mares' races.

Local Show (Ire)
8 br g Oscar - Loughaderra Rose (Roselier)

Ben Pauling   **Nicholas Piper & Claire E Piper**

PLACINGS: 1U/23U312/117-   RPR **152+c**

Starts	1st	2nd	3rd	4th	Win & Pl
9	3	2	2	-	£16,008
	1/16	Kemp	3m Cls4 Nov Ch soft		£4,660
125	12/15	Newb	2m7¹/₂f Cls3 Nov 121-133 Ch Hcap soft		£6,498
	2/15	Ffos	3m Cls5 Mdn Hdl soft		£2,599

Much improved when sent over fences last season, winning his first two chases including a short-head defeat of Onenightinvienna at Kempton; fair seventh in the National Hunt Chase when hampered at a key stage; open to improvement after just three chases.

Long House Hall (Ire)
8 b g Saddlers' Hall - Brackenvale (Strong Gale)

Dan Skelton   **Carl Hinchy**

PLACINGS: 3P1/91026611/1U25-41   RPR **156+c**

Starts	1st	2nd	3rd	4th	Win & Pl
14	5	2	-	1	£82,094
143	7/16	MRas	2m5¹/₂f Cls1 List 131-157 Ch Hcap good		£28,475
	5/15	Bang	2m1¹/₂f Cls4 Nov Ch good		£3,899
125	4/15	Chel	2m4¹/₂f Cls2 111-135 Hdl Hcap good		£12,512
119	4/15	MRas	2m2¹/₂f Cls3 106-125 Hdl Hcap good		£9,747
	5/14	Kbgn	2m3¹/₂f Mdn Hdl good		£4,600

Finished second in last season's Coral Cup before proving even better over fences this summer, winning the Summer Plate in only his fourth chase; goes well at Cheltenham (also won a handicap hurdle there in 2015) and likely to be lined up for a festival handicap.

Lord Scoundrel (Ire)
7 b g Presenting - Noble Choice (Dahar)

Gordon Elliott (Ir)   **Gigginstown House Stud**

PLACINGS: 3484334/111223312-51   RPR **154+c**

Starts	1st	2nd	3rd	4th	Win & Pl
25	7	7	5	4	£187,039
145	7/16	Gway	2m6¹/₂f Cls4 134-162 Ch Hcap yield		£95,441
	2/16	Thur	2m2f Ch soft		£11,305
	11/15	Cork	2m4f Nov Gd3 Ch soft		£18,895
	10/15	Gway	2m2f Nov Ch yield		£9,995
	10/15	Limk	2m3¹/₂f Ch yield		£7,756
	10/14	Punc	2m4f Mdn Hdl gd-fm		£5,750
	3/14	Clon	2m1¹/₂f NHF 4-7yo sft-hvy		£4,313

Won his first three novice chases last season, including a Grade 3 at Cork, and finally built on that promise when winning the Galway Plate in July; not quite as effective on softer ground over the winter, though he still won on soft at Thurles.

Lucky Pass (Fr)

5 ch g Ultimately Lucky - Fuela Pass (Astarabad)

Willie Mullins (Ir)   **Gigginstown House Stud**

PLACINGS: 1/11-					RPR **131+b**
Starts	1st	2nd	3rd	4th	Win & Pl
2	2	-	-	-	£10,697
12/15	Leop	2m NHF 4-7yo heavy			£5,884
11/15	Fair	2m NHF 4yo soft			£4,814

Won both bumpers in good style last season, most notably at Leopardstown over Christmas; also won sole point-to-point in 2015 and seems sure to take well to jumping; all wins on soft or heavy ground and connections unsure how he'll cope with quicker.

Ma Du Fou (Fr)

6 b/br g Le Fou - Belle Du Ma (Zamindar)

Warren Greatrex   **Walters Plant Hire & James & Jean Potter**

PLACINGS: 1/32/111P6-					RPR **140+h**
Starts	1st	2nd	3rd	4th	Win & Pl
8	4	1	1		£28,012
2/16	Hntg	2m3¹/₂f Cls1 Nov List Hdl gd-sft			£14,860
12/15	Bang	2m¹/₂f Cls4 Nov Hdl soft			£4,549
11/15	Ffos	2m Cls4 Nnv Hdl heavy			£5,198
4/14	Weth	2m Cls6 NHF 4-6yo gd-sft			£1,643

Won three novice hurdles last season, most notably a Listed contest at Huntingdon from North Hill Harvey; twice disappointing in the spring but very green when favourite at Aintree (twice jumped paths) and remains capable of better.

Mala Beach (Ire)

8 b g Beneficial - Peppardstown (Old Vic)

Gordon Elliott (Ir)   **C Jones**

PLACINGS: 30121/231/214/F22FP-					RPR **157+c**
Starts	1st	2nd	3rd	4th	Win & Pl
19	4	5	2	1	£96,552
12/14	Punc	2m6f Ch gd-yld			£6,900
1/14	Gowr	3m Gd2 Hdl soft			£21,667
3/13	Fair	2m4f Nov Gd2 Hdl soft			£21,138
1/13	Leop	2m4f Mdn Hdl heavy			£6,171

Smart staying chaser who has been unlucky not to add to his sole win over fences in 2014; missed the rest of that season through injury and ran well in defeat last term when a close second in the Thyestes and falling two out when going well in front in the Bobbyjo.

Mall Dini (Ire)

6 b g Milan - Winsome Breeze (Glacial Storm)

Patrick Kelly (Ir)   **Philip J Reynolds**

PLACINGS: 1121/46314331-					RPR **144+h**
Starts	1st	2nd	3rd	4th	Win & Pl
10	3	1	3	2	£69,185
139	3/16	Chel	3m Cls1 List 135-154 Hdl Hcap good		£51,255
	12/15	Thur	2m6¹/₂f Mdn Hdl sft-hvy		£6,953
	3/15	Cork	2m NHF 4-7yo heavy		£4,814

Game winner of last season's Pertemps Final at Cheltenham less than five months after hurdling debut; probably a shade fortunate in a messy finish but remains unexposed as a stayer and interesting in a higher grade.

Lil Rockerfeller: tough hurdler can be found more winning opportunities

Many Clouds (Ire)

9 br g Cloudings - Bobbing Back (Bob Back)

Oliver Sherwood   **Trevor Hemmings**

PLACINGS: /1212B4/11161/62210-   RPR **168** + c

Starts	1st	2nd	3rd	4th	Win & Pl
25	10	7	-	1	£847,734
	3/16	Kels	2m7¹/₂f Cls1 List Ch soft		£18,509
160	4/15	Aint	4m2¹/₂f Cls1 Gd3 139-161 Ch Hcap gd-sft		£561,300
	1/15	Chel	3m1¹/₂f Cls1 Gd2 Ch soft		£56,950
151	11/14	Newb	3m2f Cls1 Gd3 138-157 Ch Hcap soft		£99,663
	11/14	Carl	2m4f Cls1 List Ch soft		£15,735
	12/13	Weth	2m3¹/₂f Cls3 Nov Ch soft		£6,498
	11/13	Carl	2m4f Cls4 Ch heavy		£6,498
	2/13	Extr	2m2¹/₂f Cls4 Nov Hdl heavy		£4,549
	11/12	Asct	2m3¹/₂f Cls3 Mdn Hdl soft		£6,256
	2/12	Weth	2m Cls6 NHF 4-5yo gd-sft		£1,437

Produced a mighty weight-carrying performance to win the 2015 Grand National and confirmed himself a high-class stayer with several big efforts last season; faded quickly when attempted an Aintree repeat and has since had a wind operation.

Marlbrook (Ire)

8 b g Beneficial - Drinadaly (Oscar)

Colm Murphy (Ir)   **John P McManus**

PLACINGS: 11/3F0/P211-P   RPR **146** + c

Starts	1st	2nd	3rd	4th	Win & Pl
9	3	1	1	-	£39,279
132	2/16	Naas	2m4f Nov 118-134 Ch Hcap sft-hvy		£21,691
	1/16	Fair	2m4f Nov Ch heavy		£9,559
	3/13	Gowr	2m Mdn Hdl 4-5yo heavy		£5,610

Failed to build on debut win over hurdles but fared much better when switched to fences last season, winning twice; sent off favourite for a big novice handicap at Punchestown in April but swiftly pulled up after a bad mistake at the first.

Many Clouds: 2015 Grand National hero will be back for more next April

Martello Tower (Ire)

8 b g Milan - Johnsalice (Zaffaran)

Margaret Mullins (Ir)				Barry Connell
PLACINGS: 11/41/11F121/337-				RPR **154**h

Starts	1st	2nd	3rd	4th	Win & Pl
12	6	1	2	1	£137,736

	3/15	Chel	3m Cls1 Nov Gd1 Hdl soft	£68,340
	12/14	Limk	3m Nov Gd3 Hdl heavy	£17,063
	11/14	Cork	3m Nov Gd3 Hdl soft	£20,313
	5/14	Klny	2m4f Mdn Hdl gd-yld	£4,600
	4/14	Fair	2m NHF 4-7yo soft	£7,188
	4/13	Punc	2m NHF 4-7yo heavy	£5,049

Crowned a fine novice campaign two seasons ago by winning the Albert Bartlett at Cheltenham on soft ground; failed to build on that last season when no better than third in three runs; could do better when switched to fences.

Measureofmydreams (Ire)

8 b g Shantou - Le Ravellen (Le Bavard)

Willie Mullins (Ir)				Gigginstown House Stud
PLACINGS: 21/212/13148/0113F0-				RPR **153**c

Starts	1st	2nd	3rd	4th	Win & Pl
14	5	2	2	1	£56,280

	2/16	Navn	3m Nov Gd2 Ch heavy	£18,438
	1/16	Punc	2m4f Ch heavy	£7,103
	1/15	Thur	2m6f Nov Hdl sft-hvy	£6,419
	11/14	WxfR	2m2f Mdn Hdl sft-hvy	£4,600
	3/14	Navn	2m NHF 5-7yo sft-hvy	£4,600

Much improved for the switch to fences last season, winning his first two chases and finishing a fine third in what looked a very strong National Hunt Chase; early faller in the Scottish National and faded after running well for a long way in the bet365 Gold Cup.

Might Bite (Ire)

7 b g Scorpion - Knotted Midge (Presenting)

Nicky Henderson				The Knot Again Partnership
PLACINGS: 311/517-				RPR **150+**h

Starts	1st	2nd	3rd	4th	Win & Pl
6	3	-	1	-	£34,999

	138	3/16	Kemp	2m5f Cls2 127-138 Hdl Hcap good	£20,645
		4/15	Chel	2m4½f Cls2 Nov Hdl good	£10,102
		3/15	Newb	2m4½f Cls4 Nov Hdl gd sft	£3,422

Very lightly raced and reportedly slow to come to hand last season but returned from a long absence in style when winning at Kempton in March; not beaten far off 10lb higher next time and an exciting prospect back over fences (fifth on sole start last autumn).

Milansbar (Ire)

9 b g Milan - Ardenbar (Ardross)

Neil King				Robert Bothway
PLACINGS: /408/1/11231/342129-				RPR **151**c

Starts	1st	2nd	3rd	4th	Win & Pl
16	5	3	2	2	£69,328

	137	2/16	Extr	3m Cls3 Nov 127-142 Ch Hcap soft	£6,564
	141	3/15	Kels	3m2f Cls2 120-141 Hdl Hcap gd-sft	£16,245
	119	12/14	Uttx	3m Cls4 95-120 Hdl Hcap heavy	£3,249
	112	12/14	Uttx	2m4f Cls4 106-119 Hdl Hcap soft	£3,769
		12/12	Folk	2m6½f Cls5 Mdn Hdl heavy	£2,053

Real mudlark who flourished when granted an extreme test of stamina last season, finishing a terrific second in the Midlands National under top weight; remains on the same mark and should be a force in similar races on soft or heavy ground.

Milsean (Ire)

7 b g Milan - Boro Supreme (Supreme Leader)

Willie Mullins (Ir)				Gigginstown House Stud
PLACINGS: 1/121/1222/				RPR **153**h

Starts	1st	2nd	3rd	4th	Win & Pl
7	3	4	-	-	£51,607

	11/14	Navn	2m Mdn Hdl soft	£6,900
	3/14	Limk	2m3f NHF 5-7yo heavy	£5,750
	1/14	Navn	2m NHF 5-7yo soft	£4,600

Long seen as an exciting prospect (sent off odds-on for first six runs under rules) but only fulfilled potential when granted an extreme test of stamina with 33-1 second in the 2015 Albert Bartlett at Cheltenham; missed last season through injury.

Min (Fr)

5 b g Walk In The Park - Phemyka (Saint Estephe)

Willie Mullins (Ir)				Mrs S Ricci
PLACINGS: 43/112-				RPR **157+**h

Starts	1st	2nd	3rd	4th	Win & Pl
5	2	1	1	1	£61,084

	1/16	Punc	2m Nov Gd2 Hdl heavy	£18,529
	12/15	Punc	2m2f Mdn Hdl soft	£5,349

No match for Altior in last season's Supreme Novices' Hurdle but still ran a cracker to beat the rest comfortably on only his third run since moving from France; likely to go novice chasing given his yard's hurdling strength and should be fairly high in the pecking order.

Racing Post iPad app
30-day free trial. On the App Store now.
Available on the App Store

Minella Foru (Ire)

7 b g King's Theatre - Shannon Rose (Topanoora)

Edward Harty (Ir)   **John P McManus**

PLACINGS: 1/11736/3565/121-   RPR **145**+c

Starts	1st	2nd	3rd	4th		Win & Pl
12	4	1	2	-		£123,643
134	12/15	Leop	3m¹/₂f 122-150 Ch Hcap heavy			£82,791
	5/15	Limk	2m3¹/₂f Ch good			£6,953
	11/13	Navn	2m Nov Gd3 Hdl yield			£15,325
	9/13	List	2m Mdn Hdl 4yo yield			£6,171

Won last season's Paddy Power Chase at Leopardstown, improving massively for a stiff test of stamina having never raced beyond 2m4f previously; raised 12lb for that victory but remains unexposed over fences and may well progress again.

Minella Present (Ire)

7 b g Presenting - Dabaya (In The Wings)

Neil Mulholland   **Mrs Jane Gerard-Pearse**

PLACINGS: 3313/115P02/3122P-1   RPR **144**+c

Starts	1st	2nd	3rd	4th		Win & Pl
16	5	3	4	-		£41,525
134	5/16	Uttx	2m4f Cls2 123-146 Ch Hcap good			£16,245
	6/15	Font	2m1¹/₂f Cls4 Nov Ch gd-sft			£3,899
	10/14	Uttx	2m4f Cls4 Nov Hdl gd-sft			£3,249
	10/14	Uttx	2m4f Cls5 Cond Mdn Hdl good			£2,599
	3/14	Chep	2m Cls6 Mdn NHF 4-6yo soft			£1,560

Lightly raced chaser who progressed well over fences early last season and finished a close second at Cheltenham before a winter break; pulled muscles behind on his return at Aintree but won well at Uttoxeter when stepped up to 2m4f.

Minella Rocco (Ire)

6 b g Shirocco - Petralona (Alleged)

Jonjo O'Neill   **John P McManus**

PLACINGS: 1/11/3P621-   RPR **160**+c

Starts	1st	2nd	3rd	4th		Win & Pl
7	3	1	1	-		£77,927
	3/16	Chel	4m Cls1 Nov List Am Ch gd-sft			£59,960
	2/15	Newb	2m4¹/₂f Cls4 Nov Hdl soft			£3,249
	2/15	Kemp	2m5f Cls4 Nov Hdl soft			£3,249

Took time to find his feet over fences last season but delivered in style when winning the National Hunt Chase (first time on ground better than soft); relished extreme test of stamina that day and interesting to see if he has the class to become a Gold Cup candidate.

Missed Approach (Ire)

6 b g Golan - Polly's Dream (Beau Sher)

Warren Greatrex   **Alan & Andrew Turner**

PLACINGS: 1113/1P2-   RPR **147**+h

Starts	1st	2nd	3rd	4th		Win & Pl
6	3	1	1	-		£17,185
123	11/15	Newb	3m Cls3 120-142 Hdl Hcap soft			£9,384
	11/14	Ffos	2m4f Cls5 Mdn Hdl soft			£1,949
	10/14	Uttx	2m Cls6 NHF 4-6yo good			£1,560

Easy winner at Newbury on his return from nearly a year out last season, rocketing 20lb up the handicap; pulled up when second favourite for the Pertemps Final but bounced back with a good second over an inadequate trip at Ayr.

Missy Tata (Fr)

4 b f Astarabad - Queen Running (Cadoudal)

Gordon Elliott (Ir) — Simon Munir & Isaac Souede

PLACINGS: 53/3124-11 — RPR **140+h**

Starts	1st	2nd	3rd	4th	Win & Pl
8	3	1	2	1	£48,328

5/16	Klny	2m1f Hdl good	£7,914
4/16	Punc	2m Nov Hdl yield	£11,305
10/15	DRoy	2m Hdl 3yo yld-sft	£7,488

Pulled a muscle when failing to build on a fine debut win for new connections last season but shrugged off the layoff to run a big race when fourth in the Fred Winter at Cheltenham; won twice more in the spring and still on an upward curve.

Mister Miyagi (Ire)

7 b g Zagreb - Muckle Flugga (Karinga Bay)

Dan Skelton — Den Turner & Jay Tabb

PLACINGS: 3FF/2311/1161- — RPR **150+h**

Starts	1st	2nd	3rd	4th	Win & Pl
8	5	1	1	-	£28,939

4/16	Chel	2m4¹/₂f Cls2 Nov Hdl gd-sft	£10,010
11/15	Tntn	2m¹/₂f Cls4 Nov Hdl gd-stt	£4,549
10/15	Chel	2m¹/₂f Cls3 Mdn Hdl good	£6,279
3/15	Strf	2m¹/₂f Cls5 NHF 4-6yo good	£2,599
3/15	Strf	2m¹/₂f Cls5 Mdn NHF 4-6yo gd-sft	£2,599

Won his first two races over hurdles last autumn and excelled in the spring after a break, finishing sixth in the Supreme Novices' Hurdle and winning back at Cheltenham; well-beaten favourite in a bumper on only run under rules on soft ground.

Moabit (Ger)

4 b g Azamour - Moonlight Danceuse (Bering)

Paul Nicholls — Owners Group 014

PLACINGS: 2-11115P — RPR **131h**

Starts	1st	2nd	3rd	4th	Win & Pl
7	4	1	-	-	£27,761

6/16	NAbb	2m1f Cls3 Nov Hdl gd-sft	£7,280
123 5/16	Strf	2m¹/₂f Cls2 123-140 Hdl Hcap gd-sft	£11,711
5/16	Winc	1m7¹/₂f Cls4 Nov Hdl gd-fm	£3,249
5/16	Extr	2m1f Cls4 Mdn Hdl gd-fm	£3,249

Three-time winner on the Flat in France in 2015 and made a bright start over hurdles this summer, completing a four-timer in June before not beaten far when fifth on a sharp rise in class for the Summer Hurdle at Market Rasen.

Modus

6 ch g Motivator - Alessandra (Generous)

Paul Nicholls — John P McManus

PLACINGS: 1180/2/311300- — RPR **139+h**

Starts	1st	2nd	3rd	4th	Win & Pl
11	4	1	2	-	£45,541

11/15	Newb	2m¹/₂f Cls3 Nov Hdl soft	£6,279
11/15	Tntn	2m3f Cls3 Nov Hdl good	£5,697
1/14	Chel	1m6f Cls1 List NHF 4yo soft	£11,888
10/13	Extr	1m5f Cls6 NHF 3yo gd-sft	£1,560

Finished second of 23 in the 2015 Champion Bumper but not suited by big fields according to his rider when well beaten in the Betfair and County Hurdles last season; had won two out of three in novice hurdles and looks capable of better.

Minella Rocco: powering up the hill to win Cheltenham's four-miler

Monksland (Ire)

9 b g Beneficial - Cush Jewel (Executive Perk)

Noel Meade (Ir)				Mrs Patricia Hunt
PLACINGS: O1113/121/320/21232-				RPR **153h**

Starts	1st	2nd	3rd	4th	Win & Pl
15	6	5	3	-	£160,099

	11/15	Gowr	2m4f Ch heavy	£8,558
	12/12	Leop	3m Gd2 Hdl soft	£21,667
	11/12	DRoy	2m Gd2 Hdl yld-sft	£27,083
	1/12	Naas	2m4f Nov Gd2 Hdl sft-hvy	£20,313
	12/11	Navn	2m Mdn Hdl 4yo sft-hvy	£5,948
	11/11	DRoy	2m NHF 4-7yo soft	£5,056

Finally got the chance to go chasing last season having missed two years through injury earlier in his career; won on his chasing debut at Gowran Park and ran well when placed three times at Grade 1 level; should improve granted a stiff test of stamina.

Moon Racer (Ire)

7 b g Saffron Walden - Angel's Folly (Wesaam)

David Pipe			Professor Caroline Tisdall & Bryan Drew
PLACINGS: 1/11/2			RPR **135+b**

Starts	1st	2nd	3rd	4th	Win & Pl
4	3	1	-	-	£101,855

	3/15	Chel	2m¹/₂f Cls1 Gd1 NHF 4-6yo good	£34,170
	10/14	Chel	2m¹/₂f Cls4 NHF 4-6yo gd-sft	£4,549
	4/14	Fair	2m NHF 4-5yo gd-yld	£49,167

Hugely impressive winner of the Champion Bumper at Cheltenham in 2015, overcoming a slow start before powering through the field; subsequently held up by injury but made a solid return when second in Grade 1 bumper at Punchestown in April.

More Of That (Ire)

8 b g Beneficial - Guigone (Esprit Du Nord)

Jonjo O'Neill				John P McManus
PLACINGS: 1/1111/3/113-				RPR **162+c**

Starts	1st	2nd	3rd	4th	Win & Pl
9	7		2	-	£261,557

		12/15	Chel	2m5f Cls2 Nov Ch soft	£15,451
		11/15	Chel	2m4¹/₂f Cls2 Nov Ch good	£14,389
		3/14	Chel	3m Cls1 Gd1 Hdl good	£156,613
		12/13	Chel	2m4¹/₂f Cls1 Gd2 Hdl good	£22,780
137	11/13	Hayd	2m3f Cls2 121-147 Hdl Hcap soft	£24,692
130	11/13	Weth	2m4f Cls3 110-131 Hdl Hcap gd-sft	£5,523
		12/12	Folk	2m1¹/₂f Cls5 Mdn Hdl soft	£1,779

Brilliant winner of the World Hurdle in 2014 but has run only four times since then due to injury and breathing issues; won first two chases last season but broke blood vessels when third in the RSA Chase; could be a Gold Cup horse if finally getting a clear run.

Morning Assembly (Ire)

9 b g Shantou - Barrack Village (Montelimar)

Pat Fahy (Ir)				Clipper Logistics Group Ltd
PLACINGS: 13/21F1/1123/3/2248-				RPR **156+c**

Starts	1st	2nd	3rd	4th	Win & Pl
15	5	4	3	1	£135,735

	11/13	Punc	2m6f Nov Gd2 Ch yield	£20,874
	10/13	Punc	2m4f Ch yld-sft	£6,732
	4/13	Punc	3m Nov Gd1 Hdl soft	£40,325
	1/13	Naas	2m3f Mdn Hdl heavy	£7,854
	2/12	Punc	2m NHF 4-7yo heavy	£4,888

Finished third in the RSA Chase before missing more than 18 months through injury, returning only last spring; soon back to his best and finished a fine fourth behind Un Temps Pour

WALKERS
Beware of Racehorses
Please cross gallops here
with extreme caution →

Jackdaws Castle
Private Property
Beyond this point

Tout at Cheltenham before going well for a long way when a non-stayer in the Grand National.

Mr Mix (Fr)

5 gr g Al Namix - Royale Surabaya (Turgeon)

Paul Nicholls   **Ian Fogg & Potensis Bloodstock Ltd**

PLACINGS: 3/3312F-   **RPR 143h**

Starts	1st	2nd	3rd	4th	Win & Pl
6	1	1	3	-	£18,230
	1/16	Tntn	2m3f Cls4 Nov Hdl 4-7yo heavy		£4,549

Useful novice hurdler last season; most impressive when winning easily on heavy ground at Taunton and ran Yala Enki close at Ascot, though not in contention when a faller in the Fred Winter; looks the type to improve again over fences.

Muthaza (Fr)

4 ch f Muhtathir - John Quatz (Johann Quatz)

Willie Mullins (Ir)   **Mrs J Donnelly**

PLACINGS: 111F   **RPR 128+h**

Starts	1st	2nd	3rd	4th	Win & Pl
4	3	-	-	-	£19,444
	7/16	Gway	2m¹/₂f Nov Hdl 4yo good		£9,044
	6/16	Bell	2m1f Nov Hdl 4yo yield		£5,879
	6/16	Tram	2m5f Mdn Hdl good		£4,522

French recruit who made a bright start for new connections this summer, most notably when easily winning at the Galway Festival; seems sure to be a leading contender for the mares' novice hurdle at Cheltenham.

My Murphy (Ire)

10 b g Presenting - Fine De Claire (Teenoso)

Liam Burke (Ir)   **Hans Joerg Zindel**

PLACINGS: P/41421P/69237/3P1P-   **RPR 151+c**

Starts	1st	2nd	3rd	4th	Win & Pl
27	6	2	5	5	£139,680
139	1/16	Gowr	3m1f 131-156 Ch Hcap heavy	£44,118
135	3/14	Navn	3m Nov 107-135 Ch Hcap soft	£27,083
	12/13	Fair	3m Ch soft	£4,488
	3/12	Navn	2m7f Nov Hdl soft	£9,200
	12/11	Limk	3m Nov Gd3 Hdl heavy	£15,409
	10/11	WxfR	2m2f Mdn Hdl soft	£4,461

Gutsy stayer who loves heavy ground and has found the Thyestes right up his street in the last two seasons, winning in January having beaten all bar handicap snip Djakadam (albeit left in second at the last) in 2015; will surely be aimed at a repeat.

My Tent Or Yours (Ire)

9 b g Desert Prince - Spartan Girl (Ela-Mana Mou)

Nicky Henderson   **John P McManus**

PLACINGS: 122/121121/1123/22-3   **RPR 167h**

Starts	1st	2nd	3rd	4th	Win & Pl
16	7	7	2	-	£535,371
	2/14	Kemp	2m Cls3 NHF std-slw	£6,330
	12/13	Kemp	2m Cls1 Gd1 Hdl soft	£56,950
	11/13	Newc	2m¹/₂f Cls1 Gd1 Hdl good	£56,270
	4/13	Aint	2m¹/₂f Cls1 Nov Gd2 Hdl gd-sft	£34,170
149	2/13	Newb	2m¹/₂f Cls1 Gd3 133-159 Hdl Hcap soft	£86,849
	1/13	Hntg	2m Cls4 Nov Hdl 4-7yo soft	£3,444
	11/12	Asct	1m7¹/₂f Cls3 Nov Hdl gd-sft	£7,507
	12/11	Ludl	1m6f Cls5 NHF 4-5yo gd-sft	£2,274

Off the track for nearly two years before a tremendous return in the Champion Hurdle,

More Of That: 2014 World Hurdle winner might finally get a chance to shine over fences

finishing second in the race for the second time; form tailed off subsequently but still looks the best 2m hurdler in Britain; yet to prove he stays 2m4f.

Nambour (Ger)

6 b g Sholokhov - Nanouska (Dashing Blade)

Willie Mullins (Ir) **Gigginstown House Stud**

PLACINGS: 1/113222- RPR **143**h

Starts		1st	2nd	3rd	4th	Win & Pl
6		2	3	1	-	£31,132
	11/15	Fair	2m2f Mdn Hdl sft-hvy			£6,419
	5/15	Punc	2m NHF 4-7yo gd-sft			£5,884

Unlucky not to add to victory on hurdling debut last season, twice finishing second to Acapella Bourgeois (by a head on second occasion) and again behind Up For Review, progressing throughout; has the size to make a better chaser.

Native River (Ire)

6 ch g Indian River - Native Mo (Be My Native)

Colin Tizzard **Brocade Racing**

PLACINGS: U/3116F19/3113321- RPR **165**+c

Starts		1st	2nd	3rd	4th	Win & Pl
14		6	1	4		£148,144
	4/16	Aint	3m1f Cls1 Nov Gd1 Ch gd-sft			£56,319
	11/15	Newb	2m7½f Cls1 Nov Gd2 Ch gd-sft			£20,284
	11/15	Extr	3m Cls2 Nov Ch soft			£12,974
	2/15	Extr	2m1f Cls1 Nov List Hdl gd-sft			£11,390
	11/14	Newc	2m6f Cls2 Nov Hdl soft			£11,261
	10/14	Strf	2m6f Cls5 Mdn Hdl good			£2,599

Smart novice chaser last season when well suited by a thorough test of stamina; second in the National Hunt Chase at Cheltenham before winning a 3m1f Grade 1 at Aintree under an aggressive ride; likely to be aimed at top staying handicaps.

Nearly Nama'd (Ire)

8 b g Millenary - Coca's Well (Religiously)

Sandra Hughes (Ir) **John P McManus**

PLACINGS: 6897/8126219F/86113- RPR **145**+c

Starts		1st	2nd	3rd	4th	Win & Pl
23		6	3	1		£114,065
134	1/16	Fair	2m1f 132-153 Ch Hcap heavy			£44,118
127	11/15	Fair	2m1f 119-142 Ch Hcap sft-hvy			£23,256
	9/14	Navn	2m4f Ch gd-fm			£10,833
	5/14	Kbgn	2m4f Ch good			£5,175
120	10/13	Gway	2m 107-134 Ch Hcap heavy			£12,683
	3/13	Navn	2m Mdn Hdl heavy			£5,610

Proved a revelation when winning twice over 2m1f at Fairyhouse last winter, including a valuable handicap in January, relishing testing conditions having previously raced mainly over further on summer ground (had even won on good to firm); may be up to Graded level.

Nichols Canyon

6 b g Authorized - Zam Zoom (Dalakhani)

Willie Mullins (Ir) **Andrea & Graham Wylie**

PLACINGS: 11U131/111333-3 RPR **168**+h

Starts		1st	2nd	3rd	4th	Win & Pl
13		7	4	5	-	£362,799
	12/15	Leop	2m Gd1 Hdl heavy			£46,512
	11/15	Punc	2m Gd1 Hdl soft			£39,535
	5/15	Punc	2m4f Nov Gd1 Hdl gd-yld			£44,186
	4/15	Aint	2m4f Cls1 Nov Gd1 Hdl good			£42,203
	2/15	Leop	2m2f Nov Gd1 Hdl yield			£41,860
	11/14	Fair	2m Nov Gd1 Hdl yield			£40,625
	11/14	Cork	2m Mdn Hdl 4yo soft			£5,750

Became the only horse to beat Faugheen on his return last season; clearly flattered by that success but still proved himself a very smart hurdler, most notably when third in the Champion Hurdle; equally effective over 2m4f and could stay further again.

Noble Endeavor (Ire)

7 b g Flemensfirth - Old Moon (Old Vic)

Gordon Elliott (Ir) **C Jones**

PLACINGS: 01416/22125/2312F-P RPR **146**c

Starts		1st	2nd	3rd	4th	Win & Pl
16		4	5	1	1	£52,078
	12/15	DRoy	2m4f Ch heavy			£7,488
	1/15	Punc	2m4f Hdl soft			£6,953
	2/14	Punc	2m4f Mdn Hdl heavy			£6,325
	12/13	Leop	2m NHF 4yo soft			£5,049

Beaten a head by Killultagh Vic in the Martin Pipe Hurdle two seasons ago but didn't quite reach that level over fences last season; probably running his best race when falling two out in the National Hunt Chase (had been expected to relish step up to 4m).

O O Seven (Ire)

6 b g Flemensfirth - Kestral Heights (Eagle Eyed)

Nicky Henderson **Triermore Stud**

PLACINGS: 120/11218-2 RPR **148**h

Starts		1st	2nd	3rd	4th	Win & Pl
9		4	3	-	-	£48,309
	2/16	Muss	3m Cls2 Hdl soft			£14,389
	12/15	Sand	2m Cls3 Nov Hdl soft			£6,498
	11/15	Hntg	2m Cls5 Mdn Hdl gd-sft			£2,599
	12/14	Hntg	2m Cls6 NHF 4-6yo gd-sft			£1,560

Won three times over hurdles last season and twice second at Grade 1 level, albeit well beaten by Yorkhill and Jer's Girl; described by his trainer as a 'baby' and should have lots more to come; looked in need of further when second over 2m4f last time.

Native River: could find himself lining up in the Cheltenham Gold Cup if he continues to progress – where he could meet stablemates Cue Card and Thistlecrack

O'Faolains Boy (Ire)

9 b g Oscar - Lisa's Storm (Glacial Storm)

Rebecca Curtis　　　　　**Trembath, Hyde, Outhart & Hill**

PLACINGS: 1/31114/2P115/P1P87-　　　　RPR **163+c**

Starts	1st	2nd	3rd	4th	Win & Pl
15	6	1	1	1	£142,421

12/15	Newb	2m7¹/₂f Cls2 Ch soft	£14,427
3/14	Chel	3m¹/₂f Cls1 Gd1 Ch good	£85,425
2/14	Asct	3m Cls1 Nov Gd2 Ch soft	£18,092
2/13	Bang	2m7f Cls3 Nov Hdl heavy	£5,393
1/13	Chep	2m3¹/₂f Cls4 Mdn Hdl heavy	£3,249
12/12	Chep	2m Cls6 NHF 4-6yo heavy	£1,754

Won the RSA Chase in 2014 but missed the following campaign through injury; mixed form last season but won well at Newbury and ran well for a long way in the Gold Cup (still upsides four out); down to an interesting mark for good staying handicaps.

Old Guard

5 b g Notnowcato - Dolma (Marchand De Sable)

Paul Nicholls　　　　**The Brooks, Kyle & Stewart Families**

PLACINGS: 1P293/1114-　　　　RPR **159+h**

Starts	1st	2nd	3rd	4th	Win & Pl
9	4	1	1	1	£155,597

12/15	Chel	2m1f Cls1 Gd2 Hdl soft	£74,035
145 11/15	Chel	2m¹/₂f Cls1 Gd3 128-147 Hdl Hcap gd-sft	£56,950
137 10/15	Chel	2m¹/₂f Cls3 116-139 Cond Hdl Hcap good	£6,256
11/14	Newb	2m1¹/₂f Cls3 Hdl 3yo soft	£6,498

Sharply progressive during the first half of last season when winning three times at Cheltenham, most notably in the International Hurdle after two handicap victories; over the top when well beaten in the Christmas Hurdle; could be a dark horse for top 2m hurdles.

ON THE FIGURES

Native River Benefited from more positive tactics when landing a Grade 1 at Aintree last season. Jumping errors had rather hindered his progress up to that stage, but that April success was worth an RPR of 165 and, although he will need to find upwards of 10lb improvement to make his mark at the very top level, an official mark of 154 marks him down as an obvious Hennessy Gold Cup candidate. [Steve Mason, Racing Post Ratings]

On The Fringe (Ire)

11 b g Exit To Nowhere - Love And Porter (Sheer Grit)

Enda Bolger (Ir) **John P McManus**

PLACINGS: /1/123/112211/1711-1 **RPR 145+c**

Starts	1st	2nd	3rd	4th	Win & Pl
21	12	4	2	1	£185,649

	4/16	Punc	3m1f Hunt Ch yield	£11,305
	4/16	Aint	2m5f Cls2 Am Hunt Ch soft	£23,720
	3/16	Chel	3m2½f Cls2 Hunt Ch good	£23,984
	5/15	Punc	3m1f Hunt Ch gd-yld	£11,085
	4/15	Aint	2m5f Cls2 Am Hunt Ch gd-sft	£23,720
	3/15	Chel	3m2½f Cls2 Hunt Ch soft	£23,984
	5/14	Klny	2m6f Hunt Ch yld-sft	£4,600
	5/14	Punc	3m1f Hunt Ch gd-yld	£11,917
	12/13	DRoy	2m7f Hunt Ch soft	£3,927
	5/12	Punc	3m1f Hunt Ch yield	£11,917
	2/11	Leop	3m Hunt Ch heavy	£8,922
	4/10	Punc	3m1f Hunt Ch good	£14,381

The outstanding hunter chaser in the last two seasons, pulling off the Cheltenham-Aintree-Punchestown treble in both campaigns; seems sure to be a leading player again next spring even at the age of 12.

One Track Mind (Ire)

6 b g Flemensfirth - Lady Petit (Beneficial)

Warren Greatrex **Andy Weller**

PLACINGS: 1/1U41/512-1 **RPR 154h**

Starts	1st	2nd	3rd	4th	Win & Pl
9	5	1	-	1	£117,443

	4/16	Punc	3m Gd1 Hdl yield	£86,765
140	12/15	Newb	2m4½f Cls2 125-140 Hdl Hcap soft	£11,574
	2/15	Weth	2m3½f Cls4 Nov Hdl good	£3,119
	11/14	Weth	2m3½f Cls4 Nov Hdl soft	£3,422
	4/14	Weth	2m Cls6 NHF 4-6yo gd-sft	£1,643

Lightly raced in two seasons over hurdles and made steady progress before winning a Grade 1 at Punchestown last season; form is probably weak for the grade but should have more to come over fences and looks a terrific prospect for novice chases.

Onenightinvienna (Ire)

7 b g Oscar - Be My Granny (Needle Gun)

Philip Hobbs **Mrs Judith Luff**

PLACINGS: 4/13213/211/1225U- **RPR 157c**

Starts	1st	2nd	3rd	4th	Win & Pl
12	4	4	2	-	£33,865

	11/15	Extr	3m Cls3 Nov Ch heavy	£9,495
	4/15	Prth	3m Cls2 Nov Hdl gd-sft	£9,495
	3/15	Hexm	2m7½f Cls4 Nov Hdl gd-sft	£3,422
	2/14	Tntn	2m½f Cls5 Am NHF 4-6yo heavy	£2,053

Useful novice chaser last season; always likely to struggle when thrown in at the deep end in the Grand National on fifth run over fences (in rear when departing) but such placing underlined need for extreme trips and should progress.

Open Eagle (Ire)

7 b g Montjeu - Princesse De Viane (Kaldoun)

Willie Mullins (Ir) **Supreme Horse Racing Club/Colin Gray**

PLACINGS: 3/12218- **RPR 142h**

Starts	1st	2nd	3rd	4th	Win & Pl
6	2	2	1	-	£22,423

	2/16	Wwck	2m5f Cls3 Nov Hdl soft	£6,498
	11/15	Fair	2m Mdn Hdl heavy	£5,349

Smart Flat horse (won the 2014 November Handicap by 12 lengths) who proved a useful novice hurdler last season, winning twice and finishing second to Altior and Thomas Hobson; travelled well but failed to stay 3m in the Albert Bartlett last time.

Orbasa (Fr)

5 b g Full Of Gold - Ierbasa De Kerpaul (Cadoubel)

Paul Nicholls **Potensis Bloodstock Limited**

PLACINGS: 5P12/261431422- **RPR 144+c**

Starts	1st	2nd	3rd	4th	Win & Pl
13	3	4	1	2	£74,138

	2/16	Font	2m1½f Cls2 Nov Ch gd-sft	£18,270
	7/15	Le L	2m4f Ch 4-5yo good	£8,930
	2/15	Fntb	2m2f Hdl 4yo v soft	£7,814

Chase and hurdle winner in France who finished alone when making a successful British debut at Fontwell in February; beaten three times after but ran with great credit when second at Ascot and Ayr; may well have benefited from a break.

Oscar Rock (Ire)

8 b g Oscar - Cash And New (Supreme Leader)

Malcolm Jefferson **Mr & Mrs G Calder**

PLACINGS: 11/12332/7211F/1007- **RPR 155+c**

Starts	1st	2nd	3rd	4th	Win & Pl
17	6	4	2	-	£80,505

147	9/15	MRas	2m5½f Cls1 List 135-155 Ch Hcap good	£28,475
138	3/15	Kels	2m5½f Cls2 Nov 129-138 Ch Hcap gd-sft	£14,621
132	2/15	Newc	2m4f Cls3 116-135 Ch Hcap gd-sft	£6,498
	11/13	Weth	2m4f Cls4 Nov Hdl gd-sft	£3,422
	2/13	Newb	2m½f Cls1 List NHF 4-6yo soft	£8,543
	11/12	Newb	2m½f Cls6 NHF 4-6yo soft	£1,949

Took plenty of time to find his feet over jumps after winning a Listed bumper in 2013 but flourished in 2015 when winning three out of four; twice disappointing at Cheltenham but shaped with a lot more promise in the bet365 Gold Cup and on a fair mark.

Onenightinvienna: could do well in staying handicap chases this season

'He should have more to come over fences and looks a terrific prospect for novice chases'

Otago Trail (Ire)

8 b g Heron Island - Cool Chic (Roselier)

Venetia Williams　　　　　　　　　　**Mrs Marie Shone**

PLACINGS: **S/1312/1132/2113P3-**　　　　RPR **157+c**

Starts		1st	2nd	3rd	4th	Win & Pl
13		5	3	4	-	£58,714
141	1/16	Chep	2m3¹/₂f Cls2 123-141 Ch Hcap heavy			£19,166
133	12/15	Extr	2m3f Cls3 119-133 Ch Hcap heavy			£15,698
	1/15	Winc	1m7¹/₂f Cls3 Nov Hdl heavy			£5,523
	11/14	Carl	2m4f Cls4 Nov Hdl soft			£3,249
	2/14	Font	2m1¹/₂f Cls6 NHF 4-6yo heavy			£1,560

Revels in heavy ground and won handicap chases in those conditions at Exeter and Chepstow during a bright start to his career over fences last winter; much less effective during the spring but remains one to watch when the mud is flying.

Our Kaempfer (Ire)

7 b g Oscar - Gra-Bri (Rashar)

Charlie Longsdon　　　　　　　**Swanee River Partnership**

PLACINGS: **3/1305/43113/42B5-**　　　　RPR **141h**

Starts		1st	2nd	3rd	4th	Win & Pl
13		3	1	3	2	£32,090
	3/15	Kemp	2m5f Cls4 Nov Hdl good			£3,899
	2/15	MRas	2m4¹/₂f Cls4 Nov Hdl gd-sft			£3,769
	10/13	Worc	2m Cls6 NHF 4-6yo good			£1,560

Dual novice hurdle winner two seasons ago who has looked better since stepped up to 3m despite failing to win again, finishing second and fifth in hot handicaps at Aintree and Cheltenham (Pertemps Final) last season when given plenty to do.

Out Sam

7 b g Multiplex - Tintera (King's Theatre)

Warren Greatrex				Swanee River Partnership
PLACINGS: 22/11F/631177-				RPR **153+c**

Starts	1st	2nd	3rd	4th	Win & Pl
9	4	-	1	-	£30,126
	2/16	Newb	2m7¹/₂f Cls3 Nov Ch soft		£7,798
	1/16	Catt	2m3f Cls4 Nov Ch soft		£4,883
	1/15	Asct	2m5¹/₂f Cls3 Nov Hdl 4-7yo soft		£6,498
	11/14	Newb	2m4¹/₂f Cls3 Nov Hdl soft		£6,498

Very impressive when winning his first two chases last season, albeit in three-runner races and disappointed in bigger fields at Cheltenham and Aintree; something to prove now but could still be a force in good staying handicaps.

Outlander (Ire)

8 b g Stowaway - Western Whisper (Supreme Leader)

Willie Mullins (Ir)				Gigginstown House Stud
PLACINGS: /1116/12162/3111F2-2				RPR **156c**

Starts	1st	2nd	3rd	4th	Win & Pl
16	8	4	1	-	£155,704
	2/16	Leop	2m5¹/₂f Nov Ch sft-hvy		£36,875
	12/15	Limk	2m3¹/₂f Nov Gd2 Ch heavy		£21,163
	11/15	Punc	2m4f Ch soft		£6,953
	1/15	Leop	2m4f Nov Gd2 Hdl yield		£19,903
	11/14	Fair	2m Mdn Hdl sft-hvy		£4,600
	2/13	Naas	2m NHF 4-7yo sft-hvy		£7,573
	12/12	Leop	2m NHF 4-7yo soft		£6,325
	12/12	Fair	2m NHF 4yo soft		£4,888

High-class novice chaser last season, winning his first three chases including a Grade 1 at Leopardstown; kept busy during the spring (second at Fairyhouse and Punchestown after falling four out in the JLT) and may prove better still when freshened up.

Ozzie The Oscar (Ire)

5 b g Oscar - Private Official (Beneficial)

Philip Hobbs				Bradley Partnership
PLACINGS: 3111-2				RPR **140+h**

Starts	1st	2nd	3rd	4th	Win & Pl
5	3	1	1	-	£15,000
	4/16	Ludl	2m Cls4 Nov Hdl gd-sft		£3,899
	4/16	Newb	2m1¹/₂f Cls4 Nov Hdl good		£4,549
	3/16	Tntn	2m Cls4 Mdn Hdl soft		£3,249

Gained a quickfire hat-trick in novice hurdles last spring, all at a modest level, and perhaps went to the well once too often when beaten at Newton Abbot; has done all his racing at around 2m but ought to get further; likely to go novice chasing.

Pain Au Chocolat (Fr)

5 b g Enrique - Clair Chene (Solido)

Dan Skelton				Mike & Eileen Newbould
PLACINGS: 2/2110/53113F-8				RPR **150+c**

Starts	1st	2nd	3rd	4th	Win & Pl
12	4	2	2	-	£40,663
	2/16	Newc	2m1¹/₂f Cls4 Nov Ch soft		£3,899
	12/15	Hayd	2m1¹/₂f Cls2 Nov Ch heavy		£12,628
	1/15	Sand	2m Cls3 Hdl 4yo soft		£6,498
	1/15	Plum	2m Cls4 Nov Hdl soft		£3,379

Did well to win novice chases at Haydock and Newcastle last season but fell on his only subsequent run over fences at Ayr (third in the Kingwell Hurdle in between and well beaten over hurdles in France); should make a good 2m handicapper.

Peace And Co (Fr)

5 b g Falco - Peace Lina (Linamix)

Nicky Henderson				Simon Munir & Isaac Souede
PLACINGS: 1111/63P-				RPR **147h**

Starts	1st	2nd	3rd	4th	Win & Pl
7	4	-	1	-	£118,517
	3/15	Chel	2m1f Cls1 Gd1 Hdl 4yo soft		£68,340
	1/15	Chel	2m1f Cls1 Gd2 Hdl 4yo soft		£17,085
	12/14	Donc	2m1¹/₂f Cls1 Gd2 Hdl 3yo soft		£15,876
	6/14	Claf	2m1f Hdl 3yo soft		£12,800

Won the Triumph Hurdle in 2015 during a brilliant unbeaten juvenile campaign but proved bitterly disappointing last season; twice well beaten at odds-on and breathing operation seemed to make no difference when pulled up in the Champion Hurdle.

Pendra (Ire)

8 ch g Old Vic - Mariah Rollins (Over The River)

Charlie Longsdon				John P McManus
PLACINGS: 1/1120/11730/45/150-				RPR **149+c**

Starts	1st	2nd	3rd	4th	Win & Pl
15	6	2	1	1	£94,926
140	10/15	Asct	3m Cls1 Gd3 137-159 Ch Hcap good		£56,950
	11/13	Ling	2m Cls4 Nov Ch heavy		£3,769
	10/13	Carl	2m Cls4 Ch gd-sft		£4,549
	12/12	Plum	2m Cls4 Nov Hdl soft		£4,106
	11/12	Plum	2m Cls5 Mdn Hdl soft		£2,053
	3/12	Hntg	2m Cls6 NHF 4-6yo good		£1,365

Hasn't quite lived up to expectations over the years (sent off at 9-1 or less for three Cheltenham Festival handicaps) but gained biggest success at Ascot last season; also ran well in the Silver Cup and could win another good staying handicap.

ON THE CLOCK

Peace And Co Retained his unblemished record in the 2015 Triumph Hurdle but the wheels came off last term. If he can be taught to settle there are good races to be won. Nicky Henderson's five-year-old should not be written off prematurely. *[Dave Edwards, Topspeed]*

Perfect Candidate (Ire)

9 b g Winged Love - Dansana (Insan)

Fergal O'Brien — **ISL Recruitment**

PLACINGS: /2445/1715150/25101-   RPR **155+c**

Starts	1st	2nd	3rd	4th	Win & Pl
21	5	2	1	3	£52,407
142	4/16	Chel	3m2f Cls2 122-148 Ch Hcap good		£12,512
134	1/16	Chel	3m2¹/₂f Cls2 119-139 Ch Hcap heavy		£12,512
124	1/15	Leic	2m6¹/₂f Cls3 Nov 117-132 Ch Hcap gd-sft		£6,330
115	11/14	Bang	2m4¹/₂f Cls4 97-120 Ch Hcap soft		£3,994
	5/14	Weth	3m1¹/₂f Cls4 Nov Hdl soft		£3,119

Did all of his racing at Cheltenham last season and progressed throughout, winning twice at around 3m2f; thorough stayer who is now more likely to get in the Grand National after his latest win in April (just missed out on a spot last season).

Petit Mouchoir (Fr)

5 gr g Al Namix - Arnette (Denham Red)

Willie Mullins (Ir) — **Gigginstown House Stud**

PLACINGS: 1/113482-2   RPR **154h**

Starts	1st	2nd	3rd	4th	Win & Pl
7	2	2		1	£89,533
	11/15	Thur	2m Mdn Hdl 4yo soft		£5,349
	4/15	Punc	2m NHF 4 5yo gd-yld		£45,736

Ran a string of good races in Grade 1 novice hurdles last season, going closest at Aintree when just touched off by Buveur D'Air on soft ground; should improve over further and looks a good prospect for novice chases (already a point-to-point winner).

Pleasant Company (Ire)

8 b g Presenting - Katie Flame (Alderbrook)

Willie Mullins (Ir) — **Malcolm C Denmark**

PLACINGS: 2/1134/43/3413P-1   RPR **145c**

Starts	1st	2nd	3rd	4th	Win & Pl
11	3	2	4	3	£48,696
139	4/16	Punc	3m1f 120-145 Ch Hcap yield		£26,029
	12/15	Punc	3m1f Ch heavy		£6,953
	11/13	Asct	1m7¹/₂f Cls4 NHF 4 6yo gd-sft		£3,128

Won a 3m1f handicap chase at Punchestown at the end of April having won over the same course and distance on his chasing debut last season; lightly raced for his age and seen by his trainer as a Grand National contender.

Politologue (Fr)

5 gr g Poliglote - Scarlet Row (Turgeon)

Paul Nicholls — **J Hales**

PLACINGS: 21U210-   RPR **141+h**

Starts	1st	2nd	3rd	4th	Win & Pl
6	2	2			£42,025
	2/16	Extr	2m1f Cls1 Nov List Hdl heavy		£11,524
	6/15	Autl	2m2f Hdl 4yo soft		£17,860

Shaped with great promise in four starts following move from France last season; unseated

his rider when challenging at Cheltenham and travelled strongly before being outstayed by Barters Hill in the Challow Hurdle; top prospect.

Potters Legend

6 b g Midnight Legend - Loose Morals (Luso)

Lucy Wadham — **Mrs J May**

PLACINGS: 1221223-   RPR **141h**

Starts	1st	2nd	3rd	4th	Win & Pl
7	2	4	1	-	£34,895
	1/16	Hntg	2m Cls5 Mdn Hdl soft		£2,274
	10/15	Fknm	2m Cls6 Am NHF 4-6yo gd-sft		£2,053

Won twice last season and knocked on the door at a higher level, finishing second to Ballyandy in a Listed bumper, second in the EBF Final and third in a Grade 1 novice hurdle at Aintree; should make a fine staying chaser.

Prince Of Scars (Ire)

6 b g Flemensfirth - Spirit Leader (Supreme Leader)

Gordon Elliott (Ir) — **Gigginstown House Stud**

PLACINGS: 5/125/81113-   RPR **163+h**

Starts	1st	2nd	3rd	4th	Win & Pl
8	4	1	1	-	£89,965
	12/15	Leop	3m Gd1 Hdl heavy		£39,535
139	11/15	Navn	2m7f 111-139 Hdl Hcap soft		£15,116
130	11/15	Clon	3m 109-136 Hdl Hcap heavy		£12,093
	1/15	Leop	2m Mdn Hdl yield		£3,624

Made rapid progress last season, winning two handicaps before easily beating Alpha Des Obeaux in a Grade 1 over Christmas; unsuited by a slow pace next time at Aintree; exciting novice chase prospect given testing conditions (missed World Hurdle due to good ground).

Ptit Zig (Fr)

7 b g Great Pretender - Red Rym (Denham Red)

Paul Nicholls — **Barry Fulton, Chris Giles & Richard Webb**

PLACINGS: 264/1111F5/12FU21-41   RPR **168c**

Starts	1st	2nd	3rd	4th	Win & Pl
26	10	6	1	3	£518,337
	6/16	Autl	3m1¹/₂f Gd1 Hdl soft		£122,426
	4/16	Sand	2m5¹/₂f Cls1 List Hdl good		£28,475
	10/15	DRoy	2m4f Gd2 Ch yld-sft		£23,256
	1/15	Chel	2m5f Cls1 Nov Gd2 Ch soft		£18,310
	12/14	Asct	2m3f Cls1 Nov Gd2 Ch soft		£15,162
	11/14	Wrck	2m Cls3 Nov Ch 4-5yo soft		£9,384
	11/14	Extr	2m1¹/₂f Cls4 Ch soft		£4,660
	11/13	Autl	2m3¹/₂f Gd1 Hdl 4yo heavy		£98,780
134	4/13	Sand	2m Cls2 112-134 Hdl 4yo Hcap good		£15,640
	2/13	Ludl	2m Cls4 Mdn Hdl soft		£3,249

Looked a very smart chasing prospect early last season but was let down by his jumping; did well reverting to hurdles, finishing second in the Cleeve before wins at Sandown and Auteuil (French Champion Hurdle); can win more good staying hurdles.

Pylonthepressure (Ire)

6 b g Darsi - Minnie O'Grady (Welsh Term)

Willie Mullins (Ir)   Mrs S Ricci

PLACINGS: **111/522-**   RPR **130h**

Starts	1st	2nd	3rd	4th	Win & Pl
5	2	2	-	-	£14,151

2/15	Naas	2m3f NHF 5-7yo soft	£5,349
12/14	Thur	2m NHF 4-7yo sft-hvy	£4,313

Smart bumper performer two seasons ago but beaten at odds-on in both maiden hurdles last term; still ran well to finish second to two good opponents and seems sure to benefit from a step up in trip and switch to fences.

Pylonthepressure: dual bumper winner can surely improve on what he managed last season

Rayvin Black

7 b g Halling - Optimistic (Reprimand)

Oliver Sherwood   R White & V J Walsh

PLACINGS: **16/251527/032012216-**   RPR **153+h**

Starts	1st	2nd	3rd	4th	Win & Pl
21	5	8	1	-	£122,099

2/16	Winc	1m7¹/₂f Cls1 Gd2 Hdl soft	£34,170
137 1/16	Sand	2m Cls2 124-150 Hdl Hcap heavy	£15,640
119 1/15	Sand	2m Cls2 119-144 Hdl Hcap soft	£15,640
10/13	Extr	2m1f Cls4 Nov Hdl gd-fm	£3,249
4/13	Ludl	2m Cls4 Mdn Hdl good	£3,249

Much improved over hurdles last season, winning a Sandown handicap off 137 before finishing second in the Haydock Champion Hurdle Trial and winning the Kingwell; has shown best hurdles form on soft or heavy ground but won on good on the Flat in April.

Red Sherlock

7 ch g Shirocco - Lady Cricket (Cricket Ball)

David Pipe — **The Johnson Family**

PLACINGS: **11/11119/**   RPR **148h**

Starts 7	1st 6	2nd -	3rd -	4th -	Win & Pl £39,082
1/14	Chel	2m4½f Cls1 Nov Gd2 Hdl heavy			£17,165
1/14	Weth	2m4f Cls4 Nov Hdl 4-7yo soft			£3,769
12/13	Sthl	2m4½f Cls5 Mdn Hdl good			£1,949
11/13	Chel	2m½f Cls1 List NHF 4-6yo good			£11,390
2/13	Asct	1m7½f Cls4 NHF 4-6yo soft			£3,249
1/13	Towc	2m Cls6 NHF 4-6yo heavy			£1,560

On the comeback trail again after a nightmare run of setbacks that has seen him miss last two seasons through injury; had looked hugely exciting in bumpers and novice hurdles, winning six out of six before disappointing in 2014 Neptune Hurdle.

Red Spinner (Ire)

6 b g Redback - Massalia (Montjeu)

Kim Bailey — **Paul & Clare Rooney**

PLACINGS: **6617211/11452-**   RPR **148+c**

Starts 12	1st 5	2nd 2	3rd -	4th 1	Win & Pl £30,213
135	12/15	Wwck	2m Cls3 Nov 122-135 Ch Hcap soft		£6,498
	11/15	Leic	2m Cls3 Ch gd-fm		£6,486
	3/15	Bang	2m½f Cls4 Nov Hdl gd-sft		£3,249
	2/15	Muss	2m3½f Cls5 Mdn Hdl good		£3,249
	8/14	Rosc	2m NHF 4yo yield		£4,313

Progressed rapidly during 2015, winning his last two novice hurdles and returning from a summer break to add his first two novice chases; ran a fine race when fifth in the Grand Annual (still in front approaching the last) and open to further improvement.

Red Tornado (Fr)

4 ch g Dr Fong - Encircle (Spinning World)

Dan Skelton   Notalotterry

PLACINGS: **311-111**   RPR **130**h

Starts		1st	2nd	3rd	4th	Win & Pl
6		5	-	1	-	£35,450
129	7/16	MRas	2m¹/₂f Cls1 List 118-144 Hdl Hcap good			£19,933
	6/16	Uttx	2m Cls4 Nov Hdl good			£3,639
	5/16	Ludl	2m Cls4 Nov Hdl good			£3,899
	4/16	Sedg	2m1f Cls4 Nov Hdl gd-sft			£3,509
	4/16	Ludl	2m Cls4 Nov Hdl gd-sft			£3,899

Smart Flat recruit (rated 99 at his peak and third at Listed level) who thrived over hurdles during the summer, most notably when winning the Summer Hurdle at Market Rasen; prefers good ground and could again thrive if getting those conditions in the spring.

Regal Encore (Ire)

8 b g King's Theatre - Go On Eileen (Bob Back)

Anthony Honeyball   John P McManus

PLACINGS: **124/840174/53F1PPP-2**   RPR **144+**c

Starts		1st	2nd	3rd	4th	Win & Pl
20		4	4	1	3	£56,578
129	12/15	Plum	2m1f Cls3 Nov Ch soft			£6,498
	2/15	Extr	2m7f Cls2 127-153 Hdl Hcap gd-sft			£12,512
	11/13	Plum	2m Cls4 Nov Hdl gd-sft			£3,249
	10/12	Chep	2m Cls6 NHF 4-6yo gd-sft			£1,754
	2/12	Sthl	2m Cls6 NHF 4-6yo std-slw			£1,437

Taking an age to fulfil rich bumper promise (second in 2013 Champion Bumper) but produced a career-best when a close second in a 3m1f handicap chase at Punchestown at the end of April; could yet become a useful staying chaser.

Reve De Sivola (Fr)

11 b g Assessor - Eva De Chalamont (Iron Duke)

Nick Williams   Paul Duffy Diamond Partnership

PLACINGS: **/013148/757120/6251-**   RPR **163**h

Starts		1st	2nd	3rd	4th	Win & Pl
41		10	7	7	4	£616,019
	2/16	Hayd	2m7f Cls1 Gd2 Hdl heavy			£22,780
	12/14	Asct	3m¹/₂f Cls1 Gd1 Hdl gd-sft			£56,270
	12/13	Asct	3m¹/₂f Cls1 Gd1 Hdl soft			£42,701
	11/13	Autl	3m Gd1 Hdl heavy			£135,366
	1/13	Chel	3m Cls1 Gd2 Hdl heavy			£34,170
	12/12	Asct	3m¹/₂f Cls1 Gd1 Hdl heavy			£42,203
	12/10	Chel	2m5f Cls2 Nov Ch good			£9,798
	4/10	Punc	2m4f Nov Gd1 Hdl good			£46,637
	12/09	Newb	2m4¹/₂f Cls1 Nov Gd1 Hdl heavy			£24,229
	10/09	Chep	2m3¹/₂f Cls1 Nov Gd2 Hdl soft			£17,103

Famous for winning three successive runnings of the Long Walk Hurdle from 2012 to 2014 and beaten only by Thistlecrack at Ascot last season;

won the Rendlesham Hurdle to show he was no back-number and could have more life in him yet.

Road To Riches (Ire)

9 b g Gamut - Bellora (Over The River)

Noel Meade (Ir)   Gigginstown House Stud

PLACINGS: **3P41/212113/31232-FP**   RPR **169+**c

Starts		1st	2nd	3rd	4th	Win & Pl
23		9	4	4	1	£475,951
	11/15	Clon	2m4f Gd2 Ch sft-hvy			£23,934
	12/14	Leop	3m Gd1 Ch sft-hvy			£75,000
	11/14	DRoy	3m Gd1 Ch yield			£70,000
149	7/14	Gway	2m6¹/₂f 134-155 Ch Hcap good			£100,313
	4/14	Fair	2m1f Nov Ch gd-yld			£9,488
	11/13	Naas	2m3f Ch yld-sft			£6,732
	12/12	Cork	3m Nov Gd3 Hdl soft			£14,896
	11/12	Punc	2m4f Mdn Hdl heavy			£7,763
	10/12	Naas	2m3f NHF 4-7yo heavy			£5,750

Dual Grade 1 winner two seasons ago when also third in the Gold Cup; endured a frustrating campaign last season but ran well over an inadequate trip in the Ryanair Chase and looked a likely winner when falling two out in the Punchestown Gold Cup.

Rock On Oscar (Ire)

6 b g Oscar - Brogeen Lady (Phardante)

Paul Nicholls   I Fogg, C Barber, D Bennett & D Macdonald

PLACINGS: **16/22113-2**   RPR **138**h

Starts		1st	2nd	3rd	4th	Win & Pl
7		2	3	1	-	£12,901
	3/16	Tntn	2m3f Cls4 Nov Hdl good			£3,899
	2/16	Donc	2m3¹/₂f Cls4 Nov Hdl 4-7yo gd-sft			£3,899

Steadily progressive over hurdles and won at Doncaster and Taunton before probably stepping up again when third to Mister Miyagi at Cheltenham; bumped into a very smart rival in Virgilio when second on his chasing debut and could make a useful novice.

Rock The Kasbah (Ire)

6 ch g Shirocco - Impudent (In The Wings)

Philip Hobbs   Mrs Diana L Whateley

PLACINGS: **2/11321P/21100-**   RPR **152+**h

Starts		1st	2nd	3rd	4th	Win & Pl
12		5	3	1	-	£77,045
144	1/16	Asct	2m3¹/₂f Cls1 Gd3 125-151 Hdl Hcap soft			£28,475
136	11/15	Hayd	2m3f Cls2 121-139 Hdl Hcap soft			£25,024
	3/15	Newb	2m4¹/₂f Cls3 Nov Hdl gd-sft			£5,848
	11/14	Font	2m3f Cls4 Nov Cond Hdl soft			£3,119
	10/14	Ffos	2m Cls6 Mdn NHF 4-6yo soft			£1,643

Won twice and finished second in good handicap

'This smart Flat recruit thrived over hurdles during the summer, most notably when winning the Summer Hurdle – he could again thrive if getting the right conditions'

hurdles last season; much better on soft ground according to connections and failed to run to form on good when favourite for the Coral Cup at Cheltenham; looks a fine prospect for novice chases.

Rocky Creek (Ire)
10 b g Dr Massini - Kissantell (Broken Hearted)

Paul Nicholls   **The Johnson & Stewart Families**

PLACINGS: 13/225/2P10P/2P40P3-					RPR **160c**
Starts	1st	2nd	3rd	4th	Win & Pl
22	5	6	2	1	£253,287
154	2/15	Kemp	3m Cls1 Gd3 130-155 Ch Hcap soft		£56,950
	2/13	Asct	3m Cls1 Nov Gd2 Ch soft		£18,855
	1/13	Wwck	3m¹/₂f Cls2 Nov Ch soft		£12,001
	12/12	Donc	3m Cls4 Nov Ch gd-sft		£3,899
	1/12	Donc	3m¹/₂f Cls1 Nov Gd2 Hdl gd-sft		£14,305

Brilliant winner of the BetBright Chase in 2015 but seemingly soured since then by repeated exposure to Grand National fences (disappointing three times at the course since National fifth in 2014); no surprise if his outstanding trainer can spark a revival.

Rogue Angel (Ire)
8 b g Presenting - Carrigeen Kohleria (Luso)

Mouse Morris (Ir)   **Gigginstown House Stud**

PLACINGS: 2B0P2PU/P541216P41-0					RPR **150c**
Starts	1st	2nd	3rd	4th	Win & Pl
33	5	5	4	5	£252,290
137	3/16	Fair	3m5f 124-150 Ch Hcap yld-sft		£111,765
133	9/15	List	3m 130-147 Ch Hcap heavy		£81,589
177	7/15	Gway	2mG¹/₂f 114-135 Ch Hcap yield		£13,353
	12/13	Punc	3m Ch heavy		£6,732
	10/12	Gway	2m Mdn Hdl 4yo gd-sft		£6,325

Tremendous jumper who won last season's Irish Grand National and Kerry National, both by a short head having made most of the running; should continue to be a force in top staying handicaps, especially when able to dominate.

Roi Des Francs (Fr)
7 b g Poliglote - Grande Souveraine (Sillery)

Willie Mullins (Ir)   **Gigginstown House Stud**

PLACINGS: 0/33/12113P/621166-					RPR **151+c**
Starts	1st	2nd	3rd	4th	Win & Pl
14	5	2	2	-	£61,587
	1/16	Naas	3m Nov Gd2 Ch sft-hvy		£18,750
	12/15	Fair	3m Ch heavy		£5,884
	2/15	Clon	2m6f Nov Gd3 Hdl yld-sft		£15,872
	1/15	Thur	2m6f Mdn Hdl sft-hvy		£4,279
	10/14	Tipp	2m4f NHF 5-7yo gd-sft		£4,313

Very highly rated at home (even backed down to 3-1 favouritism for the Martin Pipe Hurdle at Cheltenham in 2015) but hasn't quite reproduced that form on the track yet; still won twice over fences last season and should have plenty more to offer.

Romain De Senam (Fr)
4 b g Saint Des Saints - Salvatrixe (Housamix)

Paul Nicholls   **Chris Giles & Dan Macdonald**

PLACINGS: 621/132525-					RPR **139+h**
Starts	1st	2nd	3rd	4th	Win & Pl
9	2	3	1	-	£50,938
	10/15	Winc	1m7¹/₂f Cls4 Hdl 3yo good		£5,198
	4/15	Engh	2m¹/₂f Hdl 3yo v soft		£17,860

Raced far too freely for much of last season but settled better in the Fred Winter and stormed home to finish second having been given lots to do; more to come in big handicaps on that evidence, although well beaten in a higher grade at Aintree next time.

Royal Caviar (Ire)
8 b g Vinnie Roe - Blackwater Babe (Arctic Lord)

Willie Mullins (Ir)   **Mrs S Ricci**

PLACINGS: 1/11d/222/1222-					RPR **142+h**
Starts	1st	2nd	3rd	4th	Win & Pl
9	2	7	-	-	£31,945
	11/15	Thur	2m Mdn Hdl soft		£5,349
	11/13	Fair	2m2f NHF 4-7yo soft		£3,927

Very lightly raced for his age and went the right way last season despite finishing second on his last three runs, getting close to Sutton Place in a Grade 2 on his final run; point-to-point winner who could do better over fences.

Royal Regatta (Ire)
8 b g King's Theatre - Friendly Craic (Mister Lord)

Philip Hobbs   **Mrs Lesley Field & Mrs Eileen Murphy**

PLACINGS: 1150P/313152P/65123-					RPR **161+c**
Starts	1st	2nd	3rd	4th	Win & Pl
18	6	2	1	-	£93,340
	12/15	Asct	2m5f Cls2 Ch gd-sft		£15,857
138	1/15	Donc	2m¹/₂f Cls2 127-143 Ch Hcap gd-sft		£11,886
130	11/14	Newb	2m¹/₂f Cls3 Nov 128-139 Ch Hcap soft		£10,948
	12/13	Leic	2m4¹/₂f Cls4 Nov Hdl gd-sft		£4,549
	10/13	Aint	2m4f Cls4 Nov Hdl 4-6yo good		£5,198
	3/13	Hayd	1m7¹/₂f Cls5 NHF 4-5yo gd-sft		£1,949

Took form to a new level in final three runs last season, all over 2m5f at Ascot, and even ran well for a long way in the Ascot Chase before being outstayed by Silviniaco Conti; could do better still on decent ground and remains on a fair mark.

RACING POST
MIND-BLOWING

iPad Daily Edition
£99 for 5 months.
To claim this offer visit
Racingpost.com/ipad5months

Available on the App Store

Saint Are (Fr)

10 b/br g Network - Fortanea (Video Rock)

Tom George   **D W Fox**

PLACINGS: 90/84PF/33312/671P0-   RPR **155c**

Starts		1st	2nd	3rd	4th	Win & Pl
37		5	4	6	3	£380,686
146	2/16	Donc	3m Cls2 121-147 Ch Hcap good			£18,768
129	2/15	Catt	3m1f Cls3 117-134 Ch Hcap gd-sft			£7,798
137	4/12	Aint	3m1f Cls1 List 124-150 Ch Hcap good			£34,170
	4/11	Aint	3m¹/₂f Cls1 Nov Gd1 Hdl good			£56,520
	6/10	Sabl	2m1f Hdl 4yo gd-sft			£8,920

Nursed back to form in the last two seasons and nearly won the Grand National in 2015 when second to Many Clouds; primed for a repeat last season and won a veterans' chase on his prep run but was pulled up.

Sametegal (Fr)

7 b g Saint Des Saints - Loya Lescribaa (Robin Des Champs)

Paul Nicholls   **Mr & Mrs J D Cotton**

PLACINGS: /121332/12358/1U221-   RPR **154+c**

Starts		1st	2nd	3rd	4th	Win & Pl
18		6	6	3	-	£171,626
143	3/16	Newb	2m4f Cls1 Gd3 127-152 Ch Hcap soft			£28,475
	11/15	Hntg	2m4f Cls3 Nov Ch gd-sft			£6,498
	10/13	Chel	2m¹/₂f Cls2 Hdl 4yo good			£18,768
	2/13	Muss	1m7¹/₂f Cls2 Hdl 4yo gd-sft			£12,512
	11/12	Weth	2m Cls1 List Hdl 3yo gd-sft			£8,583
	4/12	Engh	2m¹/₂f Hdl 3yo v soft			£19,200

Missed 18 months through injury prior to return last season but won on his chasing debut and made steady progress before landing the Greatwood Gold Cup; still just lower than peak hurdles mark after a 5lb rise and open to improvement.

Saphir Du Rheu (Fr)

7 gr g Al Namix - Dona Du Rheu (Dom Pasquini)

Paul Nicholls   **The Stewart Family**

PLACINGS: 41114/U1F121/155665-   RPR **164+c**

Starts		1st	2nd	3rd	4th	Win & Pl
22		8	1	2	2	£279,321
	11/15	Carl	2m4f Cls1 Cls1 Ch gd-sft			£15,661
	4/15	Aint	3m1f Cls1 Nov Gd1 Ch good			£50,793
	1/15	Chel	3m Cls1 Gd2 Hdl soft			£34,170
	12/14	Extr	2m5f Cls2 Nov Ch gd-sft			£12,512
158	2/14	Ffos	2m4f Cls2 130-158 Hdl Hcap heavy			£31,280
145	1/14	Kemp	2m5f Cls1 List 121-145 Hdl Hcap good			£25,628
130	12/13	Sand	2m6f Cls2 120-142 Hdl Hcap gd-sft			£12,512
	1/13	Tntn	2m¹/₂f Cls4 Nov Hdl heavy			£4,106

Disappointing last season when chasing career was put on hold for second time following fifth in Hennessy Gold Cup but return to hurdles failed to spark revival; still interesting based on World Hurdle second and Grade 1 novice chase win.

Sausalito Sunrise (Ire)

8 b g Gold Well - Villaflor (Religiously)

Philip Hobbs   **Mrs Diana L Whateley**

PLACINGS: 3115611/122F/P12143-   RPR **166c**

Starts		1st	2nd	3rd	4th	Win & Pl
20		5	3	1		£122,318
150	2/16	Asct	3m Cls1 List 132-150 Ch Hcap soft			£25,628
144	11/15	Chel	3m3¹/₂f Cls1 Gd3 129-153 Ch Hcap gd-sft			£28,475
	10/14	Chep	2m7¹/₂f Cls4 Nov Ch soft			£4,549
	4/14	Prth	3m Cls2 Nov Hdl gd-sft			£9,747
	4/14	Bang	2m7f Cls4 Nov Hdl gd-sft			£3,899
129	12/13	Hayd	2m7f Cls3 120-140 Hdl Hcap soft			£9,495
	12/13	Chep	2m7¹/₂f Cls4 Nov Hdl gd-sft			£3,119

Progressive staying chaser last season, winning good handicaps at Cheltenham and Ascot; hit hard by the handicapper for those wins but fine third in the bet365 Gold Cup (just outstayed from the last) suggested he may have more to give.

Sceau Royal (Fr)

4 b g Doctor Dino - Sandside (Marchand De Sable)

Alan King   **Simon Munir & Isaac Souede**

PLACINGS: 71/1d211106-   RPR **137+h**

Starts		1st	2nd	3rd	4th	Win & Pl
9		4	2	-	-	£43,117
	1/16	Hntg	2m Cls2 Hdl 4yo soft			£12,512
	12/15	Chel	2m1f Cls2 Hdl 3yo soft			£12,628
	11/15	Wwck	2m Cls4 Hdl 3yo gd-sft			£3,249
	3/15	Bord	2m¹/₂f Hdl 3yo v soft			£7,814

Quickly developed into one of the leading juvenile hurdlers in Britain last season when first past the post (placed second once) on four of first five runs following move from France; disappointing at Cheltenham and Aintree but eased by the handicapper for those runs.

Seeyouatmidnight

8 b g Midnight Legend - Morsky Baloo (Morpeth)

Sandy Thomson   **Mrs A M Thomson**

PLACINGS: P3F/11113/27/311173-   RPR **161+c**

Starts		1st	2nd	3rd	4th	Win & Pl
12		6	1	3	-	£119,841
	2/16	Newc	2m7¹/₂f Cls2 Nov Ch gd-sft			£12,660
	1/16	Chel	2m5f Cls1 Nov Gd2 Ch heavy			£18,224
	12/15	Kels	2m7¹/₂f Cls3 Nov Ch heavy			£10,222
	2/14	Hayd	2m7f Cls1 Gd2 Hdl heavy			£20,787
	2/14	Muss	3m1¹/₂f Cls2 Hdl soft			£12,996
	12/13	Hexm	2m Cls4 Nov Hdl soft			£3,119

Smart hurdler who was even better when sent chasing last season, comfortably beating RSA winner Blaklion at Cheltenham; just outstayed when a fine third in the Scottish National and could win good handicaps over slightly shorter.

ON THE CLOCK

Seeyouatmidnight Beat only one home in the RSA but earned a personal best on the clock when third in the Scottish National. Looks a leading Hennessy contender. *[Dave Edwards, Topspeed]*

Sempre Medici (Fr)

6 b g Medicean - Sambala (Danehill Dancer)

Willie Mullins (Ir)   Mrs S Ricci

PLACINGS: **12761/4211P-52**   RPR **158+h**

Starts		1st	2nd	3rd	4th	Win & Pl
12		4	3	-	1	£106,566
	2/16	Gowr	2m Gd2 Hdl heavy			£19,522
	1/16	Naas	2m3f Gd3 Hdl sft-hvy			£14,338
	4/15	Fair	2m Nov Gd2 Hdl soft			£21,415
	11/14	Cork	2m Mdn Hdl 4yo heavy			£5,750

Progressed well over hurdles last season, going close in the International at Cheltenham before winning a couple of Graded races; limitations exposed subsequently, including when pulled up in the Champion Hurdle and fifth behind Vroum Vroum Mag at Punchestown.

Shades Of Midnight

6 b g Midnight Legend - Hannah Park (Lycius)

Donald Whillans   The Potassium Partnership

PLACINGS: **31/05141/033112-**   RPR **148h**

Starts		1st	2nd	3rd	4th	Win & Pl
13		5	4	3	1	£32,729
137	3/16	Ayr	2m4¹/₂f Cls3 122-137 Hdl Hcap heavy			£9,747
124	7/16	Kels	2m6¹/₂f Cls3 104 124 Hdl Hcap heavy			£6,498
	4/15	Carl	2m3¹/₂f Cls4 Nov Hdl soft			£3,574
	1/15	Kels	2m Cls4 Nov Hdl heavy			£3,249
	4/14	Hexm	2m Cls6 NHF 4-5yo gd-sft			£1,643

Thorough stayer who flourished when stepped up to trips around 3m last season, winning handicap hurdles at Kelso and Ayr on heavy ground; improved again on quicker ground over 3m2f when second at Kelso last time; useful novice chase prospect.

Shaneshill (Ire)

7 b g King's Theatre - Durubuku (Topanoru)

Willie Mullins (Ir)   Andrea & Graham Wylie

PLACINGS: **/112/11221/311422-F2**   RPR **162+c**

Starts		1st	2nd	3rd	4th	Win & Pl
16		7	6	1	1	£242,024
	1/16	Naas	2m Nov Ch heavy			£10,037
	11/15	Thur	2m2f Ch soft			£5,884
	4/15	Fair	2m4f Nov Gd2 Hdl soft			£21,415
	11/14	Fair	2m4f Mdn Hdl sft-hvy			£4,600
	4/14	Punc	2m Gd1 NHF 4-7yo gd-yld			£48,750
	11/13	Fair	2m NHF 4-7yo gd-yld			£5,610
	11/13	Naas	2m NHF 4yo yld-sft			£4,488

Never entirely convincing when sent chasing last season so says much about his ability that he still finished second in the RSA; subsequently reverted to hurdles, finishing second at Aintree and falling at the last when challenging at Punchestown; likely to stay hurdling.

Shantou Village (Ire)

6 b g Shantou - Village Queen (King's Theatre)

Neil Mulholland   Mrs Jane Gerard-Pearse

PLACINGS: **11/112P-1**   RPR **147h**

Starts		1st	2nd	3rd	4th	Win & Pl
6		4	1	-	-	£33,115
	8/16	Font	2m5f Cls4 Nov Ch good			£4,660
	11/15	Chel	2m5f Cls1 Nov Gd2 Hdl good			£17,085
	10/15	Carl	2m4f Cls4 Nov Hdl good			£3,249
	3/15	Weth	2m Cls6 NHF 4-6yo good			£1,711

Runaway winner of his first two races over hurdles last season, including a Grade 2 at Cheltenham by 15 lengths; much better than he showed in two more runs, struggling on heavy ground behind and struck into when favourite for the Albert Bartlett; won on his chasing debut in August; interesting.

Sharp Rise (Ire)

9 b g Croco Rouge - Missouna (King's Ride)

Charlie Longsdon   Robert Aplin

PLACINGS: **65351/11U12F1U-1121U**   RPR **160+c**

Starts		1st	2nd	3rd	4th	Win & Pl
18		8	2	1		£67,252
150	7/16	Uttx	2m4f Cls2 124-150 Ch Hcap good			£18,768
145	6/16	Uttx	2m Cls2 119-145 Ch Hcap good			£12,512
133	6/16	Worc	2m¹/₂f Cls3 111-135 Ch Hcap good			£9,384
	4/16	Kels	2m2f Cls4 Nov Hdl gd-sft			£3,899
	7/15	Prth	2m4f Cls4 Nov Hdl good			£3,899
117	5/15	Sedg	2m3¹/₂f Cls4 93-119 Ch Hcap good			£4,159
	5/15	Sedg	2m3f Cls4 Nov Hdl soft			£3,249
107	10/14	Sedg	2m3¹/₂f Cls4 Nov 105-115 Ch Hcap gd-sft			£6,256

Made remarkable progress this summer following switch to Charlie Longsdon's yard, winning three of first four races for new trainer despite soaring handicap mark (all on good ground from 2m to 2m4f); will be aimed at stronger handicaps now.

Shutthefrontdoor (Ire)

9 b/br g Accordion - Hurricane Girl (Strong Gale)

Jonjo O'Neill   John P McManus

PLACINGS: **/31114/12461/15/3P9-**   RPR **144h**

Starts		1st	2nd	3rd	4th	Win & Pl
18		9	1	2	2	£209,567
	11/14	Carl	3m¹/₂f Cls2 Ch soft			£12,517
142	4/14	Fair	3m5f 129-150 Ch Hcap gd-yld			£117,500
	10/13	Aint	2m4f Cls3 Nov Ch good			£7,507
135	2/13	Carl	3m1f Cls2 121-145 Hdl Hcap soft			£11,574
	1/13	Winc	1m7¹/₂f Cls4 Nov Hdl soft			£3,899
	12/12	Uttx	2m Cls5 Mdn Hdl heavy			£1,689
	2/12	Newb	2m¹/₂f Cls1 List NHF 4 6yo gd-sft			£5,695
	12/11	Asct	1m7¹/₂f Cls1 List NHF 4-6yo soft			£7,290
	11/11	Ffos	2m Cls6 NHF 4-6yo soft			£1,506

Won the Irish Grand National in 2014 and has run only five times since then; trained for the Grand National in last two seasons but has twice failed to see out the trip, though still a good fifth in 2015; has slipped to a fair mark.

> ## 'Thorough stayer flourished when stepped up to 3m last season. He looks a useful novice chase prospect'

Silsol (Ger)

7 b g Soldier Hollow - Silveria (Groom Dancer)

Paul Nicholls   **Michelle & Dan Macdonald**

PLACINGS: 211/1512/611243132-8   RPR **159**h

Starts		1st	2nd	3rd	4th	Win & Pl
19		7	5	2	2	£143,884
152	4/16	Kels	3m2f Cls2 133-152 Hdl Hcap gd-sft..........£12,996
	11/15	Hayd	2m5¹/₂f Cls2 Nov Ch soft £16,245
	11/15	Carl	2m4f Cls3 Nov Ch heavy..........................£6,498
151	1/15	Ffos	2m4f Cls2 131-151 Hdl Hcap heavy..........£31,280
144	11/14	Newb	2m3f Cls2 124-144 Hdl Hcap soft............£19,494
	4/14	NAbb	2m5¹/₂f Cls2 Nov Hdl gd-sft......................£3,509
124	4/14	Ayr	2m4f Cls3 102-128 Hdl Hcap gd-sft..........£7,798

Slightly lost his way over fences after winning his first two chases last season but did well reverting to hurdles, winning at Kelso and finishing a fine third at Aintree; on a much lower chase mark and could be a contender for good staying handicaps.

Silvergrove

8 b g Old Vic - Classic Gale (Classic Cliche)

Ben Pauling   **Nicholas Piper & Claire E Piper**

PLACINGS: 95568/523122P2/U113-   RPR **141**c

Starts		1st	2nd	3rd	4th	Win & Pl
17		3	4	2		£43,066
130	2/16	Kemp	3m Cls3 122-137 Ch Hcap soft £6,498
124	12/15	Newb	3m2f Cls3 107-129 Ch Hcap soft................£7,798
103	1/15	Extr	3m Cls4 101-110 Ch Hcap soft £6,498

Progressive staying chaser last season, winning well at Newbury and Kempton before a fine third in the Kim Muir at Cheltenham (best of prominently ridden horses, winner held up a long way off pace); still looks on the upgrade.

Silviniaco Conti (Fr)

10 ch g Dom Alco - Gazelle Lulu (Altayan)

Paul Nicholls   **Potensis Bloodstock Ltd & Chris Giles**

PLACINGS: F3/3141/51171/22P1P-   RPR **175**c

Starts		1st	2nd	3rd	4th	Win & Pl
31		16	3	4	3	£1,088,777
	2/16	Asct	2m5f Cls1 Gd1 Ch soft £85,425
	4/15	Aint	3m1f Cls1 Gd1 Ch soft £84,570
	12/14	Kemp	3m Cls1 Gd1 Ch gd-sft.........................£113,900
	11/14	Hayd	3m Cls1 Gd1 Ch soft.............................£112,873
	4/14	Aint	3m1f Cls1 Gd1 Ch good.........................£84,405
	12/13	Kemp	3m Cls1 Gd1 Ch gd-sft.........................£114,436
	2/13	Newb	2m7¹/₂f Cls1 Gd2 Ch soft........................£25,628
	11/12	Hayd	2m7f Cls1 Gd1 Ch soft..........................£112,540
	11/12	Weth	3m1f Cls1 Gd2 Ch gd-sft.........................£56,950
	4/12	Aint	3m1f Cls1 Nov Gd2 Ch good....................£42,713
	11/11	Winc	2m5f Cls1 Nov Gd2 Ch gd-sft...................£20,093
	11/10	Asct	2m3¹/₂f Cls1 Gd2 Hdl gd-sft......................£50,697
	10/10	Chep	2m3¹/₂f Cls1 Nov Hdl soft.........................£14,253
	10/10	Bang	2m1¹/₂f Cls3 Nov Hdl good.........................£4,879
	4/10	Nanc	2m1f Hdl 4yo good................................£12,743
	3/10	Seno	2m2f Hdl 4yo gd-sft.................................£5,097

Seven-time Grade 1 winner who added to his tally last season despite a largely indifferent campaign, bouncing back from health issues to win the Ascot Chase; didn't take to the Grand National next time but could still run well in top staying chases.

Simonsig

10 gr g Fair Mix - Dusty Too (Terimon)

Nicky Henderson   **R A Bartlett**

PLACINGS: 1F1/112111/111/2-30   RPR **166**c

Starts		1st	2nd	3rd	4th	Win & Pl
12		8	2	1	-	£267,724
	3/13	Chel	2m Cls1 Gd1 Ch soft.............................£85,425
	12/12	Kemp	2m Cls1 Nov Gd2 Ch heavy....................£13,326
	12/12	Asct	2m3f Cls1 Nov Gd2 Ch heavy..................£19,667
	4/12	Aint	2m4f Cls1 Nov Gd1 Hdl good...................£28,475
	3/12	Chel	2m5f Cls1 Nov Gd1 Hdl good...................£56,950
	2/12	Kels	2m2f Cls1 Hdl good.................................£9,747
	11/11	Asct	2m3¹/₂f Cls3 Nov Hdl good........................£5,005
	4/11	Fair	2m2f NHF 4-6yo good............................£25,647

Once seen as a future superstar but barely sighted since winning the 2013 Arkle due to injury; finally raced again last season and went on to run a cracker when third at Punchestown; further progress can't be ruled out given trainer's amazing touch with difficult veterans.

Simply Ned (Ire)

9 ch g Fruits Of Love - Bishops Lass (Marju)

Nicky Richards   **David & Nicky Robinson**

PLACINGS: 122132/12356/14253P-   RPR **164+**c

Starts		1st	2nd	3rd	4th	Win & Pl
28		8	6	4	3	£159,550
157	10/15	Kels	2m1f Cls2 131-157 Ch Hcap gd-fm...........£13,986
157	10/14	Kels	2m1f Cls2 132-157 Ch Hcap gd-sft...........£14,115
138	1/14	Donc	2m¹/₂f Cls2 130-153 Ch Hcap gd-sft...........£14,076
130	11/13	Ayr	1m7¹/₂f Cls3 109-130 Ch Hcap soft.............£7,798
127	2/13	Kels	2m Cls3 112-133 Hdl Hcap soft..................£5,523
117	12/11	Muss	1m7¹/₂f Cls3 95-121 Hdl Hcap gd-sft.............£6,498
	11/11	Sedg	2m1f Cls4 Nov Hdl 4-6yo good..................£2,534
	10/11	Kels	2m Cls5 Mdn Hdl gd-sft...........................£1,819

Has started the last two seasons with victory off 157 in the same Kelso handicap chase but just come up short at a higher level; missed a big opportunity when second to Flemenstar in a Grade 1 at Leopardstown last season; prefers good ground.

Sire De Grugy (Fr)

10 ch g My Risk - Hirlish (Passing Sale)

Gary Moore   **The Preston Family & Friends Ltd**

PLACINGS: 1211111/U14F/512284-   RPR **171**c

Starts		1st	2nd	3rd	4th	Win & Pl
34		16	6	2	4	£785,855
	12/15	Sand	1m7¹/₂f Cls1 Gd1 Ch gd-sft.......................£85,425
172	2/15	Chep	2m Cls2 146-172 Ch Hcap soft..................£15,825
	4/14	Sand	1m7¹/₂f Cls1 Gd1 Ch gd-sft.......................£71,188
	3/14	Chel	2m Cls1 Gd1 Ch good...........................£199,325
	1/14	Asct	2m1f Cls1 Gd1 Ch heavy.........................£59,199
	12/13	Kemp	2m Cls1 Gd2 Ch soft..............................£45,774
	12/13	Sand	1m7¹/₂f Cls1 Gd1 Ch good.......................£76,883
161	10/13	Chep	2m Cls2 135-161 Ch Hcap gd-sft..............£16,245
	4/13	Sand	1m7¹/₂f Cls1 Gd2 Ch good........................£56,950
	4/13	Strf	2m1f Cls4 Nov Ch good...........................£4,549
	11/12	Kemp	2m Cls4 Nov Ch heavy.............................£3,217
	10/12	Kemp	2m Cls4 Ch good....................................£3,899
141	2/12	Tntn	2m2f Cls2 121-147 Hdl Hcap gd-sft..........£12,660
	2/11	Kemp	2m Cls1 Nov Gd2 Hdl gd-sft....................£12,086
	2/11	Folk	2m1¹/₂f Cls4 Nov Hdl soft..........................£1,918
	1/11	Fknm	2m Cls5 Mdn Hdl soft...............................£1,713

Former Champion Chase winner who again

showed plenty of his old spark last season, most notably when winning the Tingle Creek at Sandown; no match for top two-milers in the spring but could still have more to offer back on softer ground.

Sizing Granite (Ire)

8 br g Milan - Hazel's Tisrara (Mandalus)

Colm Murphy (Ir)   **Ann & Alan Potts Partnership**

PLACINGS: U/321/91U111/25P2-   RPR **159 + c**

Starts	1st	2nd	3rd	4th	Win & Pl
13	5	3	1	-	£110,288
	4/15	Aint	2m Cls1 Nov Gd1 Ch good		£61,897
	2/15	Leop	2m1f Nov Ch soft		£10,581
	1/15	Naas	2m Nov Ch soft		£10,078
	11/14	Naas	2m Ch yield		£8,050
	3/14	Gowr	2m Mdn Hdl soft		£5,750

Won what now looks a red-hot Grade 1 novice chase at Aintree in 2015 from God's Own and Traffic Fluide; well below that level last season when let down by jumping errors, though he did better when second at Fairyhouse last time and has the talent to put that right.

Sizing John

6 b g Midnight Legend - La Perrotine (Northern Crystal)

Jessica Harrington (Ir)   **Ann & Alan Potts Partnership**

PLACINGS: 6/41213/211223-3   RPR **156c**

Starts	1st	2nd	3rd	4th	Win & Pl
13	4	4	3	1	£171,312
	11/15	Punc	2m Nov Gd2 Ch sft-hvy		£21,163
	10/15	Punc	2m Ch yield		£7,488
	12/14	Leop	2m Nov Gd1 Hdl heavy		£43,333
	11/14	Naas	2m Mdn Hdl 4yo yield		£5,750

Unlucky to be part of the same generation as Douvan, finishing second to that horse on four occasions including in last season's Racing Post Arkle; fortunate to fill that position, though, after late carnage and disappointed at Aintree and Punchestown.

Smad Place (Fr)

9 gr g Smadoun - Bienna Star (Village Star)

Alan King   **Mrs Peter Andrews**

PLACINGS: 233/U112/5284/11416-   RPR **173 + c**

Starts		1st	2nd	3rd	4th	Win & Pl
27		8	5	5	2	£420,171
	1/16	Chel	3m1½f Cls1 Gd2 Ch heavy			£57,218
155	11/15	Newb	3m2f Cls3 Gd3 139-163 Ch Hcap soft			£113,900
	11/15	Kemp	2m4½f Cls2 Ch good			£12,996
	2/14	Extr	2m7½f Cls3 Nov Ch heavy			£7,798
	11/13	Extr	3m Cls3 Nov Ch gd-sft			£6,330
144	1/12	Asct	2m3½f Cls1 Gd2 125-145 Ch Hcap gd-sft			£22,780
	2/11	Winc	1m7½f Cls4 Nov Hdl gd-sft			£2,439
	11/10	Newb	2m1½f Cls3 Hdl 3yo gd-sft			£6,505

Came of age last season with a thrilling success in the Hennessy Gold Cup and proved that was no fluke when easily adding the BetBright Trial Chase, both in testing conditions; better than he

showed in the King George and the Cheltenham Gold Cup.

Smart Talk (Ire)

6 b m Hubbly Bubbly - Belon Breeze (Strong Gale)

Brian Ellison   **Mrs J A Martin**

PLACINGS: 41/22113110-   RPR **145 + h**

Starts	1st	2nd	3rd	4th	Win & Pl
8	4	2	1	-	£50,215
	1/16	Donc	2m1½f Cls1 Gd2 Hdl good		£28,475
	12/15	Hayd	2m3f Cls1 Nov List Hdl heavy		£11,591
	11/15	Sedg	2m4f Nov Hdl gd-sft		£3,769
	10/15	Worc	2m Cls4 Nov Hdl gd-sft		£3,899

Went from strength to strength last season, with victory in a Grade 2 mares' hurdle at Doncaster in February her fourth in last five races; disappointing next time at Cheltenham but may be better back at 2m4f and has the scope for fences.

Smashing (Fr)

7 gr g Smadoun - Faragreen (Green Tune)

Mouse Morris (Ir)   **Ann & Alan Potts Partnership**

PLACINGS: 321194/032173/111P1-   RPR **166 + c**

Starts	1st	2nd	3rd	4th	Win & Pl
29	8	4	3	4	£179,014
	4/16	Navn	2m4f Gd2 Ch sft-hvy		£18,438
	2/16	Gowr	2m4f Gd2 Ch heavy		£19,522
	1/16	Thur	2m2f List Ch heavy		£17,476
	11/15	Gowr	2m4f Ch heavy		£9,360
	1/15	Gowr	2m2f Ch heavy		£6,686
	12/13	Limk	2m Hdl 4yo heavy		£10,833
	11/13	Fair	2m4f Hdl gd-yld		£8,134
	6/12	Autl	2m1½f Hdl 3yo heavy		£9,200

Won all four starts in Ireland last season, improving throughout and claiming notable scalp of Road To Riches in a Grade 2 at Navan in April; disappointing for the second time at Cheltenham but has shown all his best form on much softer ground.

Snow Falcon (Ire)

6 b g Presenting - Flocon De Neige (Kahyasi)

Noel Meade (Ir)   **Mrs Patricia Hunt**

PLACINGS: 21222156/315F1-1   RPR **154 + h**

Starts	1st	2nd	3rd	4th	Win & Pl
14	5	4	1	-	£73,607
	8/16	Rosc	3m1½f Hdl good		£8,366
	2/16	Navn	2m5f Gd2 Hdl heavy		£19,522
	11/15	Naas	2m4f Hdl yield		£10,078
	1/15	Naas	2m7f Mdn Hdl soft		£5,349
	10/14	Fair	2m NHF 4-7yo good		£4,313

Has been troubled by back problems, exacerbated by a fall at Leopardstown last season, but very smart on his day as he showed when bouncing back to win the Boyne Hurdle; thorough stayer who relishes heavy ground but ran well on good when fifth in the 2015 Neptune.

Solstice Star

6 b g Kayf Tara - Clover Green (Presenting)

Martin Keighley   **E&G Racing Ltd**

PLACINGS: 3/2330785/491111122-   RPR **142h**

Starts		1st	2nd	3rd	4th	Win & Pl
17		5	3	3	1	£57,420
127	1/16	Chel	2m1f Cls2 127-153 Hdl Hcap heavy			£16,245
113	12/15	Chel	2m1f Cls3 109-135 Hdl Hcap soft			£7,507
106	12/15	Ling	2m3¹/₂f Cls4 102-110 Hdl Hcap heavy			£3,994
93	11/15	Ling	2m Cls4 93-110 Hdl Hcap soft			£5,848
93	11/15	Chep	2m Cls5 73-99 Cond Hdl Hcap soft			£2,274

Showed remarkable improvement last season, winning five successive handicap hurdles and climbing from 93 to 140; second off that mark at Cheltenham on good to soft having been felt to need much softer so could do even better back on heavy ground.

Sound Investment (Ire)

8 b g Dr Massini - Drumcay Polly (Le Bavard)

Paul Nicholls   **Owners Group 001**

PLACINGS: 56521103/21251/8135-   RPR **166c**

Starts		1st	2nd	3rd	4th	Win & Pl
22		7	3	3	-	£149,273
155	10/15	Aint	2m4f Cls1 Gd2 142-162 Ch Hcap good			£33,762
149	2/15	Newb	2m4f Cls1 Gd3 126-149 Ch Hcap gd-sft			£28,475
142	11/14	Sand	2m4f Cls2 123-142 Ch Hcap gd-sft			£25,024
	3/14	Sand	1m7¹/₂f Cls3 Nov Ch gd-sft			£6,498
125	2/14	Tntn	2m Cls3 Nov 119-138 Ch Hcap heavy			£6,498
	4/13	Winc	2m4f Cls4 Nov Hdl good			£3,899
	1/13	Tntn	2m3f Cls5 Mdn Hdl soft			£2,738

Has progressed throughout last two seasons apart from failing to stay on only attempt at 3m; won Greatwood Gold Cup and Old Roan Chase on next two runs over fences before third in the Paddy Power Gold Cup; not far off the best at around 2m4f.

Southfield Royale

6 b g Presenting - Chamoss Royale (Garde Royale)

Neil Mulholland   **Mrs Angela Yeoman**

PLACINGS: 112201/21124-7   RPR **158+c**

Starts		1st	2nd	3rd	4th	Win & Pl
12		5	4	-	1	£56,085
	12/15	Donc	3m Cls1 Nov Gd2 Ch heavy			£19,221
	10/15	Weth	3m Cls4 Nov Ch soft			£3,861
	3/15	Hntg	2m3¹/₂f Cls4 Nov Hdl gd-sft			£3,899
	11/14	Font	2m3f Cls4 Nov Hdl heavy			£3,899
	6/14	MRas	2m¹/₂f Cls6 NHF 4-6yo good			£1,560

Made a big impression with wide-margin wins in novice chases at Wetherby and Doncaster last season; outpaced by Tea For Two next time before a good fourth in the National Hunt Chase

(every chance when blundered two out); should make a good staying handicapper.

Southfield Theatre (Ire)

8 b g King's Theatre - Chamoss Royale (Garde Royale)

Paul Nicholls   **Mrs Angela Yeoman**

PLACINGS: 1/134321/11212/34B4-   RPR **152c**

Starts		1st	2nd	3rd	4th	Win & Pl
21		8	3	5	4	£157,921
	2/15	Extr	2m3f Cls3 Nov Ch gd-sft			£6,498
	11/14	Winc	2m4f Cls1 Nov Gd2 Ch gd-sft			£17,655
	10/14	Chep	2m3¹/₂f Cls2 Nov Ch gd-sft			£12,996
	4/14	Sand	2m6f Cls1 List Hdl gd-sft			£28,475
	10/13	Winc	2m5¹/₂f Cls4 Nov Hdl good			£3,249
	4/13	Winc	2m Cls4 Nov Hdl soft			£3,249
	3/13	Extr	2m7f Cls4 Nov Hdl good			£3,249
	10/12	Chel	2m1¹/₂f Cls4 NHF 4-6yo gd-sft			£4,549

Smart staying novice two seasons ago and perhaps unlucky when second to Don Poli in the RSA (suffered a badly cut leg); out of sorts early last season and brought down when returning at Cheltenham but back on track with a good fourth in the bet365 Gold Cup.

Special Tiara

9 b g Kayf Tara - Special Choice (Bob Back)

Henry De Bromhead (Ir)   **Mrs S Rowley-Williams**

PLACINGS: 3/U3463/534131/423-6   RPR **170c**

Starts		1st	2nd	3rd	4th	Win & Pl
23		5	4	6	3	£339,929
	4/15	Sand	1m7¹/₂f Cls1 Gd1 Ch good			£71,188
	12/14	Kemp	2m Cls1 Gd2 Ch soft			£46,096
	4/13	Aint	2m Cls1 Nov Gd1 Ch good			£62,190
	9/12	Baln	2m1f Ch yld-sft			£4,600
	7/12	Kbgn	2m Mdn Hdl 4-5yo yield			£4,313

As good as ever last season despite not winning, looking particularly unlucky when narrowly beaten in the Tingle Creek (badly hampered by winner); ran another big race when third in the Champion Chase; has won on soft ground but much better on quicker.

Spookydooky (Ire)

8 b g Winged Love - Kiora Lady (King's Ride)

Jonjo O'Neill   **The Piranha Partnership**

PLACINGS: 1/5454/23113/41244P-   RPR **143c**

Starts		1st	2nd	3rd	4th	Win & Pl
15		3	2	2	5	£40,268
134	11/15	Newb	2m6¹/₂f Cls3 Nov 118-135 Ch Hcap soft			£7,507
122	2/15	Sthl	3m Cls3 118-139 Hdl Hcap soft			£7,666
113	1/15	Donc	3m1¹/₂f Cls4 97-120 Hdl Hcap gd-sft			£3,249

Set some stiff tasks for an inexperienced horse

'Showed remarkable improvement last season, winning five successive handicap hurdles and climbing from 93 to 140. He could do better back on heavy ground' last season, finishing second in the Tommy Whittle and not beaten far when fourth in the Midlands National; thorough stayer who should progress after just six runs over fences.

Sprinter Sacre (Fr)

10 b/br g Network - Fatima III (Bayolidaan)

Nicky Henderson	**Mrs Caroline Mould**

PLACINGS: **11/11111/P/2P2/1111-** RPR **176+c**

Starts	1st	2nd	3rd	4th	Win & Pl
24	18	3	1	-	£1,136,883

4/16	Sand	1m7¹/₂f Cls1 Gd1 Ch good		£71,188
3/16	Chel	2m Cls1 Gd1 Ch good		£199,325
12/15	Kemp	2m Cls1 Gd2 Ch gd-sft		£45,560
11/15	Chel	2m Cls1 Gd2 Ch gd-sft		£42,713
4/13	Punc	2m Gd1 Ch soft		£100,813
4/13	Aint	2m4f Cls1 Gd1 Ch good		£113,072
3/13	Chel	2m Cls1 Gd1 Ch gd-sft		£208,300
1/13	Chel	2m¹/₂f Cls1 Gd1 Ch heavy		£39,389
12/12	Sand	1m7¹/₂f Cls1 Gd1 Ch soft		£68,340
4/12	Aint	2m Cls1 Nov Gd1 Ch good		£56,270
3/12	Chel	2m Cls1 Gd1 Ch good		£74,035
2/12	Newb	2m¹/₂f Cls1 Gd2 Ch gd-sft		£17,085
12/11	Kemp	2m Cls1 Nov Gd2 Ch good		£13,326
12/11	Donc	2m¹/₂f Cls1 Nov Gd2 Ch good		£3,444
2/11	Asct	1m7¹/₂f Cls2 Nov Hdl soft		£6,262
2/11	Pfos	2m Nov Hdl gd-sft		£2,602
4/10	Ayr	2m Cls4 NHF 4-6yo good		£4,554
2/10	Asct	1m7¹/₂f Cls3 NHF 4-6yo gd-sft		£3,204

One of the greatest 2m chasers of all time until struck down by health issues in 2013, but rolled back the years last season to reclaim his Champion Chase crown; will be hard pushed to maintain his dominance rising 11 but remains a phenomenal talent who can win more races.

Squouateur (Fr)

5 gr g Martaline - Samansonnienne (Mansonnien)

Gordon Elliott (Ir)	**John P McManus**

PLACINGS: **4/121176-** RPR **140+h**

Starts	1st	2nd	3rd	4th	Win & Pl
7	3	1	-	1	£32,657

128	2/16	Fair	2m4f 120-136 Hdl Hcap heavy	£10,853
120	12/15	Leop	2m4f Nov 109-128 Hdl Hcap heavy	£13,605
	11/15	Fair	2m Mdn Hdl 4yo yield	£5,349

Won three of first four races over hurdles last season, with easy victory in a handicap at Fairyhouse leading to a huge gamble down to 9-4 for the Martin Pipe at Cheltenham, but could manage only seventh; may still have a big race in him, perhaps back on heavy ground.

Starchitect (Ire)

5 b g Sea The Stars - Humilis (Sadler's Wells)

David Pipe	**Paul & Clare Rooney**

PLACINGS: **11224F/253-1** RPR **151+h**

Starts	1st	2nd	3rd	4th	Win & Pl
10	3	3	1	1	£77,099

143	5/16	NAbb	2m5¹/₂f Cls2 117-143 Hdl Hcap gd-fm	£12,512
	10/14	Aint	2m1f Cls4 Hdl 3yo good	£5,198
	10/14	Bang	2m¹/₂f Cls4 Hdl 3yo good	£3,249

Useful juvenile hurdler two seasons ago who ran well in several top handicaps last season, notably when second in the Betfair Hurdle; deservedly won at Newton Abbot in May when stepped up in trip but raised 7lb for that success.

Sternrubin (Ger)

5 b g Authorized - Sworn Mum (Samum)

Philip Hobbs	**Terry Warner**

PLACINGS: **42222/111P30-** RPR **144h**

Starts	1st	2nd	3rd	4th	Win & Pl
11	3	4	1	1	£116,598

134	12/15	Asct	1m7¹/₂f Cls1 Gd3 131-150 Hdl Hcap gd-sft	£58,740
128	11/15	Newb	2m¹/₂f Cls1 List 128-137 Hdl Hcap soft	£25,628
	5/15	Extr	2m1f Cls4 Mdn Hdl good	£3,249

Just about completed a hat-trick when dead-heating in the Ladbroke at Ascot last season; inconsistent subsequently but ran another cracker when third at 33-1 in the County Hurdle and should again be a force in top 2m handicaps.

Supasundae

6 b g Galileo - Distinctive Look (Danehill)

Jessica Harrington (Ir)	**Ann & Alan Potts Partnership**

PLACINGS: **1/16/9317-4** RPR **150h**

Starts	1st	2nd	3rd	4th	Win & Pl
8	1	-	1	1	£22,779

12/15	Leop	2m Mdn Hdl heavy	£7,488
12/14	Asct	1m7¹/₂f Cls1 List NHF 4-6yo soft	£11,390
3/14	Weth	2m Cls6 NHF 4-6yo good	£1,711

Promising in bumpers and novice hurdles, finishing sixth in the Champion Bumper and seventh in last season's Supreme, though he twice disappointed at Punchestown and doesn't seem to take much racing; may well leave previous form behind when he goes novice chasing.

Superb Story (Ire)

5 b g Duke Of Marmalade - Yes My Love (Anabaa)

Dan Skelton	**A Holt, J Robinson, A Taylor & S Miller**

PLACINGS: **1444/121-P** RPR **148+h**

Starts	1st	2nd	3rd	4th	Win & Pl
8	3	1	-	3	£89,776

138	3/16	Chel	2m1f Cls1 Gd3 138-152 Hdl Hcap good	£51,255
120	10/15	Weth	2m Cls3 119-133 Hdl Hcap good	£5,523
	1/15	Muss	1m7¹/₂f Cls3 Hdl 4yo gd-sft	£9,747

Much improved last season and made the most of a lenient handicap mark, winning the County Hurdle at Cheltenham having been put away for the race since his Greatwood second; raised just 7lb for that and could win another top 2m handicap.

'One of the greatest 2m chasers of all time is still a phenomenal talent'

Sutton Place (Ire)

5 b g Mahler - Glebe Beauty (Good Thyne)

Gordon Elliott (Ir)   **John P McManus**

PLACINGS: 3111-					RPR **144+h**
Starts	1st	2nd	3rd	4th	Win & Pl
4	3	-		1	£37,283
	3/16	Fair	2m Nov Gd2 Hdl yld-sft..................................		£19,522
	3/16	Naas	2m Nov List Hdl sft-hvy...................................		£12,436
	1/16	Fair	2m NHF 5-7yo heavy..		£4,566

Won two novice hurdles and a bumper last season, finishing off with a narrow Grade 2 win at Fairyhouse; still green and awkward that day and should get much better with experience; looks a potential star over fences.

Taglietelle

7 b g Tagula - Averami (Averti)

Gordon Elliott (Ir)   **Olduvai Syndicate**

PLACINGS: 1/2111441/4347347-4F					RPR **157h**
Starts	1st	2nd	3rd	4th	Win & Pl
20	5	1	2	6	£70,067
145	4/15	Aint	3m¹/₂f Cls1 Gd3 136-151 Hdl Hcap gd-sft............		£28,135
	10/14	Punc	2m Hdl gd-fm..		£10,833
	9/14	Prth	2m¹/₂f Cls4 Nov Hdl good...............................		£3,119
	8/14	Ctml	2m1f Cls4 Nov Hdl good.................................		£3,249
	3/14	Dpat	2m2f Mdn Hdl soft..		£4,600

Failed to win last season but ran some terrific races off stiff marks, notably when fourth in the Pertemps Final at Cheltenham; began chasing this summer and could be one for good novice handicaps as he gains experience.

Tango De Juilley (Fr)

8 b g Lesotho - Lasalsa De Juilley (Le Balafre)

Venetia Williams   **Muhammad Nadeem Khan**

PLACINGS: 51224/83/122U161/2-					RPR **153c**
Starts	1st	2nd	3rd	4th	Win & Pl
15	4	5	1	1	£64,849
	4/15	Carl	2m4f Cls3 Nov Ch soft....................................		£6,498
	2/15	Hntg	2m¹/₂f Cls3 Nov Ch soft..................................		£6,498
	11/14	Kemp	2m Cls4 Ch good..		£4,660
	7/11	Claf	2m1f Hdl 3yo v soft.......................................		£12,414

Missed virtually all of last season but did remarkably well to finish second in the Brown Advisory & Merriebelle Stable Plate at Cheltenham first time out; had progressed

ON THE CLOCK

Tea For Two A convincing winner on his chasing bow at Exeter, he was a cut above his Kempton rivals over 3m on Boxing Day. Nick Williams' seven-year-old is suited by that trip on a right-handed flat track with ease in the ground and can continue on the up. *[Dave Edwards, Topspeed]*

throughout his novice campaign and still seems to be going the right way.

Taquin Du Seuil (Fr)

9 b/br g Voix Du Nord - Sweet Laly (Marchand De Sable)

Jonjo O'Neill   **Martin Broughton & Friends**

PLACINGS: 16/113211/32P49/165-					RPR **164c**
Starts	1st	2nd	3rd	4th	Win & Pl
19	8	3	2	1	£204,431
152	2/16	Wwck	2m4f Cls2 130-152 Ch Hcap soft......................		£18,768
	3/14	Chel	2m4f Cls1 Nov Gd1 Ch good............................		£68,340
	1/14	Hayd	2m4f Cls1 Nov Gd2 Ch heavy...........................		£17,912
	11/13	Chel	2m4¹/₂f Cls2 Nov Ch good...............................		£12,512
	10/13	Ffos	2m Cls4 Nov Ch heavy....................................		£4,549
	12/12	Newb	2m4¹/₂f Cls1 Nov Gd1 Hdl heavy......................		£17,165
	12/12	Sand	2m4f Cls1 Nov Gd2 Hdl heavy..........................		£12,676
	10/12	Uttx	2m Cls5 Mdn Hdl gd-sft..................................		£2,144

Largely disappointing since winning the JLT Novices' Chase at Cheltenham in 2014 but won his first race since then on his belated return last season and came a fair sixth in the Ryanair Chase; remains unconvincing over 3m but can win good races over shorter.

Tea For Two

7 b g Kayf Tara - One For Me (Tragic Role)

Nick Williams   **Mrs Jane Williams & Len Jakeman**

PLACINGS: 1/221/13112P/67113-					RPR **161+c**
Starts	1st	2nd	3rd	4th	Win & Pl
15	7	3	2	-	£113,412
	12/15	Kemp	3m Cls1 Nov Gd1 Ch gd-sft..............................		£39,865
	12/15	Extr	2m3f Cls2 Nov Ch heavy..................................		£12,686
134	1/15	Kemp	2m5f Cls1 List 129-155 Hdl Hcap soft..............		£25,628
	12/14	Towc	2m5f Cls4 Nov Hdl 4-6yo gd-sft........................		£3,249
	10/14	Kemp	2m5f Cls4 Nov Hdl gd-sft................................		£3,899
	4/14	Extr	2m1f Cls6 NHF 4-6yo good.............................		£1,625
	3/14	Winc	1m7¹/₂f Cls6 NHF 4-6yo good..........................		£1,625

Stormed to a memorable Grade 1 victory under Lizzie Kelly at Kempton last season on only his second run over fences, proving stamina over 3m; had also gained biggest hurdles win at that track and yet to prove he can be equally effective elsewhere.

The Druids Nephew (Ire)

9 b g King's Theatre - Gifted (Shareef Dancer)

Neil Mulholland   **The Stonehenge Druids**

PLACINGS: 6/4F2P/12751F/662P5-					RPR **155c**
Starts	1st	2nd	3rd	4th	Win & Pl
24	4	4	2	1	£108,424
146	3/15	Chel	3m1f Cls1 Gd3 133-155 Ch Hcap gd-sft..............		£51,255
132	10/14	Hntg	2m7¹/₂f Cls3 122-132 Ch Hcap soft....................		£6,657
	1/13	Winc	2m5f Cls3 Nov Ch soft....................................		£6,975
	1/12	Kemp	2m5f Cls3 Nov Hdl good.................................		£5,848

Cheltenham Festival winner in 2015 and may well have followed up in the Grand National but for falling in front five out; laid out for a repeat last season but was pulled up; good fifth in the bet365 Gold Cup next time and dropped 5lb following that run.

The Eaglehaslanded (Ire)

6 b g Milan - Vallee Doree (Neverneyev)

Paul Nicholls   Mrs Angela Tincknell & W Tincknell

PLACINGS: 11F1/124P11-8   RPR **140+h**

Starts		1st	2nd	3rd	4th	Win & Pl
10		5	1	-	1	£27,750
132	4/16	Wwck	3m1f Cls3 111-133 Hdl Hcap good			£7,148
125	4/16	Chel	3m Cls2 122-145 Hdl Hcap good			£10,010
	10/15	Extr	2m7f Cls4 Nov Am Hdl gd-fm			£3,120
	3/15	Chep	2m3¹/₂f Cls4 Nov Hdl soft			£3,249
	1/15	Extr	2m1f Cls6 Mdn NHF 4-6yo soft			£1,625

Won twice on soft ground two seasons ago but much better on good according to connections and proved the point last spring, taking his form to a new level with handicap wins at Cheltenham and Warwick; likely to go novice chasing.

The Game Changer (Ire)

7 b g Arcadio - Gilt Ridden (Heron Island)

Gordon Elliott (Ir)   Gigginstown House Stud

PLACINGS: 0392/311210211142-22   RPR **156+c**

Starts		1st	2nd	3rd	4th	Win & Pl
32		10	9	4	2	£215,699
	10/15	Punc	2m2f Nov Gd3 Ch good			£15,116
	10/15	Tipp	2m4f Nov Gd3 Ch good			£15,116
	9/15	Rosc	2m Nov Gd3 Ch good			£17,636
	7/15	Limk	2m3¹/₂f Nov Ch good			£9,360
	6/15	Rosc	2m Nov Ch good			£8,023
	5/15	Punc	2m Ch good			£6,953
137	8/14	Klny	2m1f 109-137 Hdl Hcap good			£17,063
	12/13	Punc	2m Nov Hdl gd-yld			£7,573
	11/13	Cork	2m Mdn Hdl 4yo soft			£5,610
	3/13	Cork	2m NHF 4-7yo heavy			£4,488

Prolific over fences early last season and unlucky to come up against Douvan when returning in the spring (would have been second in the Arkle but for being hampered and twice second to him subsequently); needs good ground.

The Last Samuri (Ire)

8 ch g Flemensfirth - Howaboutthis (Oscar)

Kim Bailey   Paul & Clare Rooney

PLACINGS: /121119/211U12/3112-   RPR **160+c**

Starts		1st	2nd	3rd	4th	Win & Pl
15		8	4	1	-	£325,042
149	3/16	Donc	3m2f Cls2 132-155 Ch Hcap soft			£34,536
140	12/15	Kemp	3m Cls2 127-145 Ch Hcap gd-sft			£25,992
132	3/15	Kels	2m4f Cls2 125-150 Ch Hcap gd sft			£16,245
	1/15	Ayr	3m1¹/₂f Cls4 Nov Ch soft			£4,029
	11/14	Bang	3m Cls3 Nov Ch soft			£8,406
	1/14	Catt	3m1¹/₂f Cls4 Nov Hdl soft			£3,249
	11/13	Bang	2m3¹/₂f Cls4 Nov Hdl soft			£3,249
	11/13	Kels	2m6¹/₂f Cls4 Nov Hdl gd-sft			£3,899

Went from strength to strength last season, winning two good handicaps including the Grimthorpe before a fine second in the Grand National; may have missed his chance given he starts this campaign 10lb higher, although connections think he will be better on good ground.

The New One (Ire)

8 b g King's Theatre - Thuringe (Turgeon)

Nigel Twiston-Davies   S Such & Cg Paletta

PLACINGS: 2/11231/11115/1214F-   RPR **163h**

Starts		1st	2nd	3rd	4th	Win & Pl
25		16	4	1	1	£745,525
	1/16	Hayd	1m7¹/₂f Cls1 Gd2 Hdl heavy			£42,713
	10/15	Kemp	2m Cls1 List Hdl good			£17,085
	1/15	Hayd	2m Cls1 Gd2 Hdl heavy			£42,713
	12/14	Chel	2m1f Cls1 Gd2 Hdl gd-sft			£74,035
	11/14	Hayd	2m Cls2 Hdl soft			£61,900
	10/14	Kemp	2m Cls1 List Hdl gd-sft			£14,238
	4/14	Aint	2m4f Cls1 Gd1 Hdl good			£112,540
	12/13	Chel	2m1f Cls1 Gd2 Hdl good			£74,035
	10/13	Kemp	2m Cls1 List Hdl gd-sft			£14,238
	3/13	Chel	2m5f Cls1 Nov Gd1 Hdl gd-sft			£68,340
	1/13	Wwck	2m5f Cls1 Nov Gd2 Hdl soft			£15,735
	10/12	Chel	2m5f Cls2 Nov Hdl gd-sft			£10,635
	10/12	NAbb	2m2¹/₂f Cls4 Nov Hdl soft			£2,924
	4/12	Aint	2m1f Cls1 Gd2 NHF 4-6yo good			£14,238
	1/12	Chel	1m6f Cls1 List NHF 4yo gd-sft			£7,133
	11/11	Wwck	1m6f Cls6 NHF 3yo good			£2,053

Has failed three times in the Champion Hurdle but continues to run well, last season's fourth following a second successive win in the Haydock trial; proven over 2m4f (has won Neptune and Aintree Hurdles) and may need that sort of trip these days.

The Nipper (Ire)

5 b m Scorpion - Sharp Single (Supreme Leader)

Warren Greatrex   Smith, Ratcliffe & Bowring

PLACINGS: 111-O   RPR **125+b**

Starts		1st	2nd	3rd	4th	Win & Pl
4		3	-	-	-	£16,523
	3/16	Sand	2m Cls1 List NHF 4 7yo soft			£11,390
	11/15	Bang	2m1¹/₂f Cls6 NHF 4-6yo heavy			£2,053
	5/15	Bang	2m1¹/₂f Cls5 NHF 4-6yo good			£3,080

Hugely talented mare who completed a hat-trick in a Listed bumper at Sandown despite hanging across the track; rider put that down to greenness but then ran out at Punchestown to raise further temperament issues.

The Organist (Ire)

5 b m Alkaadhem - Go On Eileen (Bob Back)

Oliver Sherwood   JP McManus

PLACINGS: 11121F-   RPR **140+h**

Starts		1st	2nd	3rd	4th	Win & Pl
6		4	1	-	-	£28,236
	3/16	Donc	3m1¹/₂f Cls1 Nov List Hdl soft			£17,165
	12/15	Font	2m3f Cls4 Nov Hdl heavy			£3,249
	11/15	Hntg	2m3¹/₂f Cls4 Nov Hdl gd-sft			£3,899
	5/15	Prth	2m1¹/₂f Cls6 NHF 4-6yo soft			£2,053

Fast-improving mare who would have made it five wins out of six but for falling at the last when three lengths clear at Cheltenham in April; sold for 260,000gns the following month; likely contender for top mares' hurdles.

The Romford Pele (Ire)

9 b g Accordion - Back And Fore (Bob Back)

Rebecca Curtis   **Trembath & Outhart**

PLACINGS: 233246/3111/77F38U-2   RPR **149c**

Starts	1st	2nd	3rd	4th	Win & Pl
28	6	7	4	2	£111,404

	10/14	Chel	3m¹/₂f Cls2 Nov Ch good	£12,628
	139 6/14	Uttx	3m2f Cls1 List 127-146 Ch Hcap good	£34,170
	128 6/14	Worc	2m4f Cls3 111-132 Ch Hcap gd-sft	£7,666
	12/12	Chep	2m3¹/₂f Cls4 Nov Hdl heavy	£3,249
	11/12	Tntn	2m¹/₂f Cls3 Nov Hdl good	£5,198
	2/12	Bang	2m¹/₂f Cls6 NHF 4-6yo good	£1,437

Has failed to complete in last two runs over fences and did better reverting to hurdles last season, finishing third in the Cleeve Hurdle and eighth in the Coral Cup before a close second at Punchestown; on a fair mark over hurdles and fences.

The Saint James (Fr)

5 b g Saint Des Saints - Aimela (Sagamix)

Jonjo O'Neill   **John P McManus**

PLACINGS: 211/242432/025FP-2   RPR **138+c**

Starts	1st	2nd	3rd	4th	Win & Pl
15	2	6	1	2	£132,752

	4/14	Autl	1m7f Hdl 3yo v soft	£24,000
	3/14	Engh	2m Hdl 3yo v soft	£20,000

Very smart juvenile hurdler two seasons ago (placed at Cheltenham and Aintree) but failed to jump well enough over fences last term, including when falling when likely to win the Pendil at Kempton; starts on a very good mark if jumping improves.

The Young Master

7 b g Echo Of Light - Fine Frenzy (Great Commotion)

Neil Mulholland   **Dajam & The Old Masters**

PLACINGS: 921F11/111d17/2U4631-   RPR **155c**

Starts	1st	2nd	3rd	4th	Win & Pl
23	7	2	2	1	£184,949

	148 4/16	Sand	3m5f Cls1 Gd3 144-159 Ch Hcap good	£84,405
	144 12/14	Asct	3m Cls1 List 135-161 Ch Hcap gd-sft	£56,270
	121 10/14	Chel	3m1f Cls3 107-125 Am Ch Hcap good	£7,195
	9/14	Worc	2m7f Cls4 Ch good	£4,327
	110 1/14	Sedg	3m3f Cls4 100-112 Hdl Hcap heavy	£3,899
	103 1/14	Fknm	2m7¹/₂f Cls4 102-108 Hdl Hcap heavy	£3,249
	94 11/13	Font	2m5¹/₂f Cls5 Nov 69-95 Hdl Hcap heavy	£1,949

Won the Silver Cup at Ascot two seasons ago to make up for luckless disqualification in the Badger Ales Trophy when ineligible; back to winning ways last spring in the bet365 Gold Cup having run a couple of fine races in third in other good staying handicaps.

Theatre Guide (Ire)

9 b g King's Theatre - Erintante (Denel)

Colin Tizzard   **Mrs Jean R Bishop**

PLACINGS: P1/332/1640R/3231F8-   RPR **154+c**

Starts	1st	2nd	3rd	4th	Win & Pl
26	6	3	5	2	£205,729

	139 2/16	Kemp	3m Cls1 Gd3 133-159 Ch Hcap gd-sft	£56,950
	11/14	Kemp	2m4¹/₂f Cls2 Ch soft	£8,412
	4/13	NAbb	2m5f Cls3 Nov Ch gd-sft	£8,578
	11/12	Extr	2m7¹/₂f Cls4 Nov Hdl gd-sft	£9,902
	2/12	Winc	1m7¹/₂f Cls4 Nov Hdl soft	£3,249
	4/11	Chep	2m Cls6 NHF 4-6yo gd-sft	£1,821

Had long threatened to land a big handicap (twice placed in the Hennessy Gold Cup) before running away with the BetBright Chase by ten lengths last season; travelled well for a long way when eighth in bet365 Gold Cup on final start (possible non-stayer).

Theinval (Fr)

6 b g Smadoun - Kinevees (Hard Leaf)

Nicky Henderson   **Mr & Mrs Sandy Orr**

PLACINGS: 2242/615211/3P09-313   RPR **146c**

Starts	1st	2nd	3rd	4th	Win & Pl
23	4	4	3	3	£96,562

	5/16	Uttx	2m4f Cls4 Ch good	£4,431
	144 4/15	Aint	2m4f Cls1 Gd3 127-149 Hdl Hcap gd-sft	£28,135
	134 3/15	Kemp	2m5f Cls2 115-135 Hdl Hcap good	£22,743
	119 11/14	Kemp	2m Cls3 105-129 Cond Hdl Hcap soft	£5,393

Disappointing last season having won a handicap hurdle at the Grand National meeting in 2015; bounced back over fences this summer when a smooth winner at Uttoxeter and a fine third in the Summer Plate in only his fourth chase.

Third Intention (Ire)

9 b g Azamour - Third Dimension (Suave Dancer)

Colin Tizzard   **Robert & Sarah Tizzard**

PLACINGS: 35/153F103/22366434-   RPR **164c**

Starts	1st	2nd	3rd	4th	Win & Pl
40	6	9	10	3	£219,212

	2/15	Kemp	2m4¹/₂f Cls2 Ch gd-sft	£12,996
	11/14	Hayd	2m¹/₂f Cls2 Ch soft	£16,245
	10/13	Chel	2m4f Cls2 Nov Ch good	£12,512
	2/12	Font	2m3f Cls1 Gd2 Hdl gd-sft	£16,800
	4/11	Chel	2m1f Cls2 Nov Hdl good	£6,262
	12/10	Newb	2m¹/₂f Cls4 Hdl 3yo good	£3,903

Began last season in excellent form (twice second including the Haldon Gold Cup) but paid the price with his mark and struggled; given a chance by the handicapper now (7lb lower than when third in the Topham) and could take advantage.

ON THE FIGURES

Thistlecrack The RPR of 178 he earned when landing the World Hurdle was the highest figure recorded by a hurdler at the Cheltenham Festival in the past 25 years. He looks sure to take high rank now his attentions are set to be switched to fences. *[Steve Mason, Racing Post Ratings]*

Thistlecrack

8 b g Kayf Tara - Ardstown (Ardross)

Colin Tizzard   **John & Heather Snook**

PLACINGS: 3/1/517151/211111-   RPR **178+h**

Starts	1st	2nd	3rd	4th	Win & Pl
14	9	1	1	-	£460,000

4/16	Aint	3m¹/₂f Cls1 Gd1 Hdl soft	£84,405
3/16	Chel	3m Cls1 Gd1 Hdl good	£170,850
1/16	Chel	3m Cls1 Gd2 Hdl heavy	£34,170
12/15	Asct	3m¹/₂f Cls1 Gd1 Hdl gd-sft	£56,950
11/15	Newb	3m Cls1 Gd2 Hdl soft	£25,628
4/15	Aint	3m¹/₂f Cls1 Nov Gd1 Hdl gd-sft	£56,437
2/15	Asct	1m7¹/₂f Cls2 Nov Hdl soft	£9,384
1/15	Winc	1m7¹/₂f Cls4 Nov Hdl heavy	£3,899
4/14	Winc	1m7¹/₂f Cls6 NHF 4-6yo good	£1,625

Hugely exciting individual who dominated the staying hurdle division last season, running away with the World Hurdle at Cheltenham as part of a five-timer and proving equally effective on soft ground elsewhere; set to go chasing and could well develop into a Gold Cup candidate.

Thomas Brown

7 b g Sir Harry Lewis - Tentsmuir (Arctic Lord)

Harry Fry   **The Corse Lawners**

PLACINGS: 1/4181/121P6/121U74-   RPR **147+c**

Starts	1st	2nd	3rd	4th	Win & Pl
15	6	2		2	£43,956

1/16	Donc	3m Cls4 Nov Ch gd-sft	£5,326
11/15	Asct	2m3f Cls3 Ch soft	£7,798
1/15	Chel	2m4¹/₂f Cls3 Nov Hdl soft	£6,256
11/14	Extr	2m5¹/₂f Cls3 Nov Hdl gd-sft	£5,523
3/14	Bang	2m¹/₂f Cls5 NHF 4-6yo gd-sft	£2,053
11/13	Newb	2m¹/₂f Cls6 NHF 4-6yo gd-sft	£3,249

Won two of his first three chases last season but let down by his jumping in handicap company, including when favourite for the BetBright Chase; should get better with experience and on a fair mark for good staying handicaps.

Thomas Hobson

6 b g Halling - La Spezia (Danehill Dancer)

Willie Mullins (Ir)   **Mrs S Ricci**

PLACINGS: F1211P-3   RPR **148+h**

Starts	1st	2nd	3rd	4th	Win & Pl
7	3	1	1	-	£42,864

1/16	Wwck	2m5f Cls1 Nov Gd2 Hdl heavy	£17,165
12/15	Punc	2m4f Hdl soft	£6,686
7/15	Gway	2m Mdn Hdl good	£7,756

Smart Flat horse who began to translate that ability to hurdles last season, most notably when winning a Grade 2 at Warwick, although sloppy jumping held him back at other times; may well prove better than his mark once ironing out those issues.

'He's been given plenty of time to develop and should progress again'

Three Musketeers (Ire)

6 b g Flemensfirth - Friendly Craic (Mister Lord)

Dan Skelton   **Mrs G Widdowson & Mrs R Kelvin-Hughes**

PLACINGS: 2113/3154-   RPR **158c**

Starts	1st	2nd	3rd	4th	Win & Pl
7	3		2	1	£55,919

11/15	Newb	2m4f Cls1 Nov Gd2 Ch soft	£20,026
1/15	Wwck	2m5f Cls1 Nov Gd2 Hdl soft	£15,946
12/14	Weth	2m5¹/₂f Cls4 Nov Hdl soft	£3,263

Has been given plenty of time to develop and remains very lightly raced; looked a fine prospect when winning easily at Newbury last season and bounced back to form with a close fourth in the JLT Novices' Chase at Cheltenham; should progress again.

Tombstone (Ire)

6 ch g Robin Des Champs - Connaught Hall (Un Desperado)

Gordon Elliott (Ir)   **Gigginstown House Stud**

PLACINGS: 31/11224-   RPR **150h**

Starts	1st	2nd	3rd	4th	Win & Pl
7	3	2	1	1	£49,606

11/15	Fair	2m2f Mdn Hdl sft-hvy	£6,419
10/15	DRoy	2m NHF 4-7yo yld-sft	£6,953
1/15	Naas	2m3f NHF 5-7yo soft	£4,279

High-class novice hurdler last season, twice finishing second at Grade 1 level in Ireland before a fine fourth in the Supreme Novices' Hurdle; looked to find even a stiff 2m too sharp that day and should improve over further; good chasing prospect.

Tomngerry (Ire)

6 b g Craigsteel - Lady Vic (Old Vic)

Brian Ellison   **Mrs J A Martin**

PLACINGS: 11111P-   RPR **134+h**

Starts	1st	2nd	3rd	4th	Win & Pl
5	4	-	-	-	£13,255

2/16	Newc	2m6f Cls3 Nov Hdl gd-sft	£6,498
2/16	Weth	2m5¹/₂f Cls4 Nov Hdl heavy	£3,249
1/16	Catt	1m7¹/₂f Cls6 NHF 4-6yo soft	£1,949
12/15	Sedg	2m1f Cls6 NHF 4-6yo heavy	£1,560

Prolific last season when winning two bumpers and two novice hurdles to add to point-to-point success; disappointing he couldn't make a better fist of step up in class when pulled up in the Sefton at Aintree but worth another chance.

RACING POST

MIND-BLOWING

iPad Daily Edition £99 for 5 months.

To claim this offer visit
Racingpost.com/ipad5months

Available on the App Store

Top Gamble (Ire)

8 ch g Presenting - Zeferina (Sadler's Wells)

Kerry Lee   **Walters Plant Hire & James & Jean Potter**

PLACINGS: 11/9FF/111251/P3311-   RPR **165+c**

Starts	1st	2nd	3rd	4th	Win & Pl
17	8	2	2	-	£117,566

3/16	Fair	2m1f Gd2 Ch yield	£18,438
2/16	Newb	2m¹/₂f Cls1 Gd2 Ch soft	£28,475
4/15	Ayr	2m4¹/₂f Cls1 Nov Gd2 Ch good	£27,197
1/15	Newb	2m¹/₂f Cls3 Nov 125-144 Ch Hcap good	£6,498
12/14	Wwck	2m Cls3 Nov 124-135 Ch Hcap soft	£6,498
11/14	Weth	1m7f Cls4 Nov Ch soft	£4,106
2/13	Ffos	2m Cls4 Nov Hdl heavy	£3,899
12/12	Ffos	2m Cls6 Mdn NHF 4-6yo heavy	£1,430

Progressed well to win a couple of Grade 2 contests towards the end of last season at around 2m after good efforts in handicaps over further; has to improve again to make a mark at the top level but could be a surprise package on soft ground.

Top Notch (Fr)

5 b g Poliglote - Topira (Pistolet Bleu)

Nicky Henderson   **Simon Munir & Isaac Souede**

PLACINGS: 11/1112/22515-   RPR **162h**

Starts	1st	2nd	3rd	4th	Win & Pl
11	3	5	-	-	£147,324

2/16	Kels	2m2f Cls2 Hdl heavy	£16,245
2/15	Hayd	1m7¹/₂f Cls2 Hdl 4yo soft	£9,747
1/15	Asct	1m7¹/₂f Cls3 Hdl 4yo soft	£6,498
12/14	Newb	2m¹/₂f Cls3 Hdl 3yo gd-sft	£6,498
4/14	Engh	2m¹/₂f Hdl 3yo v soft	£19,200
3/14	Bord	2m¹/₂f Hdl 3yo heavy	£8,400

Smart hurdler who ran some big races in defeat last season, going close in the Fighting Fifth and finishing fifth in the Champion Hurdle on ground quicker than ideal; open to further progress and should continue to run well in good 2m hurdles.

Traffic Fluide (Fr)

6 b g Astarabad - Petale Rouge (Bonnet Rouge)

Gary Moore   **Galloping On The South Downs Partnership**

PLACINGS: P37142113/3-   RPR **165c**

Starts	1st	2nd	3rd	4th	Win & Pl
10	3	1	2	1	£54,910

3/15	Sand	1m7¹/₂f Cls3 Nov 122-140 Ch Hcap good	£6,498
2/15	Plum	2m1f Cls3 Nov 129-145 Ch Hcap gd-sft	£7,988
10/14	Stra	2m4f Ch 4yo heavy	£8,800

Ran a huge race on his only run last season when a 33-1 third in the Clarence House Chase behind Un De Sceaux, beaten only five lengths; open to plenty more improvement after just seven runs over fences and could be a contender for top 2m chases.

Triolo D'Alene (Fr)

9 ch g Epalo - Joliette D'Alene (Garde Royale)

Nicky Henderson   **Mr & Mrs Sandy Orr**

PLACINGS: /2P381/1310P/P3/150-   RPR **160+c**

Starts	1st	2nd	3rd	4th	Win & Pl
22	7	1	3	2	£257,625

	1/16	Kemp	2m4¹/₂f Cls1 List Ch soft	£18,690
147	11/13	Newb	3m2f Cls1 Gd3 132-158 Ch Hcap good	£99,663
139	4/13	Hntg	2m7¹/₂f Cls2 130-156 Ch Hcap good	£14,076
132	4/13	Aint	2m5f Cls1 Gd3 125-151 Ch Hcap gd-sft	£67,524
127	1/12	Asct	2m3f Cls3 Nov 120-134 Ch Hcap gd-sft	£9,495
	11/11	Fntb	2m2f Ch 4yo v soft	£9,103
	10/11	Mlns	2m2f Ch 4yo soft	£6,621

Won the Topham and Hennessy Gold Cup in 2013 but has been restricted to just five runs in the last two seasons; suggested he retains plenty of ability with easy win at Kempton last term but disappointed in the Grand National for the second time.

Ttebbob (Ire)

7 b g Milan - Our Dream (Bob Back)

Jessica Harrington (Ir)   **David Bobbett**

PLACINGS: 9021/3601B2/511P2-5   RPR **151+c**

Starts	1st	2nd	3rd	4th	Win & Pl
16	4	3	1	-	£53,260

12/15	Navn	2m1f Nov Gd3 Ch heavy	£17,636
11/15	Thur	2m2f Ch soft	£5,884
2/15	Clon	2m3¹/₂f Hdl soft	£6,686
3/14	Naas	3m Mdn Hdl yld-sft	£5,750

Looked a terrific prospect in his first two chases last season, building on progressive hurdles form with thrilling all-the-way wins; destroyed by Douvan next time and nowhere near as good in two more runs; could do well back at a slightly lower level.

Two Taffs (Ire)

6 b g Flemensfirth - Richs Mermaid (Saddlers' Hall)

Dan Skelton   **Walters Plant Hire & James & Jean Potter**

PLACINGS: 1/32341-   RPR **135+h**

Starts	1st	2nd	3rd	4th	Win & Pl
6	2	1	2	1	£21,569

129	4/16	Ayr	2m5¹/₂f Cls2 124-150 Hdl Hcap gd-sft	£12,996
	3/15	MRas	2m¹/₂f Cls6 Mdn NHF 4-6yo good	£1,560

Finally got off the mark over hurdles when comfortably landing a handicap at Ayr in April, benefiting from step up in trip; had shaped with great promise over shorter and even sent off favourite when fourth in EBF Final at Sandown.

Picture Perfect
Moments made into memories

ORDER NOW *RACING POST*.com/photos

Ubak (Fr)

8 b g Kapgarde - Gesse Parade (Dress Parade)

Gary Moore   Nick Peacock

PLACINGS: **3P4/234712/4U42314-0**   RPR **153h**

Starts 17	1st 2	2nd 3	3rd 3	4th 5	Win & Pl £124,909
146	4/16	Aint	3m¹/₂f Cls1 Gd3 132-158 Hdl Hcap soft		£28,135
	4/13	Aint	2m4f Cls1 Nov Gd2 Hdl gd-sft		£34,170

Very talented novice hurdler four seasons ago only to miss more than two and a half years through injury; struggled over fences when returning last season but flourished back over hurdles, finishing third in the Coral Cup before winning at Aintree.

Ucello Conti (Fr)

8 b g Martaline - Gazelle Lulu (Altayan)

Gordon Elliott (Ir)   Simon Munir & Isaac Souede

PLACINGS: **26/5312P/69/1P/6236**   RPR **149c**

Starts 25	1st 8	2nd 5	3rd 2	4th 1	Win & Pl £304,664
	6/14	Rost	2m5f Ch grd-fm		£6,000
	8/12	Roya	1m6¹/₂f NHF		£6,667
	2/12	Ange	2m1f Hdl 4yo gd-sft		£10,400
	11/11	Engh	2m1f List Ch 3yo v soft		£35,172
	9/11	Autl	2m1¹/₂f Ch 3yo v soft		£23,172
	7/11	Sabl	1m5¹/₂f NHF 3yo gd-sft		£6,034
	7/11	Claf	2m1f Hdl 3yo soft		£13,241
	5/11	Nanc	2m1f Hdl 3yo gd-fm		£8,276

Joined Gordon Elliott from France last season and ran well in several top staying handicaps, getting placed in the Paddy Power Chase and the Thyestes before a fine sixth in the Grand National; made several blunders that day and capable of better.

Un De Sceaux (Fr)

8 b g Denham Red - Hotesse De Sceaux (April Night)

Willie Mullins (Ir)   Edward O'Connell

PLACINGS: **/11111/F111/1F122-16**   RPR **172+c**

Starts 20	1st 15	2nd -	3rd -	4th -	Win & Pl £605,020
	5/16	Autl	2m5¹/₂f Gd2 Hdl v soft		£57,904
	1/16	Asct	2m1f Cls1 Gd1 Ch soft		£71,188
	4/15	Punc	2m Nov Gd1 Ch soft		£53,488
	3/15	Chel	2m Cls1 Gd1 Ch gd-sft		£85,425
	1/15	Leop	2m1f Nov Gd1 Ch yld-sft		£37,209
	12/14	Fair	2m Ch soft		£6,900
	4/14	Autl	2m3¹/₂f Gd2 Hdl heavy		£65,625
	3/14	Autl	2m3¹/₂f Gd3 Hdl v soft		£50,625
	2/14	Gowr	2m Gd2 Hdl heavy		£21,667
	1/14	Navn	2m Hdl soft		£10,833
	12/13	Thur	2m Hdl soft		£8,695
	4/13	Punc	2m Nov Hdl heavy		£11,890
	2/13	Punc	2m Mdn Hdl sft-hvy		£4,207
	10/12	Sbri	1m4f NHF 4yo v soft		£4,167
	2/12	Mchl	1m4f NHF 4yo gd-sft		£4,167

Exciting front-running chaser who has been beaten just twice when completing, both times by Sprinter Sacre at Cheltenham and Sandown (may have found ground quicker than ideal); subsequent win over 2m5f in France gives connections more options.

Un Temps Pour Tout (Ire)

7 b g Robin Des Champs - Rougedespoir (Bonnet Rouge)

David Pipe   Professor Caroline Tisdall & Bryan Drew

PLACINGS: **1331321/3363/122414-**   RPR **164+c**

Starts 21	1st 6	2nd 3	3rd 9	4th 2	Win & Pl £407,819
148	3/16	Chel	3m1f Cls1 Gd3 131-153 Ch Hcap gd-sft		£56,950
	6/15	Autl	3m1¹/₂f Gd1 Hdl v soft		£129,070
	2/14	Asct	2m3¹/₂f Cls2 Nov Hdl heavy		£15,640
	9/13	Autl	2m2f Gd3 Hdl 4yo v soft		£49,390
0	5/13	Autl	2m3¹/₂f List Hdl 4yo Hcap heavy		£34,756
	5/13	Bord	2m2¹/₂f Hdl 4yo gd-sft		£8,585

High-class staying hurdler (won the French Champion Hurdle in 2015) who left behind a slow start to his chasing career with a brilliant win in the 3m handicap chase at the Cheltenham Festival; looks a Grade 1 chaser on that evidence and had excuses (finished lame) at Aintree next time.

Unioniste (Fr)

8 gr g Dom Alco - Gleep Will (Laniste)

Paul Nicholls   J Hales

PLACINGS: **/31838/613F8/803120-**   RPR **155c**

Starts 29	1st 8	2nd 4	3rd 5	4th 2	Win & Pl £241,167
	2/16	Kels	3m2f Cls2 Ch heavy		£14,102
148	1/15	Sand	3m Cls2 128 154 Ch Hcap soft		£31,280
	12/13	Aint	3m1f Cls1 List Ch gd-sft		£17,387
	2/13	Newb	2m7¹/₂f Cls3 Nov Ch soft		£8,123
143	12/12	Chel	2m5f Cls1 Gd3 136-150 Ch Hcap heavy		£56,950
	10/12	Aint	2m4f Cls3 Nov Ch good		£6,963
	5/12	Autl	2m3¹/₂f Ch 4yo heavy		£21,200
	2/12	Pau	2m3f Hdl soft		£13,600

Largely disappointing since remarkable win in the December Gold Cup at Cheltenham as a four-year-old in 2012; back down to mark of 149, though, and has a decent record from just three runs in handicaps below 151 (first and third at Sandown before third failure over Grand National fences).

Unowhatimeanharry

8 b g Sir Harry Lewis - Red Nose Lady (Teenoso)

Harry Fry   Harry Fry Racing Club

PLACINGS: **/33353/34237P/11111-**   RPR **149h**

Starts 18	1st 6	2nd 1	3rd 6	4th 2	Win & Pl £119,730
138	3/16	Chel	3m Cls1 Nov Gd1 Hdl good		£68,340
	2/16	Extr	2m5f Cls2 124-139 Hdl Hcap heavy		£11,617
	12/15	Chel	3m Cls1 Nov Gd2 Hdl soft		£17,165
123	11/15	Newb	2m4¹/₂f Cls4 Nov 109-123 Hdl Hcap gd-sft		£6,498
123	11/15	Chel	2m5f Cls3 118-125 Cond Hdl Hcap gd-sft		£7,507
	2/13	Font	2m1¹/₂f Cls6 NHF 4-6yo soft		£1,625

Improved out of all recognition for a change of yard last season and completed a stunning five-timer with victory in the Albert Bartlett Hurdle at Cheltenham; fascinating to see how far he can go, though that race may have been set up for him from the rear.

Up For Review (Ire)

7 br g Presenting - Coolsilver (Good Thyne)

Willie Mullins (Ir)   **Andrea & Graham Wylie**

PLACINGS: 3/1/120/3114P1-   RPR **151+h**

Starts	1st	2nd	3rd	4th	Win & Pl
9	4	1	1	1	£46,952

4/16	Prth	3m Cls2 Nov Hdl good		£11,261
12/15	Punc	3m Nov Gd2 Hdl heavy		£21,163
11/15	Fair	2m4f Mdn Hdl heavy		£5,349
12/14	Leop	2m NHF 4-6yo soft		£5,175

Powerful front-running stayer who won three times over hurdles last season, though he fluffed his lines on his two biggest tests when taken on for the lead both times and racing too keenly;

has plenty of scope for fences and seems to act on any going.

Upswing (Ire)

8 b g Beneficial - Native Country (Be My Native)

Jonjo O'Neill   **John P McManus**

PLACINGS: 1/164F1/80520/212P9-   RPR **143+c**

Starts	1st	2nd	3rd	4th	Win & Pl
19	4	3	1	3	£46,873

128	10/15	Worc	2m7f Cls3 Nov 116-135 Ch Hcap gd-sft	£7,596
128	2/14	Newb	3m1/2f Cls2 115-139 Hdl Hcap heavy	£12,512
114	10/13	Carl	2m1f Cls2 108-122 Hdl Hcap gd-sft	£6,498
108	3/13	Carl	2m1f Cls4 89-115 Hdl Hcap heavy	£4,224

Disappointing when well fancied for the Welsh National and Kim Muir last season but now looks even better handicapped on form of close second to Sausalito Sunrise at Cheltenham in November; open to improvement after just five runs over fences.

Valseur Lido: can be expected to take high rank in top staying chases in Ireland during the winter

Uxizandre (Fr)

8 ch g Fragrant Mix - Jolisandre (Dear Doctor)

Alan King   **John P McManus**

PLACINGS: 2312315/11521/418U1/   RPR **174**c

Starts		1st	2nd	3rd	4th	Win & Pl
17		7	3	2	1	£330,365
	3/15	Chel	2m5f Cls1 Gd1 Ch good £178,538			
	11/14	Chel	2m Cls1 List Ch soft £39,865			
	4/14	Aint	2m4f Cls1 Nov Gd1 Ch good £50,643			
	11/13	Plum	2m3¹/₂f Cls3 Nov Ch gd-sft £6,498			
135	10/13	Plum	2m3¹/₂f Cls3 Nov 123-137 Ch Hcap soft £8,123			
	3/13	Wwck	3m1f Cls4 Nov Hdl soft £3,899			
	12/12	Newb	2m3f Cls4 Nov Hdl 4-6yo soft £3,899			

Cheltenham specialist who has a habit of improving on good ground in March, with 16-1 win in the Ryanair Chase in 2015 following 33-1 second in the JLT Novices' Chase; has also won a Shloer Chase on soft ground at the track; missed last season through injury.

Valseur Lido (Fr)

7 b g Anzillero - Libido Rock (Video Rock)

Willie Mullins (Ir)   **Gigginstown House Stud**

PLACINGS: /1101/211236/12FU22-   RPR **168**c

Starts		1st	2nd	3rd	4th	Win & Pl
18		7	5	1	-	£269,364
	4/15	Punc	3m1f Nov Gd1 Ch gd-yld £44,186			
	11/14	Fair	2m4f Nov Gd1 Ch yld-sft £40,625			
	11/14	Punc	2m4f Ch yield £6,900			
	4/14	Fair	2m Nov Gd2 Hdl soft £21,667			
	12/13	Navn	2m Nov Hdl sft-hvy £7,293			
	11/13	Cork	2m Mdn Hdl 4yo sft-hvy £5,610			
	11/12	Pari	1m4f NHF 3yo v soft £12,500			

Ran several good races in defeat last season, most notably when a staying-on second to Vautour in the Ryanair Chase; trainer convinced his future lies over further and might have won the Irish Gold Cup but for unseating at the last.

Value At Risk

7 b g Kayf Tara - Miss Orchestra (Orchestra)

Dan Skelton   **D M Huglin**

PLACINGS: 2/110/3125/FF921-   RPR **151**h

Starts		1st	2nd	3rd	4th	Win & Pl
13		4	3	1	-	£62,230
	3/16	Fair	2m4f Gd2 Hdl yld-sft £26,029			
	12/14	Newb	2m3f Cls4 Nov Hdl 4-6yo soft £3,899			
	12/13	Leop	2m NHF 4-7yo soft £6,171			
	12/13	Fair	2m NHF 4yo gd-yld £4,768			

Smart bumper/hurdles performer who was expected to thrive over fences last season but fell at the second in both chases; steadily rediscovered his form back hurdling and finished with a fine Grade 2 win at Fairyhouse; likely to try chasing again.

Vaniteux (Fr)

7 br g Voix Du Nord - Expoville (Video Rock)

Nicky Henderson   **Mr & Mrs R Kelvin-Hughes**

PLACINGS: 34/1413/22285/121U3-   RPR **162+**c

Starts		1st	2nd	3rd	4th	Win & Pl
14		4	4	2	1	£120,649
	1/16	Donc	2m¹/₂f Cls2 Nov Gd2 Ch good £19,933			
	11/15	Kemp	2m Cls4 Nov Ch gd-sft £4,660			
	2/14	Donc	2m3¹/₂f Cls4 Nov Hdl 4-7yo gd-sft £3,574			
	12/13	Sand	2m Cls3 Nov Hdl gd-sft £6,498			

Took well to fences last season, winning twice either side of a good run behind Ar Mad and looking set for second in the Arkle until unseating his rider two out; outstayed when stepped up in trip back over hurdles on final start.

Vautour (Fr)

7 b g Robin Des Champs - Gazelle De Mai (Dom Pasquini)

Willie Mullins (Ir)   **Mrs S Ricci**

PLACINGS: 22/1111/11211/121F-2   RPR **180**c

Starts		1st	2nd	3rd	4th	Win & Pl
16		10	5			£596,177
	3/16	Chel	2m5f Cls1 Gd1 Ch good £178,538			
	11/15	Asct	2m5f Cls1 Gd2 Ch gd-sft £40,334			
	3/15	Chel	7m4f Cls1 Nov Gd1 Ch good £68,340			
	1/15	Leop	2m3f Nov Gd2 Ch soft £18,895			
	11/14	Navn	2m1f Ch soft £8,625			
	5/14	Punc	2m4f Nov Gd1 Hdl gd-yld £46,500			
	3/14	Chel	2m¹/₂f Cls1 Nov Gd1 Hdl gd-sft £68,340			
	2/14	Leop	2m2f Nov Gd1 Hdl sft-hvy £43,333			
	1/14	Punc	2m Nov Gd2 Hdl sft-hvy £20,313			
	12/13	Navn	2m Mdn Hdl 4yo gd-yld £5,019			

Has won at the Cheltenham Festival for the last three seasons, most recently running away with the Ryanair Chase; had been controversially rerouted from the Gold Cup and yet to prove his stamina as a stayer having been pipped on the line in the King George.

Venitien De Mai (Fr)

7 b g Network - Meylba (Grand Tresor)

Jim Dreaper (Ir)   **Ann & Alan Potts Partnership**

PLACINGS: 111/122321/F3119-   RPR **138+**c

Starts		1st	2nd	3rd	4th	Win & Pl
10		3	3	2	-	£38,291
127	3/16	Naas	3m 120-148 Ch Hcap heavy £21,691			
	2/16	DRoy	2m4f Ch heavy £4,974			
	3/15	Limk	2m5f Mdn Hdl heavy £6,419			

Took well to fences last season and was well backed when winning the Leinster National; finished a fair ninth in the Irish Grand National next time in only his fifth chase; open to further improvement and may well land another big staying handicap.

'He took well to fences last season and is open to further improvement. He may land another big staying handicap'

Very Wood (Fr)

7 b g Martaline - Ball Of Wood (Cadoudal)

Noel Meade (Ir) **Gigginstown House Stud**

PLACINGS: 211/12531/61PP1d0/ **RPR 153h**

Starts	1st	2nd	3rd	4th	Win & Pl
12	4	1	1	-	£96,626

10/14	Gway	2m6¹/₂f Ch gd-yld	£9,775
3/14	Chel	3m Cls1 Nov Gd1 Hdl good	£68,340
10/13	Gway	2m Mdn Hdl 4yo heavy	£6,171
4/13	Punc	2m NHF 4yo soft	£5,049

Thorough stayer who wore down rivals when winning the Albert Bartlett at Cheltenham in 2014; mixed form over fences the following season but did win a Grade 2 at Navan in good style (disqualified for banned substance); missed last season through injury.

Vibrato Valtat (Fr)

7 gr g Voix Du Nord - La Tosca Valtat (Dom Alco)

Paul Nicholls **Axom XLIII**

PLACINGS: 1/3312111424/1334F5- **RPR 162c**

Starts	1st	2nd	3rd	4th	Win & Pl
27	8	8	5	3	£234,768

11/15	Extr	2m1¹/₂f Cls1 Cls2 148-167 Ch Hcap soft	£35,594
2/15	Wwck	2m Cls1 Nov Gd2 Ch soft	£22,780
12/14	Kemp	2m Cls1 Nov Gd2 Ch soft	£20,167
12/14	Sand	1m7¹/₂f Cls1 Nov Gd1 Ch soft	£22,780
11/14	Wwck	2m Cls3 Nov Ch gd-sft	£7,596
4/14	Ayr	2m Cls3 Nov Hdl gd-sft	£6,657
2/14	Extr	2m1f Cls1 Nov List Hdl heavy	£11,390
9/12	Angl	1m5f NHF 3yo good	£4,167

Unable to make an impact in top 2m chases last season despite promising comeback win in the Haldon Gold Cup; could do better over further and was still going well when falling four out in the Ryanair, although he disappointed next time at Aintree.

Vicente (Fr)

7 b g Dom Alco - Ireland (Kadalko)

Paul Nicholls **Ian Fogg & John Hales**

PLACINGS: 2/421P/12F0/1131451- **RPR 159+c**

Starts	1st	2nd	3rd	4th	Win & Pl
18	6	3	3	2	£185,730

4/16	Ayr	4m Cls1 Gd3 135-155 Ch Hcap gd-sft	£119,595
11/15	Chel	3m¹/₂f Cls2 Nov Ch gd-sft	£14,588
5/15	Winc	3m1f Cls4 Nov Ch gd-fm	£3,994
4/15	NAbb	2m5f Cls4 Ch gd-fm	£4,328
10/14	Chel	2m5f Cls2 Nov Hdl good	£10,635
126 3/14	Winc	2m4f Cls3 113-129 Cond Hdl Hcap gd-sft	£6,330

Flourished over fences last season and signed off with a terrific success in the Scottish National having been badly hampered when fifth in the National Hunt Chase; 5lb rise for that win looks reasonable and could again be a threat in good staying handicaps.

Vieux Lion Rouge (Fr)

7 ch g Sabiango - Indecise (Cyborg)

David Pipe **Prof Caroline Tisdall & John Gent**

PLACINGS: 0/11103/390/111U267- **RPR 150+c**

Starts	1st	2nd	3rd	4th	Win & Pl
19	9	1	2		£70,378

139 11/15	Hayd	3m Cls2 128-145 Ch Hcap soft	£21,896
6/15	MRas	2m3f Cls4 Nov Ch good	£3,861
5/15	Towc	2m5¹/₂f Cls4 Nov Ch gd-sft	£3,769
2/14	Sedg	2m5f Cls4 Nov Hdl heavy	£3,379
1/14	Winc	1m7¹/₂f Cls3 Nov Hdl heavy	£5,523
1/14	Winc	1m7¹/₂f Cls4 Nov Hdl heavy	£3,899
2/13	Extr	2m1f Cls6 NHF 4-6yo heavy	£1,625
1/13	Newb	1m4¹/₂f Cls6 NHF 4yo soft	£1,643
12/12	Ffos	2m Cls6 NHF 3-5yo heavy	£1,430

Won his first two chases last summer and returned from a break to complete a hat-trick in the Tommy Whittle; ran very well for a long way in the National Hunt Chase and the Grand National, looking a non-stayer both times; should win good races back at around 3m.

Vigil (Ire)

7 b g Dansili - Magnolia Lane (Sadler's Wells)

Dermot Weld (Ir) **Noel Furlong**

PLACINGS: 215/15/316- **RPR 141h**

Starts	1st	2nd	3rd	4th	Win & Pl
8	3	2	1	-	£23,661

2/16	Naas	2m Mdn Hdl sft-hvy	£5,879
12/14	Leop	2m NHF 4-7yo soft	£6,325
2/14	Leop	2m NHF 5-7yo sft-hvy	£4,888

Fifth in two runnings of the Champion Bumper at Cheltenham before finally going hurdling last season, winning at Naas and shaping with much promise in the Neptune (never put in the race but kept on well into sixth); looks capable of better.

Village Vic (Ire)

9 b g Old Vic - Etoile Margot (Garde Royale)

Philip Hobbs **Alan Peterson**

PLACINGS: 6604/1/3412P/111190- **RPR 160+c**

Starts	1st	2nd	3rd	4th	Win & Pl
22	7	3	1	2	£131,201

144 1/16	Chel	2m5f Cls1 Gd3 136-160 Ch Hcap heavy	£34,170
136 12/15	Chel	2m5f Cls1 Gd3 136-162 Ch Hcap soft	£56,950
129 11/15	Muss	2m4f Cls3 109-135 Ch Hcap good	£11,696
125 10/15	Weth	2m3¹/₂f Cls3 110-134 Ch Hcap good	£6,256
120 2/15	Newb	2m¹/₂f Cls3 109-125 Ch Hcap gd-sft	£6,498
9/13	Worc	2m4f Cls5 Mdn Hdl good	£1,949
12/11	Chep	2m Cls6 NHF 4-6yo heavy	£1,365

Climbed through the ranks last season with a four-timer, including wins in two valuable handicaps at Cheltenham, but found out at Grade 1 level in the Ryanair; further progress can't be discounted but still 11lb higher than for latest handicap win.

'He finished fifth in two runnings of the Champion Bumper before going hurdling. He looks capable of better'

Virgilio (Fr)

7 b g Denham Red - Liesse De Marbeuf (Cyborg)

Dan Skelton   C J Edwards, D Futter & A H Rushworth

PLACINGS: 5144/111P5-1   RPR **148+c**

Starts		1st	2nd	3rd	4th	Win & Pl
10		5	-	-	2	£52,531
	5/16	Wwck	2m4f Cls4 Nov Ch gd-sft			£3,899
138	12/15	Aint	2m4f Cls2 125-144 Hdl Hcap soft			£13,763
125	5/15	Aint	2m4f Cls2 125-146 Hdl Hcap good			£11,574
118	5/15	Wwck	2m3f Cls3 118-133 Hdl Hcap soft			£6,498
	10/13	Sabl	2m1f Hdl 4yo v soft			£9,756

Won his first three starts in Britain in 2015, all in handicap hurdles starting from a mark of 118 before finishing a good fifth at Aintree in April off 148; very impressive when making a successful chasing debut at Warwick in May.

Vivaldi Collonges (Fr)

7 b g Dom Alco - Diane Collonges (El Badr)

Paul Nicholls   The Gi Gi Syndicate

PLACINGS: 2631/2442P/1511-   RPR **157+c**

Starts		1st	2nd	3rd	4th	Win & Pl
13		4	3	1	2	£59,497
143	4/16	Ayr	3m1/2f Cls2 Nov 125-143 Ch Hcap gd-sft			£16,245
	2/16	Wwck	3m1½f Cls3 Nov Ch soft			£10,077
134	12/15	Kels	2m1½f Cls2 120-142 Ch Hcap heavy			£15,013
119	4/14	Ayr	3m1½f Cls3 105-125 Hdl Hcap gd-sft			£7,798

Progressed well as a second-season novice last term, winning three out of four including a terrific performance last time out in a novice handicap at Ayr; disappointed in the Classic Chase at Warwick (second poor run in a big field) but that came on desperate ground.

Voix D'Eau (Fr)

6 b g Voix Du Nord - Eau De Chesne (R B Chesne)

Harry Fry   Harry Fry Racing Syndicate

PLACINGS: 40/153/212131-3   RPR **155c**

Starts		1st	2nd	3rd	4th	Win & Pl
12		4	2	3	1	£63,875
145	4/16	Chel	2m5f Cls1 Gd2 145-165 Ch Hcap gd-sft			£28,475
138	11/15	Donc	2m3f Cls3 115-139 Ch Hcap good			£6,498
122	10/15	Ffos	2m3½f Cls3 Nov 117-128 Ch Hcap good			£9,747
	6/14	Nanc	2m1f Hdl 4yo			£7,200

Smart novice chaser last season; returned from a four-month break to win the Silver Trophy at Cheltenham having been put away for spring ground (hasn't run on soft since career in France in 2014); should have more to offer after just six runs over fences.

Voix Du Reve (Fr)

4 br g Voix Du Nord - Pommbelle (Apple Tree)

Willie Mullins (Ir)   Andrea & Graham Wylie

PLACINGS: 2F3112F2-   RPR **144+h**

Starts		1st	2nd	3rd	4th	Win & Pl
8		2	3	1	-	£42,585
	11/15	Engh	2m1½f Hdl 3yo v soft			£17,860
	9/15	Nanc	2m1f Hdl 3yo v soft			£7,814

Bought by current connections after winning his last two in France and very unlucky not to add to his tally in the spring, falling at the last when looking likely to win the Fred Winter; ideal type for big 2m handicaps when getting a strong gallop.

Vieux Lion Rouge: three-time hurdle winner added three victories over fences to his CV last season and should do well in staying handicaps this time

Volnay De Thaix (Fr)

7 ch g Secret Singer - Mange De Thaix (Mont Basile)

Nicky Henderson — Mrs Judy Wilson

PLACINGS: 4111215/14253/14052-   RPR **154+**c

Starts	1st	2nd	3rd	4th	Win & Pl
17	6	3	1	3	£104,127

	12/15	Donc	2m3f Cls4 Nov Ch gd-sft................................£3,754
144	11/14	Hntg	2m3¹/₂f Cls2 125-144 Hdl Hcap soft..............£15,640
138	3/14	Newb	2m¹/₂f Cls2 123-138 Hdl Hcap good..................£9,747
	11/13	Newb	2m¹/₂f Cls3 Nov Hdl gd-sft............................£6,256
	11/13	Kemp	2m Cls4 Nov Hdl gd-sft...................................£3,899
	6/13	Sabl	2m1f Hdl 4yo soft..£8,195

Victory on chasing debut last season proved a false dawn as he took time to get the hang of fences but showed much more promise when second at Sandown last time; mark of 150 seems stiff based on bare form but should progress.

Vroum Vroum Mag (Fr)

7 b m Voix Du Nord - Naiade Mag (Kadalko)

Willie Mullins (Ir) — Mrs S Ricci

PLACINGS: 213122/11111/1111-1   RPR **157+**h

Starts	1st	2nd	3rd	4th	Win & Pl
16	12	3	1	-	£323,399

	4/16	Punc	2m Gd1 Hdl yield..£86,765
	3/16	Chel	2m4f Cls1 Gd1 Hdl gd-sft......................................£58,802
	1/16	Asct	2m7¹/₂f Cls1 Gd2 Hdl soft......................................£28,475
	12/15	Clon	2m¹/₂f Hdl heavy...£10,078
	11/15	Clon	2m4f Gd3 Ch sft-hvy..£17,636
	4/15	Fair	2m4f Gd3 Ch soft...£17,636
	3/15	Limk	2m6f Nov Gd2 Ch sft-hvy......................................£23,934
	1/15	Thur	2m¹/₂f Nov Gd2 Ch sft-hvy.....................................£26,453
	12/14	Cork	2m1f Nov Gd3 Ch sft-hvy......................................£20,042
	11/14	WxfR	2m3f Ch sft-hvy..£5,175
	9/13	Toul	2m1¹/₂f Hdl 4yo gd-sft...£8,195
	7/13	Lign	1m4f NHF 4-5yo gd-fm..£4,065

Brilliant mare who is unbeaten in ten races since moving to Ireland from France; gradually stepped up in class last season, winning the Mares' Hurdle at Cheltenham and beating the boys in the 2m Grade 1 at Punchestown; also won over as far as 2m7f at Ascot; sure to be a big player again.

Vyta Du Roc (Fr)

7 gr g Lion Noir - Dolce Vyta (Grand Tresor)

Nicky Henderson — Simon Munir & Isaac Souede

PLACINGS: 53/1111242/12155-   RPR **151**c

Starts	1st	2nd	3rd	4th	Win & Pl
14	6	3	1	1	£122,177

	2/16	Asct	3m Cls1 Nov Gd2 Ch soft......................................£22,887
	12/15	Bang	2m1¹/₂f Cls4 Nov Ch heavy......................................£4,660
	12/14	Sand	2m4f Cls1 Nov Gd2 Hdl soft..................................£17,085
	11/14	Chel	2m¹/₂f Cls1 Nov Gd2 Hdl soft.................................£17,085
	6/14	Hexm	2m Cls3 Nov Hdl good...£5,817
	5/14	Uttx	2m Cls5 Mdn Hdl good..£2,339

Took well to fences last season and won the Reynoldstown Chase at Ascot; only fifth in the RSA Chase and Scottish National but was sent off favourite for latter event and remains a threat for similar races (has dropped to 6lb below hurdles mark).

Wait For Me (Fr)

6 b g Saint Des Saints - Aulne River (River Mist)

Philip Hobbs — Andrew L Cohen

PLACINGS: 13/2114-8   RPR **142**h

Starts	1st	2nd	3rd	4th	Win & Pl
7	3	1	1	1	£24,171

	1/16	Kemp	2m Cls4 Nov Hdl soft...£3,249
	12/15	Newb	2m¹/₂f Cls4 Mdn Hdl soft...£3,249
	2/15	Asct	1m7¹/₂f Cls4 NHF 4-6yo soft.....................................£4,549

Third in the 2015 Champion Bumper at Cheltenham but didn't quite reach the heights expected over hurdles last season, with both wins coming at odds-on; still a good fourth in the County Hurdle and may well have a big handicap in him.

Wakanda (Ire)

7 b g Westerner - Chanson Indienne (Indian River)

Sue Smith — M B Scholey & R H Scholey

PLACINGS: 742/214312124/111PP-   RPR **157**c

Starts	1st	2nd	3rd	4th	Win & Pl
20	7	5	4	3	£167,709

151	12/15	Asct	3m Cls1 List 137-158 Ch Hcap gd-sft..................£56,950
145	11/15	Newc	2m7¹/₂f Cls1 List 128-153 Ch Hcap soft................£34,170
139	10/15	Weth	2m3¹/₂f Cls1 List 132-145 Ch Hcap soft................£15,661
	1/15	Hayd	2m4¹/₂f Cls1 Nov Gd2 Ch heavy...........................£17,370
	12/14	Kels	2m7¹/₂f Cls3 Nov Ch soft..£10,128
120	10/14	Hexm	2m4f Cls4 Nov 101-120 Ch Hcap good..................£6,844
	7/13	Slig	2m Mdn Hdl 4yo good..£4,207

Completed a hat-trick in Listed handicap chases in the first half of last season, including the Silver Cup at Ascot off 151; starts this campaign just 3lb higher after twice coming up short in better company and may do better back in handicaps again.

War Sound

7 b g Kayf Tara - Come The Dawn (Gunner B)

Philip Hobbs — The Englands & Heywoods

PLACINGS: 1519/10-   RPR **106**h

Starts	1st	2nd	3rd	4th	Win & Pl
6	3	-	-	-	£41,204

140	5/15	Hayd	1m7¹/₂f Cls1 Gd3 129-153 Hdl Hcap gd-sft...........£34,170
	3/15	Chep	2m Cls4 Nov Hdl gd-sft..£3,249
	1/15	Extr	2m2¹/₂f Cls4 Nov Hdl soft..£3,249

Progressive novice hurdler two seasons ago and went on to win the Swinton Hurdle impressively; restricted to just one subsequent run when well beaten on heavy ground in the Betfair Hurdle; has the physique to make a fine chaser.

> **'Brilliant mare who is unbeaten in ten races looks sure to be a big player again this season'**

Welsh Shadow (Ire)

6 b g Robin Des Champs - What A Mewsment (Persian Mews)

Dan Skelton   **Walters Plant Hire Ltd**

PLACINGS: 1/214351-   RPR **142h**

Starts	1st	2nd	3rd	4th	Win & Pl
7	3	1	1	1	£30,544

4/16	Ayr	2m4¹/₂f Cls3 Nov Hdl soft	£6,498
11/15	Hayd	1m7¹/₂f Cls1 Nov List Hdl soft	£11,888
3/15	Weth	2m Cls6 NHF 4-6yo good	£1,711

Highly tried in novice hurdles last season and produced his best effort when fifth in the Neptune behind Yorkhill; won two much weaker contests on soft ground but ran no race on heavy in the Tolworth; likely to go novice chasing.

Westend Story (Ire)

5 b g Westerner - Sarahall (Saddlers' Hall)

Philip Hobbs   **Mick Fitzgerald Racing Club**

PLACINGS: FF/115-   RPR **130b**

Starts	1st	2nd	3rd	4th	Win & Pl
3	2	-	-	-	£5,125

2/16	Extr	2m1f Cls6 NHF 4-6yo heavy	£1,625
12/15	Hntg	2m Cls6 NHF 4-6yo soft	£1,625

Won his first two bumpers very impressively at Exeter and Huntingdon before doing well to finish fifth in the Champion Bumper at Cheltenham having had a rough passage; fell in both point-to-points but has schooled nicely over hurdles according to connections.

Whataknight

7 b g Midnight Legend - What A Mover (Jupiter Island)

Harry Fry   **J M Dare, T Hamlin & J W Snook**

PLACINGS: 4511/11131234-1   RPR **149+h**

Starts	1st	2nd	3rd	4th	Win & Pl
6	2	1	2	1	£28,062

138	5/16	Hayd	2m7f Cls2 124-150 Hdl Hcap good	£18,768
	12/15	Tntn	3m Cls4 Nov Hdl gd-sft	£4,549

Comfortable winner of a 2m7f handicap hurdle on good ground at Haydock in May, bouncing back having seemingly gone off the boil after a bright start to his hurdling career; multiple point-to-point winner who should make a good staying chaser.

Whisper (Fr)

8 b g Astarabad - Belle Yepa (Mansonnien)

Nicky Henderson   **Walters Plant Hire Ltd**

PLACINGS: 4141/331211/251/5P8-   RPR **144h**

Starts	1st	2nd	3rd	4th	Win & Pl
18	8	2	2	2	£238,394

4/15	Aint	3m1¹/₂f Cls1 Gd1 Hdl good	£67,582
4/14	Aint	3m¹/₂f Cls1 Gd1 Hdl gd-sft	£67,524
153 3/14	Chel	2m5f Cls1 Gd3 135-154 Hdl Hcap good	£45,560
140 12/13	Newb	2m4¹/₂f Cls2 134-144 Hdl Hcap heavy	£11,574
4/13	Chel	2m4¹/₂f Cls2 Nov Hdl gd-sft	£10,010
2/13	Ffos	2m4f Cls4 Nov Hdl 4-7yo heavy	£3,574
12/12	Ffos	2m4f Cls4 Nov Hdl heavy	£2,599
4/12	Ffos	2m Cls6 NHF 4-5yo good	£1,848

Dual winner of the Grade 1 Stayers' Hurdle at Aintree in 2014 and 2015; second victory is a rare bright spot during a difficult couple of seasons but only once got preferred good ground last term and remains a talented stayer.

Who Dares Wins (Ire)

4 b g Jeremy - Savignano (Polish Precedent)

Alan King   **W H Ponsonby**

PLACINGS: 1140-   RPR **135h**

Starts	1st	2nd	3rd	4th	Win & Pl
4	2	-	-	1	£22,663

12/15	Donc	2m1¹/₂f Cls1 Gd2 Hdl 3yo heavy	£17,165
11/15	Ludl	2m Cls4 Hdl 3yo gd-sft	£3,899

Useful middle-distance horse on the Flat who took well to hurdles last season, winning twice including a 20-length victory in a Grade 2 at Doncaster; had excuses in a messy race next time before disappointing in the Triumph.

William H Bonney

5 b g Midnight Legend - Calamintha (Mtoto)

Alan King   **Mr & Mrs R Scott**

PLACINGS: 2/21210-   RPR **136h**

Starts	1st	2nd	3rd	4th	Win & Pl
6	2	3	-	-	£9,292

2/16	Towc	2m Cls4 Nov Hdl soft	£3,899
11/15	Plum	2m Cls4 Nov Hdl soft	£3,249

Won novice hurdles at Plumpton and Towcester on soft ground last season and expected to do better on quicker by his trainer, so much so he was thrown into the Supreme (fair tenth in a red-hot race); should make a good handicapper.

Racing Post iPad app

30-day free trial. On the App Store now.

MIND-BLOWING

Available on the App Store

Willow's Saviour

9 ch g Septieme Ciel - Willow Gale (Strong Gale)

Dan Skelton   Triple F Partnership

PLACINGS: 4576/2052P/111/141F-   RPR **144**c

Starts	1st	2nd	3rd	4th	Win & Pl
18	5	2	2	2	£120,970

	2/16	Fknm	2m5f Cls4 Nov Ch gd-sft	£5,198
	11/15	Wwck	2m Cls3 Nov Ch gd-sft	£7,783
130	12/13	Asct	1m7¹/₂f Cls1 Gd3 130-151 Hdl Hcap soft	£84,405
121	11/13	Muss	1m7¹/₂f Cls2 119-145 Hdl Hcap good	£12,996
115	11/13	Asct	2m3¹/₂f Cls4 Nov 100-118 Hdl Hcap gd-sft	£5,630

Out for nearly two years after winning the Ladbroke in 2013 but got back on track straight away last season, winning two of his first three chases; in contention when fell two out in the novice handicap chase at the Cheltenham Festival.

Winter Escape (Ire)

5 b g Robin Des Pres - Saddleeruppat (Saddlers' Hall)

Alan King   John P McManus

PLACINGS: 111-   RPR **140+h**

Starts	1st	2nd	3rd	4th	Win & Pl
3	3	-	-	-	£23,907

	2/16	Kemp	2m Cls1 Nov Gd2 Hdl gd-sft	£17,085
	2/16	Donc	2m¹/₂f Cls4 Nov Hdl gd-sft	£3,899
	12/15	Donc	2m¹/₂f Cls5 Mdn Hdl gd-sft	£2,924

Won three out of three last season, most notably when comfortably landing the odds in an admittedly moderate running of the Dovecote Novices' Hurdle at Kempton; exciting prospect who should climb the ladder over hurdles.

Wolf Of Windlesham (Ire)

4 ch g Mastercraftsman - Al Amlah (Riverman)

Stuart Edmunds   M W Lawrence

PLACINGS: 1161-   RPR **139+h**

Starts	1st	2nd	3rd	4th	Win & Pl
4	3	-	-	-	£52,665

137	4/16	Sand	2m Cls2 118-144 Hdl 4yo Hcap good	£31,280
	11/15	Chel	2m¹/₂f Cls1 Gd2 Hdl 3yo gd-sft	£17,085
	10/15	Ludl	2m Cls4 Hdl 3yo good	£3,899

Moderate on the Flat before switching to hurdles last season and consequently underrated throughout a stellar campaign; won three out of four and signed off by beating Voix Du Reve in a competitive juvenile handicap at Sandown.

Wonderful Charm (Fr)

8 b g Poliglote - Victoria Royale (Garde Royale)

Paul Nicholls   R J H Geffen

PLACINGS: /111253/123783P/2P7-   RPR **161**c

Starts	1st	2nd	3rd	4th	Win & Pl
24	6	5	3	2	£201,560

	10/14	NAbb	2m5f Cls2 Ch soft	£18,941
	11/13	Newb	2m4f Cls1 Nov Gd2 Ch gd-sft	£17,912
	11/13	Winc	2m5f Cls1 Nov Gd2 Ch gd-sft	£17,912
	10/13	Fknm	2m5f Cls3 Nov Ch good	£6,990
	10/12	Chep	2m3¹/₂f Cls1 Nov Gd2 Hdl gd-sft	£12,073
	3/12	Autl	2m2f Hdl 4yo v soft	£28,000

Laid out for the Grand National last season but was never a factor and pulled up after rain turned the ground against him; best form has come on good ground, notably a close third under a big weight when stepped up to 3m1f at Aintree in 2015.

Wounded Warrior (Ire)

7 b g Shantou - Sparkling Sword (Broadsword)

Noel Meade (Ir)   Gigginstown House Stud

PLACINGS: 1/31144/F221313/226-   RPR **160**c

Starts	1st	2nd	3rd	4th	Win & Pl
15	4	4	3	2	£83,166

	1/15	Naas	3m Nov Gd2 Ch soft	£20,155
	12/14	Navn	2m4f Ch yld-sft	£6,900
	1/14	Navn	2m7f Mdn Hdl soft	£5,750
	12/13	Navn	2m NHF 4-7yo sft-hvy	£4,488

Showed huge promise during his novice campaign two seasons ago, finishing third in the RSA as a six-year-old; failed to build on that in two runs last season but found 2m4f too short first time out and struggled on desperate ground in the Irish Gold Cup.

Yala Enki (Fr)

6 b/br g Nickname - Cadiane (Cadoudal)

Venetia Williams   Hills Of Ledbury (Aga)

PLACINGS: 217124/2232/15131P5-   RPR **147h**

Starts	1st	2nd	3rd	4th	Win & Pl
19	5	5	2	2	£122,745

	2/16	Asct	2m3¹/₂f Cls2 Nov Hdl soft	£15,640
130	1/16	Kemp	2m5f Cls1 List 127-153 Hdl Hcap soft	£22,780
	11/15	Extr	2m5¹/₂f Cls3 Nov Hdl gd-sft	£5,523
	2/14	Fntb	2m2f Ch 4yo v soft	£9,600
	10/13	Pari	2m1f Ch 3yo gd-sft	£7,415

Three-time winner over hurdles last season, most notably in the Lanzarote Hurdle, and went

IT'S YOUR PAPER WITHOUT THE PAPER

IF YOU'RE ON HOLIDAY OR JUST TOO BUSY TO GET TO YOUR NEWSAGENT, THE RACING POST DIGITAL NEWSPAPER IS AT HAND

View every page on your computer, tablet or smartphone, with rather clever features including language translation, downloadable editions and bookmarking. It'll even read articles OUT LOUD.

Buy single editions (from £2.10/€2.60) or save with a discounted subscription.

RACING POST.com/digitalnewspaper

close in another good handicap at Sandown; won two chases in France and could be a decent staying handicapper over fences as well as hurdles.

Yanworth
6 ch g Norse Dancer - Yota (Galetto)

Alan King				John P McManus
PLACINGS: 1124/11112-				RPR 160+h

Starts	1st	2nd	3rd	4th	Win & Pl
9	6	2	-	1	£80,022

	1/16	Chel	2m4¹/₂f Cls1 Nov Gd2 Hdl heavy	£17,085
	12/15	Asct	1m7¹/₂f Cls1 Nov Gd2 Hdl soft	£17,085
	11/15	Wwck	2m Cls4 Nov Hdl gd-sft	£3,899
	11/15	Extr	2m1f Cls3 Nov Hdl soft	£5,523
	11/14	Newb	2m¹/₂f Cls6 NHF 4-6yo soft	£1,689
	5/14	Winc	1m7¹/₂f Cls6 NHF 4-6yo gd-sft	£1,625

Won four out of five over hurdles last season, suffering only defeat when second to Yorkhill in the Neptune; had looked even better than that when winning on heavy ground on previous run at Cheltenham and could be a top hurdler at 2m4f and beyond.

Yorkhill (Ire)
6 ch g Presenting - Lightning Breeze (Saddlers' Hall)

Willie Mullins (Ir)				Andrea & Graham Wylie
PLACINGS: U11/11111-4				RPR 158+h

Starts	1st	2nd	3rd	4th	Win & Pl
7	6	-	*	1	£154,382

	4/16	Aint	2m4f Cls1 Nov Gd1 Hdl soft	£42,402
	3/16	Chel	2m5f Cls1 Nov Gd1 Hdl good	£68,340
	1/16	Sand	2m Cls1 Nov Gd1 Hdl heavy	£23,048
	12/15	Punc	2m4f Mdn Hdl heavy	£6,419
	4/15	Punc	2m NHF 4-7yo yield	£6,419
	3/15	Gowr	2m2f NHF 4-7yo soft	£4,814

Triple Grade 1 winner last season and particularly impressive in the Tolworth and the Neptune (beat the high-class Yanworth) on contrasting ground to show his versatility; clearly over the top when well beaten at Punchestown; looks a top chasing prospect.

Zabana (Ire)
7 ch g Halling - Gandia (Danehill)

Andrew Lynch (Ir)				C Jones
PLACINGS: 311015/0312/314U-1				RPR 155+c

Starts	1st	2nd	3rd	4th	Win & Pl
15	6	1	3	1	£118,752

	4/16	Punc	3m1f Nov Gd1 Ch gd-yld	£43,382
	12/15	Leop	2m3f Ch heavy	£7,488
	1/15	Navn	2m Hdl soft	£10,078
119	1/14	Leop	2m4f 102-128 Hdl Hcap soft	£8,625
	6/13	Gowr	2m Hdl 4yo gd-fm	£7,293
	5/13	Slig	2m Mdn Hdl 4-5yo sft-hvy	£4,628

Won a Grade 1 novice chase at Punchestown in April when stepped up to 3m over fences for first time; must have left connections wondering what might have been had he not unseated his

rider at the start in the JLT, especially given strong Cheltenham form (second in 2015 Coral Cup).

Zamdy Man
7 b g Authorized - Lauderdale (Nebos)

Venetia Williams				Muhammad Nadeem Khan
PLACINGS: 52208/111/25/3409-1				RPR 145h

Starts	1st	2nd	3rd	4th	Win & Pl
15	4	3	1	1	£73,036

	4/16	Uttx	2m Cls3 Ch soft	£6,330
	1/14	Hayd	1m7¹/₂f Cls1 Nov Gd2 Hdl heavy	£15,661
	11/13	Hayd	1m7¹/₂f Cls1 Nov List Hdl soft	£11,888
	11/13	Asct	1m7¹/₂f Cls3 Nov Hdl gd-sft	£7,507

Very useful novice hurdler three seasons ago but has been largely treading water since then, with an aborted chasing campaign last term after a year out; back on track with victory in a beginners' chase at the end of April and retains novice status.

Zarkandar (Ire)
9 b g Azamour - Zarkasha (Kahyasi)

Paul Nicholls				Chris Giles & Potensis Bloodstock Ltd
PLACINGS: 141/222244/631234/3-				RPR 165h

Starts	1st	2nd	3rd	4th	Win & Pl
24	9	5	3	4	£865,156

	11/14	Autl	3m Gd1 Hdl v soft	£138,750
	4/13	Aint	2m4f Cls1 Gd1 Hdl good	£112,540
	2/13	Winc	1m7¹/₂f Cls1 Gd2 Hdl heavy	£34,170
	12/12	Chel	2m1f Cls1 Gd2 Hdl heavy	£74,035
163	11/12	Winc	1m7¹/₂f Cls1 Gd2 143-163 Hdl Hcap gd-sft	£32,746
151	2/12	Newb	2m¹/₂f Cls1 Gd3 136-162 Hdl Hcap gd-sft	£86,849
	4/11	Aint	2m¹/₂f Cls1 Gd1 Hdl 4yo gd sft	£56,632
	3/11	Chel	2m1f Cls1 Gd1 Hdl 4yo good	£57,010
	2/11	Kemp	2m1f Cls1 Gd1 Hdl 4yo good	£12,086

Seemed to reach his limit in top 2m-2m4f hurdles but transformed into a leading staying hurdler two seasons ago when winning the Long Walk Hurdle and perhaps unlucky not to add the World Hurdle (bad mistake two out); missed last season through injury.

Zubayr (Ire)
4 b g Authorized - Zaziyra (Dalakhani)

Paul Nicholls				P J Vogt
PLACINGS: 101-3				RPR 139h

Starts	1st	2nd	3rd	4th	Win & Pl
4	2	-	1	-	£33,238

	4/16	Winc	1m7¹/₂f Cls4 Nov Hdl gd-sft	£3,249
	2/16	Kemp	2m Cls1 Gd2 Hdl 4yo gd-sft	£17,085

Long considered a top hurdling prospect (ante-post Triumph favourite early last season) but perhaps paid for lack of experience when well beaten at Cheltenham; still won twice either side of that and not beaten far when third in a French Grade 1 in May.

THIS SEASON'S KEY HORSES LISTED BY TRAINER

Kim Bailey
Charbel
Harry Topper
Red Spinner
The Last Samuri

Enda Bolger
Gilgamboa
Josies Orders
On The Fringe

Peter Bowen
Henri Parry Morgan

Mark Bradstock
Coneygree

W J Burke
My Murphy

Stuart Crawford
Fine Rightly

Gavin Cromwell
Jer's Girl

Rebecca Curtis
Irish Cavalier
O'Faolains Boy
The Romford Pele

Henry Daly
Briery Belle

Henry de Bromhead
Alisier D'Irlande
Identity Thief
Special Tiara

Rose Dobbin
Jonniesofa

Elizabeth Doyle
Last Goodbye

Jim Dreaper
Goonyella
Venitien De Mai

Stuart Edmunds
Wolf Of Windlesham

Gordon Elliott
Ball D'Arc
Campeador
Cause Of Causes
Clarcam
Diamond King
Don Cossack
Fagan
Free Expression
Lord Scoundrel
Mala Beach
Missy Tata
Noble Endeavor
Prince Of Scars
Squouateur
Sutton Place
Taglietelle
The Game Changer
Tombstone
Ucello Conti

Brian Ellison
Definitly Red
Smart Talk
Tomngerry

James Ewart
Aristo Du Plessis

Pat Fahy
Morning Assembly

Johnny Farrelly
Amore Alato

Alan Fleming
Blue Hell
Gwencily Berbas

Harry Fry
Activial
Charmix
Fletchers Flyer
Hell's Kitchen
Henryville
Jessber's Dream
Jolly's Cracked It
Jollyallan
Thomas Brown
Unowhatimeanharry
Voix D'Eau
Whataknight

Tom George
A Good Skin
Always On The Run
Double Shuffle
God's Own
Saint Are

Warren Greatrex
Aloomomo
Cole Harden
La Bague Au Roi
Ma Du Fou
Missed Approach
One Track Mind
Out Sam
The Nipper

Mrs John Harrington
Don't Touch It
Jezki
Sizing John
Supasundae
Ttebbob

Edward Harty
Coney Island
Minella Foru

Nicky Henderson
Altior
Beat That
Bloody Mary
Brain Power
Buveur D'Air
Cocktails At Dawn
Consul De Thaix
Cup Final
Different Gravey

Fixe Le Kap
Hargam
Josses Hill
Kayf Grace
Khezerabad
Kilcrea Vale
L'Ami Serge
Might Bite
My Tent Or Yours
O O Seven
Peace And Co
Simonsig
Sprinter Sacre
Theinval
Top Notch
Triolo D'Alene
Vaniteux
Volnay De Thaix
Vyta Du Roc
Whisper

Philip Hobbs
Brother Tedd
Champagne West
Duke Des Champs
Gala Ball
Garde La Victoire
If In Doubt
Kruzhlinin
Onenightinvienna
Ozzie The Oscar
Rock The Kasbah
Royal Regatta
Sausalito Sunrise
Sternrubin
Village Vic
Wait For Me
War Sound
Westend Story

Anthony Honeyball
Regal Encore

Ms Sandra Hughes
Acapella Bourgeois
Nearly Nama'd

Malcolm Jefferson
Cloudy Dream
Cyrus Darius
Oscar Rock

Martin Keighley
Solstice Star

Patrick G Kelly
Mall Dini

John Kiely
Carlingford Lough

Alan King
Annacotty
Karezak
Katie Too
Sceau Royal
Smad Place
Uxizandre
Who Dares Wins

William H Bonney
Winter Escape
Yanworth

Neil King
Lil Rockerfeller
Milansbar

Emma Lavelle
Junction Fourteen

Kerry Lee
Bishops Road
Grey Gold
Kylemore Lough
Top Gamble

Charlie Longsdon
Coologue
Drop Out Joe
Kilcooley
Our Kaempfer
Pendra
Sharp Rise

Andrew Lynch
Zabana

Tony Martin
Anibale Fly
Gallant Oscar

Donald McCain
Katachenko

Noel Meade
Apache Stronghold
Disko
Monksland
Road To Riches
Snow Falcon
Very Wood
Wounded Warrior

James Moffatt
Highland Lodge

Arthur Moore
Dandridge

Gary Moore
Ar Mad
Sire De Grugy
Traffic Fluide
Ubak

Mouse Morris
Alpha Des Obeaux
Rogue Angel
Smashing

Neil Mulholland
Baltimore Rock
Carole's Destrier
Fox Norton
Minella Present
Shantou Village
Southfield Royale
The Druids Nephew
The Young Master

Margaret Mullins
Martello Tower

Willie Mullins
A Toi Phil
Abbyssial
Allblak Des Places
Annie Power
Apple's Jade
Arctic Fire
Augusta Kate
Avant Tout
Bacardys
Bachasson
Ballycasey
Bamako Moriviere
Battleford
Bello Conti
Bellshill
Black Hercules
Blazer
Bleu Et Rouge
Blow By Blow
Briar Hill
Castello Sforza
Champagne Fever
Devils Bride
Diakali
Dicosimo
Djakadam
Don Poli
Douvan
Faugheen
Felix Yonger
Footpad
Gangster
Great Field
Ivan Grozny
Kalkir
Killultagh Vic
Koshari
Let's Dance
Limini
Listen Dear
Lucky Pass
Measureofmydreams
Milsean
Min
Muthaza
Nambour
Nichols Canyon
Open Eagle
Outlander
Petit Mouchoir
Pleasant Company
Pylonthepressure
Roi Des Francs
Royal Caviar
Sempre Medici
Shaneshill
Thomas Hobson
Un De Sceaux
Up For Review
Valseur Lido
Vautour
Voix Du Reve
Vroum Vroum Mag

Yorkhill

Colm Murphy
Empire Of Dirt
Marlbrook
Sizing Granite

Richard Newland
Boondooma

Paul Nicholls
Adrien Du Pont
All Set To Go
Arpege D'Alene
Art Mauresque
As De Mee
Aux Ptits Soins
Bouvreuil
Clan Des Obeaux
Connetable
Diego Du Charmil
Dodging Bullets
Emerging Talent
Frodon
Ibis Du Rheu
Irish Saint
Irving
Just A Par
Le Mercurey
Moabit
Modus
Mr Mix
Old Guard
Orbasa
Politologue
Ptit Zig
Rock On Oscar
Rocky Creek
Romain De Senam
Sametegal
Saphir Du Rheu
Silsol
Silviniaco Conti
Sound Investment
Southfield Theatre
The Eaglehaslanded
Unioniste
Vibrato Valtat
Vicente
Vivaldi Collonges
Wonderful Charm
Zarkandar
Zubayr

Joseph O'Brien
Ivanovich Gorbatov

Fergal O'Brien
Barney Dwan
Perfect Candidate

Edward O'Grady
Kitten Rock

Jonjo O'Neill
Another Hero
Beg To Differ
Eastlake

Holywell
Minella Rocco
More Of That
Shutthefrontdoor
Spookydooky
Taquin Du Seuil
The Saint James
Upswing

Ben Pauling
A Hare Breath
Barters Hill
Drumacoo
Local Show
Silvergrove

David Pipe
Ballynagour
Broadway Buffalo
Champers On Ice
Doctor Harper
Dynaste
Katkeau
Moon Racer
Red Sherlock
Starchitect
Un Temps Pour Tout
Vieux Lion Rouge

Nicky Richards
Baywing
Eduard
Simply Ned

Oliver Sherwood
Many Clouds
Rayvin Black
The Organist

Dan Skelton
Al Ferof
Azzuri
Blue Heron
Born Survivor
Ch'Tibello
Its'afreebee
Kasakh Noir
Long House Hall
Mister Miyagi
Pain Au Chocolat
Red Tornado
Superb Story
Three Musketeers
Two Taffs
Value At Risk
Virgilio
Welsh Shadow
Willow's Saviour

Sue Smith
Wakanda

Sandy Thomson
Seeyouatmidnight

Karl Thornton
Colms Dream

Colin Tizzard
Cue Card
Native River
Theatre Guide
Third Intention
Thistlecrack

W F Treacy
Fethard Player

Nigel Twiston-Davies
Ballyandy
Ballybolley
Ballyoptic
Blaklion
Bristol De Mai
Cogry
Flying Angel
The New One

Lucy Wadham
Le Reve
Potters Legend

Robert Walford
Camping Ground

Ted Walsh
Foxrock

Paul Webber
Gwafa

Dermot Weld
Vigil

Donald Whillans
Shades Of Midnight

Harry Whittington
Affaire D'Honneur
Bigmartre
Emerging Force

Evan Williams
Buywise
Court Minstrel
Firebird Flyer
King's Odyssey

Ian Williams
Ballyalton

Nick Williams
Agrapart
Aubusson
Coo Star Sivola
Reve De Sivola
Tea For Two

Venetia Williams
Arthur's Oak
Aso
Cold March
Houblon Des Obeaux
Otago Trail
Tango De Juilley
Yala Enki
Zamdy Man

LAST SEASON'S LEADING JUMPS JOCKEYS IN BRITAIN

Jockey	Wins-runs	Wins (%)	2nd	3rd	4th	Win prize	Total prize	Profit/loss (£)
Richard Johnson	235–1044	23%	186	155	120	£1,591,005	£2,339,364	-180.10
Aidan Coleman	129–741	17%	112	103	81	£879,503	£1,338,565	-217.48
Sam Twiston-Davies	128–741	17%	118	89	81	£1,238,193	£1,941,621	-165.32
Noel Fehily	122–663	18%	106	84	78	£976,041	£1,530,151	-125.14
Brian Hughes	103–735	14%	131	113	92	£558,995	£988,219	-103.00
Harry Skelton	101–452	22%	79	57	52	£718,074	£1,190,865	+3.40
Tom Scudamore	85–536	16%	70	67	80	£988,441	£1,392,504	-146.00
Paddy Brennan	75–463	16%	70	55	61	£1,078,325	£1,366,226	-45.65
Gavin Sheehan	72–440	16%	64	51	56	£459,824	£747,847	-51.84
Nico de Boinville	69–327	21%	34	34	24	£910,496	£1,069,140	+105.75
Leighton Aspell	60–428	14%	55	59	51	£343,911	£580,168	-65.42
Sean Bowen	58–358	16%	42	46	38	£364,909	£552,523	-77.36
Wayne Hutchinson	56–388	14%	55	59	47	£480,026	£727,086	-102.31
Paul Moloney	54–366	15%	27	54	37	£298,015	£527,501	-28.28
David Bass	54–311	17%	43	31	29	£386,722	£783,128	-37.31
Daryl Jacob	50–384	13%	53	48	38	£362,104	£708,602	-178.96
Tom O'Brien	49–465	11%	59	61	54	£269,237	£502,354	-201.38
Danny Cook	48–295	16%	59	41	43	£424,038	£644,818	-37.09
Will Kennedy	47–350	13%	53	49	32	£241,035	£392,863	-37.87
Nick Scholfield	44–330	13%	44	32	27	£359,498	£548,353	-40.55
Henry Brooke	42–456	9%	50	46	44	£256,966	£373,900	-164.59
Brian Harding	42–350	12%	43	31	39	£197,034	£318,565	-147.63
David Noonan	41–253	16%	34	24	25	£219,026	£311,427	-3.28
Trevor Whelan	40–307	13%	35	34	31	£227,977	£360,926	-36.73
Tom Cannon	38–384	10%	29	44	32	£165,571	£290,750	-102.61
Craig Nichol	36–292	12%	34	34	29	£167,887	£240,821	-94.58
Adam Wedge	36–284	13%	31	37	36	£228,890	£363,959	-67.10
Jamie Moore	36–282	13%	33	30	29	£415,451	£588,792	-31.22
Andrew Tinkler	36–276	13%	25	28	30	£170,649	£261,234	-76.96
Brendan Powell	35–382	9%	35	45	48	£243,695	£389,555	-28.79
Joshua Moore	34–215	16%	24	27	22	£297,575	£448,250	+4.39
Richie McLernon	32–312	10%	30	19	31	£151,182	£262,857	-72.54
Barry Geraghty	30–198	15%	30	21	22	£491,229	£930,183	-82.12
Harry Cobden	30–138	22%	30	18	13	£190,675	£381,605	+5.45
James Reveley	28–188	15%	22	25	18	£191,532	£262,964	-13.16
Derek Fox	26–205	13%	22	25	35	£149,003	£230,683	-48.17
Joe Colliver	26–166	16%	21	15	16	£118,302	£175,352	-32.38
Kielan Woods	25–261	10%	30	30	36	£135,543	£221,561	-65.75
Denis O'Regan	25–240	10%	35	23	29	£103,961	£196,977	-113.53
James Banks	24–265	9%	34	35	19	£96,725	£167,351	-16.25
Adam Nicol	23–218	11%	25	19	24	£81,918	£125,046	-18.40
Ryan Hatch	22–170	13%	14	24	11	£337,237	£490,468	-45.90
Liam Treadwell	21–300	7%	35	37	37	£203,050	£389,414	-154.75
James Davies	21–299	7%	27	33	31	£175,135	£261,462	-140.17
Peter Buchanan	21–210	10%	24	30	38	£116,321	£207,699	-55.67
Jamie Hamilton	21–157	13%	17	26	21	£88,679	£138,345	+20.38
Sean Quinlan	20–246	8%	40	28	28	£125,948	£214,857	-105.46
Jake Greenall	20–189	11%	16	18	19	£93,274	£145,619	-54.13
Jeremiah McGrath	20–151	13%	20	13	19	£96,294	£148,696	+9.93
James Best	19–257	7%	18	26	23	£82,236	£140,065	-81.77

LAST SEASON'S LEADING JUMPS TRAINERS IN BRITAIN

Trainer	Wins-runs	Wins (%)	2nd	3rd	4th	Win prize	Total prize	Profit/loss (£)
Paul Nicholls	122–568	21%	104	74	45	£1,505,434	£2,439,740	-73.23
Willie Mullins	27–159	17%	24	13	14	£1,412,457	£2,341,735	-58.18
Nicky Henderson	81–414	20%	54	49	34	£1,066,035	£1,614,348	-101.03
Colin Tizzard	50–323	15%	39	52	40	£1,147,233	£1,443,451	-46.75
Philip Hobbs	113–523	22%	82	81	47	£909,949	£1,386,468	-64.73
Dan Skelton	104–529	20%	88	70	61	£732,806	£1,255,804	-156.34
Nigel Twiston-Davies	72–482	15%	62	45	48	£822,890	£1,205,966	-79.80
David Pipe	80–571	14%	77	68	71	£653,453	£1,151,789	-111.92
Alan King	68–403	17%	60	53	50	£742,259	£1,044,468	-120.54
Venetia Williams	56–419	13%	56	63	44	£612,960	£983,247	-104.92
Jonjo O'Neill	81–560	14%	72	44	67	£534,423	£845,767	-114.49
Evan Williams	70–448	16%	52	61	46	£492,638	£809,087	+12.95
Gordon Elliott	28–147	19%	35	21	20	£507,209	£743,507	-55.35
Harry Fry	54–240	23%	53	31	18	£521,342	£718,943	-15.36
Mouse Morris	1–8	13%	1	2	0	£561,300	£653,391	+26.00
Gary Moore	54–294	18%	39	41	32	£445,273	£653,159	+80.84
Neil Mulholland	60–427	14%	58	43	60	£397,072	£637,619	-145.57
Charlie Longsdon	62–416	15%	59	34	47	£423,775	£624,143	-105.15
Kim Bailey	43–275	16%	37	34	27	£277,775	£612,728	-77.93
Tom George	38–225	17%	32	28	25	£421,616	£587,022	30.06
John Ferguson	71–251	28%	58	34	23	£385,192	£583,805	-67.02
Sue Smith	44–312	14%	63	42	38	£383,973	£576,199	-66.35
Brian Ellison	48–250	19%	37	34	32	£298,368	£453,584	-11.23
Warren Greatrex	53–254	21%	45	40	23	£267,715	£434,510	-58.89
Donald McCain	53–497	11%	60	73	67	£289,228	£430,725	-138.27
Lucinda Russell	48–376	13%	47	64	55	£243,126	£409,673	-44.21
Kerry Lee	23–110	21%	19	9	5	£313,559	£377,508	+39.06
Oliver Sherwood	32–207	15%	34	25	24	£212,975	£365,526	-50.61
Fergal O'Brien	33–237	14%	35	33	24	£218,002	£355,615	-5.50
Neil King	34–217	16%	30	30	24	£205,423	£328,386	-36.19
Peter Bowen	33–236	14%	34	28	20	£217,709	£326,520	-84.96
Nick Williams	12–112	11%	23	20	14	£209,601	£323,952	-52.20
Micky Hammond	43–347	12%	39	45	51	£193,743	£313,990	-122.72
Malcolm Jefferson	37–167	22%	31	37	17	£194,807	£297,934	+16.72
Richard Newland	28–146	19%	29	17	9	£187,006	£294,437	-9.76
Nicky Richards	40–188	21%	29	20	23	£207,902	£288,940	-13.53
Tim Vaughan	42–449	9%	56	50	44	£164,980	£277,786	-225.75
Emma Lavelle	19–163	12%	18	20	20	£131,943	£246,013	-40.42
Rebecca Curtis	24–194	12%	15	26	15	£144,306	£245,319	-34.31
Ian Williams	28–225	12%	27	22	25	£169,509	£234,371	-77.60
Harry Whittington	21–91	23%	12	19	7	£155,810	£215,762	+20.36
Anthony Honeyball	28–170	16%	27	20	13	£150,338	£212,801	-29.53
Jeremy Scott	27–192	14%	23	28	14	£104,591	£211,804	-19.51
David Dennis	27–220	12%	32	32	26	£125,968	£204,358	-81.39
Lucy Wadham	21–119	18%	16	13	20	£119,665	£203,806	+28.58
Martin Keighley	25–179	14%	11	19	23	£150,778	£203,746	+15.04
Henry de Bromhead	1–23	4%	2	4	1	£63,585	£200,992	-16.00
Ben Pauling	26–155	17%	23	7	19	£147,259	£198,601	+58.12
Henry Oliver	15–119	13%	17	10	14	£136,837	£189,229	-13.53
Enda Bolger	5–11	45%	0	1	1	£122,380	£188,996	+4.88

2016 BRITISH JUMPS FIXTURES

OCTOBER

1	Sat	Fontwell
2	Sun	Kelso, Huntingdon, Uttoxeter
3	Mon	Southwell
5	Wed	Ludlow, Towcester
6	Thu	Hereford, Exeter
7	Fri	Newton Abbot
8	Sat	Hexham, Chepstow
9	Sun	Chepstow
11	Tue	Huntingdon
12	Wed	Wetherby
13	Thu	Carlisle, Uttoxeter
14	Fri	Fakenham, Wincanton
15	Sat	Market Rasen, Stratford, Ffos Las
16	Sun	Kempton
17	Mon	Plumpton
18	Tue	Exeter
19	Wed	Fontwell, Worcester
20	Thu	Carlisle, Ludlow, Newton Abbot
21	Fri	Cheltenham
22	Sat	Cheltenham, Kelso
23	Sun	Aintree, Wincanton
24	Mon	Ayr
25	Tue	Bangor, Chepstow
26	Wed	Fakenham
27	Thu	Sedgefield, Stratford
28	Fri	Wetherby, Uttoxeter
29	Sat	Ayr, Ascot, Wetherby
30	Sun	Carlisle, Huntingdon
31	Mon	Hereford, Plumpton

NOVEMBER

1	Tue	Exeter
2	Wed	Musselburgh, Chepstow
3	Thu	Musselburgh, Market Rasen, Newbury
4	Fri	Hexham, Warwick, Fontwell
5	Sat	Aintree, Wincanton, Kelso
6	Sun	Ffos Las, Sandown
7	Mon	Carlisle, Kempton
8	Tue	Huntingdon, Lingfield, Sedgefield
9	Wed	Ayr, Bangor, Exeter
10	Thu	Ludlow, Taunton
11	Fri	Newcastle, Cheltenham
12	Sat	Wetherby, Cheltenham, Uttoxeter
13	Sun	Cheltenham, Fontwell
14	Mon	Leicester, Plumpton
15	Tue	Fakenham, Southwell
16	Wed	Hexham, Warwick, Chepstow

17	Thu	Market Rasen, Wincanton
18	Fri	Haydock, Ascot, Ffos Las
19	Sat	Haydock, Huntingdon, Ascot
20	Sun	Uttoxeter, Exeter
21	Mon	Ludlow, Kempton
22	Tue	Sedgefield, Lingfield
23	Wed	Wetherby, Hereford
24	Thu	Musselburgh, Towcester, Taunton
25	Fri	Doncaster, Newbury
26	Sat	Doncaster, Bangor, Newbury, Newcastle,
27	Sun	Carlisle, Leicester
28	Mon	Ludlow, Plumpton
29	Tue	Southwell, Lingfield
30	Wed	Catterick, Ffos Las

DECEMBER

1	Thu	Leicester, Market Rasen, Wincanton
2	Fri	Sedgefield, Exeter, Sandown
3	Sat	Aintree, Chepstow, Wetherby, Sandown,
4	Sun	Kelso, Huntingdon
5	Mon	Ayr, Ludlow
6	Tue	Fontwell, Uttoxeter
7	Wed	Hexham, Leicester
8	Thu	Newcastle, Warwick, Taunton
9	Fri	Doncaster, Bangor, Cheltenham
10	Sat	Doncaster, Cheltenham, Lingfield
11	Sun	Carlisle, Southwell
12	Mon	Ffos Las, Plumpton
13	Tue	Catterick, Wincanton
14	Wed	Musselburgh, Newbury
15	Thu	Towcester, Exeter
16	Fri	Uttoxeter, Ascot
17	Sat	Haydock, Ascot, Newcastle
18	Sun	Fakenham
19	Mon	Ayr, Hereford
20	Tue	Taunton
21	Wed	Ludlow, Ffos Las
22	Thu	Bangor
26	Mon	Sedgefield, Huntingdon, Fontwell, Wetherby, Market Rasen, Kempton, Wincanton
27	Tue	Wetherby, Chepstow, Kempton
28	Wed	Catterick, Leicester
29	Thu	Doncaster, Kelso
30	Fri	Haydock, Taunton
31	Sat	Uttoxeter, Warwick, Newbury

INDEX OF HORSES

INDEX OF HORSES

INDEX OF HORSES